Stanley Krippner

SONG
OF THE SIREN

A PARAPSYCHOLOGICAL
ODYSSEY

HARPER COLOPHON BOOKS
Harper & Row, Publishers
New York, Hagerstown, San Francisco, London

To the memory of
Charlotte Bühler,
　　　who also heard a song,
and Alan Watts,
　　　who was also lured by a siren. . . .

Acknowledgment is made for permission to reprint the following material:

From "Truckin'" by Jerry Garcia, Bob Weir, Phil Lesh, and Robert Hunter. Copyright 1971 by Ice Nine Publishing Co., Inc.

From *The I Ching: Or Book of Changes,* trans. by Richard Wilhelm, rendered into English by Cary Baynes, Bollingen Series XIX, Foreword by C. G. Jung. Copyright © 1950 and 1967 by Bollingen Foundation, reprinted by permission of Princeton University Press.

From *Mudra* by Chogyam Trungpa. Shambhala: Berkeley and London. 1972. Used by permission of the publisher.

A hardcover edition of this book is published by Harper & Row, Publishers, Inc.

First HARPER COLOPHON edition published 1977

ISBN: 0-06-090509-3
77 78 79 10 9 8 7 6 5 4 3 2 1

CONTENTS

Acknowledgments   iv

Foreword *by Rolling Thunder*   v

Introduction by *K. Ramakrishna Rao*   viii

1. FOUR UNIVERSITIES IN THREE ACTS   1

2. MUSIC TO EAT MUSHROOMS BY   19

3. PERCHANCE TO DREAM, TELEPATHICALLY   46

4. IN AND OUT OF CONSCIOUSNESS   68

5. BY THE LIGHT OF THE MOON   97

6. MISSION TO MOSCOW   135

7. BACK IN THE USSR   152

8. THE SPIRITS OF SÃO PAULO   169

9. PSYCHOTRONICS IN PRAGUE   186

10. JOURNEY TO THE EAST   211

11. BE NOT DECEIVED   246

12. THE PUZZLE OF PSI   265

References   293

Index   308

ACKNOWLEDGMENTS

Although somewhat autobiographical in nature, this book is not an autobiography. I have not mentioned many people who were significant in my life, nor several events which were critically meaningful.

I would like to give special recognition to Margaret Schneider and Irene Lozano, our two secretaries at the Maimonides Dream Laboratory. They contributed more to the success of our experimental program than anyone reading the research reports could imagine—until we ran out of money to pay them.

I am also grateful to Dr. Marvin Kranis, director of personnel health services at Maimonides for guiding me through the hazardous operation described in chapter three, and for providing me with the inoculations and vaccinations needed for my travels to the outposts of three continents. I would also like to thank Harold Friedman, director of the visual aids department at Maimonides, for his superb craft in reproducing the art prints, pictures, charts, diagrams, and Kirlian photographs that played such an important role in my work.

Gratitude is expressed to Hadley Smith for typing and editing the manuscript. Further editing was done by Cynthia Merman, and portions of the manuscript were read at my request by Frank Barron, Walter Houston Clark, Robert Craig, Richard Davidson, Charles Honorton, James Hickman, Jean Houston, Jerry Jacobs, Montague Ullman, Rhea A. White, and by my wife, Lelie Krippner, who has been a support as well as an inspiration in all my endeavors. I appreciate the comments and corrections offered by these readers; any remaining errors must be attributed to me, not to them.

STANLEY KRIPPNER

FOREWORD

What scientists call psychic phenomena, the American Indians would refer to as the "other world." These phenomena are very important. In fact, they are the most important aspects of our lives. They have to do with life and death and sickness. They even have to do with the rise and fall of governments.

Everything in the universe rises and falls and travels in cycles. These cycles are energy patterns created in the universe itself, then in the bodies of everyone living and everything that has life. I think as scientists go more into explorations in this area, they will find that these energy patterns explain a lot. Scientists have done some photographic experiments on the life force in plants and animals; I think this is the deepest aspect of what you call psychic phenomena. The meaning of life itself seems to be what these scientists are working on at this time, and I think it's a real good thing.

But there was a time when I was quite suspicious of scientists. I'll admit this. Like when I met Stanley Krippner for the first time at Mickey Hart's place. Mickey is one of the Grateful Dead and has been associated with rock music and the rock people. I've known those people for many years, and it was through the efforts of Mickey Hart that I first met Stanley.

For some reason they seemed to want to bring us together. I never push to meet anyone, and I admit that at that time I was in no hurry to meet anybody. They had wanted me to meet a lot of different people and I had been disappointed a few times in some religious leaders they wanted me to meet. So when they came and told me they wanted me to meet a man named Stanley Krippner, at first I was skeptical. And I was even a little suspicious when I first met him. And I know we both tested each other.

From my pagan or primitive point of view, I wondered if a person with scientific training could be sincere in studying the "other world." That was the reason for my skepticism. It wasn't a personal thing, I admit, because I couldn't find any fault with Stanley personally. As a matter of fact, I liked him from the beginning when I first met him. But I think it was the scientific terms—the high language and words that I didn't always understand.

I know that Stanley felt a bit skeptical too, and he knew many of my thoughts the same as I knew many of his thoughts. And I knew, even though he didn't say so, that he thought he was meeting with a pagan and a savage. And most people would think that these two—the savage and the scientist—couldn't be one and the same and probably couldn't get along together.

But I've found since that time that many of the findings of parapsychology reflect the teachings that many of our people have known from old civilizations, ancient times, and even other worlds. Much knowledge has been handed down to us about such things as how the pyramids were built, how to reverse the law of gravity through magic and through mathematics, how to communicate with other people in dreams; how to use the electrical force that you find in all living things, and many other things that are assumed to be lost. But they are only lost temporarily, until the people are able to handle this wisdom without destroying themselves and without destroying the world.

Modern people think we're uncivilized, and we think many times that because they use big words like "genocide," and because they can't get along among themselves, that they are uncivilized. So it's just a matter of opinion. And it is a matter, too, of our mistrust of science, and their misuse of science. That was the reason I was suspicious of Stanley in the beginning. But as time went on, I came to know of his work, and was able to see some of it, and was able to grasp his reasons for knowing about the "other world." Then I began to understand that there are some people working in science who want to understand these things and who don't have any ulterior motives at all.

It is too bad that there aren't more people who have the same viewpoints and the same object in mind that Stanley has in rediscovering these things that were well known in ancient civilizations. I think that through his efforts great progress is being made not only in bringing about better understanding among people, but also to help modern people to understand the "other world" which they have lost. This loss has caused much of the confusion and misunderstanding among modern people today.

American Indians also have been victims of some of it, and now that we are finding our way back, our people are getting strong again and breaking away from what they call modern life and its falseness and dishonesty. Our people, in truth, are learning how to live and how to be honest with themselves. Then we can attain a higher state of consciousness with open minds and fresh attitudes. And then we can also be friends with other people, and we will find people that we can trust—first among some of the younger generation and then, later, among people of science and parapsychology like Stanley Krippner. I've even found many good people among doctors. And while I know that there has been a lot of misunderstanding, I have come to understand that not all doctors are bad and that there are many good doctors.

As a matter of fact, sometimes I have hopes that we'll even find some good politicians. And while I'm not overly optimistic, I'm still hopeful because we understand too that there are good and bad among all people. We haven't seen it happen yet, but I think the time will come that some politicians might themselves become interested in parapsychology and things like that, and it will do them a lot of good.

I'm not only talking about this country, although we need to make a lot of changes before our land is completely destroyed and before the people are completely ruined. I'm also talking about a lot of other countries on both sides of the ocean. There is a great deal of wisdom that has been lost —of the "other world," of the nature of matter, and of the life force. These are the things that Stanley Krippner has been studying. I wish that more people would follow his example.

ROLLING THUNDER
Medicine Man
Western Shoshone Nation

INTRODUCTION

The duality of human nature has been a subject of philosophical disputation ever since people began to speculate about themselves and their place in the universe. While the reality of the psychic and the somatic aspects of human existence has not been questioned at the phenomenological level, there has never been an agreement on their ontological status. The nature of the relation between the "inner" and the "outer" worlds has formed a significant part of many philosophical discussions.

When human beings were relatively ignorant of the nature of the external forces acting on them and unable to exercise an appreciable measure of control on these forces, they tended to pay more attention to their internal states. Such a situation favored a climate of opinion that looked upon these internal, invisible forces as compelling realities. Inner experiences became important referents in the universe of human discourse.

The rapid advance of science and the progressive control of natural forces achieved through technology led to a situation in which one's inner life was interpreted in terms of external forces acting on the person. The subjective, speculative resolution of problems was replaced by the experimental manipulation of variables.

And then, just when scientific consensus had all but denied the reality of one's inner world, there emerged a disturbing body of evidence in support of parapsychological phenomena. These data simply did not fit into the neat framework that was so elegantly conceived by the scientific establishment of the time.

The evidence in support of parapsychological phenomena came from the work of some people whose scientific training reflected backgrounds in some of the world's most prestigious universities. These scientists employed the same techniques of investigation and methods of evaluation that had been accepted as legitimate in other and more conventional areas of inquiry. Therefore, it soon became apparent that the massive evidence demonstrating parapsychological phenomena could not be dismissed without assuming a gigantic conspiracy entered into by dozens of investigators scattered all over the globe.

Yet another jolt to the scientific establishment grew out of the psychedelic drug scene in the United States and Western Europe. Scientific researchers as well as curious artists and students discovered that familiar models of experience could be shattered by the ingestion of small doses of certain chemicals. Chemically-induced alterations of consciousness produced a variety of phenomenologically distinguishable experiences that no longer admitted familiar categorizations. The new vistas of inner experience made possible by the advent of mind-altering drugs are too significant and absorbing to be ignored or dismissed as aberrations.

It did not take investigators long to realize that significant alterations of consciousness could be brought about without drugs by such means as yoga, meditation, and other practices which have been known for centuries. Further, developments in biofeedback research demonstrated that some of our bodily functions which were traditionally regarded as involuntary could be brought under conscious control. All these developments made it again less plausible to maintain that a person's inner life could be explained completely through the manipulation of external variables. And individuals altering their consciousness both inside and outside of scientific laboratories began to report spontaneous instances of parapsychological phenomena occurring while their inner world was shifting from one state to another.

The reaction to methodologically sound, parapsychological research ranged between two extremes. At one end were those who held the view that no amount of evidence would convince them of the reality of parapsychological phenomena because these events did not fit into the worldview of the scientific establishment. At the other end were those who considered parapsychological phenomena as evidence for the existence of "mind," thus supporting a radical dualistic position.

It is a pity that the atmosphere has been muddled by the prejudices and preconceptions of the extremists. A less passionate appraisal of these phenomena would reveal that there is nothing threatening about them. All that parapsychological phenomena imply is that the traditional notions of cause and effect are insufficient to explain human behavior fully. Furthermore, it appears possible for one to obtain information which is not "caused" by an external source. What we regard as ordinary awareness is merely one of many states of consciousness. Other states exist and are worthy of attention. We have all experienced these nonordinary states of consciousness in sleep and in dreams. Each of these nonordinary states may well have its own logic and order. The concepts and models derived from ordinary consciousness may be inadequate and even misleading to explain phenomena generated in other states of consciousness. Parapsychological phenomena may be just as natural to certain states of consciousness as ordinary perception and cognition are to ordinary consciousness. There is nothing new about this idea; the traditional writings on yoga have repeatedly emphasized similar concepts.

If these assumptions are correct, parapsychological investigations and studies of altered states of consciousness will benefit by closer association. Such an association is likely to lead not only to a better understanding of these phenomena but also to a fuller understanding of human nature. Some significant attempts have already been made. Indeed, the work at the Dream Laboratory of the Maimonides Medical Center in Brooklyn, New York, is the most outstanding of these attempts so far. Dr. Stanley Krippner served as director of this laboratory and, in this book, brings to bear his acknowledged expertise and authority in the areas of parapsychology and altered states of consciousness. He guides us through these fascinating fields with ease and with care. As we go through these pages, many interesting ideas unfold. The result is an inescapable impression that a reasonable control over parapsychological phenomena eventually may be achieved through the understanding of consciousness.

Finally, the intimate personal narrative of Dr. Krippner's book is deeply absorbing and informative. It demonstrates the excitement of conducting pioneering, scientific work as well as the personal sacrifices that a pioneer must make. The narrative also demonstrates the disciplined balance between hard-nosed skepticism and reasonable open-mindedness which must be maintained by a parapsychologist. I hope that this book will reach a wide audience and help bring greater support for further exploration of this "other side" of consciousness that seems to hold the key to parapsychological phenomena.

K. RAMAKRISHNA RAO, PH.D.
Senior Professor and Head,
Department of Psychology and Parapsychology
Andhra University
Visakhapatnam, India

1

FOUR UNIVERSITIES IN THREE ACTS

> As the solar system is reckoned in terms of light-years, so may
> the inner light be what we are calling humanity. . . . Science
> seems to be going toward the physical discovery that light is the
> essence of the human being. . . . There is nothing higher in human
> consciousness than beams of this interior light.
>
> *Frank Lloyd Wright*

Act I: Wisconsin; Prologue

I was fourteen years old when I had my first paranormal experience. I
wanted a set of encyclopedias very badly, but my parents had explained to
me that we could not afford it. They owned an orchard, and the weather
conditions over the past year had not been favorable for a bumper crop of
apples, their chief source of income. I went to my room and began to cry. I
enjoyed reading and I enjoyed travel; both experiences cost money, and my
parents' financial status was dependent upon such unpredictable forces as
the weather and the economy. Where was the money to come from? I had
an uncle who was fairly well to do. I stopped crying for a moment and
began to consider how I would make my funding appeal to Uncle Max.

Suddenly, I bolted upright in my bed. A horrible thought flooded my
consciousness: "Uncle Max can't help me because he's dead." At that
moment I heard the telephone ring. My mother answered the phone, then
began sobbing as my cousin told her that Max had unexpectedly taken ill,
was rushed to the hospital, and had just died.

Many years later I was to learn how typical this sort of frightening
occurrence is for people experiencing psychic, or psi, phenomena spontaneously. These experiences ordinarily occur in altered states of consciousness—an emotional state (such as I went through), while dreaming, while
relaxing, while drugged, or following some external manipulation 'such as
hypnotic suggestion.

1

Later, I also realized that my financial disadvantages were more than offset by the advantage of living on a farm, growing up in the country, hunting for Sauk, Potawatomi, and Fox Indian arrowheads in freshly plowed soil, and having time between chores in the orchard and the garden to explore the inner life, to daydream, to read Greek mythology, American Indian legends, and science-fiction novels, to compose music, to write poetry, and to sketch some of the fantastic images which emerged from my nighttime dreams. Before going to sleep at night, I enjoyed listening to the radio, especially mystery dramas, classical music, and live performances of Joseph Dunninger, the mentalist who read thoughts, predicted newspaper headlines, and broke glass—all by the power of his amazing mind.

About this time, J. Leon Buchen, a celebrated magician known professionally as "The Great Oscar," began to spend his summers at Lake Ripley, a nearby resort area. A gregarious man with a mustache that molded itself to his flashing smile, The Great Oscar bought apples, raspberries, and plums at our farm and used to entertain us with impromptu card tricks, vanishing coins, and severed rope which mysteriously restored itself following the pronouncement of a few well-chosen magical words. I was somewhat disillusioned when The Great Oscar told me that Dunninger was basically a clever magician whose demonstrations of mentalism were elaborately planned feats of legerdemain. Indeed, The Great Oscar taught me several coin, card, and rope tricks, as well as a few techniques of mentalism. I began to read books about magic, started to construct my own magical equipment, and soon was performing before groups of relatives and friends.

Sometimes I had members of my audience write down questions on pieces of paper, fold them, and drop them into my magician's hat. I would randomly select a folded piece of paper, hold it to my head, silently "read" the question, give it a humorous answer, unfold the paper and read the question out loud, then go on to the next question. At other times my sister Donna and I would work as a team. She would leave the room and the audience would decide on an item in the room for her to identify. Upon her return, I would ask, "Is it the table lamp?" "Is it Aunt Pearle's necklace?" Invariably Donna would correctly identify the object and thank everyone for their splendid telepathic concentration.

Once in a while Donna would tell me, "I knew it was Aunt Pearle's necklace even before you gave me the code word." And once in a while I knew one of the questions that would be asked even before I started to unfold the papers during my mentalism act. These experiences were exciting because they allowed me to glimpse a type of reality beyond the imagination or comprehension of most people. Each time this happened, I felt in some way transformed, as if I had a toehold in an extra dimension of life that expanded the boundaries of my identity. But these experiences also convinced me that psi phenomena were too unpredictable and fragile for anyone to utilize for a stage performance. Sleight of hand, although a difficult art to perfect, was still more dependable than psychic talent.

Scene 1: High School

My days as a performing magician ended once I entered high school. However, I would sometimes perform feats of mentalism at parties, usually with a confederate. Whenever anyone guessed how it was done, he or she became a confederate for the next demonstration at the next party. It was not unusual for a demonstration of mentalism to be performed for an audience, over half of whom were aware of the code utilized.

The same pattern emerged for a new party pastime, "hypnotism by candlelight." I would have the subject stare at a candle in a dark room. I would ask the subject to follow instructions, stating that the hypnotic experience would deepen with each instruction followed. The subject would raise a hand, touch an ear, say a strange word or two, and finally would hold a dish or plate with one hand while rubbing the bottom of it with the other. I would say:

> Rub the bottom of the plate very slowly in a counterclockwise manner. If it took you a moment to decide which direction was counterclockwise, you must be very, very deeply in hypnosis. Now, rub the plate in a clockwise direction, making sure that all five fingers are touching the bottom of the plate. Now quickly bring your fingers up to your forehead. Move them from left to right across your forehead. Again, if you had some trouble identifying left and right, your mind must be behaving in a very unusual manner, and the hypnosis must be working very well. Now touch your chin with your hand and bring the fingers up to your left cheek, across your nose and over to your right cheek. Now hold out your hand and I will place a mirror in it. You are now so deeply hypnotized that you see whatever I tell you to see. As you look into the mirror, you will see that your face looks like that of a zebra, with dark black stripes alternating with flesh-colored stripes.

The demonstration was always successful. The plate had been held over the candle earlier that evening so that it was covered with soot. Once the subject looked into the mirror, the other guests at the party began to laugh. The subject also began to laugh. The only people who did not laugh were the occasional guests who had actually become hypnotized, returned to their ordinary state of awareness when the lights were turned on, and had partial or total amnesia for the event.

During my high school days, some of us experimented with other techniques to alter consciousness. By standing against a wall and pressing one's arms tightly against the wall, one could observe one's arms rise effortlessly upon suddenly relaxing them. Sports, of course, alter one's awareness; in retrospect I can see that the sense of "oneness" I felt while swimming or while cascading down a hill on a sled represented shifts in consciousness. And if people took ten deep breaths and then had friends circle their waists and squeeze hard, they would experience a physiological "rush" accompanied by a momentary blanking out of conscious awareness.

My own favorite alterations in consciousness remained dreams and daydreams. To daydream, I would go to a large mound on our farm after a rain, look for arrowheads, and—whether or not I found any—sit quietly and think of the marvelous scientific discoveries I would someday make. Or I would go to a marsh by Red Cedar Lake, sit among the wildflowers in the one stretch of dry land, and compose operas or create dramas. Red Cedar Lake stirred my imagination because more than one neighbor or relative told how, as children, they had seen sea serpents rise from the waters of both Red Cedar and Lake Ripley. Another relative used the sea serpent on his business stationery in an attempt to stimulate the tourist trade.

Across our farm ran an Indian path known as the Black Hawk Trail because it had been used by Chief Black Hawk and his warriors. In 1832, Henry Atkinson's forces attacked Indian envoys sent by Black Hawk to discuss a peaceful settlement of their differences. The resulting conflict raged for five months and became known as the Black Hawk War. The noble Sauk chief was defeated at the Battle of Bad Ax River in Wisconsin, and Atkinson proceeded to punish the Indian tribes which had supported Black Hawk's cause.

Until my sophomore year in high school, I had a frontal lisp which made me the object of much teasing and taunting from my peers. A visiting speech correctionist from the University of Wisconsin taught me how to pronounce my *s* sounds without lisping. This dramatic event opened up entire new worlds for me. I was able to participate in dramatic presentations, debate tournaments, and public speaking events. I discovered that the stage was an arena in which I felt very much at home, and I began to appreciate the power of the spoken word. My days as an amateur magician were behind me; I realized that words had a magic of their own. I resolved to study speech pathology in college to help open up this universe of communication to other people with language defects.

I graduated from Fort Atkinson Senior High School in 1950 and was one of three student commencement speakers. We gave short presentations on the world's three principal economic systems: communism, socialism, and capitalism—renamed "Americanism" so that no one would think it was meant to have equal consideration with the two alien systems under discussion. I felt fortunate that I was selected to speak on communism, which I considered the most interesting of the topics. In preparation for the speech, I read Lenin and Marx for the first time, so felt quite knowledgeable on the topic when later that year Wisconsin's junior senator, Joseph McCarthy, began his vendetta against Marxists, Communists, and fellow travelers in "high places."

Scene 2: Madison

By that time I was at the University of Wisconsin, taking courses in the field of special education and speech correction. While at the university I met Senator McCarthy and heard him speak on several occasions. One of my classmates was Henry Wortis whose father, Joseph Wortis, a psychiatrist, had the distinction of appearing before McCarthy's investigative committee. Dr. Wortis had been to the USSR and was on suspiciously good terms with several Soviet physicians and scientists. Another incriminating fact was Henry's membership in the Labor Youth League, purportedly a Communist-front organization whose presence on a university campus in McCarthy's home state was a source of constant embarrassment to the senator and his supporters. While I felt no intrinsic sympathy for Communist philosophy, I did feel that all ideas should be allowed to compete in a university setting. And, at that time, I had no idea that Dr. Wortis and I would meet each other in Brooklyn several years later.

I studied Greek mythology under Walter Agard who noticed the apathy among most of the university students (later to be called "the silent generation") and organized the "Stick-Out-Your-Neck Club." I joined the club and also became active in the Union Forum Committee, the student group which invited guest speakers to the campus. Owen Lattimore, a political scientist, was one of the committee's guests; Senator McCarthy had accused Lattimore of helping to "sell out" China to the Communists, so his campus appearance brought about controversy, conflict, and extensive newspaper coverage. His lecture was one of the few to counteract student apathy and attract an overflow crowd. During my junior year at the university, I became chairman of the committee. We brought other McCarthy targets to the campus (Eleanor Roosevelt and Arthur Schlesinger, Jr.), as well as speakers who were sympathetic to McCarthy—William Buckley and John Dos Passos, and the anthropologist, William McGovern.

In an effort to broaden our programs, we also arranged lectures by significant persons in other fields; Trygve Lie, the former UN secretary-general spoke for us and charged one thousand dollars. This seemed like an incredible sum of money to me, so I was equally surprised when Frank Lloyd Wright, the Wisconsin-born architect, spoke to us free of charge. And one day we received word that Joseph Dunninger, billed as "the world's most amazing mentalist," was available. Originally, I was very excited about the prospect of bringing Dunninger to the campus. However, his fee was as high as Trygve Lie's, on whom we had lost money. The students rarely filled the auditorium for any of our events and we finally decided that if there was general apathy on the topic of politics, there would be almost total apathy on the topic of mentalism.

However, a strange event took place. I was taking a philosophy course from A. C. Garnett. He surprised me by introducing the topic of parapsychology into his lectures. In his opinion, a small group of scientists had established the existence of such psychic means of gaining knowledge as telepathy, clairvoyance, and precognition, and had grouped them together under the label of extrasensory perception or ESP. They had also established the existence of paranormal means of influencing objects at a distance; this phenomenon was referred to as psychokinesis or PK.

When I told Dr. Garnett about my interest in obtaining a speaker on this topic for the Forum Committee, he said, "Dunninger probably has a certain degree of ESP, but his stage performances are based on magic and trickery. Why don't you invite a reputable scientist such as Gardner Murphy or J. B. Rhine to speak on scientific parapsychology?" Garnett gave me the addresses of Murphy and Rhine whom I proceeded to contact. Murphy sent us a gracious letter in which he declined the invitation and noted, "It is strange that you speak of Dunninger, a performer who has never been tested in a scientific laboratory." Rhine, who expressed interest in speaking on our campus, noted that he had invited Dunninger to his laboratory at Duke University for experiments, only to receive the reply, "I have performed before the great Edison. I have performed before the great Steinmetz. What more can I do for science?"

Rhine requested a modest honorarium of three hundred dollars plus expenses. Our only alternative was to appeal to the All-University Lecture Committee, a faculty group, for cosponsorship.

The All-University Lecture Committee contacted the acting chairman of the psychology department, asking for his reaction to the proposed Rhine lecture. In a letter to us, he responded that a lecture on parapsychology would attract a large audience because, as he put it, ESP has a deep appeal to individuals who have suffered great personal loss and to individuals who are emotionally unstable. However, the professor noted, such a lecture would leave an unfortunate "emotional aura" and would confuse people as to what psychology really is. Needless to say, the committee turned down our request for funds.

On May 28, 1953, the Forum Committee voted unanimously to try to bring Rhine to the campus. Rhine, who had been invited to address a chemical society in Chicago that following December, suggested that he address the Wisconsin students at the same time, forgoing an honorarium. We immediately accepted his offer and, after clearing the idea with Rhine, invited the acting chairman of the psychology department to debate the proposition that the existence of psychic events had been experimentally demonstrated.

The psychologist wrote back stating that the end result would be similar to that which would ensue if a scientifically trained atheist were invited to debate with Bishop Sheen on the topic, "Resolved: That immaculate conception has been experimentally proved." Again, he predicted that "unfortunate emotional consequences" would doubtless follow. He closed his letter by advising that if we held the Rhine lecture, we follow it by a lecture in which Father Divine would speak on the topic "Recent Advances in the Art of Healing."

As publicity for the program was released during the fall semester, other psychologists made less clever but equally denigrating remarks. One professor advised his class, "If you are interested in ESP, you might as well hear about it from the horse's mouth—and from the biggest horse's ass of them all." The Forum Committee had stumbled upon its most controversial speaker since Owen Lattimore.

Ironically, the faculty members who heaped ridicule upon Rhine had staunchly defended Lattimore's appearance. The psychologists who criticized the Forum Committee's decision to bring Rhine to the campus were, without exception, liberal-minded and intelligent.

It is an easy matter to ascribe all scientific opposition toward parapsychology to an excessively physicalistic worldview that psi phenomena seem to contradict. However, the issue is not that simple. Many of the psychologists who oppose acceptance of parapsychological data are churchgoers who believe in a "soul" and other concepts which are nonphysical in nature. At the same time, several parapsychologists are agnostics or atheists who believe there is a completely "physical" explanation for even the most unusual psychic events.

Many scientists take a skeptical attitude toward psi phenomena but do not become emotionally agitated when the topic is discussed. Other scientists are open-minded but confess their ignorance; they simply have not had enough time to study the research reports and make a rational decision on the issue. The scientists who become most irritated when psychic phenomena are discussed are often those who take the standards of their discipline very seriously. Even though statistical tests demonstrate that certain subjects perform at above-chance levels, much more needs to be done to establish the validity of parapsychological concepts. Was there any possibility of fraud? Was the entire test series published or were data thrown away? Can the effect be replicated by other researchers? And, finally, what is the mechanism by which the effect takes place? Contemporary parapsychologists can answer the first two questions and demonstrate elaborate precautions against fraud or experimental "fudging." However, the last two questions cannot be answered in a positive, satisfying manner. And scientific purists can make a case for the assertion that without some degree of repeatability and explanation, psi phenomena can never find their way into the mainstream of science. Instead, they serve as pollutants, siphoning talented researchers, badly needed funds, and public interest away from scientific phenomena which can be tamed, disciplined, examined, understood, and put to worthwhile uses.

Scene 3: Rhine Arrives

When we met Rhine at the train station on December 9, we were surprised at his gentle manner and good humor. A stocky man with deep-set eyes and a mane of silver hair, Rhine was delighted to hear that we had arranged a dinner with Dr. Garnett, the philosophy professor who had first told me of Rhine's work. We also noticed that the weather had taken a turn for the worse. By the time of Rhine's lecture, one of Wisconsin's famous snowstorms was raging. In addition, we knew that most students were preparing for their examinations and that a popular theatrical event in the Union building was competing for the student's attention. Nevertheless, over one thousand students filled the Union's lecture hall past its capacity.

The student who had been designated to introduce Rhine suddenly bowed out, feeling that too close an identification with our speaker might lower the grades which his psychology professors were to bestow, and affect the recommendations he needed for applying to medical school. As a result, I introduced Rhine myself, thus validating my membership in Dr. Agard's Stick-Out-Your-Neck Club.

Rhine centered his talk around the themes of how new ideas emerge in science, why they arouse dissent, and gave suggestions as to in what way they might be judged. In the case of parapsychology, he simply asked that the data themselves be examined as well as the methods by which the data were obtained.

To objectify psi phenomena, Rhine and his associates had designed a special series of ESP cards. The cards bore five symbols: a square, circle, cross, star, and wavy lines, usually in decks of twenty-five cards with five cards for each symbol. By having subjects guess the order of the cards in a shuffled deck under various conditions, Rhine was able to study ESP—perception without the assistance of the recognized senses—in the laboratory and identify three basic forms.

Telepathy was defined by Rhine as "extrasensory perception of the mental processes of another person." In one of the Duke University experiments, a subject named Ownbey noted the designs on a deck of cards being viewed by a subject named Turner. As there were five different designs in each deck of twenty-five cards, chance results would have resulted in five correct guesses. Rather, Ownbey correctly guessed an average of seventeen cards per deck over a three-day period. Furthermore, Turner was 250 miles away from Ownbey while the experiment was taking place.

Rhine defined clairvoyance as knowing "events beyond the range of the senses," and illustrated the phenomena with the case of a subject who guessed all twenty-five cards in a shuffled deck correctly. The odds against this event being coincidence would have been several million to one.

Rhine illustrated precognition, "extrasensory perception of future events," by citing an example from his wife's collection of spontaneous cases. A young woman from Brooklyn was unable to see her mother very often, so was pleased when her brother came for a visit, reporting that their mother was in good health. In the middle of the night, however, she awakened with the conviction that her mother would be hospitalized exactly eight days from the following morning. Her brother criticized her for such a silly notion. Yet their mother took sick exactly eight days later, was hospitalized, and died. Rhine noted that this case could not by itself serve as evidence; furthermore, he doubted that psychic dreams could ever be tested under experimental conditions. However, precognition could be tested with ESP cards; many subjects had guessed the order of cards in decks which had not yet been shuffled—and did so at statistically significant levels.*

Somewhat different from ESP, the receptive, perceptual type of psi, is psychokinesis, the expressive, motor activity type of psi. Rhine noted that

---

*To indicate whether psi is happening, statistics are used to evaluate if the number of correct guesses exceeds what would happen by chance alone. For example, if a person repeatedly tries to guess the color of the next car to drive around the corner, sooner or later he or she will be correct. This means nothing about how well the person can tell what colors of cars are coming around the corner, unless the person can do it consistently. So if someone makes consistently correct guesses in a psi experiment, this is not due to chance. When two things correspond by chance alone, nothing meaningful is happening. But if they correspond more often than is expected by chance, we call the results "statistically significant."

PK produces "a change in physical events" through mental activity. He told us of experiments in which subjects tried to influence dice to fall in a certain way through thoughts alone. Chance, for example, would bring up two sevens in every twelve throws. His use of dice was stimulated by a gambler who told Rhine that he often had a "feeling" that he would be lucky; this "feeling" was invariably associated with success at "willing" the dice to perform appropriately.

In closing, Rhine admitted that his work had aroused skepticism and hostility among many of his scientific colleagues. He noted, "Science, too, can be functionally blind when it would shock her complacency to see." Rhine noted that we live in an era of conformity but urged the students to question traditional ways of thinking and to hold fast to their convictions once they had been formed through reason and experience.

Rhine received what he later told me was one of the greatest ovations of his career. And a few days later, he wrote, "I had a good stirring time with the chemists in Chicago, although it was not nearly so exciting as my experience in Madison. In fact, I have not had more fun in years than I had up there with you folks."

Scene 4: The Rhine Aftermath

On January 11, 1954, *Life* magazine published Aldous Huxley's article, "The Case for ESP, PK, and Psi"; the Forum Committee's status on campus received a boost because we had ventured into the area before this highly favorable article was published. In addition, Rhine's lecture was discussed in various university classes for several months. Only one psychology professor had accepted our invitation to meet Rhine at a discussion session after the lecture. Although he asked only one question and made no critical comment at that time, the next week he was quoted in the student newspaper as saying, "Rhine throws away data just below or just above chance on the theory that the subject wasn't working right." When we sent Rhine a copy of this statement, he fired back a reply that the professor's statement "would be, to the scientist, the most libelous thing that could be said; it would represent an implication of scientific dishonesty." Of course, I sent a copy of Rhine's letter to the professor, noting that this opinion should have been aired directly when he was with Rhine.

The same professor was reported to have singled me out personally as being responsible for creating bad feelings and bad publicity for his department. Finally, he stated at a public forum, which I was chairing, that no one had replicated Rhine's work. I replied that although a repeatable ESP experiment had not been devised, basic results had been replicated by a dozen or more investigators throughout the world. The psychologist snapped that I, as chairman, had no business interjecting my own opinions into the discussion. Admittedly, I was not kindly disposed toward the professor. In addition to his attacks on Dr. Rhine, he had stated during a psychology course I took with him that only schizophrenics dreamed in color. At that time, I had never had a single black-and-white dream, and refused to accept the diagnosis of schizophrenia.

Shortly thereafter, the psychologist in question left for another university and became one of the world's most eminent authorities on visual perception. He published one experiment in which individuals were hypnotized, "regressed" to earlier age levels, and performed as if they were children on visual perception tests. Another psychologist, T. X. Barber, performed the same experiment but could not replicate the results.

By 1954 I had graduated from the University of Wisconsin and had begun to work with handicapped children in Illinois and in Virginia. While living in Virginia, I paid several visits to Duke University, spent many delightful days with J. B. and Louisa Rhine at their farm, and talked with such interesting members of the Parapsychology Laboratory staff as Karlis Osis, W. E. Cox, and J. G. Pratt. I remember the day when one of Rhine's associates asked me if I knew of anyone who wanted to buy his car; he was short of cash and needed the money. I was shocked to realize that such an important figure in the field of psychical research was having financial problems. As the years went by, however, I was to realize that parapsychology was one of the most financially hazardous of professions. Rhine's staff meetings frequently took up the issue of money, how much was needed to keep the research going, and where it might be obtained. I even met one parapsychologist, a former president of the Parapsychological Association, who took a bus to his out-of-town lectures rather than an airplane. As he had been given air-travel expenses, he was able to pocket the difference and devote it to his research.

I was also present at a Parapsychology Laboratory staff meeting in 1955 when the news arrived that a medical researcher, G. R. Price, published an article critical of parapsychology in *Science,* the official journal of the prestigious American Association for the Advancement of Science. To explain ESP and PK data, Price suggested experimenter fraud as "the one explanation that is simplest and most in accord with everyday experiment." Price directed most of his criticism to ESP card tests by Rhine and by S. G. Soal, a prominent British parapsychologist, pointing out several ways in which the results could be "fudged" so as to produce significant results. This article received an incredible amount of publicity and was hailed by many critics as the "definitive" exposé of parapsychologists and their methods. Rhine's response was surprisingly muted; he announced he would initiate a correspondence with Price in an attempt to explain the laboratory's procedures and thus counteract Price's charges. Rhine's patience apparently paid off. In 1972, *Science* published a letter titled "Apology to Rhine and Soal," in which Price retracted his former statements.

What effect did this unjustified criticism of parapsychology have on me? For one thing, it reminded me of the teasing I had put up with for most of my childhood and a good share of my adolescence. Perhaps parapsychology had a "lisp"—the fact that ESP and PK experiments could not be easily repeated. This defect, however, was no cause for assertions that parapsychologists were inept at best and fradulent at worst. The issue of repeatability, however, did prevent parapsychological findings from entering the front door of science. Slowly, I was resolving that in some small way I would help to move parapsychology from the back door to the front door and find a room in the halls of science for parapsychology from which it could never be evicted.

Act II: Northwestern and Hawaii

In 1956, Northwestern University granted me a fellowship for graduate study. I stayed on the Evanston, Illinois campus until I obtained my doctorate in 1961, working with Paul Witty in the field of special education and learning disabilities. Dr. Witty was also well known for his pioneering work in creativity, another area in which I was developing a strong interest.

Scene 1: Rhine Revisited

Dr. Rhine returned to Chicago in May 1958; on behalf of Phi Delta Kappa, a professional educational society, I invited him to speak on the campus. Our group arranged a dinner for him while he was on campus, inviting all members of the education and psychology departments. Several faculty members from education accepted the invitation. However, we were informed that the chairman of the psychology department had warned his faculty members that to accept the invitation would be to disgrace the department.

Two psychologists came anyway. One of the psychologists had an engrossing discussion with Rhine in which he noted the three reasons why he remained skeptical of the existence of paranormal phenomena. First, the experiments could not be guaranteed to produce repeatable results if done by different researchers. Second, there was no mechanism that he knew of which would explain ESP or PK. And finally, Rhine's claim that distance made no difference in telepathy tests violated the inverse square ratio established by physicists in which an effect diminishes in a predictable proportion over distance.

Despite these objections, the dinner was pleasant. As the years went by, I was glad to note that one of the two psychologists later became department chairman at Northwestern University while the other was elected president of the American Psychological Association.

Rhine's lecture went well and my interest in parapsychology was rekindled. In 1960, Rhine telephoned me with a report that had come his way of poltergeist phenomena in the nearby town of Guttenberg, Iowa. An elderly couple, cared for by their grandson, found themselves immersed in a series of alarming incidents which included explosions, flying objects, and furniture which crashed to the floor. A visiting sailor who weighed 265 pounds claimed that his mattress rose in the air and tossed him out of bed. By the time we arrived, the house had been studied by physicists and geologists armed with an ion counter, an oscilloscope, a Geiger counter, and an argon radiation counter. No disturbances were recorded, the house's foundations were pronounced sound, and the bedrock was judged to be solid. Many people concluded that a poltergeist or "noisy ghost" was at work.

By the time Arthur Hastings, a fellow Northwestern student, and I arrived, thousands of curiosity seekers and souvenir hunters had rampaged their way through the house doing more damage than any number of poltergeists. After interviewing the family members, we established the time of each untoward incident as well as the location of everyone at the time of each disturbance. After collecting the facts, it became apparent to us that there was no incident that could not have been caused by the grandson. If the disturbance took place in the dark, the grandson was in the same room with his grandparents. If the incident took place in daylight, it happened in a *different* room from the one where the grandparents were located and at a time when the grandson's whereabouts were unknown. The motivation was clear; the grandson was tired of baby-sitting for the elderly couple. After they fled the house, he resumed his former lifestyle as an Iowa playboy.

And what about the sailor who was thrown from his bed? Simple questioning revealed that he had imbibed several bottles of beer before retiring. If there were active spirits in this case, we concluded they were inside the sailor rather than inside the mattress. This whole saga taught us the importance of retaining a critical position when encountering unusual phenomena, and checking out simple explanations before taking a position that complex forces could be at work.

Scene 2: With Gardner Murphy in Honolulu

In 1959, Gardner Murphy accepted an invitation to lecture for Northwestern's psychology department. Murphy also accepted my invitation to meet with a small group of graduate students interested in parapsychology. We were joined by one of the professors who had attended the Rhine dinner.

Murphy, wispy-haired and slender, had just written a provocative book, *Human Potentialities,* and we had several questions for him about its contents. *Human Potentialities* was one of the first significant books to be published in what would later be called "humanistic psychology"; like other writings in this field, Murphy's book emphasized a holistic approach to the study of the person, stressing positive, growth-oriented personality traits rather than the pathological descriptions so common at that time.

Murphy devoted a great deal of *Human Potentialities* to creativity and its relationship to ESP. For example, he noted that both abilities often occur in altered states of consciousness, such as dreams, reverie, and relaxation. He also noted the phenomenon of periods of creativity within a given culture, suggesting that people working together or in close proximity could reinforce each other's ideas telepathically. He wrote:

> In every one of these periods of rapid cultural acceleration, there is, of course, some interdependence among the various styles of human expression. We take it as a matter of course that Velasquez and Cervantes appear in the same period in Spanish history. Even between artistic and scientific waves of creativeness there is often a close affiliation. We take it as a matter of course that the Netherlands which produced the great physicist Huygens and the great microscopist Leeuwenhoek, was the Netherlands which produced Terborch, Vermeer, and Rembrandt.

Murphy was making the point that historians and social psychologists typically ignore the possibility that psychic phenomena may play a role in the creative development of a person or of a culture.

It was snowing when we drove Murphy to the train station that afternoon and he remarked how much he was looking forward to spending the summer teaching at the University of Hawaii. I remarked that I had been invited to Honolulu to participate in a friend's wedding and had been promised living quarters for the summer. Murphy suggested that I work as his teaching assistant.

The summer of 1960 was everything I could have hoped for. Each morning I assisted Murphy in his two classes on social psychology. At noon, I had lunch with the Murphys and discussed parapsychology, social issues, personality theory, and a host of other topics on which Murphy was one of the world's leading authorities. Every night was an international adventure; I had friends among the Japanese, Chinese, Filipino, and Hawaiian ethnic groups who enjoyed taking me to different parts of the island for new experiences with food, music, or tropical entertainment.

One morning we received word that a group of townspeople had discovered Murphy's presence on campus and threatened to picket his classes because of his purported "Communist" leanings. We hoped for some excitement, but the picketers never arrived; perhaps they were victims of the "Polynesian island paralysis"—the benign climate which is supposed to decrease motivation among people visiting or holding residency in Hawaii.

At the end of the summer, I presented my first professional paper; it described our poltergeist investigation and was read at an international general semantics meeting presided over by S. I. Hayakawa. My last assignment for Murphy was to buy him a Russian-English dictionary; he was leaving for Moscow immediately after our final class meeting. He said that there were rumors that some type of parapsychological work was going on in the Soviet Union.

Act III: Kent State

I graduated from Northwestern University in 1961 and moved to Ohio, having been appointed director of the Kent State University Child Study Center. During my final year at Northwestern, I had started to keep a dream diary. Once I began receiving my first paychecks from Kent State, I began psychoanalytically oriented psychotherapy with a local psychiatrist. During my therapy sessions, my psychiatrist emphasized the interpretation of dreams, one of which was especially puzzling:

> I was in Wisconsin, on my parents' farm, walking through the swamp. I was surrounded by several dozen wild turkeys. Suddenly, there appeared a row of uniformed men who opened fire. Most of the turkeys flew away but four of them did not escape. Their bodies were ripped open by the bullets and as the blood poured forth, I could see their heads change into human faces.

The obvious interpretation had to do with unresolved childhood problems and unmet oral needs. I had been having stomach problems at the time, and the Thanksgiving turkey was an appropriate symbol of both food and family. However, I remembered the dream in May 1970, when units of the Ohio national guard opened fire on a group of Kent State University students during a demonstration protesting the Cambodian incursion. When the smoke cleared away, four students lay dead in pools of their own blood. Could my dream have been precognitive of this tragic event?

My work at the university involved children with reading problems and learning disabilities for whom we had a remedial clinic every summer. In 1963, I ran my first parapsychological experiment with students attending the clinic.

The experiment was based on earlier findings that when "normal" and "distorted" materials were used in testing ESP, significant differences were yielded favoring "normal" material. One of the parapsychologists who had done the most work in this area was Dr. K. Ramakrishna Rao, whom I had met at Rhine's laboratory. Rao referred to the difference between target materials as the "preferential effect" and devised an experiment in which subjects brought in their own ESP symbols. Rao's study demonstrated that the subjects did better on their own preferred symbols than on the standard ESP cards depicting crosses, stars, circles, squares, and wavy lines. The preferential effect in paranormal perception thus seemed to resemble variables in ordinary perception because people will more clearly see or hear material that is familiar and of interest to them than uninteresting, unfamiliar material.

Because all thirty-seven pupils in our summer clinic had learning problems, I thought that a difference might emerge between ESP cards on which a word appeared and cards containing "coded" pictures of those cards. To translate the pictures into words would involve a "decoding" process which most pupils with learning problems would find difficult if done with ordinary perception and possibly even more difficult when done with paranormal perception.

One deck of ESP cards contained twenty-five uncoded white cards on which the words *dogs, cats, fish, boat,* or *ship* had been typed (in equal numbers of five). A coded deck contained twenty-five cards of equal size picturing dogs, cats, a fish, a boat, or a ship.

The decks were shuffled by an assistant who did not look at the cards and who did not stay in the room once the shuffling was completed. Therefore, this was a clairvoyance test rather than a telepathy or precognition test. The shuffled cards were placed face down in an opaque envelope which was placed on a table. The pupils were tested in small groups; a different shuffling was used for each group to avoid a "stacking effect" in which the order of the cards might just happen to match the order in which most people would guess the cards. The instructions given on the pupils' multiple choice answer sheets (and read aloud) were similar for both decks:

There are five types of cards in this pile. On some cards the word "dogs" is typed. On other cards the words "cats," "fish," "boat," or "ship" are typed. Each card contains only one word. You are to circle the name of the word on the list below that you think matches the word on the card in the pile. The order of the cards is indicated by the number on the left-hand side of the page.

There are five types of pictures in this pile. Some show dogs, some show cats, some show a fish, some show a boat, some show a ship. You are to circle the name of the picture on the list below that you think matches the picture in the pile. The order of the pictures is indicated by the number on the left-hand side of the page.

Samples of each card were displayed visually when the students made their guesses. For some groups, the deck of words was used first; for other groups, the deck of pictures was used first.

A transistor radio was on view during the testing period. The pupils were told that the person making the most correct guesses would receive the radio as a prize. The expected number of correct guesses was five cards per deck. The pupil who won the transistor radio made ten correct guesses on one deck and nine on the other. The odds against this happening by chance are several hundred to one.

The pupils made an average score of 6.0 correct guesses on the card deck containing words and an average of 5.4 on the card deck containing pictures. In the first instance, the results were statistically significant while in the second case the data were not significant. Thus, the "preferential effect" appeared to be operating.

I had attended most of the annual conventions of the Parapsychological Association since its formation in 1957. At the 1963 meeting Gardner Murphy introduced me to Montague Ullman, a New York psychiatrist who had been interested in paranormal phenomena since his college years. At that time, he and a few friends held weekly meetings in which they attempted to move into a "group consciousness" that appeared to facilitate such phenomena as poltergeist activity and psychic photography. The results were provocative enough to encourage Ullman to track down Murphy and ask his advice. Murphy encouraged Ullman to maintain an interest in the field and when, in 1948, Murphy organized a special medical section of the American Society for Psychical Research, he asked Ullman to become a member. This special group, which was composed of psychoanalysts such as Ullman, Jule Eisenbud, and Jan Ehrenwald, discussed paranormal phenomena in the psychoanalytic situation.

In 1950, Ullman reported a patient's dreams from the night of February 24:

> There was a bottle on the table containing part alcohol and part cream. It was sort of a white, foamy stuff. . . . I looked at the label. It read "appealing nausea." I meant to drink it when we went to bed. . . . I had a small leopard. It was very dangerous.

It happened that on the evening of February 24, Ullman had attended a lecture on the induction of neuroses in cats. A film was shown in which alcoholism was induced in cats by mixing alcohol with their milk.

On December 21, 1951, one of Ullman's patients dreamed about taking a chromium soap dish from an industrial exhibit, and about feeling guilty and blushing. On the day of the patient's dream, Ullman had told a friend, in great confidence, how some of the workmen engaged in building his house had spotted a chromium soap dish which had been shipped to Ullman by mistake but which he had no intention of returning. One of the workmen made a wisecrack about Ullman's having gotten away with theft. Perhaps the patient had picked up Ullman's remark to the friend by means of telepathy—and had supplied his own guilt.

Ullman invited me to serve as a consultant to a project he was initiating in New York City which would explore scientifically the topic of telepathic dreaming. He was also eager to have me discuss my ideas about altered states of consciousness with his staff, as well as my experience with psilocybin, a psychedelic drug. I had been a subject in the Harvard Psilocybin Research Project, had told Murphy about my entry into the realms of psychedelia, and was flattered to know that a group of New York psychotherapists wanted to hear what I had to say.

2

MUSIC TO EAT MUSHROOMS BY

Under the influence of the drug . . . all sorts of biologically useless things start to happen. There may be extrasensory perceptions. Other persons discover a world of visionary beauty. To others again is revealed the glory, the infinite value and meaningfulness of naked existence, of the given, unconceptualized event.

Aldous Huxley

A Quarter of a Million Indians Can't Be Wrong

As a child, I had read about the Oracle of Delphi and how she gave cryptic predictions of the future following ingestion of mind-altering fumes which seeped up from a nearby crack in the earth. I was also intrigued by the mystery ritual of Eleusis; a fresco in Pompeii indicated that during these rituals a potion was imbibed which stimulated astonishing visions. Later, I learned that the Native American church, said to number a quarter of a million adherents, is a federation of North American Indian users of peyote, a consciousness-changing substance prepared from the bud of a cactus plant. For many years, these Indians were harassed by governmental agents and church missionaries who claimed that peyote produced insanity and immorality.

Mescaline, the chemical synthesis of peyote, was ingested by Aldous Huxley in 1953; it also began to be utilized in several scientific investigations of creativity and psychotherapy. Simultaneously under investigation was LSD, synthesized in 1938, and dubbed "psychedelic" (or "mind-manifesting") by the psychiatrist, Humphry Osmond.

In 1955, a New York banker and his wife, Gordon and Valentina Wasson, became the first outsiders to report eating the "sacred mushroom" of central Mexico in a native religious ritual. Soon, the active ingredient of the mushroom was chemically synthesized and named psilocybin. I remem-

19

ber reading about the Wassons' adventure in *Life* magazine and envying their experience.

In the summer of 1960, Timothy Leary, a newly appointed faculty member of Harvard University, ingested the psilocybe mushrooms in Cuernavaca, Mexico.

In his book, *High Priest*, Leary wrote:

> It was the classic visionary voyage and I came back a changed man. You are never the same after you've had that one glimpse down the cellular time tunnel. You are never the same after you've had the veil drawn. . . . Since eating seven mushrooms in a garden in Mexico, I have devoted all of my time and energy to the exploration and description of these strange deep realms.

Leary, it was alleged by his critics, had his mind "blown" by the mushrooms and began to indulge in bizarre behavior. Years earlier, however, Leary had dropped out of a Roman Catholic college and, later, from West Point. He became interested in psychology, graduated from the University of Alabama, and enlisted as an army psychologist in 1942. Upon receiving his doctorate, he became director of psychological research for the Kaiser Foundation Hospital in Oakland, California. After the suicide of his first wife and the breaking up of his second marriage, he resigned his position, sailed for Spain with his two children, and settled in a villa on the Costa del Sol. The Harvard psychologist, David McClelland, whose specialty was the stimulation of achievement in nonachieving societies, persuaded Leary to return to academia. (One wonders how often since then McClelland has wished he had allowed Leary to remain a nonachieving expatriate soaking up the Spanish sun.)

Psilocybin Goes to Harvard

I first came into contact with Leary in 1961 at the annual meeting of the American Psychological Association. In a room so crowded that I ended up on a windowsill, the Harvard psychologist told his audience how psilocybin promised to provide major breakthroughs in the social sciences. Other members of the panel were the psychologist Frank Barron and the writers William Burroughs and Gerald Heard, all of whom discussed various facets of psychedelic experience.

A striking figure, with his salt-and-pepper hair and flashing smile, Leary stressed the importance of frame of mind and physical setting for a favorable psychedelic session. He also emphasized the importance of seeing the experimenter as a part of the research project's social milieu. He said, "The psychologist does not stand outside the event but recognizes his part in it, working collaboratively with the subject towards mutually selected goals." He told how participants in his study alternated roles of experimenter and subject, how the participants were given all available information about the drug before the experiment, and how the sessions took place in pleasant, spacious, esthetic surroundings.

As for the experience itself, Leary compared it to the Magic Theater written about by Hermann Hesse in his novel, *Steppenwolf*. He explained, "Psychedelic drugs open the door to the Magic Theater, and the stages and dramas you encounter depend on what you are looking for, your state of mind when you begin, and the condition of your traveling companions."

By the time Leary finished his report, I decided that I would obtain an invitation to Harvard to participate in an experiment. After all, I had a friend, Stephen Klineberg, who was a doctoral student in the department of social relations. I would encourage Klineberg to volunteer for the project, and, later, to ask permission to bring me along for a session.

In April 1962, I arrived at the department of social relations on the Harvard campus. Following an examination of my medical report as well as my responses on a personality test, I had a personal interview with Leary. He told me about a visit he had recently made to Dr. Rhine's laboratory in North Carolina where he gave psilocybin to the entire staff. According to Leary, the parapsychologists scurried around giving each other ESP tests, guessing how many crosses or squares were in a deck of twenty-five cards.

Leary invited me to a party in his home that night honoring Alan Watts. I had been eager to meet Watts ever since reading his books on Zen Buddhism and hearing delightful stories about his five years as Episcopalian chaplain at Northwestern University's Canterbury House.

Watts had become interested in the Orient after reading a Fu Manchu story at the age of eleven. Leaving his native England for America, he became an ordained Episcopalian priest in 1945. In 1950, at the end of a period of contemplation in a farmhouse near Millbrook, New York, he left the ministry, stating, "I am now fully persuaded that the Church's claim to be the best of all ways to God is not only a mistake, but also a symptom of anxiety." Since that time, Watts had continued to study, travel, write, and lecture. Originally, Watts thought it highly improbable that a true spiritual experience could follow the ingestion of a chemical. After a few psychedelic sessions, however, he was compelled to admit that "LSD had brought me into an undeniably mystical state of consciousness." However, he added that "when one has received the message, one hangs up the phone."

Watts had been given a fellowship for study and travel by Harvard. He told us about the insights he had obtained during his psychedelic sessions when the "veil was lifted," but of the necessity of reviewing the new insights subsequently in the light of cold sobriety. Some insights remained striking in their wisdom, and others proved to be sheer nonsense. This cautionary advice was a valuable send-off for my own session on the following day.

I awakened in the middle of the night sick to my stomach, and could not get back to sleep. I was in such great pain that Klineberg had to help me into the office where two of Leary's assistants were to prepare me for the evening session. I arrived early so that they would not suspect my indisposition and stayed until they had left so that they would not notice Steve helping me back to his car.

"The President Was Shot"

The session took place at a private apartment with Leary's two graduate students taking a small amount of psilocybin in order to participate in the experience as well as to serve as guides. Klineberg and I were each given thirty milligrams by Leary at 5:30 P.M. He then left for one of the many meetings he had been holding with nervous state medical officials in which he tried to calm their anxieties about his experiments. I started to administer an intelligence test to Steve, as we had decided to investigate the effects of psilocybin upon mental ability. But after thirty minutes, we began to laugh at each question I asked and abandoned the project.

At 5:57 I closed my eyes and saw a kaleidoscopic vision of colorful shapes and swirls. I opened my eyes to find the room vibrating with brilliant colors.

My fingers were tingling and my limbs were trembling. I closed my eyes again and visualized a giant mushroom spreading over me like a magical umbrella. A spiral of letters, words, and numbers blew away in a tornado; apparently I had been stripped of my verbal ability and was left with a concrete world of sense, feeling, and direct impressions.

I was given an apple; the process of chewing seemed to take forever. My mouth was a giant cavern and I felt the pulp moving slowly down my esophagus. I groped toward the kitchen and sampled the herbs; thyme, cloves, cinnamon, and vanilla registered upon my consciousness all at once yet separately.

I worked my way back to the sofa, feeling the fabric of the carpet and the pillows, and caressing the sweater and breasts of one of my guides. By this time, my aches and pains had completely vanished and I had nothing but pleasant sensations whenever I turned my attention inward.

My sense of hearing astonished me. Every tone of Moussorgsky's *Pic-*

tures at an Exhibition and Beethoven's Seventh Symphony was an event of sheer beauty. I was inside the music, surrounded by chords and tones that submerged me with their beauty.

When I closed my eyes, I saw delicate arabesques and Persian miniatures. When I opened my eyes, each item in the apartment seemed transformed. The alarm clock was a work of art from a Cellini studio. The gaudy jewelry on the dresser was on loan from the Empress Josephine. The faces of my companions radiated light; auras shone around their bodies and I felt an inexpressible kinship with them.

But then my companions began talking. I was not at all interested in verbalizing my experience or hearing other people prattle about theirs. Not able to walk away, I slowly crawled into a nearby bedroom, taking some clove sticks and some peppermint candy with me. Sniffing the cloves, tasting the candy, looking at the paintings on the walls, listening to the music, I felt as if I were being swept into a sensory whirlpool. The vortex resembled the Yin-Yang symbol and, as it carried me downstream, the first stop was the court of Kublai Khan. With my eyes closed, I visualized the rich brocade of the emperor's gown, noticed the finely detailed embroidery of the courtier's cloaks, and watched a peacock strut by, putting everyone else's raiment to shame.

Suddenly, I was in an immense auditorium listening to a concert. The concert hall was an intricately designed geometrical structure which brought Buckminster Fuller to mind. Each member of the orchestra was dressed in an ostentatious scarlet uniform with epaulets of gold braid.

Within an instant, I was at Versailles. Benjamin Franklin was chatting with the French monarchs who were gowned elaborately in satins, furs, silks, and jewels. Franklin was modestly dressed; his sense of humor was so sparkling, however, that he was getting more attention than any member of the royal family.

The record on the turntable changed, producing a burst of flamenco music. France yielded to Spain as I visualized gypsy guitarists. A black-haired, jet-eyed Spanish dancer threw roses into the air; they exploded like firecrackers.

The scene shifted to the New World. I was with Thomas Jefferson at Monticello as he explained his newest invention, a four-sided music stand which permitted all four members of a string quartet to use the same device as they performed.

A somber note was interjected as I found myself with Edgar Allen Poe in Baltimore. He was mourning the death of his young bride; his pale complexion and sad eyes convinced me that he would like to join her and that this wish could hasten his own death.

From Baltimore, I traveled to the nation's capital where I found myself in the White House gazing at a bust of Lincoln. I was seeing Lincoln's features in profile and they began to darken. I noticed a gun at the base of the statue; someone whispered, "He was shot. The president was shot." A wisp of smoke rose from the gun and curled into the air.

Lincoln's features slowly faded away and those of John F. Kennedy took their place. The wisp of smoke was still emerging from the gun and the voice repeated, "He was shot. The president was shot." My eyes were filled with tears.

Wiping my eyes, I visualized a chaotic, turbulent sea; my three companions and I were in a small boat, trying to remain afloat. We came upon a gigantic figure standing waist deep on the churning waters. He smiled a sad smile, filled with compassion, concern, and love.

Was this the image of God? Was He caught in the storm as well? Perhaps nobody could change our course, alter our situation, or provide us with security. However, we could all express compassion, concern, and love —and in so doing, partake of divinity.

I opened my eyes, telephoned Leary, and found that he had just returned from his meeting. I told him of my experience and made special note of the Lincoln-Kennedy sequence. Meeting friends in New York City the next day, I found myself still rather high as they took me to a play, *The Golden Apple*, based on the odyssey of Ulysses after the Trojan War. The costumes and music transported me back to my expanded conscious state of the previous night.

Islands on the Reef

When Kennedy was assassinated on November 22, 1963, many of my friends credited me with having had a precognitive glimpse of the tragic event. However, at the age of ten, I had studied the American presidency, noting that, since 1840, every U.S. president elected at a twenty-year interval had died in office. The first link in the chain of deaths was William Henry Harrison, elected in 1840, who died from pneumonia in 1841. In 1860, Abraham Lincoln was elected; in 1880 James A. Garfield was elected; in 1900 William McKinley was reelected; in 1920 Warren G. Harding was elected; and in 1940 Franklin D. Roosevelt was reelected. All of them died in office. One president, Zachary Taylor, was elected in 1848 and died in 1850; with that single exception, all of America's chief executives who died in office fell in the twenty-year cycle.

Is this cycle a coincidence? Perhaps. Yet it may also be an example of what Carl Jung termed "synchronicity"—a series of events connected by simultaneity and meaning. Jung described "archetypes" as primitive, primordial images which are part of the "collective unconscious," the forgotten memories of all people; to Jung, synchronous happenings are coincidences which rest on an archetypal foundation. In other words, the twenty-year presidential death cycle may not be a series of discrete events, but a single event. On the surface of an ocean, one may see a dozen small islands; by looking underwater, it may be discovered that they are all the protuberances of a single reef. So it is with synchronous events and so it may be with the deaths of American presidents. The underlying archetypal foundation may be the paternal image that Americans love, need, and hate at the same time.

Jung became interested in synchronicity by studying the *I Ching,* the Chinese *Book of Changes* which was regarded as ancient even at the time of Confucius. Its verses, hexagrams, or Kua, selected by tossing coins or by manipulating stalks of the yarrow plant, give counsel on such topics as how to recover a stray dog, how to deal with a domineering mother-in-law, and how to conduct a military campaign.

Jung brought the *I Ching* to the attention of the Western world. In explaining how oriental thought connected a designated Kuan or hexagram with the person's question, Jung wrote:

> The Chinese mind, as I see it at work in the *I Ching,* seems to be exclusively preoccupied with the chance aspects of events. What we call coincidence seems to be the chief concern of this peculiar mind, and what we worship as causality passes almost unnoticed. . . . In other words, whoever invented the *I Ching* was convinced that the hexagram worked out in a certain moment coincided with the latter in quality no less than in time. To him the hexagram was the exponent of the moment in which it was cast—even more so than the hours of the clock or the divisions of the calendar could be—inasmuch as the hexagram was understood to be an indicator of the essential situation prevailing in the moment of its origin.

> This assumption involves a certain curious principle that I have termed synchronicity, a concept that formulates a point of view diametrically opposed to that of causality. Since the latter is a merely statistical truth and not absolute, it is a sort of working hypothesis of how events evolve one out of another, whereas synchronicity takes the coincidence of events in space and time as meaning something more than mere chance, namely, a peculiar interdependence of objective events among themselves as well as the subjective (psychic) states of the observer or observers.

One criterion of the *I Ching*'s validity is whether the text of the Kuan amounts to a true rendering of the observer's condition. If so, this demonstrates that the fall of the yarrow stalks or coins was indeed an indispensable part of the given situation. Furthermore, the observer must be flexible and open-minded enough to see the possibilities in the Kua—and to believe that the *I Ching* will be helpful.

Jung's theory of synchronicity has important implications for precognition. Although I do not believe that all precognition is synchronous in nature, it is likely that some premonitions represent a clairvoyant awareness of another island on the coral reef, another aspect of the total event, one that is there beyond the viewer's sight. Others represent a global assimilation of all the data on hand, and an unconscious integration of these data into an accurate statement of a future event. Still another type of precognition actually represents a form of psychokinesis—by directing our consciousness toward the future, we may actually cause an event in time to turn out the way we think it will. The Soviet astronomer, Nikolai Kozyrev, hypothesizes that time has density and that conscious attention directed toward a future event may actually influence the event in question. Arthur Koestler has also applied ideas from the field of theoretical physics to precognition in an attempt to explain the mechanisms involved. Premonitory dreams can represent all three forms of precognition.

A possible example of synchronicity occurred when my wife, Lelie, and I were attending a psychological conference in Chicago. As I waited for her to return from a shopping expedition, another psychologist and I were talking about the meetings. For no apparent reason, he abruptly changed the topic and said, "Did you know that the Wilhelm translation of the *I Ching* is now available in one volume instead of two?" At that very moment, Lelie walked into the room carrying a surprise for me—the new one-volume edition of the *I Ching*.

Here we have a meaningful coincidence divorced from cause-and-effect relationships. Perhaps Lelie and my psychologist friend were connected unconsciously in regard to the *I Ching*. Perhaps my friend's reading of the one-volume edition was part of the same underlying matrix that brought Lelie into the bookstore. Like the tips of two suddenly emerging icebergs that are joined under the ocean, both brought new and identical information to me at the same time.

A Pliable Future

Another type of precognition represents a global assimilation of all necessary information needed to make an accurate prediction. Sometimes this is not paranormal at all, but represents the intricate workings of the human mind. In one instance, a woman told me that she had a dream of her mother's death three weeks before the heart attack actually occurred. However, I discovered that the woman saw her mother several times a week. I suspected that the woman was unconsciously noticing changes in her mother's gait, color, and speech. These pieces of information eventually combined in a dream which was an accurate prediction of the future, but one which could be explained without resorting to the precognition hypothesis.

On the other hand, Abraham Lincoln's premonitions of his assassination may represent an unconscious telepathic assimilation of information from John Wilkes Booth which burst into consciousness in the form of impressions and dreams.

Abraham Lincoln once told Harriet Beecher Stowe, "Whichever way the war ends, I have the impression that I shall not last long after it is over." Three weeks before his assassination, he had a dream which may serve as an example of the telepathic type of precognition. Ward Hill Laman, U.S. marshall for the District of Columbia, wrote down Lincoln's dream exactly as the president described it during a White House celebration of Robert E. Lee's surrender:

> About ten days ago, I retired late. I had been waiting for important dispatches. . . . I soon began to dream. There seemed to be a deathlike stillness about me. Then I heard subdued sobs, as if a number of people were weeping. I thought I left my bed and wandered downstairs. There the silence was broken by the same pitiful sobbing, but the mourners were invisible. I went from room to room. No living person was in sight, but the same mournful sounds of distress met me as I passed along. It was light in all the rooms; every object was familiar to me, but where were all the people who were grieving as if their hearts would break? I was puzzled and alarmed. What could be the meaning of all this? Determined to find the cause of a state of affairs so mysterious and so shocking, I kept on until I arrived in the East Room, which I entered. There I met with a sickening surprise. Before me was a catafalque, on which rested a corpse in funeral vestments. Around it were stationed soldiers who were acting as guards; and there was a throng of people, some gazing mournfully upon the corpse, whose face was covered, others weeping pitifully. "Who is dead in the White House?" I demanded of one of the soldiers. "The President," was his answer. "He was killed by an assassin."

Does Lincoln's dream, and those like it, pose a threat to the concept of "free will" and voluntary action? Freedom to choose, or "free will," implies that an individual acts in accord with inner motives rather than in response to external circumstances, at least part of the time. Do the data on precognition threaten this concept?

Writing in the *Journal of Parapsychology*, A. C. Garnett, my University of Wisconsin philosophy professor, addressed himself to this issue. In a brilliant paper, Dr. Garnett pointed out that much of Western philosophy views the universe as dualistic—consisting of "mental" events (thoughts, images, intentions, anticipations) and "physical" events ("material" objects which occupy physical space). Rejecting this dualistic notion, Garnett proposed the conception of a unified monistic universe which would preclude separating existence into "mind" and "matter." He suggested that there was one source, one "medium of connection" among all events. The terms *mind* and *matter*, in reality, are activities of this one connecting medium. Garnett named that medium *M* for the sake of convenience in referring back to his conception.

Among the properties of M would be patterns corresponding to future events in the universe. Existing events could produce in M an instantaneous projection of their future course in accord with natural laws. The psi process, in responding to these patterns, would enable the individual to demonstrate precognition phenomena. Discussing the pattern which an event might produce in M, Garnett wrote:

> Such a pattern might not only be limited in time representing a few months or years of the future. It might also be limited in space, representing only the interrelated set of events of a single planet and incorporating into its structure a representation of only the statistical expectation of energy received into the planet's system from outside. . . . This theory of the functioning of the neutral medium "M" thus enables us to conceive of the operation of precognition without any radical change in the notion of the ordinary causal relation of physical events and without denying the possibility that human foresight, decision, and effort can change the course of behavior.

To Garnett, M would contain the present state of the world as well as a limited model of the world's future state. The present state foreshadows the future state; however, human volition might very well alter the shape of things to come.

Just as the computer of an earth satellite contains a model of its future course, so M contains a model—albeit limited and imperfect—of the forthcoming state of the universe. "Mental" processes, which are one aspect of M, are to some extent affected by this model; precognitive experiences are the result.

Any number of cases from Louisa Rhine's collection demonstrate the usefulness of human intervention following a precognitive experience. A woman awakened her husband one night, telling him of a horrifying dream. She reported seeing a large ornamental chandelier which hung over their baby's bed. The chandelier fell and crushed the baby to death. The hands on the clock in the baby's room pointed to 4:35. The husband laughed at the story and criticized his wife for bringing the baby into her own bed. He did not laugh two hours later when a crashing noise summoned them to the baby's bedchamber. The chandelier had fallen on the baby's empty crib; the clock on the dresser showed the time to be 4:35.

In this instance, Garnett's M contained a model of the future state of the world in general and of the chandelier in particular. The chandelier, at the time of the woman's dream, was ready to fall. M permitted an association to be made between the mother's "mental" events and the model of the future "material" events surrounding the chandelier, crib, and clock in her baby's room. In this instance, human volition may have been effective in altering the effects of forthcoming events, indicating that the future is not predetermined but pliable.

If the mother's dream allowed her to obtain information about the state of the chandelier, it was clairvoyant in nature, rather than telepathic—as Lincoln's dream may have been. Both examples demonstrate how information can be assimilated by paranormal means and congeal during the night in a person's dreams. In other instances, the information about future events may break into consciousness during such states of altered awareness as daytime reverie, a meditative experience, or a psychedelic session.

Do You Know Virginia Glenn?

I discussed my psilocybin experience in a paper, "Consciousness Expansion and the Extensional World," presented at an international general semantics conference held at New York University in August 1962. The meeting was presided over by S. I. Hayakawa, who had written in *Language in Thought and Action*:

> If a child grows to adulthood with a verbal world in his head which corresponds fairly closely to the extensional world that he finds around him in his widening experience, he is in relatively small danger of being shocked or hurt by what he finds, because his verbal world has told him what, more or less, to expect. . . . If, however, he grows up with a false map in his head . . . he will constantly be running into trouble, wasting his efforts, and acting like a fool. He will not be adjusted to the world as it is; he may, if the lack of adjustment is serious, end up in a mental hospital.

I discussed the possibility that psychedelic substances, if administered properly, could help a person to reestablish contact with the reality first encountered in childhood. In so doing, they could help people break through word games which trap them and release individuals from early conditionings which thwart their later development. I concluded that the drug experience lasts only a few hours before the participants return to the world of verbalized meanings and word games. However, after the trip ends, they are often able to substitute reality-oriented and socially beneficial games for those characterized by a lack of contact with reality. In addition, they can minimize the game element in esthetic and social experiences where the quality of nongame openness is appropriate.

I also noted the potential dangers of these drugs if they were incorrectly administered. I made the flat prediction that LSD, psilocybin, and mescaline were bound to become popular on college campuses and that at least one student per week would be hospitalized with a psychotic reaction if research programs were not expanded so as to permit people to have psychedelic experiences in supportive settings under medical supervision.

Immediately after my talk, I noticed a tall woman supported by a white cane, wearing a huge green hat with a floppy brim, come limping rapidly down the aisle. She wore a necklace of potbellied Buddhas, as well as a Buddha bracelet and Buddha earrings. Her first questions to me were, "Do you know Tim Leary? Do you know Alan Watts?" I acknowledged that I knew them both, and so Virginia Glenn entered my life. I discovered that she had been in the crowded convention room when I first heard Leary discuss psychedelics, and that she had an active interest in both parapsychology and altered states of consciousness.

Earlier, Virginia discovered she had acute diabetes and decided to commit suicide; she changed her mind after hearing a taped lecture by Alan Watts. In the early 1950s, she traveled between Chicago, Cleveland, New York City, and Washington, D.C., playing her collection of Alan Watts tapes for anyone interested in hearing them. She first met Watts in 1957 while working as a waitress in New York City. By then her diabetes was worse, sending her into frequent comas, and she had developed an incurable infection of the right foot. However, Virginia never complained about anything. She began to arrange talks and seminars for Watts who looked upon her as a Bodhisattva—a living Buddha.

Virginia invited me to New York City in 1964 to give a seminar on altered states of consciousness and psychical research for a group of her friends. At the seminar, I was surprised to meet such celebrated persons as William Wolf, an internationally renowned endocrinologist; Robert Masters, the sexologist; Jean Houston, a philosopher who was conducting experiments with LSD, and Zelda Suplee, a pioneer in the nudist movement. I spoke of a "Consciousness Revolution," which I felt would rival the Copernican, Darwinian, and Freudian Revolutions in its impact on science and society. Virginia, however, was too ill to attend the seminar. At the end of my presentation, I rushed to her hospital bedside. She was in good spirits, and talked excitedly about her forthcoming trip to Deaconess Hospital in

Boston where she had offered herself as a guinea pig for any new diabetic treatment. Later, she was sent by the Deaconess physicians to Harvard where a cyclotron paralyzed certain functions of her pituitary gland in an effort to halt her developing blindness—a side effect of the diabetes.

I again saw Virginia at the 1964 convention of the American Psychological Association. She had saved seats for S. I. Hayakawa and me at an address on psychedelics and religion which Leary had been invited to give for a group of Lutheran psychologists. After the lecture, Virginia and I persuaded Hayakawa to prepare a special issue of the general semantics journal, *ETC*. The special issue sold more copies than had any previous copy of the journal and contained Hayakawa's reactions to psychedelics which impressed me as one of the best critical statements ever written. It read, in part:

> The full appreciation of art or literature or music requires years of study, years of experience and exposure to masterworks. But under LSD, tremendous "esthetic" and "creative" experiences are said to be accessible instantly and without effort. . . . Perhaps my basic reason for distrusting the dependence on "mind-expanding" drugs is that most people haven't learned to use the senses they possess.

Despite the fact that I knew people whose LSD experiences had finally put them in touch with their senses, I felt Hayakawa had given generally sound advice. But as so often happens with words wisely spoken, Hayakawa's dictum was not heeded over the years to come by the people who, in retrospect, would have found it critically beneficial.

Psilocybin Drops Out

In the meantime, events had moved rapidly for Leary. The use of undergraduate students as subjects for the drug studies was criticized by several faculty members. Consequently, he and his faculty associate in the work, Richard Alpert, another McClelland protégé, agreed to confine experimentation to graduate students. Then Leary was pressured into entrusting his supply of the drugs to the director of Harvard's health services. When one student, Walter Pahnke, asked to be given enough psilocybin for his doctoral research project, this request was refused despite the fact that a Harvard-appointed doctoral committee had approved the project. Fortunately, a researcher in another city supplied Pahnke with the chemicals and his doctoral project eventually became an important part of the literature in altered states of consciousness.

In 1961, Leary, Alpert, and Ralph Metzner, a graduate student from

Oxford, had begun to give psilocybin to convicts up for parole in an attempt to assist their rehabilitation. In January 1963, the investigators reported that only 8 percent of the exconvicts had been arrested for new crimes. Leary's critics, however, pointed out that some of the "rehabilitated" convicts regularly appropriated faculty paychecks, cashing them after visiting Leary. It was also noted that certain of Leary's male associates had been arranging their own psychedelic sessions with local coeds, taking advantage of the girls' expanded awareness as an opportunity for sexual seduction. In at least one case, a male student was seduced under similar circumstances and ended up in a mental hospital.

On May 6, 1963, Leary was discharged on the grounds that he had "failed to keep his faculty appointments," a charge that Leary felt unjustified on the basis of a verbal agreement with McClelland which reshuffled Leary's academic obligations. Leary did not request a hearing, pointing out that in any event, his contract was due to expire on June 30. Others claimed that Leary had solid grounds for requesting a hearing, but knew that the malfeasance of his associates would have gained public notoriety if he had made an issue of his dismissal.

When Leary left Harvard in 1963, he organized IFIF—the International Federation for Internal Freedom. Richard Alpert had also been dismissed from Harvard and joined Leary, along with Ralph Metzner, who had now finished his doctoral studies. The stated purpose of IFIF was to allow its members to "turn on" legally by securing consciousness-altering substances within the federal regulatory framework and ingesting them in sessions supervised by a trained physician. This plan was too visionary in its nature and too impractical in its structure to win governmental sanction. Soon, the black market in illegal drugs mushroomed across the land, leaving in its wake both enlightened spirits and "blown" minds, both expanded psyches and burned-out cases.

Psychiatrists with traditional training found themselves unable to treat untoward LSD reactions effectively. Usually, they called the reactions "toxic psychoses" and administered large doses of tranquilizing drugs. This type of treatment often resulted in later "flashbacks" because tranquilizers prevented the psyche's complete processing of the material emerging suddenly from the unconscious. As an alternative to this type of treatment, a number of "free clinics" were organized to deal with adverse LSD experiences and, later, to provide health services to the members of the psychedelic counterculture. I became a consultant to many of these clinics, giving workshops on the handling of ,adverse LSD reactions at such clinics as "Room-to-Move" in Amherst, Massachusetts, "Naturalism" in Hollywood, "421" in Toronto, and the "Haight-Ashbury Free Clinic," which serviced the growing "hippie" population in San Francisco.

IFIF's projects were shelved as Leary and his entourage attempted, without success, to relocate in Mexico and, later, in the West Indies. In 1964, Leary leased an enormous, grotesque sandcastle of a house in Millbrook, New York, from William Hitchcock, the millionaire grandson of Andrew Mellon. The house was one of several buildings on a 2,500 acre estate, formerly used for cattle raising by the Hitchcock Cattle Corporation.

IFIF was transformed into Castalia, named after a Utopian community in a Hermann Hesse novel. Its stated goals were the employment of non-chemical methods for the expansion of consciousness, and the discussion of neurological, philosophical, religious, and psychological theories concerning consciousness-expansion. Leary, Alpert, and Metzner began to hold a series of "experiential weekends" at Millbrook.

On the First Day at Millbrook

In the summer of 1965 (a year before our marriage), Lelie Harris and I went to Millbrook for a weekend workshop, taking her children, Carie and Bob with us. Virginia Glenn accompanied us, bringing along her friend Don Smoot, an industrial psychologist. Upon arriving at Castalia, we noticed Leary and Metzner in the backyard. Alpert was in California, Leary's estranged third wife, bored with the country life, was in Brazil. I walked over to greet Leary and Metzner. But before I could say anything, a frowning staff member shoved a dittoed sheet in my hand which read:

> Welcome to an experiential weekend. Your weekend in Millbrook has been planned to provide a series of consciousness-expanding experiences.
>
> The first step in the process of going beyond your routine and familiar patterns is a period of absolute silence.

Because of an overflow crowd and an ensuing room shortage, our group was sexually segregated; Lelie, Carie, and Virginia were directed to a room in the main building as Don, Bob and I were taken to the bowling alley. Built in a style best described as American Gothic, the bowling alley featured two bowling lanes, pastel landscapes, oriental rugs, incense, candles, and canopied beds. After we had unpacked, a young woman appeared and pointed to Don and Bob, who dutifully followed her. I read "Message One" on the instruction sheet:

> Please do not engage in conversation of any kind until the breaking of the silence is publicly announced.
>
> For now, LOOK.
> LISTEN to the non-verbal energy around you.
> EXPERIENCE directly.

A young man arrived, followed by Lelie, and I fell in behind them. For half an hour we walked through a wooded area. The pine trees were rustling, the crickets chirping, the brook bubbling, and the wind murmuring. It was refreshing to listen to something other than verbal conversation.

Returning to the bowling alley, I read "Message Two."

Focus on the candle; see if you can turn off planning and thinking.

Concentrate on the moment-to-moment flow of time.

After contemplating the candle for several minutes, I was rejoined by Don and Bob. On our way to the main building, which we had dubbed the "mad mansion," I thought of the candle exercise in relation to the birds in Aldous Huxley's final novel, *Island*. In this utopian land, birds had been taught to crow "Attention!" By so doing they reminded the populace to attend to the present, to live in the here-and-now, and to enjoy each day to the fullest extent.

But now it was time to read "Message Three," which purported to tell us "how to play the experiential workshop game."

Goals:
> To communicate and exchange ideas about consciousness, its expansion, and its control. A wide variety of methods . . . will be employed to expand the consciousness of participants without drugs and to maintain as high a level of ecstasy as possible.

Visitor Roles:
> The roles which have been most comfortable to you and which are of most use to you in your regular life will be of lessened utility here and, indeed, may handicap you. The aim of the workshop is to get out beyond your routine robot consciousness. Thus, there is little interest in who you are and much more concern with where and how far you can go. What you can obtain during the weekend depends in part on how much of your routine ego you can leave in your room. Why don't you check it in your suitcase?

Staff Roles:
> Ten people will be present during the weekend whose jobs it is to facilitate the goals of the seminar. Their functions are assigned and scheduled.

The Seeking Help Role:
> This is not a psychotherapeutic situation and the doctor-patient game is not played. Personal problems cannot, therefore, become the focus of discussion.

Rule One:
> Be aware of and try to minimize the attempt of your robot consciousness to capture audiences for its personal dramas.

Rule Two:
> Please obey the laws of the land. In particular, do not bring marijuana, LSD, or any other illegal chemical to the weekend workshop.

Rule Three:
> Visitors are asked to maintain their own rooms during their stay.

Strategies:
> The ecstatic-psychedelic experience can be reached by several means: intellectual, emotional, bodily movement, somatic-sensory, and sexual. One of the aims of this workshop is to encourage expansion of consciousness in all five of these functions in some sort of balanced harmony. Consciousness-expansion in the sexual area will be limited to indirect methods. . . .

Values:
> "Good" is what raises the ecstasy count of all persons present and "bad" is what lowers the ecstasy count.

Ritual:
> The creation of consciousness-expansion experiences usually involves rituals. The use of these rituals—and of such materials as votive candles, mandalas, religious pictures, incense, etc.—is strictly experimental and does not involve any commitment to sectarian systems on the part of staff members or visitors.

Time and Space Limits:
> The schedule of the programs will be announced. Consult a staff member about additions and revisions to the schedule—and about leisure play. During your leisure time you are free to use any areas except the third floor.

The regimen of silence was broken as we returned to the mansion after dinner and entered the largest of its forty-five rooms. At the sound of a Chinese gong, Leary appeared, dressed in a white shirt, black pants, red socks, and sandals. He conducted a sociodrama which cast all of us in new roles. I became a visitor from outer space and played my part while a stroboscope gave the scene the appearance of a vintage film, with all of its periodic jumps and jerks.

On the Second Day at Millbrook

Ralph Metzner, recently returned from India, led the sunrise yoga session which preceded breakfast. Then Leary discussed one of his favorite topics, imprinting and psychedelic experience. He stated that the first few weeks of an organism's life are marked by a very great susceptibility to external influence. A duck will ordinarily learn how to follow its mother during this period as an early experience makes an indelible "imprint" on the baby duck's nervous system. If the duckling were separated from its mother, it might well follow the first moving object that came along—a chicken, a basketball, even the experimenter.

According to Leary, psychedelic experience allows behavior to be changed because those who participate find themselves open to new imprints. For this reason, he forecast a bright future for LSD in psychotherapy, especially with alcoholics and with chronic lawbreakers whose behavior patterns are especially resistant to change. Leary stated:

> Imprinting is a biochemical freezing of external awareness to stimuli which are presented at a critical period of neurological vulnerability which occurs very early in the life of a fowl and mammal. In addition, imprinting probably occurs at critical hormonal, biochemical stages in the life of the human being. As the result of early imprinting, ducklings follow their mother or, if the imprinting is altered, they reject their mother in favor of orange basketballs. There is the rather terrifying implication that early accidental, and involuntary external events can blindly couple the instinctual machinery to entirely inappropriate stimuli. It raises the disturbing question for each individual, "Which orange basketballs imprinted you?"

Leary also discussed the possibility that LSD suspends imprints temporarily and that psychedelic guides and therapists could take advantage of this possibility to change permanently their patients' outlook and behavior. Leary continued:

> During a psychedelic session, the nervous system, stripped of all previous learning and identity, is completely open to stimulation. We can increase the efficiency of our current imprints by recognizing clearly what we have imprinted, and by developing new chains of associations. In addition, we can suspend the imprints and reimprint ourselves, carefully choosing the persons and the ideas to which we will become voluntarily attached.

During the question period, I asked if the suspension of imprints under LSD could increase psychic ability. I mentioned the reports surrounding the coronation of Montezuma II as the ruler of Mexico in 1502 when psychedelic mushrooms were consumed by the Aztec celebrants. Many of the natives reported visions, premonitions of future events, and telepathic communication. One of my professors at Northwestern University, William McGovern, witnessed some natives in the Amazon drink *yagé*, a preparation of the *banisteria caapi* vine. As the participants entered altered states of consciousness, they reported what was happening in a distant village including the sudden death of a native chief. McGovern later verified these incidents.

Robert Masters and Jean Houston initiated a pilot study which explored the effects of LSD on telepathic ability. Finding that their experimental subjects became bored when the standard ESP cards were used, Masters and Houston shifted to pictorial scenes. When the transmitter imagined a Viking ship being thrown about on a stormy sea, the subject envisioned a "snake with an arched head swimming in tossed seas." Another scene was an Arab riding a camel near a pyramid; the subject reported a "camel passing through the inside of a vast labyrinthian tomb." Of the sixty-two subjects tested, forty-eight appeared to receive the picture two or more times out of ten attempts. A smaller number of subjects scored up to seven or eight successes. The total results far exceeded chance expectation.

Leary responded that the suspension of imprints and other culturally imposed barriers may make people more open to psychic phenomena. In addition, psychedelics help to release an upsurge of repressed material from the unconscious; this assists the manifestation of ESP, which is usually an unconscious process.

That evening Leary explained the *I Ching,* after which several of us took turns throwing the coins. The resulting pattern of "heads" and "tails" directed us to Kua 58:

> The joyous. Success. . . .
> Thus the superior man joins with his friends
> For discussion and practice.

This was a fine introduction to the simulated psychedelic session which Leary and his staff had prepared. Don, Virginia, Carie, Lelie, and I became absorbed with the multimedia production. The staff members did interpretive movement and danced to the accompaniment of stroboscopic lights, taped "concrete music," and a film and slide presentation of Buddha heads, stars, amoebae, blood cells, and flowers whirling together in kaleidoscopic array.

On the Third Day at Millbrook

Following yoga and breakfast, Leary delivered a Sunday morning sermon:

> The two new commandments required in this psychochemical age have to do with who has the right to change anyone else's consciousness.
> 1. Thou shalt not alter the consciousness of thy fellows by psychochemical means.
> 2. Thou shalt not prevent thy fellows from changing their consciousness by chemical means. If there is clear evidence that someone's change of consciousness harms society, then, and only then, can

you take preventive measures. But in every such case, the burden of proof must be on society to demonstrate that harm is being done.

Leary admitted that psychedelics were potentially dangerous, but reminded us that other psychochemicals exist that are even more dangerous, yet are in common use, nicotine and alcohol being examples.

One of the members of our group asked Leary what advice he had given his children regarding psychedelic drugs. He replied that he had counseled:

An LSD trip is a frightening experience. If you're not ready to look at yourself and your ambitions, your lusts, desires, and pride through a clear amplifying lens, stay away from psychedelic experience—drug or nondrug. Even so, the potential damage of LSD is much less than the danger from alcohol or from such toxic yet lethal drugs as nicotine. I have made it clear to my children that I prefer that they smoke marijuana rather than use liquor or nicotine, both of which are proven addictive and toxic substances.

Leary expressed his opinion regarding young people who "turn on, tune in, and drop out."

I'm not concerned about a lot of young people who are taking days, months, and even a year or two off to examine carefully what this whole business is all about. I wonder what kind of a society we have if we deprive our young people the right to take some time off for exploration, for wandering, for curious poking about. The Buddha, after all, was one of the first drop-outs. If you are concerned about your children's interest in psychedelic drugs, why don't you sit down with them and listen to everything they have to say about it? You may learn a lot. And if the evidence suggests it, take LSD with your children.

An interpretive dance session, followed by lunch, ended our experiential weekend. Leary's final advice to us concerned social "games." He made the point that most human behavior takes place on a "game level" of social arrangements characterized by goals, rules, strategies, values, rituals, and space-time limits. Only the ego-transcending moments of sexual, mystical, or psychedelic experience occasionally allow life to become nongame. What we must do, therefore, is to play social games wisely while seeking out those experiences which allow us to spend more of our time at a nongame level.

After Millbrook

In April 1966, a Buddhist monk who had been visiting Leary suddenly left the mansion after sensing "daggers of hostility" surrounding the estate. Later that night, the staff members went for a walk in a grove of trees and sat down to engage in silent meditation. Jack, Leary's son, suggested that everyone hold hands. Although the group did not realize it, a cadre of local policemen were observing every move from nearby bushes and shrubbery.

The following night, Lelie had a strange dream. She reported that, in her dream, we had returned to Millbrook. A barefoot Leary was ebullient, and was dressed in a white shirt and white pants. Suddenly, a large number of policemen broke into the house and started to carry out cardboard boxes. Leary protested, "But they're all empty!" The raid continued until Lelie awakened.

On the night of Lelie's dream, the police had indeed closed in. A sixteen-person raiding party, armed with search warrants, entered the front door and searched every room. They confiscated several boxes of books from the library and examined the personal property and clothing of all thirty residents and visitors, among them Marya Mannes, the journalist. Four people, including Leary, clad in white pajamas, were arrested on the charge of marijuana possession. The raid was led by the Duchess County assistant district attorney, G. Gordon Liddy, who continued to harass Leary until the case stemming from the April raid was dismissed by a local judge on the condition that Leary and his colony leave Millbrook. In May 1969, Leary's organization again changed its name—to the League for Spiritual Discovery (LSD)—and eventually established its headquarters in California. From there, Leary's activities took him into a fourth marriage, to jail, over the jail wall, to Algeria, to Switzerland, to Afghanistan, and back to jail. While a special type of parole was being negotiated for Leary, I recalled what the psychologist, Walter Houston Clark, in his book, *Chemical Ecstasy*, had observed:

> To most of Leary's academic associates no goal can be imagined higher than achieving a full professorship at Harvard, with tenure and the emoluments, tangible and intangible, that go with such achievement—unless it be more of the same type of reward.

> To them, any person who would knowingly pass up such an opportunity must truly be mad. It was behavior of this type that won for the psychedelic drugs the reputation for warping the judgment of those who ingested them. Nevertheless, most of those who tried them did glimpse the wider world. . . . Time will tell whether Timothy Leary is a pied piper or one of the perceptive prophets of the age.

Twenty States of Consciousness

Eventually, Richard Alpert went to India, almost in desperation. He observed how "Tim had gone to India, Ralph had gone to India," and when they came back, "there was Tim being Tim, and there was Ralph being

Ralph. . . . They had all had some lovely experiences, . . . but they were not finished looking for something."

While in India, Alpert met Maharaji, a teacher who lived in a temple at the foothills of the Himalayas. Several things about Maharaji impressed Alpert. For one thing, he took over 900 micrograms of Alpert's best LSD without any more reaction than a twinkling of an eye. For another, he reportedly told Alpert several details of his life including the fatal spleen illness of Alpert's mother. Alpert studied with Maharaji and returned to the United States as Baba Ram Dass telling his story and teaching his principles to all who would listen.

Our weekend at Millbrook stimulated my own interest in nondrug consciousness alterations. Over the next four years, I attended workshops, classes, and sessions involving yoga, zen meditation, t'ai chi, aikido, and sensory awareness. I underwent structural integration therapy (Rolfing) with Ida Rolf and her son. I heard Maharishi Mahesh Yoga speak of Transcendental Meditation, Swami Satchidananda tell of Integral Yoga, and Swami Muktananda describe Siddhi Yoga. It became apparent that people spend much of their time in unusual states of consciousness and I tried to conceptualize as many as I could.

My tabulation was crude and unverified. It included a number of states or syndromes or domains or patterns of consciousness* which clearly overlapped. Yet it helped me organize my own experiences in a comparative way that would integrate the new with the old.

1. *Dreaming* or rapid eye movement (REM) sleep is detectable on psychophysiological measuring devices through noting the synchronous and rapid movements of the eyes, the presence of desynchronized brain waves, the absence of slow brain waves, the loss of muscle tonus, the presence of sexual excitation, and irregular respiration and heartbeat patterns. One usually recalls a dream, or vivid flow of mental imagery, if one is awakened from this state. On some occasions, one realizes that he or she is dreaming; if so, the state of consciousness is referred to as "lucid dreaming."

2. *Nondream* sleep is detected by the lack of rapid eye movements (REMs) and sexual excitation, and by the presence of muscle tonus, regular respiration and heartbreak patterns, and slow brain waves—often in the delta frequency (one-half to three cycles per

---

*I prefer to use the term "consciousness" instead of "awareness" which I view somewhat differently. People can be totally unaware of what is happening to them while they are still conscious. For example, a person with a "petit mal" epileptic seizure is unaware of the surroundings but is still conscious in that the ordinary posture is maintained and the limbs can be moved. A "state of consciousness," then, is a tapestry of perceptions, conceptualizations, and feelings that can be differentiated from other such "states" through observed behavior and reported experience.

second). If one is awakened from nondream or non-REM sleep, one often recalls simple, concrete thoughts with little mental imagery.

3. *Hypnagogic* states of consciousness occur just as one is drifting into sleep at night or while napping. One notices tableaulike visual images, often accompanied by auditory imagery. There is typically an increase in the alpha brain wave frequency (eight to thirteen cycles per second) and theta frequency (four to seven cycles per second) at this time.

4. *Hypnopompic* states occur as a person is returning to wakefulness. The images are not long enough to be dreamlike, being rather brief and devoid of plot.

5. *Hyperalert* consciousness is characterized by prolonged and increased alertness and can be induced by drinking coffee or using other stimulant drugs. It can also be induced by the heightened vigilance involved in sentry duty or crow's nest watch. Frequently, there is an increase in beta brain wave frequencies (fourteen or more cycles per second).

6. *Lethargic* consciousness is characterized by dulled, sluggish mental activity and can be induced by fatigue, sleep deprivation, malnutrition, improper sugar balance, dehydration, a depressed mental state, and such depressant drugs as tranquilizers and sedatives. Frequently, a slowing down of the brain rhythm is noted.

7. *Stupor* is characterized by a greatly reduced ability to perceive incoming sensations, to carry out motor functioning, and to use language meaningfully. It may be induced by opiates such as heroin, and by large amounts of alcohol or other depressive drugs. It also accompanies certain types of psychosis and a number of other illnesses.

8. *Coma* is a condition from which it is virtually impossible to rouse an individual. Language is not used and there is little motor activity. Coma may be induced by severe illness, glandular dysfunction, poison, overdoses of certain drugs, epileptic seizures, and physical injuries to the brain.

9. *Internal scanning*, awareness of the organs, tissues, and membranes of the body's interior, is rarely noticed unless a bodily feeling is intensified (as in pain or hunger) or unless an individual makes a concerted effort to detect bodily feelings (as in some LSD sessions or sensory awareness training). This type of consciousness is one of many which coexists with other conscious states at any given moment.

10. *Stored memories* also coexist with other conscious states and

emerge when one undergoes electrical brain stimulation, free association during psychoanalysis, or makes a directed effort to recall past experiences. Revivification of these past experiences sometimes occurs with the ingestion of psychedelic drugs; sensory deprivation and massage have also been known to facilitate recall of stored memories. Spontaneous recall is also possible as these inactive memory traces are constantly filed away in the unconscious; some are more difficult to retrieve than others due to repression or disuse.

11. *Rapture* is characterized by strong feeling and overpowering emotion which one generally evaluates as positive in nature. Rapturous consciousness, or states of ecstasy, can be induced by sexual activity, frenzied dances (such as those done by the "whirling dervishes"), orgiastic rituals, rites of passage (primitive puberty initiations and marriage dances), religious conversions and "revival" meetings, and glossolalia (speaking in tongues).

12. *Hysteria* is characterized by intense feeling and overpowering emotion, generally evaluated as negative in nature. Hysterical consciousness, like rapture, is frequently accompanied by bursts of brain waves in the theta frequency; it can be induced by rage, anger, jealousy, panic, terror, horror, neurotic anxiety, fear of being "possessed" or "bewitched," violent mob activity (such as "running berserk" or "lynching parties"), and intense pain.

13. *Regression* is typified by patterns of thought or behavior clearly inappropriate in terms of a person's chronological age. States of regression include those elicited by hypnotic experiments in "age regression" as well as states manifested by mentally retarded persons, aged persons suffering from senile psychoses (the "second childhood"), feral children (individuals abandoned by their parents and raised by animals), persons suffering from sociopathic character disorders (in which social and moral standards have never been internalized producing individuals who operate on an infantile level, from an ethical standpoint), and persons from extremely deprived backgrounds (such as those locked in attics or closets by their parents for several years).

14. *Fragmentation* is marked by lack of integration among important segments, aspects, or themes of the total personality. These patterns of consciousness are associated with some types of psychosis, severe neurosis, amnesia, dissociation, "multiple personality," and fugue states (in which a person forgets his or her past and begins an entirely new life). Fragmented consciousness is not necessarily

unpleasant; most people reporting "out-of-body" experiences have rather favorable reactions to these episodes.

15. *Daydreaming* is characterized by rapidly occurring thoughts which bear little relationship to a person's external environment. It may be induced by boredom, sensory deprivation, or attention that is directed to a psychodynamic process which assumes more importance than the objects and events in the individual's immediate surroundings.

16. *Reverie* may be induced by the same factors that bring about daydreaming. However, a series of vivid images, many of them symbolic, occur instead of verbal mentation and thought patterns. In addition, brain waves in the theta frequency often are noted, an occurrence which is not typical of daydreaming.

17. *Suggestibility* is marked by focused attention upon a single stimulus such as a hypnotist's voice, a metronome, a series of orders issued in a firm voice, a group chant, or one's own heartbeat. Suggestibility may also be induced by prolonged exposure to a revolving object, a stroboscope, a lullaby, or certain types of poetry and music. One can also enter a state of suggestibility by watching a dramatic presentation and becoming "caught up" in the action, by engaging in "trance-producing" rituals, by repetitive grilling (such as the "third degree" or "brainwashing"), or by performing a task which requires attentiveness but little variation in response (driving a "snowcat" vehicle across the snow for several hours, watching a radar screen, staring at a white line in the middle of a highway while driving). Generally speaking, there are no unique brain wave patterns which characterize states of suggestibility.

18. *Meditation* is characterized by relaxation, a sense of the immediate present, and a lack of complex imagery or verbal mentation. It is typically accompanied by an increase in slower brain wave activity, generally in the alpha frequency. Meditation is induced by contemplating an external object (such as a mandala), by repeating a mantra, or by attending to a physiological function such as breathing.

19. *Expanded consciousness* is characterized by reports of alterations in one's experience of space, time, body image, sense impressions, and (with the eyes closed) vivid visual imagery. These experiences are felt to "expand" one's appreciation of art and music, to provide personal insights, to reveal personal, and archetypal symbols, and, in rare cases, to bring about "integrative" experiences of "cosmic unity" which transform one's life in ways said to be beneficial.

Expanded states of consciousness may be induced by hypnotic induction, multimedia sensory bombardment, intense interpersonal relationships, or the ingestion of psychedelic substances.

20. *Ordinary consciousness* is used by most people as the "baseline" which alerts them to shifts into altered conscious states. During ordinary consciousness, the brain waves follow a desynchronized pattern and one feels alert, "in control," and able to cope with external internal reality by logic, rationality, goal-directedness, cause-and-effect thinking, language symbolization, and traditional thought patterns.

A great deal of research needs to be done before a conclusive map of consciousness can be drawn. Many of these twenty states overlap and many can be subdivided. Furthermore, brain waves are only one of several physiological measures which correlate with one's experiential reports. And brain waves from one lobe or hemisphere of the brain may be quite different from brain waves emanating from other portions of the brain. Perhaps ESP and PK are associated with various brain wave patterns and other psychophysiological responses. If so, one could be trained to produce those responses in the hope that one's psychic ability would increase. In addition, methods of inducing those psychophysiological responses could be devised —through drugs, meditation, hypnosis, or other means.

In retrospect, it seems to me that the professional and public interest in psychedelic experience stimulated interest in all forms of altered consciousness. As curious college students reached the limit of what LSD had to teach them, they turned to meditation, hypnosis, and other approaches. This created a demand for books, courses, and research opportunities in these areas.

And what ever happened to LSD research? Timothy Leary's outrageous behavior at Harvard and Millbrook probably set psychedelic research back ten years. But the foolish actions of the U.S. government in general and the Food and Drug Administration in particular, set it back another twenty years. In 1966, the FDA demanded that Robert Masters and Jean Houston return all of their unused supplies of psychedelic chemicals despite the fact that not one of their over 200 subjects had reported a "bad trip" or an unfavorable experience. When the FDA administrator, James Goddard, was asked whether the proper use of psychedelics could enhance one's creativity, he dismissed the possibility as "pure bunk," calling for vigorous enforcement of anti-LSD legislation. Most of the pioneer LSD researchers in the country found their supplies cut off and were ordered to return their remaining stocks of the drug to Sandoz, the pharmaceutical company which had originally manufactured the substance. Finally, Sandoz announced that it had turned its remaining supplies of LSD over to the U.S. government. James Goddard stated it was "a perfectly understandable policy" for the company "to get clear of LSD as soon as possible."

By the end of 1966, there was little chance that psychedelics would be used to investigate paranormal phenomena scientifically. Thousands of students and artists were carrying out their own experiments, using black-market chemicals of dubious quality. What respectable scientists could not obtain from Sandoz or the FDA was available on the street corner. It was clear to me that psychedelics provided science an unparalleled opportunity to study human consciousness; as a result of Leary's radical actions and the U.S. government's reactionary views, this opportunity was lost. In a remarkably perceptive editorial, *Life* magazine (April 29, 1966) stated, "Controls, not prohibition, are the key to this drug's future. . . . The first effort of government should be to get respectable LSD research moving again." These were wise words, again disregarded.

Fortunately, Walter Pahnke and his associates at the Maryland Psychiatric Research Institute were allowed to carry on their work with psychedelic psychotherapy. And fortunately, the crackdown on LSD research had not affected my activities in parapsychology. Gardner Murphy and Montague Ullman had invited me to direct the newly organized Dream Laboratory at the Maimonides Medical Center in Brooklyn. Ullman was director of the department of psychiatry and had received financial grants from the Ittleson and Scaife Foundations to conduct a large scale investigation of dream telepathy.

3

PERCHANCE TO DREAM, TELEPATHICALLY

One element of the apparently intimate connection between telepathy and dreams . . . is . . . the incontestable fact that sleep creates favorable conditions for telepathy.

Sigmund Freud

The First Screening Study

By the time I moved to Brooklyn in 1964, the first experimental series had been completed at the Maimonides Dream Laboratory. Two graduate students, Joyce Polsky and Sol Feldstein, alternated as experimenter and telepathic transmitter while twelve different subjects went through the experimental procedures. The subject slept in a sound-isolated room; his or her EEG tracings were observed in a separate room by the experimenter. The transmitter selected a sealed envelope by picking a numeral from a random number table and counting down through the envelopes as many times as the number dictated. The transmitter then took the envelope to a third room, opened it, and attempted to "send" the image of the enclosed picture to the sleeping subject.

The subject was awakened following each period of rapid-eye-movement activity, reported a dream, then went back to sleep. In the morning, the experimenter would interview the subject to obtain additional details of the dream as well as any associations the subject had between the dream and events in his or her personal life.

Once the interview was finished, the subject was given a stack of art prints—copies of those in the sealed envelopes. The subject was asked to look at all the pictures and give a rank of 1 to the picture which most closely resembled the dream reports. The picture which next most closely resembled the dreams was to be given a rank of 2. All the pictures were given a different rank. If telepathy had taken place, the correct pictures would have received lower ranks (such as 1 and 2) while the incorrect pictures for any given night would have received higher ranks (such as 11 and 12).

Transcripts of the dreams and the art prints were sent to outside judges who had some background in either dream interpretation or psychical research. The judges ranked each night of dreams against each picture. By using this procedure, statistically significant results were obtained—supporting the hypothesis that dream telepathy was possible—for the first experimental series. The subjects' own judging was more accurate than chance or the evaluation done by Virginia Glenn, who worked as an outside judge.

Three other judges worked in a different capacity. They evaluated the art prints and target pictures independently from each other, but their ranks were averaged for the statistical test. Thus, if one judge had given a target-transcript pair a rank of 1, another a rank of 2, and a third a rank of 3, the average rank of 2 would be utilized by the statistician. The evaluations of these judges did not reach statistical significance. Then a separate inspection was made of the nights on which Sol Feldstein attempted to influence the subject's dreams versus the night that Joyce Polsky was at work. There was a statistically significant difference between these nights, indicating that Feldstein had been more successful in creating the telepathic effect.

Feldstein's most telepathic subject was William Erwin, who took time off from his New York psychoanalytic practice to spend a night at Maimonides. Randomly selected was Orozco's painting *Zapatistas*, which depicts a scene from the 1910 Mexican Revolution in which a number of revolutionaries are shown against a dramatic background of massive mountains and clouds. Erwin dreamed of a thundercloud, mountains, New Mexico, war, and "the Mayan-Aztec type of civilization."

The First Erwin Study

Our second experimental series involved intensive work by Feldstein with only one subject—William Erwin. The study lasted for seven nights and the results were statistically significant. In this instance, Erwin's judging was accurate at an above-chance level, as were the evaluations by Virginia Glenn and the team of three outside judges.

The art prints utilized in the study ranged in content from *School of the Dance* by Degas to Chagall's *Paris Through a Window*. And on November 8, 1964, Dali's *The Sacrament of the Last Supper* was randomly selected as the target picture. Each of Erwin's dream reports appeared to contain elements of this unusual painting which portrays Christ breaking bread with his disciples; in the background, fishing boats can be seen on a large body of water.

Dream One: . . . there was one scene of an ocean . . ., a very rough, turbulent ocean. But it still had a strange beauty about it in a strange formation.

Dream Two: . . . I haven't any reason to say this but somehow boats come to mind. Fishing boats. Small size fishing boats. . . . There was a picture in the Sea Fare restaurant that came to mind. . . . It shows . . . about a dozen or so men pulling a fishing boat ashore right after having returned from a catch. Some of the men are putting fish into different baskets.

Dream Three: . . . Something about a bathtub. . . . The bathtub was one of those real old time type of bathtubs. . . . I was looking at a catalog . . . and it was a Christmas catalog. The Christmas season.

Dream Four: I had some sort of brief dream about an M.D. Let me see. Doctors. . . . I was talking to someone and . . . the discussion had to do with . . . proof a doctor becomes a doctor because he's supposed to be an M.D., or something. . . .

Dream Five: . . . It had to do with doctors again. . . . The picture . . . I'm thinking of is how the doctor is sitting beside a child that is ill. . . . It's called "The Physician." . . .

Dream Six: . . . I was in an office going over a report for . . . a psychiatrist. A supervisor I had. Before he became a psychiatrist he was a pathologist. . . . Makes me think of . . . medical psychology.

Dream Seven: . . . I'm in this kitchen and on the shelf there are a lot of individual boxes of . . . a type of cookie that resembles some sort of spice. . . . Also in the dream there were . . . herbs, I guess, of different types. . . .

Dream Eight: . . . A grocery store. . . . Food, of course. Spices. We get back to spices. . . . I was sampling . . . spices. Herbs. . . .

In his postsleep interview, Erwin said, "I dreamed quite a bit about a doctor last night . . . and it even makes me think in terms of these spices and herbs that are connected with medicinal things." The judges gave the night an average rank of 1.3, in combination with the target. Perhaps they recalled that Christ was called the "Divine Physician" and that some of his disciples were fishermen.

The Second Screening Study

As Erwin was kept quite busy by his patients, he was unable to participate in a further study at the dream lab. In an attempt to find other psychically gifted persons, Ullman and I again implemented an experimental series involving twelve subjects. Although the results of this study were not statistically significant, several subjects had dreams which corresponded closely with the randomly selected target pictures.

One of them was Robyn Posin, a clinical psychologist who dreamed about "a lot of mountains and trees," "the country," and a group of women engaging in "some sort of tribal ritual in a jungle." The transmitter on that occasion was looking at *Mystic Night* by Sheets; it portrays a group of women performing a ritual in a country setting against a background of trees and mountains. After looking at the judge's evaluations, and noting the average rank of 1.7, one of our staff members exclaimed, "We've found another Bill Erwin!"

At this point in time, I was in the hospital. One day I was feeling ill, went to the Maimonides personnel health service, and took a number of tests, among them a blood test. A few hours later, a stretcher was sent to remove me. I was taken to the emergency room for immediate treatment due to internal bleeding.

Virginia Glenn heard of my plight and desperately telephoned Shirley Harrison, a psychic sensitive living in Maine, for advice. Ms. Harrison's daughter answered the phone and told Virginia, "Mother has flown to New York City; she said Dr. Krippner needed her and that she had to be near him." A few minutes later, Shirley Harrison phoned Virginia Glenn from a Manhattan hotel; "The ouija board tells me that Stanley is seriously ill," she reported. "He has bleeding ulcers and will be operated on before Monday evening. But he will survive. The power of love will help him through this ordeal."

On Monday morning, I was operated on for two duodenal ulcers. I lost a great deal of blood and was in horrible pain. Shirley Harrison and other friends sent love from Manhattan. Lelie Harris, who had arrived to visit me for the summer, sent love from my bedside, which she visited every day.

My duodenum was so badly ulcerated that a chunk was cut out, as well as a portion of my stomach. A hole in my side was left open to permit the wastes to drain out. When it did not close at the expected time, my physicians were puzzled and I sent for Shirley Harrison. She went to her ouija board and received a message that four stitches had to emerge from the hole before it would heal properly. The board also predicted that the hole would close within three days.

To direct the prediction toward fulfillment, I hypnotized myself several times a day and chanted the word "heal." On the second day, two double stitches oozed from the hole; apparently they had come loose and were causing a great deal of irritation. On the following day, the wound closed.

The Posin Study

By this time, our third experimental series was concluded and we were about to begin our eight-night study with Robyn Posin. Dr. Posin was somewhat of a celebrity at Maimonides during the experiment, and had been nicknamed "the witch" because of her ESP prowess. And a celebrity of a different sort had joined the Maimonides staff at that time to direct our mental retardation unit; he was Dr. Joseph Wortis—the psychiatrist who had been hauled before Senator Joseph McCarthy's investigatory committee a decade earlier.

One of our staff members had developed a 100-point scale for a more sensitive rating of target-transcript correspondences. If the similarity between dreams and picture content was very great, a mark was placed in the top part of the scale—at 70, 80, or higher. If there were very few correspondences, a mark was placed toward the bottom of the scale—30, 20, or lower. Each target-transcript pair could be rated in this way; if telepathy were operating, the correct pairs would receive higher ratings than the incorrect pairs. We eagerly anticipated using this technique with Posin's dreams and targets.

Unfortunately, Posin's performance fell short of Erwin's. The results of her experimental series were not statistically significant. Her self-ratings averaged 43.5 for the correct pairs and 24.0 for the incorrect pairs. Three judges produced averages of 42.2 for the correct pairs and 41.5 for the incorrect pairs. In neither instance were the differences large enough to confirm the hypothesis that telepathy was operating. A person with great self-insight, Posin wrote us a letter which may explain what happened to Feldstein's thwarted attempt to communicate with her telepathically.

> As I've reread the set of transcripts I first read for judging, . . . I've had a number of thoughts which seem quite relevant. . . . I now "hear" in the transcripts of my dream protocols . . . a clear sense of unwillingness to allow the ESP experience to develop and a resentment at what unconsciously I had experienced as an intrusion. . . . Reflecting from this distance in time and space on what was going on in my life at the time of the experiment, I can begin to see that the whole ESP involvement then was a great threat to my equilibrium. At the same time it is clear too that I couldn't have allowed myself the open awareness that was needed. . . . As I read

through the dream reports, . . . I hear my own fear of losing control (having an ESP experience or, more generally, allowing an impact from another person) and of being "exposed." Though I then laughed . . . about being called "a witch" (I think my skepticism about ESP became very personalized), for me to have such experiences then would have been . . . very disrupting. . . .

So we learned by our work with Posin that the dream telepathy subject needs to be sympathetic to the ESP hypothesis and open to the possibility of being influenced by someone else during sleep. Erwin had told us that he viewed Feldstein's telepathic attempts as a form of "psychic penetration." However, Erwin remarked, "I liked Sol and I didn't mind being penetrated by him." In her letter, Posin confessed to a lack of this same type of openness.

Posin's and Erwin's comments take on special significance when viewed from the perspective of a research study executed by Gertrude Schmeidler and Lawrence LeShan. The investigators used the Rorschach inkblot technique and scores from ESP card tests with fifty students who "believed" in the possibility of ESP. From this group, a subgroup of students was identified with high average ESP scores as well as high "variance," referring to the range of scores on the ESP tests. Another subgroup of students was identified with high average ESP scores and low variance. Schmeidler and LeShan felt that variance was an important factor to examine because a subject who could maintain a high overall ESP-scoring average and still jump from high to low scores on individual tests would demonstrate more spontaneity and "openness" than those subjects who varied little from ESP test to ESP test.

Schmeidler and LeShan predicted that the subgroup with high variance would give more Rorschach inkblot responses which involved penetration than would the low-variance subgroup. Penetration responses are defined by Rorschach experts as those emphasizing surfaces and structures that permit entry. The results of a statistical analysis confirmed this prediction; the students who frequently reported "open windows" and "kitchen sieves," were generally those students with a higher ESP score variance.

Schmeidler and LeShan also predicted that the students with low ESP variance would make more "barrier" responses on the Rorschach, responses emphasizing protective coverings or clothing. Again, the hypothesis was confirmed; the low-variance students typically reported such perceptions as "turtle shells" and "coats of armor" on the Rorschach. Schmeidler and LeShan performed further statistical analysis on their group and concluded, "Evidence from the barrier and penetration relationship supports our inference that subjects relatively low on barrier and high on penetration would have better ESP scores than subjects with the opposite pattern." However, they noted a great deal of overlap and admitted that other variables are important as well.

The Hypnosis Study

There is considerable evidence in the parapsychological literature that hypnotic induction can enhance ESP scores, perhaps by lowering the psychological barriers that Schmeidler and LeShan detected in their study. Thus, Ullman and I initiated our first study combining dream recall, telepathy, and hypnosis. We utilized four telepathic transmitters in this study; each transmitter was assigned four subjects.

I hypnotized two of these subjects and gave relaxation suggestions to the other two. Members of both groups were told, by the transmitters:

> I will select a target picture and will concentrate on that picture. It is very likely that you will be able to think of that target even though we are in different rooms. You will be asked to imagine what target I have selected and it is very possible that a picture, or a word, or some other image will come to mind. Be sure to mention the first image that comes to mind as well as any additional impressions you may have. . . . Then you will have an opportunity to take a nap. Once again, I will select a target picture and will concentrate on it. This may be the same target or it may be something different. In any event, it is likely that during your nap you will dream about the target. If you should not fall asleep, do not be concerned, as it is likely that you will think about the target while you are resting. When you leave the laboratory, I will again select a target picture. Recent experiments in our laboratory indicate that telepathy may occur while a person is dreaming. Therefore, you will probably dream about the target tonight and on other nights during the week. When you wake up in the morning, you may write down anything you remember about your dreams. You may even draw pictures of the dream content, if you wish. . . . Your dreams will be associated with the target picture until you return to the laboratory, bringing the records of your dreams with you.

As a matter of fact, the identical picture was used for all three conditions. Following the collection of imagery and dreams from all sixteen subjects, three outside judges utilized the new 100-point evaluation form. The averages of their scores were utilized for our statistical tests. (Virginia Glenn's eyesight was now so poor that she could no longer serve as a judge. However, she assisted the dream lab in other ways, most notably by stimulating Alan Watts's interest in our work and obtaining for us a grant from his organization, the Society for Comparative Philosophy.)

When we inspected the results, we were quite surprised by the findings.

The subjects who had been hypnotized obtained statistically significant results on the imagery they reported before leaving the lab, especially while napping. The subjects in the relaxation group obtained significant results on the imagery elicited from their nighttime dreams. It seemed that hypnosis had indeed lowered the psychological barriers to telepathy and had speeded up the processing of the target content. The subjects who were not hypnotized appeared to have received the target picture from the transmitters—but much later in the experiment.

Our results were not clear-cut. For example, when the subjects' evaluations were inspected, significant results were obtained from the subjects in the relaxation group on the set of images reported immediately following relaxation. And there were provocative instances of telepathy for subjects in both groups. In the case of one hypnotized subject, the agent transmitted Davies' picture, *Unicorns*, in which the mythical animals are portrayed against a background of clouds and mountains. Immediately after hypnotic induction, this subject reported: "I can see vague mountains and clouds—stratus clouds. I saw something flying. A man on a horse. . . . Now a horse is coming toward me from left to right with his mane flying." On the other hand, a subject in the relaxation group had a vivid image containing equally strong correspondences to a target following her nap: "A rustle of silk. . . . Female dresses. Tight bodices. Huge shirts. A jeweled brooch at the neckline. . . . The thought came, 'Beauty to beauty." This was an appropriate description of *Girls at the Piano* by Renoir, the randomly selected picture utilized by the transmitter.

It was obvious to us that dreams were not the only altered state of consciousness which could facilitate telepathy. But it was also apparent that additional research was needed to discover the ways in which hypnotic induction could be most helpful.

The Grayeb Study

At this point, the extra money from individuals such as Alan Watts enabled us to hire two additional part-time researchers. Robyn Posin's interest in the personality dynamics of telepathic subjects made her an especially acute experimenter. Virginia Glenn had introduced me to Don Smoot, the industrial psychologist whose visit to Millbrook with us had stimulated an interest in Timothy Leary's work with psychedelic drugs. Lelie Harris and I were married in 1966 and the additional staff members were a great help in assuming some of my duties while I moved to Staten Island with Lelie and her two children.

Smoot was selected to serve as transmitter for our sixth experimental series. Theresa Grayeb, a secretary at the Maimonides Medical Center, was to be the subject. In three preliminary sessions, her dreams closely resembled the target pictures; when the Rousseau picture *Merry Jesters* was used, she dreamed of "a large fur rug or an animal skin" and "a white bird." The painting shows several monkeys and a white bird in the jungle. In muted tones, the question was asked, "Have we found another William Erwin?"

For this study, we hoped to compare nights when a target picture was sent against nights when there was no target and no transmitter. Smoot and Grayeb arrived at the dream lab each of sixteen nights. When Grayeb went to bed, Smoot randomly selected an envelope. If it contained a picture, he went to a distant room and attempted telepathic transmission. If it was empty, he left the laboratory and went to sleep. Grayeb was not told about the design of this experiment because we feared that she would attempt to guess which nights Smoot was present and thus alter her motivation for the telepathy task.

At the end of the experiment, Grayeb evaluated her material. The correct target-transcript pairs obtained an average score of 52.7 while the incorrect pairs received a rating of 40.9. The results were promising, but not strong enough to be statistically significant. The outside judges gave the correct pairs an average rating of 40.5 and the incorrect pairs a rating of 52.6. Although the difference was not great enough to be statistically significant, these results were in the opposite direction of those produced by Grayeb herself. What had happened?

It is always easier to use hindsight than foresight. Nevertheless, we did observe that the very first night had been a night when no target was used causing Smoot to leave the lab. Had Grayeb telepathically looked for him and, finding no transmitter, given up in despair? Had this altered her psychic performance for the rest of the study? It was also recalled that Smoot made frequent, explicit, sexual references to Grayeb before she went to bed. This is a practice that Feldstein had scrupulously avoided so as to reduce the "penetration" anxiety which had upset Posin so much. The fear of "penetration" may have inhibited Grayeb's psi ability.

Indeed, we later examined seventy-four nighttime sessions with seventy-four different subjects. Much to our surprise, we found that male subjects did significantly better than females in reporting dreams that corresponded to the telepathic targets. Louisa Rhine had previously found that more women than men sent her spontaneous cases of dream telepathy and other forms of ESP. So why did women frequently have difficulty with our experiments?

The women's liberation movement has done a great service by reminding us that, in many respects, the American culture promulgates a sexist society. Professional women are typically paid less' than professional men and the talents of housewives are often stifled. True, women are considered more "emotional" and "intuitive," and this may account for their greater readiness to report ESP experiences. But in an experimental laboratory, women feel more nervous than men about sleeping in a strange bed and having male experimenters walk in and out of their rooms. In addition, female subjects may be queasy about having transmitters of either sex attempt to "penetrate" their dreams. Other experimenters have reported that women are less likely than men to volunteer for laboratory sleep and dream studies. Furthermore, males tend to report their dreams more fully than do females. A complete dream report would give the judges more information on which to base their evaluations than would an incomplete report. The very items which a somewhat bashful female subject might withhold could be the items most closely related to the telepathic target.

The Second Erwin Study

In 1966, we persuaded Erwin to return to the laboratory for an eight-night dream study. Once again, Feldstein served as telepathic transmitter. Feldstein recalled that some of the more dramatic correspondences in the dreams of Erwin and other subjects had occurred when the transmitter became actively involved with the target picture. Feldstein suggested that a greater opportunity be given him to act out the theme of the randomly selected art print.

We gave this assignment to Richard Davidson, a bright high school student who had wandered into my office after he found out that he could not see anyone in the heart transplant laboratory—the other highly publicized research project at Maimonides. Davidson found a boxing glove to accompany Bellow's painting of a boxing match, apparel from India to accompany the portrait of an Indian prince, and a Protestant hymnal to go along with a Daumier painting of a French religious service. For Hiroshige's painting, *Downpour at Shono*, Feldstein opened the box of accompanying materials and found the instructions to take a shower while holding a Japanese umbrella resembling those in the art print over his head. On that night, Erwin dreamed about "an Oriental man," "a fountain," "water spray," and walking down the street while "it was raining."

On the night of January 25, 1967, Beckman's *Descent from the Cross* was randomly selected as the target picture. The painting depicted the emaciated body of Christ being taken from the cross. It was accompanied by a "do-it-yourself" crucifixion kit consisting of a small wooden cross, a picture of Christ, thumb tacks, a red felt-tipped pen, and the instructions, "Nail

Christ to the cross and color his wounds red." One of Erwin's dreams involved Churchill:

> We passed by an area where Winston Churchill was making a talk . . . and there was a lot of wine that I tasted. . . . Churchill . . . was . . . old, emaciated. . . . Sort of drying up. I had remembered him as being a fat, chubby guy and here he was . . . getting thinner and drawn.

Christ was crucified on a hill, Golgotha, and this fact might have related to a dream about Churchill (Church-hill). In addition, wine was mentioned which is reminiscent of Christ's last supper and the Christian sacraments. Further, the emaciated image of Churchill in the dream resembled the portrayal of Christ in the painting.

Erwin's most vivid dream report involved a group of primitive natives who had captured him:

> It got to the point . . . where we were going to be put in the stewpot. We were going to be sacrificed . . . and there were political overtones. . . . They were busy going through a whole native-type dance—ceremony, drumbeating and all this type of thing. . . . The gods disapproved of what they were doing. . . .

The next morning, Erwin commented that in "the last stage of the ceremony, we would be the star participants. . . . There was . . . an awareness that they were going to kill us." He added:

> The Churchill one . . . seemed to have sort of a ceremonial presentation . . . and you could say the same thing about the native one. It was a very traditional, native dance—a little more primitive, true—but I would say it had its political elements too. . . . In terms of the natives, . . . it was leading to the sacrifice, . . . like the primitive trying to destroy the civilized. . . . It seemed to have an element of cannibalism in it. . . . The god was not to make them fearful. . . . This was not what he approved of.

Erwin's emphasis on ceremony, cannibalism, sacrifice, and a disapproving god led the judges to award the combination of dreams and target a score of 80.7. In fact, high ratings were obtained from the judges for every correct pair in the series; the results were highly significant—more so than during Erwin's first series with us.

Our first experiment with Erwin had been criticized by some observers who suggested that there was no cross check on the fake target-transcript correspondences. These critics suggested that we take art prints that had *not* been used in the experiment, randomly assign them to experimental nights, and subject the target-transcript pairs to a similar evaluation. We thought that this was a sensible precaution, and randomly assigned eight art prints from a different study to Erwin's eight dream transcripts from his second study. We had a judge read each of the eight transcripts in comparison with each of the eight mock targets; these were presented to the judge in a random series so that each transcript had to be read eight times. This comprised a total of sixty-four evaluations, which we delivered to our statistical consultants for analysis.

The results adequately countered the critics' objection. Only one target-transcript pair of the eight received a high rating (exactly what would be expected through coincidence). That is to say, the ratings for the false target-transcript pairs were virtually the same as the ratings for the real target-transcript pairs. One of our staff members remarked, "It really makes you believe in the laws of chance!"

The Van de Castle Study

By 1967, our work had been published in several psychiatric, psychological, and parapsychological journals. One of the hallmarks of an important scientific contribution is its ability to stimulate attempts at replication. The first three attempted replications of our dream telepathy experiments had produced encouraging but mixed, results.

Inge Strauch, a psychologist who had studied with the eminent psychical researcher, Hans Bender, at the University of Freiburg, ran a dream telepathy experiment at her laboratory in West Germany. The overall results were not statistically significant, although there appeared to be a tendency for more target-transcript correspondence to emerge during the morning post-sleep interview than during the nighttime dream reports.

A prominent sleep and dream researcher, Gordon Globus, designed a dream telepathy experiment which included two methods of evaluation; in addition to the rating of target-transcript correspondence, the judges were asked to rate their confidence in their judgments. Although the results of the first judging procedure did not produce statistically significant results, the correct target-transcript pairs received significantly higher confidence ratings than did the incorrect pairs as a result of the second judging procedure.

Calvin Hall, one of the world's most knowledgeable authorities on dreams—and an admitted skeptic on the topic of ESP—obtained statistically significant results in an attempt to replicate our work. One of his subjects was Robert Van de Castle, a psychologist who had studied with J. B. Rhine and who had already published several articles in parapsychological journals.

Ullman and I arranged for Van de Castle to come to Brooklyn each month for an eight-night experimental series. We allowed him to select his own transmitter and to spend several hours with him or her, establishing rapport and laying the groundwork for the attempted telepathic transmission. Van de Castle worked with Ullman for one night, with a psychology graduate student for two nights, and with a psychiatric social worker for five nights. As Van de Castle requested immediate feedback on his attempts to dream telepathically, we created a separate pool of art prints for each night; this enabled him to do his judging each morning (with a duplicate pool) and to meet his transmitter after breakfast to discover what procedures best facilitated the telepathic effect.

Why did he only work with Ullman—a friend of several years standing —for one night? He later answered that question in writing, also describing the other two transmitters:

> They were attractive, well-endowed, single young women about whom it would be easy to develop sexual fantasies, and I did. It was as if I were attempting to consummate a sexual relationship telepathically—consummate in its basic meaning of "bringing to completion or fulfillment."

Van de Castle's experimental series was statistically significant, both in terms of his own judging and on the basis of outside evaluation. One night Dali's painting, *Discovery of America by Christopher Columbus* was randomly selected. Van de Castle's dreams so closely corresponded to the picture that he gave that particular transcript-target pair a rating of 100 on the 100-point scale. When Cézanne's stark painting *Trees and Houses* was utilized, Van de Castle had no dreams about people, only about "a model home," "a house," "this isolated house," "dingy buildings," and "a telephone pole." He stated, "If there's a target picture in there that's a lonely shack sitting on a hillside, . . . then we've been doing tremendous." Van de Castle had indeed given an accurate description of the Cézanne picture. Several of us gleefully chanted, "We've found another Bill Erwin!"

In May 1967, I returned from a series of lectures in California shortly before Van de Castle's visit. When Lelie and I moved to Staten Island, we found it almost impossible to obtain a mortgage on the house we wanted to buy. Banks were not very impressed with my position as a parapsychologist, and the fact that I had no job security was an additional detriment. In the meantime, I had spent all my savings on rental for the house and was scheduling a number of lectures to raise additional money. When I returned from California, I found that I was twenty-five dollars short of reimbursement for travel expenses. Fortunately, one of my sponsors sent me the needed money just before Van de Castle arrived. Not wanting to bother him with such trivialities, I did not mention the incident. Nevertheless, he dreamed that:

When I was in the lab, I was lying there and there were some of Stan's expense account statements and I looked at one of them . . . and it seemed like it was his expense account for a trip to California. . . . Down underneath something was written to the effect of, "This was not enough money. Twenty-five dollars more needed to be raised." And it seemed as if somehow I knew that he didn't need to raise the money, that the twenty-five dollars had been raised in another way.

This is only one of several examples in which the sleeping subject zeroes in on the personal situation of one of the experimenters. And why not? Our studies in dream telepathy were originally suggested by real-life situations in which patients began to dream of incidents in their therapists' lives. The correspondences between the subjects' dreams and episodes from the experimenters' lives did not strengthen our statistics, but they did confirm our notions about ESP.

The Hypnotic Dream Study

Robyn Posin had left us to go into full-time practice as a psychotherapist. Sol Feldstein had left us to immerse himself in his doctoral studies. And in 1967, Don Smoot had accepted an invitation from Timothy Leary to direct the Manhattan office of the League for Spiritual Discovery.

In the meantime, J. B. Rhine had parted company with one of his research assistants, Charles Honorton—a young man whom I regarded as just about the most capable experimenter in the field. Rhine did not share Honorton's interest in altered states of consciousness as a logical area for psi investigation. Within a week, Ullman and I invited Honorton to join our staff as our first full-time research associate.

At our laboratory, Honorton pursued an interest he had been following for several years, the relation between clairvoyance and hypnotic dreams. This was our first experimental series in clairvoyance, the form of ESP in which someone identifies distant objects or events by paranormal means. (We were aware of the fact that our earlier telepathy studies might have involved a clairvoyant element. The subjects could have obtained information about the art print through clairvoyance as well as telepathy; this possibility exists so often in psychical research that the term "general ESP" has been coined to describe experiments which could involve clairvoyance as well as telepathy.) It was our second experimental series involving hypnosis —a far less expensive procedure than the nighttime dream studies which involved such equipment as the EEG, tape recorders, and microphones.

Sixty subjects were divided equally into two groups, one of which received hypnosis and one of which received instructions concerning imagination. The suggestibility of individuals in both groups had been measured with a suggestibility test devised by T. X. Barber. Both groups received average suggestibility scores that were about the same, but we had selected the subjects so that there would be ten persons in each of six groups: a high-suggestible hypnosis group, a high-suggestible imagination group, a medium-suggestible hypnosis group, a medium-suggestible imagination group, a low-suggestible hypnosis group, and a low-suggestible imagination group.

All subjects were assisted either in entering hypnosis or relaxation. A sealed envelope containing an art print was placed on the arm of each subject's chair. The hypnosis subjects were told, "You are going to have a dream; a very vivid and realistic dream about the target in the envelope." The other subjects were told, "You are going to have a daydream, a very vivid and realistic daydream about the target in the envelope." This procedure was repeated four times as four randomly selected pictures were used per subject. Also, in an interview, subjects described the quality of their dreams or daydreams and the degree to which their consciousness had been altered.

The subjects evaluated their own material immediately after their sessions. Only the high-suggestible hypnosis group attained statistically significant results. It was also observed that hypnosis (but not imagination) subjects who described their dreams as "like watching a film" or "as though I was in a dream world" did significantly better at the clairvoyance task than those subjects who said they "were just thinking" or had a minimal change in consciousness. Finally, subjects in the hypnosis (but not the imagination) group who reported major alterations in consciousness did significantly better than those reporting little change in their patterns of consciousness.

One of the subjects in the hypnosis group was Felicia Parise, a hematologist working at Maimonides. One of the target pictures was Hiroshige's painting, "The Kinryuszan Temple" which portrays a red and gold ceremonial lantern hanging down from a temple doorway. Parise reported:

> A room with party decorations . . . I saw a gold chest, like a pirate's chest, but shining and new. The party decorations were colorful. No decorations on the floor, they were on the ceiling and walls. There was a table with things on it. Red balloons, red punch bowls.

When asked to associate to the hypnotic dream, Parise recalled her "sweet sixteen" birthday party, at which her parents had strung party decorations of Japanese lanterns. A few weeks later, she brought a photograph of that party to the dream lab; it bore a striking resemblance to the Hiroshige painting.

The Bessent Studies

Over the years, several of our subjects had dreams of events which took place *after* the dream had been reported. Parapsychologists refer to this ability, the extrasensory perception of events which have not yet happened, as precognition. One subject dreamed of a distant relative, and crossed his path on the streets of Manhattan the very next day. Another subject dreamed of a high school classmate he had not seen for twenty years—and ran into him a week later, just after discussing the dream with his dinner companion. One morning in 1969, I had a telephone call from Arthur Young, inventor of the Bell helicopter and president of the Foundation for the ·Study of Consciousness. Young asked if we would be interested in making a formal study of Malcolm Bessent, a young Englishman who was the great-nephew of Annie Besant, a celebrated medium and one of the first Western writers to observe the importance of yoga for psychical research.

In 1969, Bessent produced statistically significant results in a precognitive dream experiment, so in 1970 we scheduled Bessent for another study. The experiences which Bessent would try to dream about were prepared before the study began by people who were not present while Bessent was in the laboratory. The experiences consisted of photographic slides and appropriate music or sound effects that would be listened to with stereophonic headphones. Bessent would attempt precognition on eight nights of a sixteen-night study. On alternate nights, he would go to bed immediately after experiencing the slide-and-sound sequence. This would allow us to observe how much of a direct impact the experience had upon his dreams as opposed to the precognitive impact. It also would allow him to process each experience thoroughly in his dreams and dream reports so that it would not show up on some future night.

Bessent dreamed precognitively, eliciting statistically significant results from the three judges. However, the dreams which immediately followed his exposure to the experiences were not significantly related to those slide-and-sound sequences. For example, on September 18, 1970, the sound-and-slide sequence titled "police" was randomly selected. The only statement Bessent made which was at all related to police was during the post-sleep interview when he mentioned "some sort of conflict." However, on September 17, Bessent had several dreams which correlated with the slides showing police arresting people, giving tickets, and quelling disturbances with accompanying music from the James Bond films. After one dream, he reported:

I just had this scene of a university campus with a lot of people there, and, you know, they were just sitting around and suddenly all these people in motor uniform came marching into the scene and sitting in it . . . and so it was obvious that the only outcome was going to be violence of some kind. At that point, leaders of the parties tried to assure the people in their parties . . . that . . . it wasn't going to do any good to kill a white man and not going to do any good to kill a black man. There's the point of the conflict between the students and the armed guard. . . . I started thinking about politics in general and the way that people were manipulated and exploited. . . . It tied in a lot with . . . the dream I had the other night about a police state. . . . I don't usually have those kinds of serious things. I seldom think that seriously about politics. . . . What is curious to me is that I should think of it tonight. It has, perhaps, some significance with the target or some connection with the target.

Bessent had a later dream about "five hundred National Guardsmen," and in his postsleep interview, guessed that the slide-and-sound sequence would "have something to do with authority-type figures."

Bessent's most dramatic precognition came on September 13, 1970, when he had several dreams about doves and geese, guessing that "the next target material will be about birds." The slide-and-sound sequence later chosen depicted a variety of birds accompanied by a recording of bird calls. The judges awarded the target-transcript combination an average rating of 98. However, his dreams after experiencing the bird sequence had no mention of birds whatsoever.

The Vaughan Study

Bob was now preparing for his debut as a laboratory subject, having done quite well in a pilot study. Van Gogh's painting, *The Church at Auvers*, was used and Bob reported a dream about being in Europe. He said, "We came to this building. It could have been a church." Hall and Van de Castle found in a study that churches are mentioned only six times per 500 male dreams. Bob's performance, therefore, was quite impressive.

Three other subjects were used in this study: Alan Vaughan, a well-known psychic sensitive and science writer, Iris Vaughan, his wife, and Felicia Parise, the Maimonides hematologist who had produced such striking clairvoyant effects in our hypnotic dream study.

My interest in Vaughan had been aroused when he reported from West Germany, on June 4, 1968, a series of dreams concerning the assassination of Robert Kennedy. The tragic event occurred a month later under circumstances very similar to those in Vaughan's dreams.

Each of our four subjects spent eight nights in the dream lab. On one of those nights, an art print was randomly selected. For the next three nights, the transmitter stuck with that same art print. On the other four nights, a different target picture was used each time the subject's rapid eye movements indicated that he or she was dreaming.

We felt that this procedure would be useful in exploring the role of the transmitter; for example, most people would become bored with a picture that had to be used night after night. We also felt that this technique would allow us to discern whether dream telepathy was the result of a "build-up" of information sent repeatedly by a transmitter or if there was some sort of mutual "resonance" between the transmitter and receiver that required very little time to exert its effect.

We obtained statistically significant results in this study, although not for each subject in every condition. No support was given to the notion that telepathy involved a "build-up." When the same picture was used for one night, the telepathic correspondences took place as frequently toward the beginning of the night as toward the morning. When we examined all four of the nights on which the same picture was transmitted, we found no evidence that any such "build-up" of information existed. Indeed, there were fewer and fewer correspondences as the nights proceeded, with most of the evidence for telepathy emerging from the very first night the picture was used. Furthermore, the transmitters admitted that they found it difficult to maintain interest in the pictures over a four-night period.

When a different art print was selected for each period of dreaming, the results were much more impressive. Sometimes a dream corresponded to a picture that was selected earlier that night, just as if a residue of information existed that had to be worked through. By and large, however, the correspondences were direct enough to support the theory that a mutual "resonance" between transmitter and receiver accounts for telepathy.

When the transmitter concentrated on a photograph of a medieval water vessel shaped like an armored knight, Bob reported the following dream:

> There was this war going on and they had these helmets on. . . . Both representatives of this war had these kinds of helmets and they were just about to fight. . . . Their copper helmets . . . were bluish, and the other guys' helmets were copper bluish. . . . They discovered that nobody wanted to fight.

The picture which was randomly selected for Bob to receive for four nights in a row was Dali's *Portrait of Gala* in which the artist's wife is pictured facing a mirror and wearing a multicolored jacket. On the first night that this picture was used, Bob had his most telepathic dream, one of a girl in "a ratty fur coat." However, correspondences to Gala decreased on the following nights.

The other subjects also did better when several different pictures were used each night than when one picture was selected for several nights.

When Alan Vaughan's transmitter concentrated on an untitled painting of a gruesome monster by Bacon, Vaughan dreamed of an actor "wearing either a mask or most intensive makeup, like Boris Karloff used to do in his Frankenstein movies." When Iris Vaughan was being transmitted an 1895 circus poster of a buxom female horseback rider, she reported a dream about a girl who "was very, very, very, healthy; she always had loads of . . . fruits or vegetables and . . . was a very big sports fan."

One of the pictures selected randomly for Felicia Parise to perceive telepathically was Rouault's *Punchinello*. The picture portrays a fat circus clown dressed in red, wearing makeup and a close-fitting yellow cap. Parise reported:

> Somebody was . . . hanging rubber bathing caps . . . in my room. . . . I think besides the rubber caps they were going to put masks up, you know, masks hanging all over. I was watching somebody sing. . . . I think the person was . . . dressed in a hobo style like a clown. . . . Baggy pants and suspenders and a T-shirt. The pants had something in them to make them very wide, like one of those hobo-clowns, you know. . . . I was being entertained. I was surprised, really . . . , to see this person in this costume. It reminded me of Hallowe'en.

In summary, this study supported a "resonance" theory of telepathy instead of a "build-up" theory. It also pointed out the importance of novelty for the transmitter—and suggested that the dreamer might also do better if given a variety of telepathy targets to work with rather than the same picture several nights in a row. Perhaps both the subject and the transmitter become bored if a picture is used over and over again.

The NIMH Study

Much of my time at Maimonides had been spent writing financial grant requests which were usually turned down by the foundations contacted. In addition, I helped to write several grant proposals to the National Institute for Mental Health, a government agency which had never subsidized dream telepathy research. On our third try, however, we struck pay dirt; in October 1972, Ullman, Honorton, and I were notified that the proposal we had submitted was being funded to the tune of nearly 45,000 dollars over a two-year period.

Our study was modeled after the well-known work of H. A. Witkin, an experimental design which had also influenced our second study with Malcolm Bessent. Witkin showed his subjects emotionally arousing films before they went to sleep, then examined their dream reports to see in what way the elements of the film were incorporated into the dream. Our plan was to repeat this procedure and, on half the experimental nights, show the film to a telepathic transmitter to see if the subject's dreams could be influenced by ESP.

Forty pairs of transmitters and subjects (who had passed a one-night "screening test" in which an art print was used as the transmitter's target) were used in our study. On the first experimental night, ESP was attempted as the transmitter was taken to a distant room and shown one of four possible ten-minute films, the exact selection being chosen randomly. The subject's dreams were monitored according to the procedures used in our previous studies.

On the second experimental night, ESP was again attempted. However, two of the films were emotionally arousing and two were placid and serene. If the transmitter had viewed a film of an American mountain countryside the first night, the other nonarousing film (a travelog of London) would be eliminated from the list so that an arousing film—such as the birth of a baby or an Australian aboriginal ritual in which the penis is scratched by a sharp stone—would be shown the second night. In this way, each transmitter had an opportunity to attempt transmitting both an exciting film and a serene film.

On the third night of the study, one of the two remaining films in our collection was selected randomly. This was shown to the subjects who then went to sleep. Again, the dreams were recorded and transcribed. On the fourth night, the final film was shown to the subject. In other words, each subject was exposed to two exciting and two neutral films; half of the films were exposed directly as a presleep experience while the others were presented indirectly through ESP.

Three outside judges evaluated the correspondences between the films and the dreams using a number of judging procedures. The results were clear-cut; when our subjects viewed the film before going to sleep, the film content was identified by the judges at statistically significant levels. Nonarousing film content was incorporated into the dreams about as well as the content from our emotionally arousing films. When the films were viewed by the transmitters, no statistically significant correspondences were detected by the judges.

In other words, our experiment was an important landmark in dream research in that it confirmed Witkin's findings using judging procedures which were more sophisticated than those used in his original study. In the annals of parapsychological research, however, the first federally financed dream telepathy study proved to be a complete washout.

There was one curious statistically significant result of this study. We had administered a psychological test to all the subjects to test for "field independence," the ability to remain fairly independent from environmental influence. Artists, for example, make high scores on this test; so do school children who earn superior grades. Our high scorers on this test showed an interesting result regarding ESP and the nonemotional films. The judges' ratings of the "field independent" subjects' transcripts were significantly below chance for the nonemotional films that were telepathically transmitted. But why no significant results emerged in regard to the emotional films is unknown.

Additional Replications

Robert Van de Castle, in an experimental study involving dream diaries, had obtained significant results in replicating certain aspects of our work. And a group of students at Princeton University, monitoring periods of dreaming with the EEG, had provided an additional replication. Interest was also shown by David Foulkes, director of sleep research at the University of Wyoming, who had established a reputation as one of the world's most meticulous investigators of dream phenomena. He had become intrigued by our studies on telepathic dreams and, in 1969, obtained funds from Gardner Murphy to run an eight-night study with Robert Van de Castle as the subject. Although the results were not significant, his interest persisted and, in 1971, we launched a joint project.

We wrote to Malcolm Bessent, asking him to work with us in a long-distance telepathic dream study. Bessent flew to the University of Wyoming to meet eight female students who had volunteered their services as subjects. After establishing rapport with them, he returned to New York City and spent eight nights with Robert Masters and Jean Houston at the Foundation for Mind Research.

Our previous studies with Bessent had involved precognition. Our new study called upon him to work as a telepathic transmitter. The major similarity among the experiments was the use of slide-and-sound sequences in both the precognition and the telepathy studies.

Bessent was exposed to randomly selected slide-and-sound sequences on eight different nights; which he attempted to transmit telepathically to sleeping University of Wyoming students 2,000 miles away. When the results from the three outside judges were returned, it was discovered that while there had been some evidence of telepathy on five out of the eight nights, it was not strong enough to yield statistically significant results.

The failure of our collaborative effort to produce a telepathic effect was a disappointment to all of us. Until a fairly repeatable parapsychological effect can be studied by experimenters, we told ourselves, these bizarre phenomena cannot be studied intensively and incorporated into the mainstream of science. We were convinced that Foulkes and his associates had been open-minded and given telepathy a fair chance to operate. If an investigator such as Foulkes, in a collaborative study with our laboratory, could not obtain significant results, what chance would most cynics or skeptics have to capture ESP? Dream telepathy had taught us a great deal about psychic phenomena, but it was not predictable enough to allow science to integrate it with other findings.

In the meantime, what happened to Foulkes and his interest in the field? Fortunately, he retained an open mind on the subject and wrote us the following letter:

> . . . I have experienced a personally impressive instance of apparent telepathy in another laboratory study ostensibly unrelated to ESP. While working one night on our continuing study of children's dreams, I was watching for the appearance of a REM period in the sleep record of a pre-adolescent girl. I had left a task which had been occupying my attention for some time and gone into an audio control room. I picked up and began editing a review of an article on the effects of thirst on the sleep cycle. I wrote out a revision of the commentary section. The reviewer's second point was that "the cheese and crackers bedtime snack added a new and seemingly unnecessary aspect to the deprivation condition." I silently agreed—it was unnecessary. I then copied the third point, two sentences long, and got up to inspect the polygraph [EEG] record. The subject was now in a REM period, and I initiated an awakening. Her report:

> "This lady and this man lived near us, and they came over to our house, and they saw our dog, and then he had a snack, and he asked my dad if he wanted a beer, and my daddy said no, and finally my dad decided he wanted one, but it was one of the first times he had ever had one, and that's all I can remember. Oh, wait—and then . . . there were these three boxes of crackers. . . . one box of crackers had two white pieces, white crackers and then [a] little piece of cheese between, a whole pack like that, and then the other box of crackers was white and the other packages were brown. . . ."

> A striking coincidence? Surely, for this was the twenty-fifth night on which we had observed this subject's dreams, and there were no other dreams of cheese-crackers-thirst. Nor has this particular combination of elements ever occurred in the hundreds of dreams we have collected from other children in the same study in which the subject was serving.

Foulkes concluded, "An experience such as this keeps alive one's spark of interest in telepathic dreams." Such an experience also demonstrates the provocative nature of psychic phenomena. They often elude our laboratory designs only to emerge in real life, now frustrating our efforts and destroying our hopes, and then tempting us again, reviving our interest, like a siren leading us on.

4

IN AND OUT OF CONSCIOUSNESS

The particular thing to learn is how to get to the crack between the worlds and how to enter the other world. There is a crack between the two worlds, the world of the diableros and the world of living men. There is a place where the two worlds overlap. The crack is there. It opens and closes like a door in the wind. To get there a man must exercise his will. . . . When the crack opens the man has to slide through it. . . . After your return, you will not be the same. . . .

don Juan Matus

The Hypnagogic and Hypnopompic Twins

I attended my first meeting of the Association for Humanistic Psychology in 1967, at the insistence of Virginia Glenn. Virginia attended all of the humanistic psychology events, predicting that this was the coming wave in the social sciences. She introduced me to her friends in the field: Abraham Maslow, Walter Houston Clark, Rollo May, Ira Progoff, Ida Rolf, Charlotte Selver, Huston Smith, Alec Rubin, Gertrude Enelow, A. J. Brodbeck, James Klee, and Myron Arons. Dr. Arons, who had developed an entire department of humanistic psychology at West Georgia College, introduced me to Frank Barron, Charlotte Bühler, Carmi Harari, and Sidney Jourard.

Soon I found myself invited to speak on parapsychology at humanistic psychology conferences and to direct experiential workshops on ESP and altered states of consciousness at "growth centers" such as the Esalen Institute. In so doing, I used many of the techniques I had learned from Leary during his salad days at Millbrook. I attended additional workshops myself to study Tibetan Buddhism with Lama Govinda, body movement with Melvene Dyer-Bennett, and "Mind Dynamics" with Alexander Everett.

I was especially impressed by the lectures and writings of J. Krishnamurti, whose "method of no method" paralleled the teachings of Chogyam

Trungpa. Virginia Glenn had insisted that James Hickman, Lelie, and I come with her to hear Trungpa, a Tibetan Buddhist scholar, on his first New York visit in June 1970. Krishnamurti had said that a "guru" or teacher was not essential for one's personal development as we all should be our own gurus. Trungpa concurred, writing:

> The lonely child who travels through
> The fearful waste and desolate, fields,
> And listens to their barren tune,
> Greets as an unknown and best friend
> The terror in him and he sings
> In darkness all the sweetest songs.

My continued interest in altered states of consciousness led me to analyze closely the results of our telepathic dream experiments. In so doing, I was assisted by Judith Malamud, a student at the University of Chicago, who was the first of many talented student research assistants to work in the laboratory. Some of them volunteered their time; others received a one-hundred-dollar "Gardner Murphy Fellowship," which came from a special fund Murphy had earmarked for our use. I spent what time I could with Malamud and the other student research assistants, remembering how much I had learned from both the formal and informal contact I had been fortunate enough to have had in my student days with Murphy and Rhine.

Malamud divided each typed transcript of dreams into "units of meaning," which consisted of sentences, phrases, exclamations, and interjections that carried discrete bits of information. We then had an outside judge look at the target picture utilized for that dream fragment and decide whether or not enough of a correspondence existed to rate the unit of meaning as telepathic. This procedure was followed for dream reports, hypnagogic and hypnopompic imagery reports, and statements made by the subjects while fully awake and before drifting into a hypnagogic state or going to sleep.

We obtained units of meaning by the thousand, as we worked our way through the studies with Robyn Posin, Theresa Grayeb, Robert Van de Castle, and the two studies with William Erwin. The results were about the same for all five studies. There was very little telepathy in the waking statements, but a great deal in the dream reports and the subjects' associations to their dreams. However, the twin "twilight states" of hypnagogic and hypnopompic imagery contained a higher proportion of ESP than any of the comparative conditions. There were no significant differences between the two states themselves, but great statistical differences between the "twin states" and each of the other conditions we investigated.

As usual, we were running out of funds. However, we found that we could make our money go further by studying mental images such as those occurring during hypnagogic and hypnopompic states. In so doing, we could directly investigate the issue of psi-conducive states of consciousness and determine which conscious states were most conducive to paranormal phenomena.

"Dark Star" and the ACID Chamber

For our first attempt to explore ESP performance during several different states of consciousness, we asked Jean Mayo, a well-known filmmaker and multimedia artist, to design a sensory bombardment chamber. Claiming to see auras, Ms. Mayo utilized colors and patterns for the chamber which, as she stated, "characterize the auras of individuals during their periods of greatest psychic activity." We dubbed her construction the "Altered Consciousness Induction Device," or ACID.

ACID consisted of a large circular structure placed in a multimedia environment. Mayo constructed the circular structure from clear liquid plastic which had been poured into a mold. Hollow tubes in the plastic allowed colored water to circulate through the structure while colored background lights flickered on and off in a prearranged sequence.

Testing out the new apparatus became a family affair. My wife Lelie suggested several museums where our staff members could go to obtain the art prints we used as target pictures. Bob prepared the subjects for their ACID trip, and Carie was the first subject for our preliminary sessions. As Carie entered the chamber, Bob placed stereophonic earphones on her head and seated her in front of the circular structure on a comfortable cushion. He then handed her a randomly selected sealed envelope which contained a smaller sealed envelope which contained the target picture. Finally, Bob turned on a taped recording of "Dark Star," an instrumental selection played by the Grateful Dead. "Dark Star" was selected because the complexity of the music would prevent subjects from becoming bored if they had to listen to it several times. Furthermore, the rock-and-roll style of "Dark Star" adapted well to the sensory bombardment features of ACID.

Carie's target happened to be a picture of a sailboat. She reported an image of "sailors by a waterfront," so we knew we were off and running.

Our next subject was Martha Harlin, a psychic sensitive who was a frequent volunteer for laboratory experiments at the American Society for Psychical Research. At the end of eight ACID sessions, Harlin reported that she had not grown tired of "Dark Star," but had found new elements of interest in it with each listening. And her guesses as to the clairvoyant target had yielded close correspondences in six out of eight attempts.

Now we were ready to begin our formal experiment. We would run four subjects through twenty-four sessions—eight in ordinary consciousness, eight in sensory bombardment, and eight in a state over which the subject exercised voluntary control. For example, Malcolm Bessent and Alan Vaughan utilized meditative states that they had practiced for several years. Gordon Goodman (a student research assistant attending Harpur College) used Zen meditation, and Tina Johnson (a psychic sensitive from Baltimore) utilized automatic writing.

"Dear Friends"

Ms. Johnson claimed to be able to communicate with "discarnate entities" and, in a state of reverie, quickly wrote down whatever messages they sent to her. She asked if her alleged entities would like to participate in an ESP test and they "wrote" back that it sounded like fun!

When the outside judges evaluated correspondences between each art print and each subject guess, we found that the overall results of this study were highly significant. The self-induced states of consciousness yielded slightly more ESP than the sessions in which the subjects merely sat at a desk and wrote down their guesses as to the contents of the sealed envelopes. The ACID sessions yielded more ESP than either of the other two conditions, the data from that condition being statistically significant when taken by themselves and analyzed. The fact that ACID appeared to produce a psi-favorable state of consciousness may indicate that sensory bombardment breaks up habitual perceptions, allowing paranormal information to escape the filtering devices that often exclude it from conscious awareness.

Before making a definitive statement, more research needs to be done —especially in light of the contradictory data produced when the subjects, at the end of each set of three sessions, evaluated their own material using a package of duplicate art prints. The subjects produced results that were also statistically significant but with more clairvoyance emerging during ordinary consciousness than during the other conditions. This was not the first time that subject evaluation had differed from that done by outside judges— demonstrating the weakness of our evaluation system and the need for a more objective technique.

According to evaluation by both the subjects and judges, Tina Johnson obtained more correct guesses than any of the other subjects, doing especially well in the sessions utilizing automatic writing. For example, the target picture randomly selected for Ms. Johnson's first session of contact with the entities was de Chirico's *The Enigma of Arrival*. It portrays two figures, one in blue and one in red. Johnson wrote the following comments as she entered into a dialogue with her entities, her own comments being recorded by the experimenter. The statements attributed to the entities (which she referred to as "dear friends") are italicized in this account:

> "Dear friends, are you there?"
> *"Yes, we are."*
> "I am holding an envelope with a picture inside. Can you see it?"
> *"Yes. We can sense it."*
> "What is the picture?"
> *"There is blue. A blue boy."*
> "What else do you see?"
> *"People."*
> "Are you certain?"
> *"We see a very young man in a blue suit. He is standing up."*
> "Do you see anything else?"
> *"No, we see the same thing."*

For the second session of automatic writing, *Dancers,* a painting by Zechin, was randomly selected. It portrays three oriental dancers; the predominant colors are orange, red, and pink. Johnson had another dialogue with her entities:

> "Dear friends: We are trying the second of the experiments. You had a 'hit' on the first one—the blue boy. Now I have another envelope in front of me. . . . What picture do you see?"
> *"Now hear this. . . . We see a great mountain of fire. It is orange and red with lava running down the sides."*
> "Thank you. I will let you try again in case you see other things in the picture. . . ."
> *"We are in a tropical situation. Burning and hot. . . ."*
> "Hell?"
> *"No. Not hell, but heat. Two people talking. . . ."*

In another session, Magritte's *The Tomb of the Wrestlers,* was randomly chosen. It portrays a huge rose, the sides of which touch all four walls of a room. The predominant colors are red and brown.

> "Are you ready for the new envelope?"
> *"Yes. It is of a narrow street with shops along it. . . ."*
> "Do you see any colors?"
> *"Brown. . . ."*
> "Does the picture have a name?"
> *"Yes, but it is not readable by us."*
> "Is it in a foreign language?"
> *"We can only see letters."*
> "Anything else?"

"*Yes. See if you can reach the sides of a building.*
"Reach the sides of a building?"
"*Yes. Reach. Stretch.*"
"Is this a clue?"
"*Yes.*"
"Is the picture happy?"
"*Well, neutral.*"

For the final session, a photograph by Freeman, *Five Is a Crowd,* was randomly selected. It shows five kittens in a wicker basket; the predominant colors are orange, brown, and white.

"This is the last try on this experiment. Can you sense the last envelope in front of me? Please try!"
"*Yes. We can sense it. And we see it contains a large picture of a girl. She is sitting on a chair.*"
"What colors are in the picture?"
"*Yellow. Some red and white.*"
"Are you certain? Please look again, being very careful, and tell me what you see."
"*It's a girl!*"
"Careful now."
"*This is not the way to make us work. You are hurting us.*"
"I don't mean to. Just describe the pictures once more, please."
"*A girl is sitting in a chair.*"
"I'll hold the envelope."
"*All right. She is still in the chair.*"
"Could it be a boy?"
"*No.*"

The judges picked up a relationship between felines sitting in a basket and a girl sitting in a chair, thus giving Tina Johnson and her entities an impressive overall score. However, many of her correspondences in other sessions were equally impressive.

While in the sensory bombardment chamber, Pinzzinato's *The Farmer's Family* was selected and Johnson visualized a "country scene. . . . a farmer around some place."

During another session, Johnson reported "Robes. . . . The idea of Spain. A Spanish dancer. . . . The name 'Goya.' " The target picture was Goya's painting, *The Maja Clothed,* which depicts a Spanish noblewoman reclining on a couch.

In another ACID session, Johnson described "the goddess of mercy; a white figure." Upon opening the double envelope, we discovered that the target had been Magritte's painting *Philosophy in the Boudoir,* which portrays a surrealistic female figure in a white gown.

Were Tina Johnson's "friends" discarnate entities? Or were they dissociated elements of her own personality? The closest we came to an answer
was her own description of the experience:

> When I do automatic writing, I simply relax my control over my conscious
> thoughts and let the thoughts from another source come into my brain and
> through my handwriting. It took a year before I was able to accomplish
> this. Other than a fraction of a second's warning, I am not aware until I am
> writing what I'm going to write. It is as if the conscious brain only watches
> while it relinquishes control of my writing mechanisms. I am able to switch
> back and forth to my own conscious writing during the sessions in order to
> write down questions for later reference. However, I am also able to ask the
> questions mentally and have them answered in writing.

The topic of shift in conscious awareness and ESP has been discussed
since Gardner Murphy wrote an important article in 1966 for the *Journal
of the American Society for Psychical Research*. Murphy hypothesized that
ESP activation is more often associated with a shift from one state of consciousness to another than with a steady state. Studies by the parapsychologist Rex Stanford lent indirect confirmation to this idea. Stanford had
observed a relationship between shifts in alpha frequency and ESP, as well
as more ESP during tests with an alpha increase than during tests with a
decrease in alpha frequency.

The Witches' Cradle

When Charles Honorton elicited hypnotic dreams in one of our experimental series, he taught his subjects a self-report scale. Based on a procedure described by Charles Tart, the scale was designed to measure one's
state of consciousness as well as shift or transitions between two different
states.

Tart found that his subjects produced reports which correlated with
objective tests of hypnotic depth. Honorton found that the subjects whose
state reports indicated that their consciousness had been profoundly altered
produced hypnotic dreams with more ESP than subjects whose state reports
indicated very little change in consciousness. Honorton also found most
ESP among the subjects making the greatest shift in conscious states from
the time the experiment started to the time they reported their hypnotic
dream.

When the U.S. Food and Drug Administration forced Robert Masters
and Jean Houston out of LSD research, the husband-and-wife team devised
methods to produce alterations in consciousness without drugs. One of
these techniques involved placing the subject in a "sensory bombardment"
audiovisual chamber similar to ACID.

Another technique utilized a "sensory deprivation" device known as the "witches' cradle." There are historical accounts of cradlelike contraptions which were suspended from trees for witches to enter. Upon being covered with a sheath, and after ingesting thorn apple, belladonna, or some other consciousness-altering drug, the witch would frequently have an out-of-body experience and would travel to the "Witches' Sabbath" to meet with fellow initiates in various rituals and ceremonies.

Masters and Houston studied the historical texts, then built a device which appeared to alter consciousness and facilitate visual imagery. The witches' cradle is essentially a metal swing in which a subject stands upright, supported by broad bands of canvas. The subject wears ear plugs to eliminate outside sound, and opaque goggles, to eliminate external visual stimuli. This swing acts as a pendulum, carrying the subject from side to side and rotating in response to involuntary movements from the subject's body.

Altered states of consciousness usually occur in from two to twenty minutes after the subject enters the witches' cradle. Subjects often report time and space distortions, body image changes, and intense visual imagery. One subject reported the following experience shortly after the cradle began to move:

> I am expanding, expanding. . . . And I can read secrets of the universe and glimpse the forms of things. Beautiful forms, mathematical forms, geometrical forms. They are all alive, colorful, and brilliant. It is the source of the forms . . ., the Unity unified, it is the experience of the Unity . . ., as if all were unified in me!

This subject described his session on the witches' cradle as one of the most profound and beautiful experiences of his life.

On the other hand, some subjects get dizzy while in the cradle, others become anxious, and some report no consciousness alteration at all. Therefore, we felt that the device would be well suited for our self-report scale.

A telepathy experiment was designed by Charles Honorton, Sally Ann Drucker, one of our research assistants, and Harry Hermon, a psychiatrist at Maimonides who lent us his witches' cradle for the study. Thirty subjects participated in the experiment and were told that a transmitter in a distant room would be viewing a target picture during the last ten minutes of their session in the cradle. We taught our subjects the self-report scale by telling them:

> During the course of this experiment, we will be interested in the degree to which your state of mind stays the same or changes. That is, at various times we are going to want to know what state of mind you are in. In order to make it easy and convenient for you to tell me this, I am going to teach

you a rating scale. This way, when you are asked "State?" you will just call out a number to indicate your state of mind, instead of having to explain it.

Here is what the numbers are to represent: *Zero* indicates that you are normally alert just as you are now. *One* indicates that you feel especially relaxed. In this state, you may feel more at ease, and the tension in your muscles may yield to a more peaceful state. Do you know what I mean? *Two* indicates that your attention is being focused more on internal feelings and sensations. This may be associated with a shift from your surrounding environment to your internal bodily feelings. If this shift is not only recognizable but strong, you should report *three*, and if it is strong and very impressive to you, report *four*. A report of *four* indicates that you feel more or less oblivious to your external surroundings.

Okay. Now, whenever I ask "State?" you should call out the first number that pops into your mind. We've found this generally to be more accurate than if you stop and think about what the number should be. Of course, if you feel that the number you've called out is way off, you may call out a correction. It is important that your state reports reflect, as accurately as possible, your internal state.

The subjects were asked for a state report at critical times during an experiment. This enabled us to detect shifts in consciousness as well as the conscious state associated with any particular attempt at ESP.

The subjects were encouraged to "relax as much as possible and allow yourself to flow with the experience. . . . Do not consciously try to elicit imagery, allow the imagery to flow spontaneously." They were each strapped into the cradle for thirty minutes. State reports were elicited every five minutes; during the final ten minutes, the telepathic transmitter viewed an art print which had been randomly selected from a collection of 140 pictures. The procedure involved shuffling two decks of cards. One deck contained cards numbered from one to twenty-eight; the other deck contained cards lettered A through E. After the card decks were shuffled ten times and cut, the top cards were drawn and the appropriate target selected (for example, A-16, D-5, B-27).

At the end of the session a copy of the art print, along with seven pictures which had not been used in the session, were presented to the subject. The subject ranked the eight art prints for correspondence with his or her imagery reports. Ranks of 1, 2, 3, and 4 were designated telepathic "hits" while ranks of 5, 6, 7, and 8 were designated "misses." A rank of 1 would have been a "direct" hit but ranks of 2, 3, and 4 would still have indicated some correspondence with the picture.

About 63 percent of the subjects obtained telepathic 'hits' in this study, a result which is not quite statistically significant. However, 76 percent of the subjects with high state reports (averaging two, three, or four) during their session on the cradle obtained hits, a significant result. On the other hand, only 46 percent of the subjects giving low state reports (zero or one) obtained hits, a nonsignificant result because one would expect 50 percent hits by chance alone.

Honorton then examined those subjects who made an above average shift in their state reports from the first ten-minute period to the last ten minutes. Of these subjects, 81 percent obtained telepathic hits, a highly significant result. Of those subjects making below average shifts, only 43 percent produced hits.

Finally, Honorton checked out the average shift in state report for all subjects making hits. The average shift was 1.15, compared to a shift of 0.45 for misses. This difference is statistically significant, confirming Gardner Murphy's hypothesis that shifts in consciousness are favorable to the emergence of ESP.

State Reports and Electrosleep

On May 26 1971, Judith Skutch brought an Electrosone 50 machine to the Dream Lab and I was the first subject. Skutch, an associate of the National Patent Development Corporation, told us how her firm had obtained patent rights from the Soviet Union to manufacture an American version of the machine. I was aware that electrosleep, the alteration in consciousness produced by the Electrosone 50, was used by therapists in various parts of the world to treat patients with insomnia and anxiety problems. However, I thought it also might be worthy of exploration as a parapsychological technique.

Skutch attached electrodes over my eyebrows and on the mastoid bone behind my ears. She turned the machine on; a mild current flowed over my head and I became very relaxed. Soon I began to visualize colorful images: a jungle scene in which a butterfly was perched on top of a puma, a mountain covered with snow and twisted pine trees, a picnic attended by a variety of Greek gods and goddesses. By the time the electrodes were unfastened, I had resolved to utilize the Electrosone 50 in an ESP experiment.

We also used two other consciousness-altering devices, both of which had been designed by Jean Mayo, the artist who had produced the ACID machine for our earlier study. One device was an audiovisual display which consisted of music and colored lights which flashed on and off sequentially.

Mayo's other apparatus was a stroboscopic device consisting of a film projector on a wheel which was rotated in front of the projector's bulb and lens. As the subject sat in front of the device with his or her eyes closed, the wheel rotated at 50 cycles per second, providing a flickering effect which typically stimulated visual imagery.

The study was carried out by Clark Hubbard, a student from Johns Hopkins University, and Nanette Auerhahn, who was attending Barnard College. They worked with four female subjects, one of whom was Tamara Cohen, Skutch's daughter; another was Felicia Parise. Each subject participated in eight sessions; during every session, the subject attempted to identify four art prints in four different sealed, opaque envelopes. A different envelope was used for each of four different conditions: electrosleep, the audiovisual display, the stroboscopic device, and the subject's ordinary conscious state. The order of the four conditions was determined randomly as was the collection of four pictures used during each session. A record was kept of each subject's performance so that no collection of pictures was used twice and so that the order of experimental conditions was never repeated.

Each experimental condition lasted for fifteen minutes with the exception of the stroboscopic device which produced so intense an effect that its duration was limited to five minutes. When the allotted time was up, the subject gave a state report followed by a description of what she thought was in the envelope. The attempted identification of the target was followed by a second state report. These responses were recorded and later evaluated by outside judges.

Three judges came to the laboratory on separate days, looked at the art prints, and read the subjects' guesses. Each judge ranked the four possible target pictures for each session against each of the conditions for that session. For example, a judge would read the subject's guess following electrosleep, would examine the four art prints, and would award ranks of 1, 2, 3, and 4. If the actual target were awarded a rank of 1, it was considered a clairvoyant hit, while ranks of 2, 3, and 4 were considered misses. The median rank for the three judges was identified for each condition in every session. For example, if one judge had given a target a rank of 1, while the others had ranked it 2 and 3, the rank of 2 (a miss) would be used. For a target to be a hit, at least two of the three judges would have had to award it a rank of 1.

There was one chance in four that a subject's guess would be a hit rather than a miss. For the total of 128 subject guesses, we would have expected a total of 32 hits by chance alone. Instead, there was a total of 44 hits, a highly significant result which confirmed the clairvoyance hypothesis. The subject making the most hits was Tamara Cohen who obtained 14 hits out of 32 attempts rather than the 8 hits one would expect by chance. For example, she made the following guess regarding the contents of a sealed envelope on which she concentrated during one experimental session:

> I saw a Japanese person with his fist pressed against the upper half of his chest. I only saw that one arm placed against a dark background. Then I saw a star in a circle. The last thing I saw was just a V-necked robe.

The picture in the envelope was a painting by the Japanese artist Sharaku, "The Actor Uso in the Part of the Ronim Kampei." All three of the judges awarded a rank of 1 to this picture in connection with the subject's guess.

We then analyzed the seventy-four guesses that were associated with high initial state reports (two, three, or four); twenty-seven of these attempts were hits, a significant proportion. Only seventeen of the fifty-four guesses associated with low initial state reports were hits, a nonsignificant amount.

The condition which altered consciousness the most was electrosleep. This condition was associated with thirteen hits out of thirty-two attempts rather than the eight expected by chance, a significant result. The average initial state report during electrosleep was 2.13; this was significantly greater than the average initial state report for each of the other conditions.

We had hoped to investigate shifts in consciousness, but in only two cases were the second state reports higher than the initial state reports. Therefore, we investigated a different phenomenon for which data did exist in the study. In most instances, the subject's second state report was lower than her first report, indicating a return to ordinary consciousness. In some cases, however, the state report stayed the same. We eliminated instances in which both state reports were zero, indicating no alteration in consciousness, and still found forty instances in which the subject gave the same state report at the end of a condition as she had given just before making her guess. Instead of the expected ten hits, the subjects made seventeen hits, a highly significant number. The attempts in which a subject dropped back to ordinary consciousness did not demonstrate a significantly greater number of hits.

How do we explain these results? Perhaps the fact that the subject remained in an altered state while making her guess indicates that the altered state had been especially profound. Or perhaps it suggests that guesses made in an altered state capture the flavor and contents of that state better than those made once a subject has returned to ordinary awareness.

The state reports reflected a change from externally directed to internally directed attentive activity. Here again was an instance of shifting consciousness affecting ESP scores. Unfortunately, the results were not clear-cut. Subject judging was in agreement with that of the outside judges in most comparisons, but insofar as state reports were concerned, the subjects actually awarded significantly more hits than misses to the sessions marked by their low state reports. Again, it was obvious that our judging techniques were too inadequate for conclusive statements to be made about this work.

State Reports and Three Environments

Our next attempt to study sensory bombardment and ESP was directed by Michael Bova, an art student at the Pratt Institute. Bova and I collaborated with an artist, Aleksandra Kasuba, in testing out environmental effects on clairvoyance.

Kasuba's studio was used as the location for all experimental sessions for the fifty subjects in our study. Kasuba designed a "group shelter" to alter our subjects' conscious states. It was a conical structure, the shape of which converged to a mirror mounted on the ceiling. There were no other furnishings inside; a tasseled deep pile rug of green, purple, gold, and blue was spread over a floor of small hill-like ridges. A white globe on the rug diffused light throughout the area.

Another environment designed by Kasuba was referred to as "the sensory." It was a spiral rising to a tall and hollow column of white stretch nylon. Inside, the floor area was a mirror on which a hand-sized glass ball had been placed. A light source around the perimeter of the mirror completed the interior.

While the sensory and the group shelter had been designed to alter consciousness, the "writing shelter," our third environment, was created to maintain ordinary consciousness. It consisted of a wooden chair and a plain writing desk. One of the adjoining walls was made of curved white nylon, flanked by two walls painted dark gray.

Emanuel Ghent's electronic, computer-generated music was played at low volume and could be heard in the sensory and group shelter, but not in the writing shelter.

Again, we used postcard-size reproductions of famous paintings as target pictures for this study. To create a collection of four possible target pictures with somewhat equivalent power to facilitate ESP, a laboratory staff member inspected over 100 art prints from local museums and art supply stores. She evaluated these art prints on the following scales:

A. *Simplicity*
   1. very simple
   2. fairly simple
   3. complex

B. *Emotionality*
1. generates great emotional feeling
2. generates some emotional feeling
3. generates little or no emotional feeling

C. *Vividness*
1. very colorful and vivid
2. fairly colorful and vivid
3. lacking vividness

All art prints which received one or more rating of 3 were eliminated from consideration. Four were then selected which differed thematically one from the other: *The Duelers* by Goya, *Lily and the Sparrows* by Evergood, *Witch Doctor* by Catlow, and *Battaglia* by Borra.

Each art print was placed in a small opaque envelope which was sealed and placed in a large opaque envelope which was also sealed. Duplicate copies of the four art prints were set aside for judging purposes.

The numbers 123, 231, and 312 were printed on cards; these numbers referred to the three environments. When a subject arrived at Kasuba's studio, Bova, the experimenter, closed his eyes and pointed blindly to a five-digit number in a table of hundreds of random numbers. He added and readded the five digits until a single number was obtained, then counted down a stack of cards one or more times until he located the card which matched the one-digit number. This card was used to determine the order in which the subject would enter the designated environment.

Next, Bova turned to a stack of cards designated A, B, C, and D; these letters referred to the four potential targets. Bova used a similar procedure to obtain a one-digit number which was used to determine the target used in the subject's first environment.

The subject was given the sealed envelope and sent to the designated environment where he or she spent fifteen minutes before writing a guess as to the target's identity on a sheet of paper. Upon arriving at Kasuba's studio, each subject had been taught the self-report scale and immediately gave a state report. Another state report was requested fifteen minutes after immersion in the environment and again after the subject had written down a guess as to the target's identity.

Subjects judged their own material in this study. Each subject was given duplicate target pictures and three evaluation forms, each of which stated:

1. Examine all four targets. Remember that the title and the artist may be perceived as well as the picture and the design.
2. Rank all four targets against your report. Place the picture which *most* resembles your report at rank #1 on this sheet. Place the target which *least* resembles your report at rank #4.

3. When you are finished, there should be a target associated with each rank. However, there should be no ties.

After all fifty subjects had been tested, their evaluation forms were investigated and the total numbers of hits and misses were determined.

In examining the state reports, it was discovered that almost all subjects shifted state between the administration of the first state report and the second. However, there were very few subjects who shifted conscious state between the second and third reports. Therefore, an examination of the effect of shift in consciousness upon ESP could not be ascertained.

An analysis was made of each subject's second state report, the one given after fifteen minutes in the environment. For the fifty sessions conducted in the writing shelter, the average state report was 1.50; all state reports below this figure (zero and one) were designated low state reports while those above 1.50 (two, three, and four) were designated high state reports. This was the basic procedure used in the other studies, all of which involved a technique to alter consciousness which produced an average state report between 1.00 and 2.00.

However, when we examined the fifty sessions conducted in the group shelter, the average state report was 2.32—a higher figure than that obtained in our other experiments. For sessions held in the sensory, the average state report was 2.14. So for these two environments, low state reports (below average) became zero, one, and two, while high reports (above average) became three and four.

For the 100 subject guesses in the group shelter and the sensory, 40 were associated with high state reports and 60 with low reports. There were more hits than misses during high report sessions, and more misses than hits during sessions characterized by low state reports. These results were statistically significant. More clairvoyance hits occurred in the group shelter but the sensory environment provided a more clear-cut discrimination between high and low state reports.

A striking clairvoyant hit was obtained by Felicia Parise while in the group shelter. She was working with the painting, *Lily and the Sparrows* by Evergood. If Parise could have seen through the two sealed envelopes, she would have discerned a picture of a girl at the window sill of a red brick building; there is a tree outside as well as sparrows. After giving a state report of three for the session, Parise reported:

A red brick house in the country. A little old lady putting pies on the window sill to cool. Some animals like police dogs are smelling the pies. There were some trees, but the color I feel most is red.

And what happened in the writing shelter? The results were not statistically significant, but were still intriguing. During the sessions marked by high state reports, there were more misses than hits; during low state report sessions, there were more hits than misses. This was the reverse of what occurred during sessions in the two environments held to alter consciousness, and suggests that an especially facilitating environment is needed for altered states of consciousness to encourage ESP. Not every unusual changed state of consciousness can be depended upon to aid psychic phenomena.

It is also of interest that the group shelter and the sensory environments altered consciousness more than any of the special devices used in the previous studies—the witches' cradle, the Electrosone 50, the stroboscope, or ACID. I was not surprised by the results as some of my most profound alterations in consciousness had come about while immersed in architectural environments, especially those designed by Frank Lloyd Wright.

In retrospect, our experimental studies of ESP and the self-report scale provided a type of replication lacking in most parapsychological research, including our own dream studies. We had completed four complex experiments, three with clairvoyance and one with telepathy. Whether we used hypnotic dreams, the witches' cradle, electrosleep, or artistic environments, we found that ESP was more likely to occur during altered states of consciousness (as denoted by high state reports) than during ordinary states of consciousness (as identified by low state reports).

Shortly after these studies had been concluded, Charles Honorton, drawing upon Judith Malamud's earlier work with units of meaning, evolved an objective judging procedure to help surmount the occasional conflicts in results when subject evaluations were compared to those of outside judges. Honorton suggested counting the number of individual units of information, then having a judge determine whether any correspondence existed between the individual units and the target. At this point, the judge would rate the degree of correspondence on a simple scale from one (very indirect) to ten (very direct).

For example, one subject had reported the following imagery in a clairvoyance experiment: "The Virgin Mary. A statue and Jesus Christ. An old church with two pillars overgrown with grass." The target had been El Greco's painting *The Adoration of the Shepherds*; the judge had credited four of the six units as having correspondence with the target. The judge's ratings regarding degrees of correspondence were:

1. The Virgin Mary (10)
2. A statue (no correspondence)
3. and Jesus Christ (10)

4. An old church (no correspondence)
5. with two pillars (3)
6. overgrown with grass (7)

Honorton concluded that such frequency and quality measures could then be employed as measures to test ways in which ESP is processed.

It was then questionable whether we would be able to utilize this sophisticated technique because our money was running out, and with it our time. Nevertheless, the result of our studies using self-reports on states of consciousness appeared to confirm Murphy's ideas on shifts in consciousness. These ideas had been put forth years earlier, and in a somewhat different way, by Sigmund Freud, who conducted some ESP tests with his friends, concluding that

> Strongly emotionally colored recollections can be successfully transferred without much difficulty . . . at the moment at which an idea emerges from the unconscious.

Berger and the EEG

In 1893, Hans Berger, a student of astronomy at the University of Berlin, had an experience which inspired him to study the interaction between mental phenomena and physiological processes. He later recalled:

> As a 19-year-old student, I had a serious accident . . . near Würzburg and barely escaped certain death. Riding on a narrow edge of a steep ravine through which a road led, I fell with my rearing, tumbling horse down into the path of a mounted battery and came to lie almost beneath the wheel of one of the guns. The latter, pulled by six horses, came to a stop just in time, and I escaped, having suffered no more than fright. This accident happened in the morning hours of a beautiful spring day. In the evening of the same day, I received a telegram from my father, who inquired about my well being. It was the first and only time in my life that I received such a query. My oldest sister, to whom I had always been particularly close, had occasioned this telegraphic inquiry, because she had suddenly told my parents that she knew with certainty that I had suffered an accident. . . . This is a case of spontaneous telepathy in which at a time of mortal danger, and as I contemplated certain death, I transmitted my thoughts, while my sister, who was particularly close to me, acted as the receiver.

Berger left astronomy for medicine and psychiatry, directing his activities toward identifying measurable physiological properties of the brain that represented mental activity. He was convinced that mind-body relationships would ultimately be explainable in terms of the basic laws of physics. While working with veterans of the First World War, Berger made his first successful recording of the human electroencephalogram in 1924. He devoted much attention to alpha waves, noting that they disappeared when his subjects began to engage in intellectual activities such as solving arithmetic problems.

For several years, Berger's work with the electrical activity of the brain was ignored, due to the popularity of Freudian psychoanalysis among psychiatrists. Eventually, his work was replicated by a British research team; but, by this time, Hitler had come to power in Germany and Berger was forced to submit his papers to censorship. In 1938, the Nazis ousted him from his university and dismantled his laboratory. Upset over the effects of the Second World War, Berger took his own life in 1941. Twenty years later, Montague Ullman was using the EEG to identify periods of dreaming among subjects in a pilot dream telepathy study. Thirty years later, Charles Honorton, at our laboratory in the Maimonides Medical Center, was using the EEG to explore relationships between alpha waves and ESP activity. Berger's hopes had finally been realized.

REMs and Psi

The use of the EEG and other psychophysiological techniques have proved to be especially useful in identifying bodily changes which accompany dreaming. Usually, the nighttime dream will be associated with irregularities of pulse, blood pressure, and respiration; with rapid-eye-movement activity and arousal of the sexual organs, with sporadic activity of certain muscles of the body, but a near absence of tonic antigravity muscle potential (or muscle tonus), with a high brain temperature and metabolic rate, and with a low voltage desynchronized EEG pattern from the brain cortex. The areas of the brain below the cortex also appear to be important in dreaming. R. M. Jones, in his book, *The New Psychology of Dreaming,* claims that the dream state is triggered by the pontile-limbic system, a primitive portion of the brain, characteristic only of mammals. Indeed, periods of rapid eye movement appear in all mammals that have been studied—cats, dogs, sheep, goats, monkeys, chimpanzees, donkeys, opossums, mice, rats, elephants, and humans.

One parapsychologist who became especially interested in the possible relation between rapid eye movements and psi was Douglas Dean, an instructor at the Newark College of Engineering. Dean had hypothesized that vertical, up-and-down eye movements might be psychokinetically increased by a telepathic transmitter who looked at a vertical picture, such as a skyscraper. In the same way, horizontal, back-and-forth eye movements might be amenable to influence by a transmitter who would concentrate on a horizontal picture, such as an automobile.

I was one of the subjects in a pilot study Dean carried out to test this hypothesis. When he looked at a photograph of a tall building, I dreamed of walking through the streets of a city with Theresa Grayeb, one of our former dream-telepathy subjects. Ms. Grayeb and I barely avoided falling into a chasm which was to hold the foundation for a tall office building. Later that night, Dean concentrated upon a painting of a goldfish. I had a vivid dream about a woman whose body was painted gold; she was stretched out on a bed and my association was to the film, "Goldfinger." I also recalled that a sexist colloquialism for a woman is "fish" in some segments of the American culture. The results of my session were statistically significant; I produced a high proportion of up-and-down eye movements while Dean was transmitting the building, and a high ratio of back-and-forth eye movements when the target was a goldfish.

Why do mammals dream? The newborn human infant spends half of his or her sleep time in the rapid-eye-movement stage; this percentage decreases to 40 by the age of two, 30 by the age of five, about 25 by adolescence, 20 by adulthood, and about 15 in old age. Prematurely born infants spend about 75 percent of their sleep time in the rapid-eye-movement stage. These developmental changes demonstrate to some scientists that the rapid-eye-movement activity provides a mechanism for establishing binocularly coordinated eye movements without which we would not be able to focus the eyes for depth perception. Once binocular skills are established, dreaming is still necessary to clear the nervous system of its residue of daily activities, to stimulate growth and maintenance of the brain's cortex, to keep the brain stimulated and functioning when there is little external sensory input, and to process information, engage in problem solving, and to fantasize about unfulfilled wishes. With all of these functions, what time does the dreaming process have for incorporating telepathic information being transmitted by a person in a distant room?

In an attempt to answer this question, we had one of our judges investigate each "unit of meaning" in the dreams collected from Dr. Erwin, Dr. Posin, Dr. Van de Castle, and Ms. Grayeb. Much to our surprise, the judge found that an average of 25 percent of each dream report contained material which corresponded to the target picture. Those studies for which the percentage was below 25 percent were not considered statistically significant.

We also had our judges evaluate each dream's units of meaning for the presence of such elements as color and emotion. We discovered that the telepathic elements in our subjects' dreams usually contained color references, various types of emotion, and more specific and elaborate detail than other portions of the dreams. We did *not* find unpleasant references to "penetration" in the telepathic parts of the dream, confirming Schmeidler and LeShan's work with the Rorschach inkblots that demonstrated very little fear of bodily or psychic penetration among high ESP scorers. Again, these data demonstrate that the successful subject in a telepathy experiment is likely to welcome the incorporation of a telepathically transmitted message, not worrying about possibly dreaming a dream which belongs to somebody else.

Bombarding the Senses

Our findings on color and emotion correlated with work reported by Dr. Thelma Moss, a psychologist at U.C.L.A. By incorporating vivid images in a slide-and-sound sequence for her telepathic senders, Moss was able to obtain highly significant results. Moss repeated these experiments several times, usually obtaining significant data, especially for the most dramatic of her slide-and-sound sequences.

In one experiment, a group of telepathic transmitters was exposed to pictures of explorers at the North Pole surrounded by ice and snow. The sound effects consisted of howling winds. One of the telepathic receivers had the impression of "howling winds and cold," and close correspondences were observed for most of the other subjects.

In another experiment, a slide-and-sound sequence centered around the assassination of John F. Kennedy; it included excerpts from his speeches, pictures from his years in office, and scenes from his assassination. The receiver responded:

> I seem to have the feeling of sadness or sorrow . . . as if I were crying . . . or something tragic has happened, and that I was grieving over something . . . much the same as one might feel attending a funeral of a dear friend . . . or a well-known figure in whom one had faith.

We were so intrigued by these results that Steven Zeichner, a student research assistant studying at the University of Chicago, did an intensive study of seventy-four of our target pictures used with seventy-four different subjects. Zeichner had three judges correlate these pictures with a list of twenty-five adjectives. An adjective was felt to characterize a particular art print if two of the three judges agreed on the term.

When Zeichner divided the pictures between those associated with telepathic hits and those associated with telepathic misses, he noticed some provocative differences. Of the art prints associated with hits, most had been described as "aggressive," "alert," "blue," "cold," "deliberate," "imaginative," "interesting," "masculine," and "unpleasant." Each of those adjectives resembled Moss's North Pole slide-and-sound sequence so closely that one could almost have predicted success for the target sequence. Of the targets associated with misses, more were described as "bright," "feminine," "formal," "orange," "pleasant," "unrealistic," "warm," and "yellow" than the targets involved with telepathic hits. The other adjectives on the list (such as "green" and "well-defined") were applied almost equally to hits and misses.

Zeichner also examined the number of adjectives applied to each picture. Between one and three adjectives were assigned to more of the hits (34 percent versus 22 percent for the misses), while between seven and nine adjectives were assigned to more of the misses (22 percent versus 15 percent for the hits). In other words, the simpler the target, the better. In addition, the more dynamic and the more disquieting the target, the more likely it was that the picture would facilitate a telepathic hit.

One art print containing the qualities identified by Zeichner was Bellows' painting *Dempsey and Firpo*. It portrays a scene from a boxing match at the moment that Dempsey has been knocked through the ropes by Firpo. The subject for this session dreamed about something "dark and unpleasant," and about "Madison Square Garden and a boxing fight. . . ." He continued to identify "a lot of tough punks—people connected with the fight" as well as "boxing posters."

On another night Orozco's painting, *Masks of Death*, was randomly selected. It portrays a scene from a Mexican festival which honors the dead; people are portrayed wearing grotesque masks. Our subject that night was a student research assistant, Richard Davidson. He dreamed about "someone being killed," "a violent scene," and "death." Both of these art prints are simple, dynamic, and very disquieting—the qualities that appear to comprise a conducive target for telepathic dream studies.

In an attempt to put to use what we had learned from Thelma Moss's work, as well as an analysis of our own studies, we arranged to collaborate on a pilot study with Robert Masters and Jean Houston. We saw value in utilizing telepathic target sequences in the sensory bombardment chamber at their Foundation for Mind Research in Manhattan. During each experimental session, the transmitter was taken to the Foundation (fourteen miles distant from the Dream Laboratory in Brooklyn) and placed in the center of the chamber. Several dozen slides, portraying a specific theme, were projected on a curved screen and were accompanied by a coordinated sound sequence, usually of recorded music. The sound tape controlled, at automatically programmed intervals, both the changing of the slides and the duration of the slide dissolves. The subjects, in Brooklyn, attempted to incorporate these images into their dreams.

Richard Davidson, our student research assistant from New York University, served as transmitter one night when we had two subjects—one in each sleep room. Davidson's girl friend, Susan Rubin, dreamed:

> Something about people who didn't believe in God anymore, and the sun came down to earth to find out why. And the sun was very round. It was orange. And Richie came later, dressed in like these robes—white robes with blue stitchings on them. . . . Some sort of religious theme or something like that.

The theme for the targets that night had been "Far Eastern Religions." Davidson had been exposed to dozens of slides portraying Buddha, Shiva, Krishna, Kali, Vishnu, etc., accompanied by the recorded chanting of Zen monks.

Davidson's other subject, located in a different sleep room, was Douglas Johnson, a celebrated English psychic sensitive who had undergone considerable testing with the British Society for Psychical Research. Johnson reported:

> I saw rather a beautiful face. Squarish, with slanty eyes. Eastern, I would think. Clean-shaven. . . . I don't know what nationality, but it was a very beautiful face.

Johnson's former student, Malcolm Bessent, also served as a subject in this study. His transmitter was Brian Washburn, a student research assistant attending the University of New Mexico. Washburn's other subject was his girl friend, Jane Akre, who had a series of unpleasant dreams centered around "a threat" and "something threatening." Actually, Washburn was viewing a slide sequence depicting the birth of a baby, accompanied by recorded infantile screams, squeals, and cries. Bessent dreamed:

> I kept thinking about an old friend of mine that I haven't seen for three years, and I dreamed she was . . . suddenly working here as your assistant . . . . She's probably had children by now. . . . I know she wanted children very much. . . . She's often told me she was really looking forward to being married and having children.

Another of our subjects was Jean Mayo. While the transmitter "sent" her photographs from U.S. outer space explorations, Mayo dreamed about "an endless chase," "getting ready for a long trip," and "traveling to distant points."

Alan Vaughan was also a subject. As the transmitter viewed artistic productions of a schizophrenic patient, Vaughan dreamed of "trying to help a boy with a problem, some sort of personal problem." He also dreamed of a song from the Broadway musical *Hair* which contains the line, "Crazy for the red, white, and blue." At the end of the night, he guessed that the target would be "sort of insane." The outside judges were given lists of the suggested target programs from which the slide-and-sound program had been randomly chosen. In the case of Vaughan, the list read:

1. Farm life.
2. Space exploration.
3. Expo '67—the Montreal World's Fair.
4. Tibetan scenery.
5. Artistic productions of a schizophrenic patient.
6. The birth of Christ.

All three outside judges selected the correct target program as the one utilized when Vaughan was dreaming. Our seven other sessions in this exploratory attempt at long-distance, sensory bombardment telepathy generally attained high evaluation from the judges and the overall results were statistically significant. Fourteen miles had not impeded dream telepathy—but the colorful slides and the emotional themes may have helped to span the distance.

Truckin' with the Grateful Dead

Another opportunity to affect dreams over distance arose through my contact with the Grateful Dead. Jerry Garcia asked me if I thought that the Dead's music would help transmit telepathic messages from a distance. Jean Mayo had the same idea and, in 1970, she and Ronny Mastrion, a young New York filmmaker, ran a pilot session to test out the idea.

The music at the concert was provided by a rock-and-roll group, The Holy Modal Rounders. Mayo gave the audience verbal instructions and initiated the target sequence. She had prepared a light show involving visual sequences of birds, projected from one movie projector and six slide projectors. As the audience watched the images, many of them picturing seagulls, Mayo flashed instructions from a slide projector such as "Think Birds" and "Fly High." The Holy Modal Rounders played the song, "If You Want to Be a Bird"; the final image was the polarized slide of a phoenix which appeared and disappeared in flames as the polarizing lens was moved in front of the projector.

There were five volunteer subjects for this study, all located in a 100-mile radius from the concert in Manhattan. All subjects were told the location of the concert and were directed to record their images at midnight, at which time the target material was revealed.

One subject had the impression of "something mythological, like a griffin or a phoenix or something." A second subject, Michael Bova, a student research assistant at the dream lab, reported the image of "a snake." Our third subject reported "grapes," and I visualized "an embryo in flames, growing into a tree."

Our fifth subject was Richie Havens, a celebrated singer and recording artist. Upon closing his eyes at the appointed time, Havens recorded an image of "a number of seagulls flying over water." Of the five subjects, two demonstrated a direct correspondence, two demonstrated no correspondence, and one a partial correspondence. This encouraged us to proceed with our more extensive pilot study involving the Grateful Dead. It also encouraged Richie Havens to plan a benefit concert for the dream laboratory. But the Maimonides lawyer stopped me at the last minute from signing the contract, fearing that the Medical Center might be held responsible if the concert produced a riot, a fire, or a "bust" for illegal drugs.

In February 1971, the Dead played six concerts at the Capitol Theater in Port Chester, New York, a distance of about forty-five miles from the dream laboratory. Ronald Suarez, a student research assistant from New York University, selected fourteen slides of art prints for use in the study. Each slide was sealed in a separate opaque envelope. Suarez randomly selected two of these envelopes each night and gave them to Ronny Mastrion, who ran the slide projector for us at the Capitol Theater. Mastrion marked one envelope "heads" and the other envelope "tails." At 11:30 P.M. each night, Mastrion tossed a coin to determine which envelope he would open and which slide he would project for the audience to attempt to "send" over to Brooklyn.

Suarez had chosen such art prints as *A Synthetic Emblematic Cross* and *The Seven Spinal Chakras*, both by Scralian, and *The Castle of the Pyrenees* and *Philosophy in the Boudoir*, both by Magritte. Duplicate copies of the slides were put aside for later evaluation by outside judges.

Malcolm Bessent and Felicia Parise, two psychic sensitives who had done well in other experiments, were used in this study. Bessent's dreams were monitored by the polygraph at the dream laboratory. Parise slept at her apartment and was telephoned from time to time during the night and asked for dream recall. Furthermore, the audience at the Capitol Theater was told about Bessent's participation in the experiment, but was not informed as to Parise. The difference in treatment between the two subjects was arranged so as to explore the influence of intent by the transmitters.

We had run a number of pilot sessions in which the subjects did not know that a transmitter was attempting to send them a target picture telepathically. In no instance did we obtain a close correspondence between the dreams and the target picture. We planned to reverse the procedure with Parise; she would know that a picture was being sent, but the transmitters would not be aware of her participation.

Each of the six concerts was attended by about 2,000 persons. By

11:30, Bessent and Parise were asleep and thus in an altered state of consciousness. And by 11:30 P.M., the members of the concert audience were also in various altered states of consciousness induced by marijuana, hashish, LSD, and the music itself. Then Mastrion projected a sequence of six slides upon the theater screen:

1. You are about to participate in an ESP experiment.
2. In a few seconds you will see a picture.
3. Try using your ESP to "send" this picture to Malcolm Bessent.
4. He will try to dream about the picture. Try to "send" it to him.
5. Malcolm Bessent is now at the Maimonides Dream Laboratory in Brooklyn.

At this point, Mastrion flipped the coin, opened an envelope, and projected the slide of an art print on the screen for fifteen minutes.

The Grateful Dead continued to play while the slides were projected. Occasionally, they commented on the experiment and the slides, thus drawing the audience's attention to the material. There was no light show on any of the six nights, so the experimental slides were the only projected visual stimuli during the concerts.

We sent the art prints and the dreams to our outside judges. Bessent's correspondences were statistically significant while Parise's were not. While we discovered that we could transmit material telepathically at a distance of at least forty-five miles, we obtained some evidence that the transmitters must know whom they are trying to reach in order for an experiment of this nature to be successful.

On February 19, 1971, *The Seven Spinal Chakras* was randomly selected as the target picture. The painting shows a man in a lotus position practicing yogic meditation. All seven *chakras*, or energy centers, are vividly illuminated. Bessent dreamed:

> I was very interested in . . . using natural energy. . . . I was talking to this guy who said he's invented a way of using solar energy and he showed me this box . . . to catch the light from the sun which was all we needed to generate and store the energy. . . . I was discussing with this other guy a number of other areas of communication and we were exchanging ideas on the whole thing. . . . He was suspended in mid-air or something. . . . I was thinking about rocket ships . . . , an energy box, and . . . a spinal column.

On several other nights, Bessent's dream reports also demonstrated close correspondences with the target pictures. For example, on February 20, Magritte's surrealistic painting, *Philosophy in the Boudoir,* was randomly selected; it portrays a headless woman in a sheer white gown. Bessent reported dreams about "a little girl's doll" and a "stop watch on a cord around my neck."

Each morning during this study we received telephone calls from people who anxiously asked, "Did the message get through?" In retrospect, the message did appear to get through—better than in our long-distance study involving the University of Wyoming, about as well as our study with Masters and Houston, and not as well as when the transmitter and subject were in the same building. I remembered from my days at Northwestern University that a psychology professor had told J. B. Rhine that he could not accept the evidence for ESP because it seemed to contradict the inverse-square law in physics which states that an action has a lessened effect on an object in proportion to the increase in distance between the action and the object. However, our experiments did indicate a decline in ESP as the distance between transmitter and receiver increased.

Our work, of course, was not conclusive as the studies in question were quite different, one from another, and not set up to investigate the distance question. The only parapsychologist who had attempted experiments along this line was Karlis Osis, research director for the American Society for Psychical Research. By sending a target randomizer around the world who sent target material to subjects in the United States, Osis noted that the ESP scores deteriorated as the distance between randomizer and receivers increased; the statistics indicated that the intensity of the clairvoyant transmission decreased with the square of the distance—as one would expect if the inverse-square law applied to telepathy.

Osis' results were not clear-cut and other investigators did not attempt to replicate them. However, the question of distance effects is an important one for any physicist attempting to mesh parapsychological findings with data from other sciences.

The Sirens' Song

I was thinking about the theoretical issues in psi as well as our struggles to keep the dream lab open one night when I decided to read some Greek mythology for diversion. Turning to Samuel Butler's translation of *The Odyssey,* I read the section in which Ulysses and his sailors have left Circe and are heading out to sea:

> I said to my men, "My friends, it is not right that one or two of us alone should know the prophecies that Circe has made me, I will therefore tell you about them, so that whether we live or die we may do so with our eyes open. . . . She said we were to keep clear of the Sirens, who sit and sing most beautifully in a field of flowers; but she said I might hear them myself

so long as no one else did. Therefore, take me and bind me to the cross-piece halfway up the mast; bind me as I stand upright, with a bond so fast that I cannot possibly break away. . . ."

I had hardly finished telling everything to the men before we reached the island of the two Sirens, for the wind had been very favorable. Then all of a sudden it fell dead calm. . . . So the men furled the sails and stowed them; then taking to their oars they whitened the water with the foam they raised in rowing. Meanwhile I took a large wheel of wax and cut it up small with my sword. Then I kneaded the wax in my strong hands till it became soft. . . . Then I stopped the ears of all my men, and they bound me hands and feet to the mast as I stood upright on the crosspiece; but they went on rowing themselves. When we had got within earshot of the land, and the ship was going at a good rate, the Sirens . . . began with their singing. "Come here," they sang, "renowned Ulysses . . . , and listen to our two voices. No one ever sailed past us without staying to hear the enchanting sweetness of our song—and he who listens will go on his way not only charmed, but wiser, for we . . . can tell you everything that is going to happen over the whole world."

They sang those words most musically, and as I longed to hear them fur-ther, I made signs by frowning to my men that they should set me free; but they quickened their stroke and . . . bound me with still stronger bonds till we had got out of hearing of the Sirens' voices. Then my men took the wax from their ears and unbound me.

The saga of Ulysses reminded me of *The Golden Apple,* the musical based on *The Odyssey* which I had seen a day after my psilocybin session in 1962. I played the record, reminisced a bit about the events of the inter-vening years, then drifted off to sleep.

I dreamed that I was back on the same ocean I had visualized at the end of my psilocybin experience. This time, however, the craft was Alan Watts's boat, the S.S. *Vallejo,* and it held, as well as myself and Watts, Vir-ginia Glenn and the Grateful Dead. Watts was steering the barge and it was approaching a large, dangerous rock. And on that rock were sitting two beautiful sirens with banners draped across their bosoms just as if they were contestants in a bathing beauty contest. They were singing, "We can tell you anything, anything at all. We will give you everything, come on and have a ball!"

The sirens' banners had letters printed on them. Let me see. Could I make the letters out? Oh yes. One read ESP. The other read—was it BK? No, it was PK! I knew that these were the elusive sirens who had lured many psychical researchers to the island from which they sang—only to dash their hopes, destroy their careers, and ruin their lives as their ships crashed against the rocks.

Virginia was too blind to read those letters, the Dead were too stoned, and Watts was too drunk. I told them all what was in store for us if we headed toward the sirens and warned them of the impending tragedy. Nevertheless, Watts kept steering his boat straight toward the rocks. I screamed, "Can't you see what's happening? The barge is heading for disaster! We're done for, doomed, finished!!!"

Watts replied, "But the girls are so lovely and their music is so beautiful." Then, pulling himself together for a moment, Watts mimicked a gruff sea captain, saying, "If we really are going to crash, I will consider it an honor and a duty to go down with my ship!" He laughed loudly, took another belt of booze, and passed out.

But wouldn't you know that the Dead began to sense what was happening. "There's only one thing to do at a time like this," said Garcia, "and that's to get high and play music!" They all took a toke of some super Columbian Red and began to play, softly at first, then louder, and *louder*, and *LOUDER*! There was Mickey Hart banging away at the cymbals, Bill Kreutzman on drums, Pigpen on the harmonica, Tom Constantin on the organ, and Bob Weir, Phil Lesh, and Jerry Garcia playing guitar and humming along as a backup for Virginia Glenn who hobbled to the prow of the boat to take her rightful place as lead vocalist. With the mike in one hand and with her white cane in the other, she belted out:

> Truckin'
> Up to Buffalo,
> Been thinkin'
> You got to mellow slow.
> Takes time.
> You pick a place to go,
> Just keep truckin' on.

Let me tell you, those sirens stopped singing and just stood there with their eyes wide open. Their minds were completely blown because they had never heard such music in all their lives. Virginia kept it up, her green hat flopping wildly in the wind:

> You're sick of hanging' around,
> You'd like to travel,
> Get tired of trellin',
> You want to settle down.
> I guess they can't revoke
> Your soul for tryin',
> Get out of the door,
> Light out and look all around.

The sirens just could not take it any longer. They had to be where the action was! They jumped off their rock—Kerrrrrrplash!!! They swam over to our boat just as fast as their long human arms and little fish tails could carry them.

I steered the barge away from the rocks and back toward shore. Watts revived and quickly took charge of the sirens—Ms. ESP in one arm and Ms. PK in the other. And as we brought our craft into the dock, there was a crowd of scientists truckin' down to meet us, decked out in beads, feathers, plumes, bells, chimes, flowers, robes, prayer cloths, peace symbols, and tie-dyed shirts; carryin' flags, pennants, balloons, bamboo poles, and shaman sticks; smokin' pot, burnin' incense, and cheerin' "Hooooorayyyyy!"

I woke up from the dream, those shouts still ringing in my ears. Maybe ESP and PK could be brought into the mainstream of science after all. And perhaps our work with psychic phenomena and altered states of consciousness had been of some help in that effort.

5

BY THE LIGHT OF THE MOON

The person exists as an "open system," one—which in its mutual
exchange with the environment—does not lose energy and does
not tend to move to an ultimate equilibrium. On the contrary,
it expands and grows.

Charlotte Bühler

Infiltrating the Conventions

Once our experiments at the Maimonides Dream Laboratory began to gain
attention, I found myself in a position to begin the implementation of my
goal—to bring psychical research into the mainstream of science. For many
years it had been apparent to me that it was not enough to design imaginative, rigorous, experimental studies that would permit ESP or PK to emerge
while, at the same time, eliminating any other possible explanation of the
results. Hundreds of major experiments (and thousands of minor experiments) had been executed which demonstrated the existence of psi phenomena. However, almost all of these reports had been published in the
parapsychological journals to be read by an audience consisting almost
entirely of persons sympathetic to psychical research. I attempted, with
some degree of success, to publish papers in nonparapsychological journals
and to present our research results at scientific meetings attended primarily
by people outside the field.

In 1966, I submitted my first paper on parapsychology to the American
Psychological Association for presentation at its annual convention. I had
been on the program at APA previously; however, those presentations had
been in the fields of vocational guidance or learning disabilities. I had now
decided it was time to infiltrate the conventions with parapsychological
research reports. I was pleasantly surprised when my paper was accepted.

Stanley Milgram, a social psychologist from Yale University who notified me of its acceptance, noted that hundreds of papers had been sent in to his division but that he had only selected a few dozen. The paper concerned our telepathic dream experiments with William Erwin, and I read it to an audience which overflowed the lecture hall.

The same convention featured a panel on humanistic psychology. J. B. Rhine was one of the speakers and was later cornered by Allen Ginsberg who regaled him with incredible stories of his ESP experiences in South America, following the ingestion of *yagé*. This brew is made from an exotic vine; an active chemical ingredient of the plant is harmaline, sometimes referred to as "telepathine" because of the tales surrounding its use by Amazonian shamans. In 1960, Ginsberg had written a letter to William Burroughs describing one of his experiences:

> After an hour [I] began seeing or feeling what I thought was the Great Being, or some sense of it, approaching my mind like a big wet vagina. . . . Only image I can come up with is of a big black hole of God . . . and the black hole surrounded by all creation, particularly colored snakes—all real.

Another participant on the humanistic psychology panel was Charlotte Bühler. I had always thought of Bühler as the very first humanistic psychologist. Her work with children convinced her that humor, play, and spontaneity were important factors in personality development. With Abraham Maslow, Sidney Jourard, Rollo May, Carl Rogers, S. I. Hayakawa, and others, she was a founding sponsor of the Association for Humanistic Psychology and one of its first presidents. Her earliest papers (written before I was born) demonstrated the principles which later became associated with humanistic psychology.

These principles included a concern with individual differences, studying the person as a whole, and following his or her case study through an entire life span. They emphasized the creative components of personality rather than the pathological, acknowledging the importance of values and purpose in decision making, and understanding that a person is an "open system" which expands and grows in relation to the environment.

Bühler's contribution to the panel centered around her conviction that one's greatest satisfaction in life is reached by bringing one's potentials to realization. For this to occur, three conditions must be met: the environment must be supportive, the individual must be able to find and set his or her own direction, and the opportunities available at a certain time and place must mesh with the given individual's potentials. Bühler traced these developments throughout the course of human life and into old age stating,

"Ideally, this last phase of life should be one in which *fulfillment* is experienced, but even the approximation of fulfillment in this stage seems to be the rare blessing of only relatively few human beings."

To St. Paul de Vence

At the same time that I was infiltrating "orthodox" scientific conferences and journals with reports on our parapsychological experiments, I was keeping in touch with other psychical researchers. In March 1967, I received an invitation to attend an international conference in St. Paul de Vence, France. Among the other American participants were Bernard Aaronson, Lawrence LeShan, Walter Pahnke, Charles Tart, Montague Ullman, and Alan Vaughan. Non-American participants included Raúl Hernández-Peón, John Beloff, Douglas Johnson, Humphry Osmond, K. Ramakrishna Rao, Emilio Servadio, and Albert Hoffman, the chemist who had originally synthesized LSD. Montague Ullman and I presented papers on our work in altered states of consciousness and ESP at the dream lab.

Aaronson told us about his hypnotically induced alterations in space and time. With hypnosis, he was able to increase or decrease depth perception, increase or decrease the perception of size as well as distance, produce clear or blurred vision, and either remove or expand the notions of past, present, or future. Aaronson predicted that psi phenomena could eventually be produced among subjects when the appropriate ways to manipulate time and space perception were understood.

LeShan questioned the assumption that the ordinary unaltered state of consciousness is the one which gives us the most valid picture of reality. He suggested that "our unaltered state of consciousness is simply a provincial artifact of Western mechanized civilization" and that many valid insights may come in what we consider to be altered, nonordinary states. LeShan ventured that the everyday conscious state of the Hopi Indian was one which we would consider an altered state; for example, the Hopis' sense of time is so unusual that they do not use such concepts as "before," "after," "come," or "go."

Rao spoke on yoga and psi phenomena, noting that the yogi usually does not attempt to develop ESP yet it sometimes occurs as a byproduct. Emilio Servadio recalled that Freud had once suggested that telepathy may be the original archaic method by which individuals communicated. Servadio suggested that people may fall back upon this archaic method of communicating whenever the distance between them is felt to be unbearably frustrating or when there is an urgent need for communication. He concluded, "The condition of sleep and the regressive quality of dreaming make dreams and dreamlike phenomena most suitable for this kind of event."

Raúl Hernández-Peón presented a unitary neurophysiological model of hypnosis, dreams, and ESP. In regard to ESP, Hernández-Peón hypothesized that when the brain is "disinhibited," extrasensory stimuli are capable of activating the organism's memory system which, in turn, could elicit a conscious experience. According to this view, hypnosis and other forms of "relaxed wakefulness" as well as sleep would be more favorable for the operation of psi than any state of alertness or emotional excitement. To test some of his ideas, Hernández-Peón conducted an experiment which involved recording the EEG of a subject and a transmitter. When the transmitter thought of the subject's name, the subject's alpha rhythm stopped. This occurred three times out of three attempts.

Hernández-Peón also postulated an "unknown field of energy" which operates during ESP, stimulating the organism's memory system and its coded information, resulting in conscious experiences marked by such factors as emotion, visual imagery, and auditory imagery. This neurophysiological model was enthusiastically received.

I returned to St. Paul de Vence a year later. After the conference, Walter Pahnke administered LSD to Eileen Garrett and Douglas Johnson. At one point in the session, Pahnke gave them both envelopes containing unexposed film and urged the sensitives to produce psychic photographs. "Hold the film where it will pick up the most energy," urged Pahnke. Garrett held her envelope to her breasts, Johnson clasped his envelope to his crotch, but neither attempts produced pictures on the film.

Garrett had more success with a sealed envelope I had brought with me from New York. I did not know the contents as the target picture in the envelope had been selected by Richard Davidson. Garrett stated that the envelope contained a picture of a man kneeling under an electric light fixture. Actually, the target was a photograph of the interior of a mosque in Washington, D.C.; it depicted a man on his knees in prayer underneath an electric chandelier.

Garrett went on to say, "The picture does not interest me as much as the person who prepared the picture. He is a bright young man who is interested in science; before the end of the month he will be in the newspapers, and before the end of the year there will be an addition to his family." Upon arriving back in New York City, I discovered that the newspapers had reported Davidson's winning of a city-wide button contest for originating the slogan, "Ignore this button." When I mentioned Garrett's other prediction, Davidson told me that his sister and her husband were expecting a baby but not until January. The baby was born, months later, on December 28—just in time to confirm Garrett's other prediction.

Johnson also successfully identified the contents of a sealed envelope. In this instance, the envelope had been prepared by Robert Nelson, an employee of the *New York Times*. Johnson held the envelope for a few seconds, turned to Nelson and said, "This is a photograph of your paternal grandfather. He died of a heart attack." Nelson was amazed. Each of Johnson's statements was correct.

A Teeny Bit of Evidence

In 1969, Ullman and I accepted an invitation from the Menninger Foundation to attend the First Interdisciplinary Conference on the Voluntary Control of Internal States. This was a meeting of scientists from various fields of study which involved the organism's ability to regulate its own brain waves, blood circulation, muscle tension, and other functions which my psychology professors had told me were incapable of being voluntarily controlled. Yogis, who had been accomplishing these tasks for centuries, were dismissed as charlatans until such scientists as Joe Kamiya, Neal Miller, and Barbara Brown demonstrated that human beings as well as various types of rodents could often be trained through biofeedback to manifest this ability.

At the Second Interdisciplinary Conference in 1970 the participants included Abraham Maslow, James Fadiman, Charles Tart, and Andrew Weil. We had the following exchange of views.

MASLOW: One . . . matter concerns a preface to a new edition of a little book that I did some time ago called *Religions, Values, and Peak-Experiences.* . . . In the first edition of the book I had warned about the dangers in overemphasizing the legalistic, organizational, institutional, and traditional aspects of religion. In the preface to the new edition, I speak of the dangers of overemphasizing the mystical aspects of religion; some people run the danger of turning away from the world and from other people to search for anything that will trigger peak experiences. This type of person represents the mystic gone wild.

To this preface, I added a footnote in which I speak about astrology, the *I Ching*, numerology, Tarot cards, and fortune-telling which—so far as I know—have no empirical support at all. In the footnote, I use these approaches to illustrate the point I make that a person with a truly scientific attitude can even be open—although skeptical—regarding them.

However, I began to reconsider this footnote this morning when Stan Krippner mentioned that there were personal experiences involving the *I*

Ching which had not been published. I would hold that some of these experiences, if written down and verified, might be part of the literature of science. You see, my conception of evidence is very inclusive. I write about "degrees of knowledge," and would say that one person whom I trusted, telling me that he has had an unusual private experience, would constitute evidence for me. True, it is a little teeny bit of evidence; even so, it is above zero. . . .

So what I am asking you is whether or not I should include this footnote in my book. Is there any evidence, even in the realm of private experience, to support the claims of astrology and these other approaches? If some evidence does exist, I am not justified in stating that these approaches have no empirical support at all.

JAMES FADIMAN: There was a recent study which eliminated my disbelief in astrology. It was done with Stanford University freshmen, using Strong Vocational Interest Blank data. There were significant correlations among certain astrological signs and certain vocational interest scales. . . .

CHARLES TART: There is another type of evidence that should be mentioned, and that is the laboratory work on . . . ESP. Sometimes people seem to receive information through channels totally unknown to us at the present time. The evidence for ESP is overwhelming.

MASLOW: I agree with you and wasn't even talking about laboratory ESP in my footnote.

FADIMAN: This is an important distinction because there is something unique about astrology . . . that isn't accounted for by the assumptions of ESP phenomena. You could explain the astrology experiment by claiming that ESP influenced the experimenters to select just the right Stanford students so that their vocational interest scores would correlate with the astrological signs. But the data seem to go beyond that possibility.

MASLOW: Stan, are there other examples of this type of research?

KRIPPNER: There is some evidence from a study dealing with several thousand people over two generations. Jonas, a European investigator, found that the ability of a woman to conceive tends to occur under exactly that phase of the moon which prevailed when she was born. Furthermore, the time of a woman's maximum fertility in each lunar month was at the point at which the moon reached exactly the same relationship with the sun, in degrees and minutes, as it had at the time of her own birth. Jonas noted that the two days previous to this point would be the times when sexual intercourse would be most likely to result in conception. He has applied his data to the areas of birth control, selection of the unborn child's sex, and the prevention of birth defects.

TART: There are also the studies people have made of the relationship between months of the year in which people have been born and the eminence they attain. There appear to be certain months of the year that are more closely related to future eminence than others. Presumably this involves being carried in the womb during that time of the year when the mother is most likely to be in good health.

ANDREW WEIL: I think that all of these influences from the environment might tie in with astrology. . . . RCA uses astrology to predict solar flares. It has something to do with the position of the center of gravity of our solar system. For example, when Mercury, being close to the center of gravity, moves toward the sun's surface, there are quite often huge flares. Robert Becker, in the Veterans' Administration Hospital at Syracuse, became interested in this and began to study the relationship between the body's electric potentials and illness. He found that the voltages from head to toe change as a person gets ill. He later discovered that small voltage changes impressed on a person would change that person's mood. This got him to thinking that there might be a relationship between solar flares and the rates of admittance into mental hospitals. He checked this out at several New York hospitals and found a striking association between the two events.

MASLOW: All of these data indicate that man is part of his environment—which I think is more miraculous than the astrological system.

KRIPPNER: This is the point of view taken by Michel Gauquelin in his book *The Cosmic Clocks*, in which he presents evidence that humans are related to what happens in their environment, even to events on the sun, the moon, and the planets.

MASLOW: Could I suggest something? Some of us have learned the hard way that there is no necessary relationship between phenomena and systems which try to explain the phenomena. For example, I have no doubt that ESP exists and I have read about forty-two different attempts to explain it. All forty-two systems look equally good, or equally lousy. As for astrology, it is quite conceivable that these relationships occur because there are more negative ions or sun spots or whatever, when somebody is born in April than when someone else is born in May. In the meantime, the world is being flooded with crap about astrology, Tarot cards, and the rest of this stuff. It's certainly 99 percent crap, if not more. If you are interested in it, then I would like to make a suggestion. Why don't you do some research on it?

WEIL: I think that's a very basic question. I believe in astrology and in Tarot, but have no intention of doing research on them. And I want to tell you why. I think there is a basic difference in outlook as to whether you require proof in advance of believing in something or whether you believe in something because you rely on your own intuition and on personal evidence. . . . The fact that a scientific journal has printed an article about what astrological predictions were confirmed on Stanford students is a low quality of evidence for me. If the predictions were confirmed or were not confirmed, it would not make much difference to me in terms of my own interest in astrology. . . .

I use . . . astrology as a system because it is internally consistent, it's available to anyone, and it includes the infinite. Any system which meets these criteria can be used as a system for organizing most of our perceptions. Tarot is a similar system that is internally consistent, highly ordered, interesting, and beautiful. It explains the meaning of every incident. In other words, it works. These systems work better than any other system that I've seen. So that's my personal testimony.

MASLOW: And you're not interested in research?

WEIL: I'm not interested in research. I don't need to be convinced. I'm aware now that these systems are right, that they work, and that any research I do would confirm them.

MASLOW: You know, if we had a transcript of this conversation, and if I changed the words from "Tarot cards" to "Roman Catholicism," you wouldn't have had to change another word. . . .

WEIL: We should always be on the lookout for better ways of organizing reality.

MASLOW: Yes, that is true. But in the meantime, our discussion demonstrates how the traditional model of science irritates some people. During the last few days, I've heard science being attacked—and that makes me bristle a little bit. . . .

KRIPPNER: How does our discussion affect your footnote for the book?

MASLOW: Well, I am still skeptical about astrology and these other things, but I am neutral, so I won't make any attack on them. I'll probably drop the footnote.

The discussion between Maslow and Weil impressed me. Maslow, as long as I had known him, constantly argued for "research, research, and more research." In several of his books, he attempted to expand the boundaries of science to include both individual persons and total cultures, both small samples of human behavior and consideration of the more elusive human experiences such as values, love, and peak experience. In *The Psychology of Science*, Maslow had written, "Science at its highest level is ultimately the organization of, the systematic pursuit of, and the enjoyment of wonder, awe, and mystery."

Weil, on the other hand, represented the people I frequently encountered who were intensively involved with drawing conclusions on the nature of the universe from their own personal experiences and from what they could learn from examining their own thought processes. For these people, scientific research is of little interest because private experience serves as a much better guide to the validity of their understanding of the world.

From my own point of view, I found both positions worthwhile, but felt that Maslow's concept encompassed that of Weil, and went beyond it. A person's private reports can suggest research strategies from which we can understand how that individual's experience is woven into the grand tapestry of human life processes throughout time and over geographical space. However, science does not move ahead by accumulating thousands of anecdotal reports; the work of J. B. Rhine and Louisa Rhine demonstrates how a collection of spontaneous ESP and PK cases can be analyzed both for information regarding the processing of psi phenomena and for hints as to how experiments might be designed. It was a gambler's personal report on the type of "feeling" he had before winning at dice that led to a series of carefully controlled experiments involving the influence of dice by subjects' psychokinetic efforts.

To Witness the World

Maslow also spoke about his heart attack and how it brought about a confrontation with death. He said:

> Ever since then, I've been living what I've been calling "the post-mortem life." I've already gone through the process of dying, so everything from then on is gravy. If you've gone through this experience, you can be more in the here and now than with all the spiritual exercises that there are. It's just a kind of spontaneous exercise in hanging on to the moment, because the moment is precious. . . . The dominance hierarchy, the competition, the competitiveness and glory, certainly become foolish. . . . I think if it were possible for us to die and be resurrected, it might then be possible for more people to have this post-mortem life.

I told Maslow about the time I was hospitalized and operated on for internal bleeding. I was sure I was going to die. After I survived, I was able to react to the stresses of life with less anxiety simply because I was grateful to be alive. When I faced hostility and criticism, I reminded myself that it was better to be alive and controversial than to be dead and revered.

We continued to speak about death informally that evening and Maslow asked about Virginia Glenn. I reminisced about Virginia's practice of giving Maslow a back rub or a foot massage after he had finished a lecture—sometimes within full view of hundreds of spectators. I also told Maslow that my wife and I, concerned about Virginia's deteriorating health, had asked the *I Ching* for advice shortly before I came to Kansas for the conference. Throwing the coins, we arrived at Kua 51, which read:

> . . . Shock comes—oh, oh!
> Laughing words—ha, ha!

We read on to discover that "the image of shock" should cause the superior person to set one's life "in order." Could the image have referred to insulin shock, the perilous condition which had already endangered Virginia's life several times? In each case, her response had been the "laughing words" of Kua 51. And Virginia's life was always "in order" because she knew only too well that each day could be her last.

Abraham Maslow suffered a fatal heart attack on June 6, 1970. Virginia Glenn and I both mourned Maslow's passing. More than any other person, he had initiated a new approach to psychology and had demonstrated that psychology could, indeed, concern itself with values, human potential, creativity, psychic phenomena—and still remain a science. I told Virginia about Maslow's discovery that, as he grew older, he had "plateau experiences" in which he was able to "witness the world" differently, noticing various levels of reality in much the same way that don Juan described "seeing" to Carlos Castaneda. Maslow had given me an example of what he meant by "witnessing":

> You just see things, but you can see them well. I had a vision once at Brandeis University. It was Commencement. I had ducked Commencement for years, but this one I couldn't duck. I was corralled and I felt there was something sort of stupid about these processions and these idiotic and medieval caps and gowns. . . . Well, this time as the faculty stood waiting for the procession to begin, for some reason, and I don't know why—there was suddenly this vision. It wasn't an hallucination. It was as if I could imagine very, very vividly a long academic procession. It went way the hell into the future, into some kind of a misty, cloudy thing. The procession contained all my colleagues, all the people I like, you know—Erasmus, Socrates, etc. In fact, Socrates was at the head of the procession. Then, behind me the procession extended into a dim cloud in which were all sorts of people, not yet born—and these were also my colleagues. I felt very brotherly towards them, these future ones. Well, you can do that all the time when you attain the plateau experience. It's the transcending of time and space which becomes quite normal, so to speak.

This conversation had great meaning to Virginia because she had been on a personal quest for many years, yet had never had a "mystical experience," had never taken LSD, and had never studied meditation. However, she recalled episodes of "witnessing" events in the way described by Maslow. Like Maslow, Virginia found that "witnessing eternity" was a profound experience because it reminds you of your own mortality.

The Bodhisattva

On July 3, 1970, Virginia, Lelie, and I had dinner in Greenwich Village. Virginia had just returned from Boston where the physicians had examined her thoroughly and, as she put it, had "readjusted my chemicals." She reached into her ever-present bag to pull out a number of articles and announcements she knew would interest me. The next day, Virginia went into a coma, was rushed to a hospital, and died.

Alan Watts was in Europe at the time, but on his return he wrote:

> There is a certain dimension of life which runs from the esoterica of Vajrayana Buddhism, Tantra, and Zen, through a more general mysticism to transpersonal psychology and psychedelic research, and then on to Jungian, humanistic, and Gestalt psychology, sensory awareness training and encounter groups, to psychodrama, Rorschach testing, and psychoanalysis. Somewhere between general mysticism and transpersonal psychology is a branch leading off to parapsychology, psychic research, astrology, spiritual healing, and magic. The only term anyone has been able to invent for this dimension of life is "These Things," as in asking, "Are you interested in these things?"

> Virginia Glenn was very definitely interested in "These Things," and in her relatively short lifetime managed to bring together many of the great workers in these fields who had hitherto only read or heard of each other. . . .

> . . . What always interested me was her discrimination and good taste in a dimension thronged with charlatans. . . . Above all, Virginia's genius was to bring together people who . . . would fertilize each other's insight and imagination. She must have been the catalyst of hundreds of friendships.

> After . . . her death . . . , I made her an ihai or memorial tablet inscribed in Chinese characters with the posthumous name *Raku-ge Bosatsu* . . . happiness and music. *Ge* means flower, gaudy, elegant, and sometimes, lotus. *Bosatsu* is Bodhisattva, a title she surely deserved.

In the Buddhist tradition, a Bodhisattva is a person who has attained Nirvana but who refuses to accept eternal bliss, preferring to return to earth to help other people develop their potentials and attain enlightenment. Virginia undoubtedly deserved this title. She knew how to love unselfishly, requesting absolutely nothing in return from me or from other friends whose lives were transformed by her presence and her efforts.

The Mother Earth

In 1971, I planned the program for the Third Interdisciplinary Conference on the Voluntary Control of Internal States. I had designed a program that would demonstrate the relationship between parapsychology and altered states of consciousness featuring many of my colleagues and friends as guest speakers. For example, Shirley Harrison, the psychic sensitive from Maine, gave the keynote presentation. Among other examples of her own ESP, she told the group of her predictions—when I was hospitalized—of the time I would be operated on, and the progress of my recovery.

Charles Honorton presented a paper on our work at Maimonides, while Gay Luce, a science writer, discussed biological rhythms and their relationship to consciousness. Robert Monroe, a Virginia business executive, described his "out-of-body" experiences to our group in great detail and told of serving as an experimental subject in Charles Tart's laboratory. Monroe's brain waves altered when he felt he was "out" of his body. Stanislav Grof discussed an international yoga conference he attended in India—and how it ended when several of the "gurus" argued about whose system was better; one yogi pulled out a knife, and Krishnamurti arrived to tell the assemblage that they did not really need gurus.

I asked Arthur Hastings to discuss the phenomenon of "state-specific learning" in which information learned in one state of consciousness cannot be recalled when another state of consciousness is entered. Hastings cited many experiments including one in which forty-eight subjects memorized nonsense syllables while they were intoxicated with alcohol. When sober, these subjects had difficulty recalling what they had learned, but they were able to recall the syllables once they were drunk again. In another experiment, subjects learned geometric configurations while under the influence of either an amphetamine or a barbiturate. In both instances, their recall was better when they again took the drug than when they were in an ordinary state of consciousness.

Roland Fischer has cited instances where a single real-life experience may produce the same effect. In LSD "flashbacks," one only has to see a symbol of one's previous LSD "trip" to reexperience part of that "trip." And in the film *City Lights,* Charlie Chaplin saves a drunken millionaire from attempted suicide, and so becomes his good friend. When sober, however, the millionaire does not remember Chaplin. However, when the millionaire is drunk again, he spots Chaplin, treats him as a long-lost friend, and takes him home. In the morning, when he is sober, he does not recognize Charlie Chaplin and has the butler throw him out.

The implications of "state-specific learning" extend to parapsychology.

Many psychic sensitives cannot do well on ESP tests in a laboratory. They are used to manifesting psychic ability in a special state of consciousness they have developed over the years. A laboratory technician might not understand this, and may become irritated when the psychic does not perform well on ESP tests. However, there is no reason why ESP tests could not be constructed that allow psychics to enter the appropriate state of consciousness before an ESP test is administered.

Charles Tart continued to develop this theme in his paper on "state-specific sciences." He suggested training a select group of individuals to enter a common altered conscious state. While in that state, they could investigate areas of specific interest: the physical reactions and internal phenomena of the state, as well as the interaction of that state with external reality. Tart predicted that "state-specific sciences" could be created for self-hypnosis, meditation, biofeedback, reverie, states induced by marijuana and LSD-type drugs, and "lucid dreaming" in which one realizes that one is dreaming while in the middle of the dream.

As I listened to Tart's description of "state-specific sciences," I realized that shamans and mystics would be excellent candidates for his program. I recalled that Mircea Eliade had written about "sacred reality" and "profane reality," the former being the world perceived by the shaman during altered states of consciousness and the latter indicating ordinary reality. To represent the shaman's point of view, I had brought Rolling Thunder, the Shoshone medicine man, to the conference.

Rolling Thunder spent two days quietly evaluating the eighty participants at the meeting. When he was satisfied that they were earnest and sincere in their desire to learn about "the other world," he agreed to lead the group in an American Indian ritual to the sun. For those of us willing to rise early to see the sunrise, Rolling Thunder performed a special ceremony. After lighting a fire, he prayed:

> Great Spirit, creator of all things, I ask that this prayer be heard and carried on the wind. I pray that we can recognize and appreciate those things given by the Great Spirit and placed on the Mother Earth for us. I ask that we give thanks to the Father Son which brings forth life on this land.

He then passed around a peace pipe as we watched the sun break through the horizon to illuminate the flat Kansas plain.

Rolling Thunder had told me that he would discuss his work in healing only if he felt "good feelings" from the assembled scientists. By the third day of the conference, Rolling Thunder had nothing but praise for the people in our group and I arranged a discussion session for him.

According to Rolling Thunder, psychic healing is something with which a person is born. He said, "When a baby is born, Indians have a way of knowing if he is supposed to be a medicine man." As the young Indian brave grows up, seven ceremonies await him as he undergoes his training as a medicine man. He learns that the love of all life is basic to his expertise as a healer, and that he must have a proper attitude to do healing or "doctoring." Rolling Thunder said, "Many times I don't know what medicine I'm going to use until the 'doctoring' starts. I'll automatically select a medicine, and when the 'doctoring' is over, I sometimes can't remember what I've used. That's because it's not me doing the 'doctoring.' It's the Great Spirit working through me."

Rolling Thunder also noted that the patient must have a proper attitude to get the most out of the healing. "The people who are being 'doctored' have to have cleared up their thinking so that they can accept the Great Spirit's work. And after the 'doctoring' is over, we don't take any pay for what we do. But we do feel good when a person gets better and appreciates what has been done."

Rolling Thunder stated that one's health could be maintained by keeping a balance among the "energy centers" of the body as well as keeping the "energy channels" free from clogging. He advised:

> If you can purify your mind, you don't need drugs and you don't need liquor. You can get high any time, just with your good feelings. And if you want to be even higher, you can go out on a hill. Fast and pray until you see a vision; this will tell you your purpose in life.

We asked about acupuncture. Rolling Thunder was of the opinion that it was an excellent form of healing; the acupuncture "meridians" resemble the "energy channels" in some Indian traditions. When we asked about meditation, we were told that medicine men rub a natural substance on their faces and bodies while meditating to protect themselves. Rolling Thunder said, "Meditation is a fine thing, but if it is not done correctly, evil spirits can get into people while they are meditating."

Rolling Thunder had a chance to demonstrate his healing ability when Arthur Becker, a research assistant at the dream lab who was studying at Bennington College, complained of a swollen ankle which had been injured during a game of touch football. Rolling Thunder asked me to find him some raw meat and a pail of water. I asked the kitchen staff for some raw hamburger. They simply could not comprehend what use Rolling Thunder and I would have for uncooked meat and surrendered a piece only with the greatest skepticism.

Before the healing ritual began, Dr. William McGarey, director of a medical clinic in Arizona, measured the swollen ankle and observed the discoloration. Then Rolling Thunder prayed to the four winds, observing that "from the winds we gain our strength as we breathe the air." He lit a fire in the dining hall fireplace and made a sacrifice of the raw hamburger. He then pressed his mouth to Becker's swollen ankle, held it there for a minute, and then spat a bilious fluid into the pail of water. He followed this procedure several times, and fanned the ankle with a bird's wing. He uttered a silent prayer and then asked me to bury the contents of the water pail.

McGarey again inspected Becker's ankle. The swelling had gone down and the discoloration was less noticeable. Becker stated that he had entered a profoundly altered state of consciousness during the ceremony, especially after the fire began to consume the raw meat. Rolling Thunder extolled the role of fire, noting that "it enables us to cook our meals, warm our bodies, and conduct our ceremonies." McGarey noted some resemblance between Rolling Thunder's ritual and those he had read about in descriptions of Tibetan practices. In any event, the swelling in Becker's ankle disappeared during the next few days. Rolling Thunder told us that this had been the first "doctoring" he had done before a large group of professional people.

Rolling Thunder concluded by recalling a recent vision of his—a red horse and a white horse. He felt that this symbolized an end to the struggle for Indian freedom, and a peaceful reconciliation with whites. He said, "We are meant to live in peace and beauty on this land as there is room for everyone. The different races are made like the flowers. Some are red, some are white, some are black, and some are yellow. We are all meant to be here with no one people being better than any other people."

PK and the Knitting Needle

On the following day, Elmer and Alyce Green reported on studies they had done at the Menninger Foundation with Swami Rama, an Indian yogi. The Swami was able to make the temperature of the little finger side of his right palm differ from the temperature of the thumb side by ten degrees Fahrenheit. He did this by controlling the flow of blood in the large radial and ulnar arteries of his wrist. Without moving his arm or using muscle tension, he appeared to "turn on" the blood flow in one artery and "turn off" the flow in the other. He also demonstrated that he could stop his heart from pumping blood, and could produce specific brain waves on demand, including delta waves which usually occur only in nondreaming sleep.

Swami Rama spoke of the ten *prânas*, or energy pathways, inside the body, that he could control. But he also said it was possible to control certain pathways of energy outside of the body. The Greens asked him if he could control an object outside of his body. The swami confidently asserted that he could do so but that he would need nine days of preparation. During this period, he practiced a special type of meditation in which he repeated special mantras (Sanskrit words used in certain meditative disciplines which supposedly activate the *chakras* or bodily energy centers) over 140,000 times.

On the predetermined date, the Greens bored a hole in a fourteen-inch aluminum knitting needle, mounting it horizontally on a vertical shaft. The swami was fitted with a plastic mask that covered his nose and mouth. He breathed through a foam rubber insert which was covered by a plexiglass shield to deflect any air currents down to the sides. His body was covered with a plastic sheet which enveloped everything except his eyes.

Swami Rama sat in a lotus position and stared at the knitting needle, which was five feet from him, while seven staff members of the Menninger Foundation watched. The knitting needle rotated toward him through ten degrees of arc, as measured by a protractor. After the knitting needle returned to its original position, the swami was asked to repeat the demonstration. Again the knitting needle moved ten degrees.

Six of the observers were convinced that the swami had demonstrated psychokinesis. The seventh suggested that Swami Rama had passed gas through his anus, had directed it to his chest, and had bounced the air off his chest, through the opening in the plastic sheet around his eyes, and over to the knitting needle. The swami's comment on this explanation was, "Every man can have his own hypothesis."

Open Systems

My opportunity to bring parapsychology to the attention of participants at an international conference came in 1970 when Charlotte Bühler asked me to be program chairperson for the First International Conference on Humanistic Psychology, in Amsterdam.

I gave the conference's banquet address at an Amsterdam restaurant, describing our work at Maimonides in parapsychology. However, the highlight of our conference was an address by Charlotte Bühler in which she outlined the basic theoretical foundations of humanistic psychology. She spoke of the importance of person-to-person relationships in education and psychotherapy, of following individuals through their life histories as a valid research technique, and of conceiving the person as an "open system" in constant exchange with the environment. She suggested that creativity was a basic human potential, rather than a sublimation of neurotic traits (a position taken by many Freudians) or a failure of an individual to obtain the standard cultural reinforcements (a position taken by many behaviorists). The conference in general and Bühler's address in particular gave humanistic psychology an international perspective with solid theoretical foundations.

The Second International Conference on Humanistic Psychology was held in July 1971, at the University of Würzburg in West Germany. Again I served as program chairperson; Bob accompanied me and three of our dream lab assistants, Donadrian Rice, Stuart Fischer, and Richard Davidson, read papers at the conference. Charlotte Bühler was to have been conference president, but illness prevented her from making the trip. Bühler had asked me to read her presidential address, in which she outlined the contributions which humanistic psychology could make in confronting many of the world's serious social problems. Her words and ideas were well received.

On the last day of the Würzburg conference, Frank Barron, Rollo May, and I initiated a petition on behalf of Timothy Leary. Having escaped from prison by scaling a wall and propelling himself hand over hand across a wire to freedom, Leary had joined the Black Panthers in Algeria. However, he soon parted company with the Black Panthers after Eldridge Cleaver proclaimed that LSD had damaged Leary's mind and that there was "no room in the revolutionary struggle for hippies, Yippies, and trippies." Leary was in Switzerland and the government was deliberating whether or not to grant him asylum. We later discovered that our petition (signed by over 100 participants at the conference) had been pivotal in persuading the Swiss to allow Leary to remain in their country. Unfortunately, Leary did not remain long. He flew to Afghanistan, was arrested, and returned to an American prison.

On the same day, I told the conference participants about Walter Pahnke's death in a drowning accident and requested a silent tribute for him. Pahnke's death left me with a feeling of great loss; he had been a source of friendship, support, and stimulation in my parapsychological odyssey as well as my psychedelic explorations.

The Predictive Power of Astrology

One of the conference participants in Würzburg had been Françoise Gauquelin who spoke on the investigations she and her husband had been making of planetary influences on human behavior. I had met her husband, Michel Gauquelin, at a New York City meeting of the Society for the Investigation of Recurring Events in 1969 and, sometime later, had given him a tour of the dream laboratory. The Gauquelins had found a slight but statistically significant correlation between the positions of the moon and certain planets at an infant's birth and the career later chosen by that person.

The Gauquelins' experiment raised the question as to astrology's validity. After all, this ancient practice can be dated back at least to the time of Hammurabi in Babylonia—nearly 1,800 years before Christ. It was inevitable, therefore, that scientific workers in parapsychology would at some point check out the interface between astrology and psychic phenomena.

In Würzburg, I told Françoise Gauquelin how one of our research assistants, who took great stock in traditional astrology, examined the date of the first dream telepathy sessions of our initial eighty subjects. The dates were divided into the corresponding "signs" of the zodiac and grouped into "air signs" (Gemini, Libra, Aquarius), "water signs" (Scorpio, Cancer, Pisces), "earth signs" (Taurus, Capricorn, Virgo), and "fire signs" (Aries, Leo, Sagittarius). The results were very heartening—for those who believe in the laws of chance but who are skeptical about traditional astrology. Just about equal numbers of ESP "hits" and "misses" adhered to each of the four groups of signs. On the other hand, several sophisticated astrologers told us that this was too simple-minded a way to make our division and that chance results were all that could have been expected.

In 1972, Gardner Murphy was approached by an astrologer who wanted to take part in a scientific evaluation of astrology. I obtained sixteen volunteers who gave me their birth information. The astrologer proceeded to construct horoscopes for each of the subjects.

Murphy and I had decided to enlist the cooperation of two types of subjects. Therefore, half the subjects were almost completely naive as to astrology while the other half read astrology columns in the newspaper and knew their "sun sign," "moon sign," and "rising sign." Many members of this latter group had already had their horoscopes plotted by an astronomer or by an astrological computer service.

We gave the members of the latter group eight personality descriptions based on their horoscopes. Two people were able to identify correctly which description belonged to them—an above-chance proportion, but not one which is statistically significant. When the eight subjects who were naive about astrology examined the personality descriptions, only one was able to make a correct identification. This is exactly what would be expected by chance.

What were Murphy and I to conclude? It appeared that the sophisticated group had slightly better success than the naive group, probably because they knew enough about astrology to identify the terms which matched their horoscope. For example, a person with an Aries "sun sign" is often described as "headstrong" and "determined." These words would be a clue to the Aries individual attempting a correct identification of the personality description.

The possibility also exists that the astrologer we used was not very competent. Therefore, our study did not pretend to present a definitive case against the validity of astrology; however, it did present a useful design which could be replicated by other people interested in studying astrology on a scientific basis.

Many people read their horoscopes and feel that the astrological statements are quite accurate. But does this confirm astrology, or does it indicate that a highly sensitive person can use an astrological chart as a focusing device? The chart may facilitate the astrologer's unconscious observation of subtle clues to combine with ESP to produce a fairly valid statement about the individual in question.

And what part does the horoscope play in one's life pattern? Carroll Righter, a celebrated astrologer, has stated that each human life takes its own course, guided as much by the individual's experience as by the stars under which that person was born. However, I have met astrologers who are much more dogmatic, allowing less leeway for the effect of experience and individual decision making. And I have rarely met an astrologer who is interested in the fact that, due to the gradual shifting of the earth in relation to the stars, the Zodiac constellations no longer govern the periods commonly ascribed to them.

Our dream lab study and an investigation by J. T. Bennett and J. R. Barth centered around "sun signs," based on the constellation which the sun was traversing at one's time of birth. Bennett and Barth concluded that "the empirical evidence offers little support for the predictive power of astrology as the basis for a theory of human behavior." I discovered that Michel Gauquelin had also looked into "sun signs" and had found that they did not correlate significantly with peoples' careers.

Roulette Wheels in the Sky

Gauquelin next investigated the "rising sign," which is the constellation ascending over the eastern horizon at birth. Again there were no significant relations with career choices. Nor did Gauquelin observe any striking results when he investigated the "aspects" or the angles between planets at the time of birth.

Gauquelin even checked into the twelve astrological "houses" through which the constellations and planets "cross." The tenth "house" represents one's career and Gauquelin found it to be without value as a prediction of vocation.

However, his study of "houses" forced him to collect data concerning the time the moon and the planets were seen to "rise" on the eastern horizon, "culminate" at the meridian of the sky, and "set" on the western horizon.

Gauquelin divided the daily motion of the moon and each planet into thirty-six sectors, starting from the heavenly body's point of "rising" and forming a giant roulette wheel. The moon or planet would "rise" at number 1, 2, or 3, have its upper "culmination" between numbers 10 and 12, "set" at 19, 20, or 21, and have its invisible lower "culmination" between 28 and 30. Each number represented two hours of the heavenly body's diurnal motion.

If a roulette wheel is spun 3,600 times, the thirty-six numbers of the wheel will appear about 100 times each. If a planet is investigated in regard to 3,600 births, the thirty-six numbers of the wheel should appear about 100 times each. The Gauquelins chose 3,600 names at random from French birth registers and located the hour of each person's birth. They found that each of the thirty-six numbers of the roulette wheel corresponding to the thirty-six positions of Mars was occupied by about 100 birth hours. In conducting similar experiments with the other planets of the solar system, they obtained the same findings. Each time they matched the birth hours of 3,600 randomly selected persons against the thirty-six possible positions of a planet, about 100 names fell into each slot.

And then the fun began. The Gauquelins examined the planetary positions of 576 members of the French Academy of Medicine. There seemed to be an odd preference of people who were later to become eminent doctors to be born at the moment when Mars had just risen over the horizon or culminated at the meridian—at numbers 1, 2, and 3, or 10, 11, and 12 on the roulette wheel. An identical relationship was observed concerning Saturn. There appeared to be a statistically significant relationship between a birth time occurring when Mars or Saturn was rising or culminating and the likelihood of becoming a prominent physician.

Michel and Françoise Gauquelin then collected over 27,000 birth records from archives in France, Italy, Belgium, the Netherlands, and West Germany. Of these births, about 16,000 represented famous personalities and about 11,000 represented people who worked in the same professions but without obtaining unusual attention or eminence. Statistical analysis demonstrated that the celebrities tended to be born just after the moon, Mars, Jupiter, and Saturn had risen or culminated at midday. There were slots on the roulette wheel which the celebrities tended to avoid when being born; thus, there were "busy hours" and "slack hours" which did not occur in the birth patterns of the less renowned people.

Among the approximately 16,000 celebrities were 3,647 physicians and scientists. One would expect 626 of them to be born after the rise or the culmination of Mars (numbers 1, 2, 3, 10, 11, and 12 on the roulette wheel). Instead, 724 births fell into these slots; the probability of this happening by chance is only one in 500,000. In the same group, 704 physicians and scientists were born after the rise or culmination of Saturn, the probability being one in 300,000. The Gauquelins preformed the same investigations on soldiers, sports champions, actors, industrial leaders, and writers. The results were identical.

The deviations from expectancy did not always occur in excess. They sometimes occurred too seldom for chance. Among 1,473 great painters, Mars and Saturn were rarely observed after their rise or culmination. The same phenomenon was noted with 866 famous musicians in regard to Mars, with both writers and journalists in regard to Saturn, and with physicians and scientists regarding Jupiter. All of these deviations are statistically significant.

When the birth hours of less renowned professional workers were examined, none of the relationships were observed which characterized celebrities. For example, of the 717 athletes in the less celebrated group, 124 were born after Mars had risen or culminated; 122 is the expected number.

The Planetary Temperaments

Obviously, there are many, many exceptions to the Gauquelins' findings. Eminence is dependent upon several other factors than the position of the moon or the planets at the time of one's birth. Social and genetic components of the personality are of critical importance. The Gauquelins have studied some of these components as well.

Michel and Françoise Gauquelin constructed a questionnaire containing 100 traits felt to be related to professional eminence or the lack of it ("enthusiastic," "pompous," "realistic," "sociable," "studious," "theatrical," "timid," "verbose," "witty," etc.). After administering this questionnaire to thousands of professional people, a "psychological portrait" was drawn of each career the Gauquelins had studied.

It was found that physicians presented a psychological portrait which included such traits as "attentive," "realistic," and "unemotional" and which did not include certain other traits such as "capricious," "dreaming," "eccentric," and "impressionable." Painters, on the other hand, tended to have a psychological portrait which did include such descriptive traits as "capricious," "dreaming," "eccentric," and "impressionable." Physicians showed a preference to be born when Mars or Saturn crossed the horizon or the meridian while painters did not. Therefore, the Mars "temperament" and the Saturn "temperament" would be more likely to include a tendency toward attentiveness than toward capriciousness.

Actors, journalists, and politicians of prominence tended to be born when Jupiter was rising or culminating. Success in all three professional groups was related to argumentativeness, brilliance, eloquence, exuberance, lack of modesty, opportunism, pretentiousness, relaxation, self-assurance, self-satisfaction, sociability, talkativeness, the tendency to be pleased with themselves, boastfulness, theatricality, and verbosity. These traits, then, would be included in the Jupiter "temperament."

By studying biographies and autobiographies, the Gauquelins discovered that many "exceptions" to their findings regarding heavenly bodies and careers were not exceptions at all. The Gauquelins observed that although there are no "professional planets" *per se*, people with certain temperaments enter certain professions, thus they decided to concentrate on "temperamental planets."

To investigate the topic of "planetary temperaments," the Gauquelins collected the dates and times of birth for 16,000 famous European men and women. They instigated a series of biographical studies of these people, paying special attention to character evaluations, behavioral descriptions, and anecdotal material. The Gauquelins collected information on approximately 1,000 athletes, actors, and actresses. From this work emerged descriptions of a "Mars temperament," a "Jupiter temperament," a "Saturn temperament," and a "lunar temperament." Apparently, these were the only heavenly bodies by virtue of their size and their distance from earth, to exert enough of an influence on human beings to produce statistically significant data in the Gauquelins' research.

The "Mars temperament" characterized people born when Mars was either rising or at its upper culmination. It was described by the Gauquelins as: active, eager, quarrelsome, reckless, combative, courageous, dynamic, energetic, fiery, untiring, fighting, aggressive, afraid of nothing, straightforward, strong, daring, valiant, full of vitality, lively, and self-willed. In comparing athletes who became prize-winning champions with other athletes, the Gauquelins found that the former were twice as likely as the latter to be born after Mars had crossed the horizon or the meridian. They also concluded that the position of Mars at birth is more likely to relate to the expression of a temperament than to affect one's professional destiny.

The Gauquelins described the "Jupiter temperament" as: at ease, ambitious, opportunistic, authoritarian, talkative, likes to assert himself, sense of the comical, communicative, debonair, spendthrift, gesticulating often, good-humored, independent, happy, worldly, prodigal, bantering, likable, and vain. It was found the actors possessing these characteristics were born more frequently after Jupiter had crossed the horizon or the meridian than other actors. Many politicians and soldiers were also found to be characterized by this temperament. There was some overlapping between the "Mars temperament" and the "Jupiter temperament" just as there were some professions—such as the military—in which eminent people were more likely to be born when Jupiter or Mars rather than Saturn or the moon were crossing the horizon or the meridian.

Physicians and scientists were more likely to characterize the "Saturn temperament" and to be: formal, reserved, conscientious, cold, methodical, meticulous, modest, observant, organized, not talkative, precise, reflective, retiring, reserved, wise, melancholy, timid, industrious, silent, and sad. It was noted that there were also extroverted scientists and physicians, but that they were not born when Saturn was rising or culminating. The Gauquelins added that "intuitive" scientists were not generally born at this time. The "Saturn temperament" most often applied to scientists who "measure, compare, and weigh the pros and cons of their observations." At the same time, a number of actors were born when Saturn was rising or culminating, but they tended to be more modest and less flamboyant than actors with a "Jupiter temperament." Once again, a planet's influence was found to be more closely tied to temperament than to profession.

The "lunar temperament" was found by the Gauquelins to characterize people born when the moon was on the horizon or the meridian. These individuals were: amiable, having many friends, simple, good company, good-hearted, accommodating, disorderly, absent-minded, generous, imaginative, easily influenced, fashionable, worldly, nonchalant, poetic, dreaming, obliging, rather snobbish, superficial, and tolerant. The Gauquelins classified their authors according to their form of literary output, finding that the "lunar temperament" most often applied to novelists and poets. The characterization applied to some essayists, literary critics, historians, and philosophers; many of these individuals, however, were born when Mars or Saturn was on the horizon or the meridian. The characterization applied to a few playwrights, although more of them were born when Jupiter was at its rise or culmination. The "lunar temperament" was rarely found among athletes, soldiers, physicians, or scientists. The "lunar temperament" was found to be the most flexible of the characterological syndromes identified by the Gauquelins; thus, it typified a greater variety of professional workers than did temperaments associated with Mars, Jupiter, or Saturn.

The Magnetic Tails

Is it so surprising that these four heavenly bodies should exert a discernible effect upon human personality? The earth is affected in many ways by the planets and the moon. The relationship between the lunar cycle and tides is one example; another example is the decline of the earth's magnetic field on the days when Mars and Jupiter are opposed in relation to the earth.

In 1955, a radio emission was detected coming from Jupiter. This emission could not be explained in terms of heat from the sun. These waves were traced to the radiation belts surrounding Jupiter. Later, scientists intercepted radio emission coming from each of the planets, from Mercury to Saturn. The radio waves coming from Jupiter were especially interesting because they were found to vary in activity with the sun's eleven-year sunspot cycle. They were also found to be affected by the rotation of Jupiter's satellites, especially Io, the largest satellite.

It has also been observed that the sun can be affected by the planets; the surface area of sunspots fluctuates in relation to planetary tides. And the effect of sunspots on radio broadcasts is modulated by the position of certain planets in regard to the sun.

What is the explanation for these interactions among planets, their satellites, and the sun? Contemporary astronomers and physicists realize that there is no interplanetary "void." This portion of space is filled with fragments of larger bodies, subatomic particles or "plasma," and electromagnetic waves. Some of these emissions come from the galactic spaces, but most emanate from the celestial bodies of the solar system. The sun, for example, regularly emits "solar wind"—a beam of protons and electrons which extends beyond the earth's orbit. Thus, the earth is within the "field" of the sun.

Artificial satellites have produced data indicating that the planets leave trails behind them called "magnetic tails." These "tails" are the result of the meeting of "solar wind" with the planets' electromagnetic fields. The magnetic lines of force are compressed on the side facing the sun, but not on the side away from the sun. Hence, there is a long "magnetic tail" following all the planets on the side opposite the sun.

It has been estimated that the earth's magnetic tail extends at least twenty times the distance between the earth and the moon. The discovery of these "magnetic tails" may provide an explanation for the observation that the earth's magnetism declines during periods of a full moon. Perhaps, at this time, the moon is crossing the earth's "magnetic tail." And, perhaps, these "magnetic tails" are involved in the subtle interactions among Mars, Jupiter, Saturn, the moon, and the earth that account for the "planetary temperaments."

Cosmic Genetics

The relative effects of heredity and environment upon personality traits has been a controversial topic for many years. It might appear that the influence of celestial bodies, as identified by the Gauquelins, can be numbered among the various environmental factors. However, the Gauquelins have produced some surprising data which focus upon hereditary factors and planetary influences.

As was true in the study of "planetary temperaments," the effect seemed related to both the distance of the planet from the earth and to the planet's mass. For example, the moon, Venus, and Mars are closer to the earth than Jupiter or Saturn—and the effect was more pronounced with the first three bodies than for the latter two. Furthermore, no similar tendency was found to exist in the case of Mercury, the smallest planet, or for Uranus, Neptune, or Pluto, the most distant planets from the earth.

The Gauquelins examined over 25,000 dates and times of birth of parents and their children. For every birth, they calculated the position of all the planets, using the thirty-six-slot roulette wheel. For every planet, they compared the area in which the planet was located at the time of birth of both the parents and the child. A total of over 160,000 planetary comparisons were analyzed statistically to investigate parent-child similarities.

What eventually emerged from the data were significant correlations between the cosmic conditions of parental births with those of their children. This effect was noticed with the moon, Mars, Jupiter, Saturn, and Venus. In other words, if parents were born after the rise or culmination of one of these five celestial bodies, their children tended to be born then also. The possibility of this being a coincidence is one in 500,000.

The Gauquelins' further investigations determined planetary similarities at the horizon and meridian during birth to be more frequent between siblings than between unrelated children. All of these data point to hereditary factors as being involved. For example, geneticists have stated that if both parents of a child have the same hereditary factor, the chances of the child's inheriting it will be doubled. The Gauquelins' statistics indicated that if both the mother and father had been born when a certain planet was crossing the horizons or the meridian, the tendency for the child to be born under the same position was twice as great as when only one of the parents was born under this configuration. On the other hand, if neither parent had been born under a certain planet, it was quite unlikely that their child was born under that planet. In the first case, the child would have been twice as likely to inherit the "planetary temperament" of his parents than if only one parent had been born under the planet. In the second case, it would have been very unusual for the child to inherit a "planetary temperament" not indicated by his parents' birth data—unless this temperament could be traced back to a previous generation. The Gauquelins concluded that "planetary temperament is part of the individual's genetic predisposition."

When I heard Françoise Gauquelin present these findings in Würzburg, it occurred to me that the traditional separation of genetic and environmental factors in personality development is overly simplistic. The Gauquelins' data serve as connecting links between heredity and environment. It should be obvious that these two factors simply cannot be separated. Zen masters will often have two students look at a rock garden from different perspectives and count the rocks. Each student comes up with a different answer. Then the Zen master takes them to a hill where they can obtain an aerial view of the garden. This time both students give the identical number—one much larger than those given from a limited perspective. So it is with heredity and environment; one's perspective is the key to the importance attributed to each factor. Yet the biased observer overlooks the fact that both work together so closely they cannot really be studied in isolation.

The Fetus Gives the Signal

Perhaps the most provocative notion put forward by the Gauquelins concerns the timing of a baby's birth. It is known that the fetus's placenta secretes both estrogen and progesterone. The latter diminishes the contractile capacity of the uterus while the former has the opposite effect. Progesterone seems to be a "brake" while estrogen appears to be an "accelerator" in the birth process. The Gauquelins have suggested that the placenta may be sensitive to planetary rhythms and the "magnetic tails" of celestial bodies. If so, the fetus itself may in some way give the signal as to the best time of birth, that time being determined by the inherited "planetary temperament" which matches the time of the rising or culmination of the appropriate heavenly body.

Evidence for this hypothesis comes from data collected on the birth times of babies. The start of labor pains does not occur at even intervals throughout the day. In a study of 500,000 cases reported by researchers in Prague, it was found not only that normal childbirth is more likely to begin at midnight than at midday, but that night deliveries are easier, faster and less painful for the mother.

The Gauquelins investigated cases where labor had been artificially induced as well as instances where the delivery was done by Caesarean section. In these cases, the planetary distribution was roughly what would be predicted by chance; there were no significant planetary groupings because the fetus and the planets had been denied their part in choosing the time of birth. Michel Gauquelin asked:

Are there some subtle directives coming from above whose orders modern medicine, with its drugs, is disturbing like an elephant entering a china shop? Do we have the right to cast aside the role of the cosmos in this way and deprive ourselves of natural data on the temperament of the newborn?

If the baby is born at a time set by the physician, this appointment with specific celestial bodies will not be kept.

The Sun and Planetary Influences

Scientists who have studied the natural rhythms of living organisms have pointed out that creatures have "biological clocks," which regulate their activity in relation to time, and "biological compasses" which help to orient them in space. One important influence on these "biological compasses" is the earth's magnetic field. This field is not constant but fluctuates. Robert Becker has found that admission rates to mental hospitals vary accordingly with changes in the earth's magnetic field.

The Gauquelins were eager to see whether these geomagnetic fluctuations affected the planetary effect through heredity. They divided their cases into two groups, those individuals born on "quiet" days and those born on "disturbed" days. They found that the number of hereditary similarities between children and parents was two and one half times greater if the child was born on a geomagnetically "disturbed" day. This relationship was noted for Mars, Jupiter, Saturn, Venus, and the moon. Therefore, the "planetary temperament" of a child is more readily manifested if the child is born in a disturbed magnetic atmosphere.

It is felt by many investigators that the sun's activity influences the earth's magnetic field. Increases in the intensity of solar flares appear to intensify geomagnetic disturbances in the earth's field. Michel Gauquelin, in his book, *Cosmic Influences on Human Behavior*, describes why the planetary effect increases during solar activity by using the analogy of rocks in a stream. If the stream flows gently, the rocks will have no great influence on the current. But, if after a large storm, the stream swells so that the rate of flow is greatly increased, it will be violently altered by the presence of the rocks in the river bed. Anyone swimming in the river on that day could be carried along by the current. Naturally, if some of the rocks are large, the swimmers will feel the violent effects of the current as they get closer to the rocks.

The cosmos in which we live is comparable to this rocky stream. The stream represents the "solar wind" which blows over us. The rocks are the planets, varying in size and distance from our terrestrial globe. The intensity of the "solar wind" varies in relation to the sun's activity. When this stream of particles and waves suddenly increases, it strikes with greater force against any obstruction, which in this case is the planets. The new currents created by this encounter leave a wake behind them called "magnetic tails." And the greater the impact is, the larger the "tails" become. These impacts cause the earth's magnetic field to be disrupted, and everything living on earth experiences their effects to a greater or lesser degree.

Under these conditions, the planetary sensitivity of a child about to be born is increased. Perhaps the magnetism facilitates a biological alteration. Perhaps the planetary signals to which the fetus reacts arrive more intensly on those days. However, on days when the sun is calm and the "solar wind" is weak, the planetary and magnetic signals are also reduced. On those days, the planetary sensitivity of the child will not be manifested so readily and the hereditary evidence will not be so apparent.

Therefore, without the sun, there would be no planetary effects on human beings. The sun is the "energy power station," the planets are "transformers," and the fetus is the "resonator" on an earth whose magnetic agitation functions as a "facilitator." The fetus must be able to discriminate sensitively from the thousands of influences surrounding it those forces originating from a celestial body and suited to its temperament.

What is the mechanism involved in the fetus' sensitivity? The Gauquelins have suggested that the planets' "magnetic tails" may affect the fetus' brain. For some time, low frequency electromagnetic waves from space have been known to affect the germination of corn, the growth of bacteria, and the hatching of insect eggs. They also affect human beings by slowing the speed of their reflexes. One investigator, J. R. Hamer, noted that the rhythm of the human brain's alpha waves is of the same frequency as these low-frequency waves from space. It could very well be the case that the alpha rhythm of the fetus's brain enters into synchrony with the electromagnetic waves from space. The brain may then facilitate hormonal secretions that cause birth to occur when the appropriate planet is rising or culminating. Of course, the placenta itself may be sensitive to planetary rhythms and "magnetic tails" thus increasing the chance that the time of birth will be appropriate in regard to one's "planetary temperament." In summation, Michel Gauquelin has written:

> Do the planets influence a child at birth by according him a specific character? No. The planetary effect simply triggers the birth for a given time as a result of the genetic sensitivity which the child has inherited from his parents. Do the planets therefore act directly on the child? This appears unlikely. The planets, it seems, act solely as disrupters of the primary action of the sun. The relationship between the planetary effect and variations in terrestrial magnetic activity which results from solar activity seems to be a rather convincing proof of this.

The work of the Gauquelins has produced a new field of science which some people label "astrobiology." In so doing, they have demonstrated in a different way the same phenomenon long noted by parapyschologists: the human being is linked by many threads with the fabric of the universe.

A Replication from Belgium

If planetary influences are as important as the Gauquelins have claimed, could not these findings be easily replicated? Unfortunately, geneticists, astronomers, and social scientists have demonstrated an almost total lack of interest in the Gauquelins' work, despite the important implications the studies have for various areas of science. Those scientists who have heard of the Gauquelins' studies often write them off as "mere astrology," despite the fact that the Gauquelins have also matched the "signs," "aspects," and "houses" of traditional astrology with their large collection of individuals, obtaining no significant results whatsoever.

In 1968, however, a replication of one of the Gauquelins' studies was attempted by the Belgian Committee for the Scientific Study of So-Called Paranormal Phenomena. The committee members gathered birth dates for a group of 535 Belgian and French sport champions, making sure that none of the athletes had been studied by the Gauquelins. The birth data were submitted to a computer which had been programmed with the movements of the planet Mars.

The results of this analysis were almost identical to those obtained earlier by the Gauquelins; significantly more athletes had been born when Mars was rising or culminating than at other times.

The members of the Belgian committee were surprised at their own findings. For four years they studied all possible objections to these findings and organized a number of control experiments. But a cross-examination of the data at the Royal Observatory of Belgium again demonstrated a link between the positions of Mars and the birth of sports champions. Finally, the committee gave its report to Michel Gauquelin and allowed him to publish it in a 1972 issue of the *Journal of Interdisciplinary Cycle Research*.

In his important book, *The Structure of Scientific Revolutions,* T. S. Kuhn pointed out that science is far from open-minded. Instead of accepting factual evidence, and revising its models of the universe to fit this evidence, science typically rejects knowledge that conflicts with its preconceptions. However, younger scientists who are not as committed to the old explanations begin to accept the new evidence and the older, narrow-minded scientists begin to die off. Eventually, new models of the universe are created which can explain the new evidence.

Both "astrobiology" and parapsychology threaten the world-view which sees people as complete within their skins, cut off from any type of direct union with other people or contact with their environment. But the findings of the Gauquelins and of the parapsychologists indicate that the universe is of one piece; a person is connected with distant people and events in many ways. It is impossible to ascertain with definitiveness where one person leaves off and where another person begins.

It would be very helpful to combine "astrobiology" and parapsychology. Is there a "planetary temperament" for psychics? If so, these are the people who should be studied in parapsychological research laboratories. Does a different "planetary temperament" typify PK rather than ESP? These are important questions, and cooperation between parapsychologists and the Gauquelins could help to answer them.

Inextricable Links

The Gauquelins' work was of special interest to me for several reasons. On my parents' farm in Wisconsin, I could see how life was affected by seasonal changes. Later, while I was studying at Northwestern University, I had several provocative discussions with F. A. Brown, Jr., a biologist.

Brown told me how he had kept rats inside a closed room for several months, in laboratory conditions of constant light, temperature, and pressure. Even so, the rats' peaks of activity were related to the position of the moon, being greater during the times when the moon was beneath the horizon and less when it was above. Brown concluded that the person "is unquestionably and inextricably linked . . . with the rest of the universe, not only by way of the physical instruments he had invented and constructed, but also by way of the amazing sensitivities of his own living substance."

Lee Sechrest, one of my psychology professors at Northwestern University, read the studies that had been done on the effect of the physical environment on human behavior. He found considerable evidence that behavioral aberrations were frequently linked with weather, climate, geomagnetic storms, and atmospheric oxygen levels.

Shortly after I moved to New York City, I met Andrija Puharich, a neurologist and inventor who had written a book about parapsychological theory called *Beyond Telepathy*. In it, Puharich mentioned a pilot study he had designed involving ESP cards. The proportion of correct guesses by the subjects appeared to increase during the nights of the full moon and the new moon. Puharich suggested that during the full moon, when the moon's gravitational pull is opposite to that of the sun, the lower gravity condition helps the telepathic receivers, while during the new moon, when the moon acts in concord with the sun's gravitational pull, the telepathic transmitters are assisted. Puharich's notion was supported, to some degree, by records of precognitive dreams kept by Franz Matauschek, whom I had met in Vienna. He would attempt to dream about the numbers to be drawn in the Austrian lottery; reportedly, more of his "hits" occurred during nights of the full moon than on other nights in the lunar cycle.

In an experiment executed by J. S. Setzer, a New York educator and theologian, several quarts of water were placed inside three different churches during services. Other quarts of water from the same tap were put aside as "controls." Ten radish seeds were placed in each of several clay pots, and the pots were watered with either the "church" water or "control" water. The person doing the watering was "blind" as to which water had been in the church and which served as the "control."

Significant results were obtained from the study. The plants nurtured with "church" water outgrew plants receiving the "control" water during the second and fourth lunar quarters. A weaker but still significant effect was observed during the first and third lunar quarters; at these times, the "control" water caused plants to outgrow those given the "church" water. Setzer suggested that, as the gravitational pull of the moon is weak but increasing during the second and fourth quarters, this was the optimum time for the "church" water to exert its effect.

The Lunar Cycle

The cumulative effects of these experiences made me eager to find out if the lunar cycle could have had any influence on our experiments in dream telepathy. Not knowing which item to use, we prepared four envelopes. One contained a card on which had been written, "traditional astrology." The other cards read "geomagnetic fluctuations," "sunspots," and "lunar cycle."

We gave each envelope to Malcolm Bessent, asking him to relate the information in each envelope to new approaches in psychical research. When holding the envelope containing the words "traditional astrology," Bessent remarked, "This is wrong. It is incomplete." When holding the "geomagnetic fluctuations" envelope, he remarked, "This is almost there, but not quite. . . . This is but a part of a whole." For the "sunspots" envelope, Bessent said, "This is the second most important. There seems to be a misunderstanding or misinterpretation, but in the main, it is very accurate. . . ." Discussing the "lunar cycle" envelope, he reported, "Very complex. . . . The contents are accurate. . . . This is the most important. The best." And so we decided to explore the relationship between dream telepathy and the lunar cycle.

Three of our student research assistants—Arthur Becker, Michael Cavallo, and Brian Washburn—took the files of the first eighty subjects who had visited our laboratory and noted in which phase of the moon they were tested. They used the *Ephemiris and Nautical Almanac*, published by the U.S. Nautical Almanac Office, to insure accuracy.

For the eighty sessions, there were fifty-nine telepathic "hits" and twenty-one "misses." On nights when the moon was in its second phase or full quarter, twenty-three sessions were run, twenty-one of which were "hits." Of the sessions run on nights during other phases of the lunar cycle, thirty-eight were "hits" and nineteen were "misses." The difference was statistically significant, suggesting a positive association between ESP success and nights of the full moon.

Cosmic Cycles

Why would this be so? I recalled Charles Darwin once suggested humans, being related to fish, demonstrate a special sensitivity to lunar influence. And Rolling Thunder once told me, "The moon controls the waters and, as our bodies are mostly water, the moon influences our thinking." Investigators of "living clocks" have found that some biological cycles are inherited and impervious to cosmic influences, while others are meshed with environmental influences such as the lunar cycle.

Life on earth appears to be influenced by the astrophysical environment and by cosmic cycles in several different ways. Fiddler crabs, for example, show a rhythm of color change each day in an exact twenty-four hour rhythm, even in isolation. Also, there is an association between cosmic ray changes and the oxygen consumption cycles of potatoes, carrots, shellfish, and rats.

Not only does the moon have a strong effect upon the sea, as is demonstrated by tidal patterns, but upon sea life as well. The California cuttlefish always spawns at the mouths of rivers three days after the full moon. The kammuschel, a shell fish, produces eggs from January to July once a month, always when the moon is full. The *Convoluta paradox,* a mollusk, keeps in rhythm even when removed to a laboratory and kept in tideless waters.

Even under laboratory conditions, many forms of life demonstrate sensitivity to lunar influence. For example, there is a relationship between the moon's cycle and the birth cycle of *Clunio marinus,* an insect which spends its larval stage in seaweed accumulations. After the full moon and after the new moon, when the tide is low, it turns into a mosquito. Researchers have taken seaweed containing the larva into a laboratory and have placed it in an aquarium. They have tried to modify the time of the transformation by inducing artificial tides and by lighting the aquarium on days other than those of the full moon. However, the transformation always takes place according to the moon's phases, unconnected with secondary causes like height of tides or moonlight.

In 1971, I was invited to speak on our work at the dream laboratory before R. Buckminster Fuller's staff in Carbondale, Illinois. Some of the staff members arranged for me to see Fuller privately after my lecture. I was pleasantly surprised to hear Fuller express an interest in parapsychology and to hypothesize that it would be more fully understood when a "tetrahedron" model of the universe was accepted by scientific theorists.

Fuller also speculated that the eyes, being the only extension of the brain that faces the external world, are the most important organs of the body insofar as psychic phenomena are concerned. He further stated that, at an early age, he had made up his mind "to understand how the universe works." Parapsychological findings, he said, had to be taken into account for a complete understanding of the cosmic workings.

I told Fuller about our data regarding ESP and the lunar cycle. Fuller produced three-dimensional models of the earth and moon, patiently explaining to me what happens during the lunar cycle.

As the moon orbits around the earth, it enters into its first quarter, a time when the line between the earth and the moon is perpendicular to a line drawn between the earth and the sun. This is the time of least tidal influence, although not the least gravitational pull. This is also the time of the "neap tide," when there are lower high tides and higher low tides.

As the moon enters its second quarter, its gravitational pull is counteracting that of the sun. The pull between moon and earth is constant, but because of the changing position of the three bodies, the net forces change. This is again the time of the "spring tide" when the tide levels increase.

The third quarter of the lunar cycle is a time when the moon is once more perpendicular to a line drawn between the earth and sun. This is again a time for "neap tide" and the time of least tidal influence.

During the new moon, or fourth quarter, the moon is between the earth and the sun. The moon's gravitational pull is thus adding to that of the sun and causes again a "spring tide." This is the time of both the highest and lowest tides. Fuller concluded our discussion by remarking, "I am firmly convinced that only the impossible happens."

After hearing Fuller's description, I conjectured that ESP may ebb and flow in a way analogous to the tides. As tide levels increase during nights of the second quarter—when the earth experiences a time of least gravitational interaction with the moon—so may ESP change significantly. As tide levels also increase during the fourth quarter, this phase of the lunar cycle should also be investigated by parapsychologists. I assumed the change would involve an enhancement of ESP, but Fuller cautioned that it could just as easily bring about decreased ESP scores. In either case, the interaction might involve the moon's effects on bodily fluids, hence on such subtle abilities as ESP.

Lunacy

Shortly after my conversation with Fuller, I read a research report from Miami. Approximately 1,900 Miami-area murders that occurred between 1956 and 1970 were correlated with the lunar cycle. It was found that the area's murder rate began to rise about twenty-four hours before the full moon, reached a peak at the full moon, then dropped back before climbing again to a secondary peak at the new moon.

William Wolf, my endocrinologist friend in New York City, had told me that hemorrhages in throat operations were 82 percent higher in the second quarter of the moon than at other times. In an address to the New York Academy of Sciences, Wolf discussed drug effects at different points in a biological cycle:

> We know that periodic variations may go so far that the same agent may have a favorable effect when given at one phase of a periodic cycle and may kill when given in another phase. We shall thus find that much of the current and past literature may well acquire entirely new meanings or even become meaningless when pursued in the light of biological rhythms.

Wolf predicted that various inexplicable variations in drug reactions such as LSD, would be more easily understood once they were seen in the context of rhythms. Even the time of day the drug was administered might make a major difference in the person's reaction to it.

I came across another example of lunar influence at the 1972 meeting of the American Society of Clinical Hypnosis. Leonard Ravitz, a scientist working in the area of hypnosis, was at the meeting. I asked him to tell us precisely what his experiments involved. He did so, detailing his work in electric potential differences, in a very lucid way. He later sent me many of his reprints which were extremely impressive and convinced me of the importance of his line of investigation.

In one of the articles, Ravitz described his findings that differences in electric potential between the head and chest of mental patients varied in accordance with seasonal and lunar changes. He found that the effects of the moon were more pronounced on mental patients than on nonpatients, noting one schizophrenic whose symptoms grew worse at the full moon and the new moon—just when the differences in electrical potential between his head and chest were greatest. (It will be recalled that the word "lunatic" originated among people who believed that the mentally ill grew worse during nights of the full moon when lunar influence on the psyche was believed to be at its peak.)

In our analysis of ESP and the lunar cycle, we found it of interest that more of the eighty dream telepathy experiments had been run during the moon's second quarter than during any of the other three quarters. Also, the success of the experiments run during this phase tended to be statistically significant. Was this coincidence? Or had we unconsciously known of the ESP-full moon link and scheduled our subjects accordingly?

One of Felicia Parise's first sessions with us was scheduled in June 1969, on a night of the full moon. The target picture being "sent" to her by the transmitter was *Departure of a Friend,* by de Chirico. The painting portrays two individuals shaking hands in front of a large gray building with a train in the background. It is sundown and the setting sun is casting shadows of the men near the building. Parise's dream reports read, in part:

> I was looking for a garage for Michael, my boy friend. . . . I was looking in the neighborhood for a garage for his motorcycle. . . . It was sundown. . . . I saw an enormous orange sun setting. . . . I remember the bank. . . . It's a pretty tall building. It's gray.

Parise had given us a report which corresponded closely to the target picture.

Later, we also investigated the other three variables for which we had solicited reactions from Bessent. We obtained purely chance results when we correlated the telepathic transmitter's "sun sign" with ESP "hits" and "misses." For both geomagnetic fluctuations and sunspots, however, we found a marked, but not significant, association with telepathic success. This was especially noticeable in the latter case; an above average number of sunspots tended to be associated with ESP "hits." Clearly this was an area worthy of further investigation.

About this time, I received a provocative letter from Ilmar Soomere, a Soviet psychiatrist. He wrote me that he had tabulated lunar-cycle data on ninety-six spontaneous cases of telepathy which he had collected. Of these ninety-six cases, twenty-seven occurred in the first lunar quarter, seventeen in the second quarter, twenty-three during the third quarter, and twenty-nine during the fourth quarter. The seventeen cases occurring in the second quarter, around the time of the full moon, were significantly *fewer* than one would expect by chance, while the twenty-nine cases during the fourth quarter were somewhat *more* than one would expect by chance. Both quarters represent times when the tide levels change, thus strengthening the possibility that ESP is associated with the lunar cycle, although the full moon may sometimes decrease rather than increase the possibility.

Soomere also observed that in three out of four cases, the lunar quarter in which the telepathic experience took place was the same quarter as that of the birthdate of the individual having the experience. Furthermore, the telepathic message came in the form of a dream (rather than during wakefulness) in forty-six out of the ninety-six instances. Of these cases, eighteen occurred during the fourth quarter—significantly *more* than would be expected by chance. Only six took place during the second quarter—significantly *fewer* than would be anticipated. Soomere concluded that "the full moon is the time when psi abilities are diminished. These abilities are increased in the new moon."

Clairvoyance at the Country Place

An opportunity arose to make a formal investigation of psychic phenomena and the lunar cycle when Renée Nell, director of the Country Place, told me that her patients were eager to participate in an ESP experiment. The Country Place, located in Litchfield, Connecticut, has gained renown for its innovative work with young adults with severe emotional problems. The patients' difficulties usually center around addiction to drugs, alcohol, or food. These patients live at the Country Place and are assisted through a combination of Jungian psychotherapy, dream analysis, occupational therapy, and nutritional alteration which usually involves a restriction on sugar and other carbohydrates as well as the intake of massive amounts of vitamins.

The subjects for this study were four female and five male patients; I trained a number of staff members to serve as the experimenters.

We used 144 postcard-size art prints for the target materials. These were divided into pairs by a staff member at the Maimonides Dream Laboratory. Pairing was done in a way that emphasized differences between the two prints, thus assisting the evaluation process.

There were two copies available of each art print. One copy of each pair was shielded on both sides with cardboard and placed in a small envelope marked "pool." The other copy also was shielded on both sides with cardboard and placed individually into a small envelope marked "heads," or "tails." These three small envelopes (marked "heads," "tails," or "pool") were placed inside a large envelope. Thus, there were seventy-two target envelopes available for the experiment; each large envelope contained three smaller envelopes—"heads," "tails," and "pool."

We designed the experiment to last for sixty days. Each day one of the experimenters consulted a random number table and, with eyes closed, pointed to a four-digit number. The digits in this number were added, producing either one-digit or two-digit numerals. The experimenter counted down the pile of seventy-two large envelopes, until the envelope matching the randomly selected number was reached. Then the experimenter tossed a coin to determine whether the envelope marked "heads" or the one marked "tails" would be the target for that session. The large envelope was opened and the small envelope marked "heads" or "tails" was taken out and used for the clairvoyance experiment.

The nine subjects were tested individually every evening by a second experimenter. The subjects recorded their guesses concerning the target on a sheet of paper; all subjects attempted to identify the same target. After each subject had recorded his or her impressions, the second experimenter administered an evaluation form which stated, "Once you have seen the two possible targets, write down the identity which you think is in the envelope." The "pool" envelope was then opened and the subjects made their selections as to which of the two targets actually had been used.

After all nine subjects had completed their evaluation forms, the target envelope was opened and the subjects saw what the target had been. We felt that this type of feedback would maintain the motivation of the subjects during the two months of the study. Also, we made a rule that a subject had to complete the evaluation form before participating in the next ESP session.

A third experimenter marked "hit" or "miss" on each subject's evaluation form. In addition, the third experimenter entered the following information on the sheet: the time of day, temperature, humidity, barometric pressure, and quarter of the moon as determined by the *Ephemeris and Nautical Almanac*. The three experimenters at the Country Place did not know that the purpose of the experiment centered around ESP and the lunar cycle. It was necessary to introduce several other variables for measurement in order to keep the experimenters from consciously or unconsciously influencing the results of the experiment through their own preconceived ideas.

Following the determination of the correct target picture for a session, the third experimenter placed all three envelopes, as well as the subjects' responses and evaluation sheets, into the larger envelopes. The stack of unopened envelopes was shuffled so that the first experimenter could repeat the process on the following day.

There was a total of 456 guesses during the sixty nights of the study. The nine subjects participated in an average of 51 guesses during the study.

Of these guesses, exactly 100 occurred when the moon was in its second quarter. Of these 100 guesses, 35 were hits and 65 were misses, although chance would dictate 50 hits and 50 misses. Guesses for the other quarters totaled 186 hits and 170 misses. The difference was statistically significant; clairvoyance at the Country Place was less successful at the time of the full moon.

Hits and misses were tabulated by Paul Ritvo, a laboratory assistant who was a student at the University of Michigan. He did not know the purpose of the study so was unlikely to bias the results unconsciously through incorrect tabulation procedures. He also analyzed the other variables (such as temperature and humidity), none of which produced significant results.

This was a carefully controlled study which attempted to investigate lunar influence on ESP experimentally. The findings resembled those of Ilmar Soomere, rather than the results of our earlier analysis at the dream lab. However, in all three cases, significant results were obtained. Certainly these findings are provocative enough to encourage other parapsychologists to repeat the experiments—or at least to keep a record of the lunar quarter in which their other ESP sessions are done.

6

MISSION TO MOSCOW

Some Soviet researchers have . . . theorized . . . that all living things have not only a physical body, but also an "energy body" consisting of "bioplasma". . . . which consists of ionized electrons, photons, and possibly other particles which react to the environment in which we live. . . . Such exotic environmental influences as solar flares and cosmic rays can cause changes in the bioplasmic body.

Thelma Moss

As Maine Goes . . .

In July 1970, Shirley Harrison organized a parapsychology symposium at the University of Maine's Gorham campus. Harrison had become well known in Maine for her psychic abilities and the meetings drew a large crowd. Zelda Suplee, Thelma Moss, Richard Davidson, Geraldine Lenz, and I made the trip, arriving in time to hear Gardner Murphy's eloquent keynote address. In it, he paid special attention to our work at Maimonides and to Thelma Moss's experiments at UCLA. He noted that Moss had used colorful slide programs and audiovisual effects while our group at Maimonides had utilized postcard-size reproductions of art prints. Nevertheless, the telepathic effects were similar and resembled phenomena characterizing ordinary perception.

After describing our two experimental series with William Erwin, both of which demonstrated ESP at statistically significant levels, Murphy stated the need in parapsychology for "people who understand the concept of replication of experimental findings." He concluded, "We need people to develop repeatable experiments, the corners of solid fact that allow the filling out of a new kind of science, one that deals with parameters of personality of which we are almost totally ignorant."

Moss and I presented papers at the Maine symposium and recalled her first visit to the Maimonides Dream Laboratory some years earlier. We had discussed psychedelic experience and I gave her a copy of a reading list I had prepared. One of the books on the list was *My Self and I* by Constance Newland; it portrayed the story of a young widow who entered LSD psychotherapy, giving a fascinating portrayal of each session. I praised the book very highly, whereupon Moss casually said, "Well, I happen to be Constance Newland."

What the book did not mention was that Moss's experiences with LSD stimulated an interest in the workings of the human mind. Before her husband's death, Moss had been involved in the entertainment world. Following LSD psychotherapy, she returned to college and, in 1966, received her doctorate in psychology from UCLA. She was immediately hired by the University as a medical psychologist in its Neuropsychiatric Institute. All her parapsychological work was done on a spare time basis, funded by her own money—not an unusual situation for parapsychologists. In addition, she had initiated several conferences as well as a course on psychical research at UCLA.

Montague Ullman was also present at the Maine symposium; at lunch, he and Moss discussed their forthcoming trips to the Soviet Union. A few months later, I had individual talks with each of them about their experiences. They had both been told about the electrophotography process developed by Semyon and Valentina Kirlian, both had met with Soviet scientists doing work in parapsychology, and both had seen Nina Kulagina, the Leningrad housewife whose reputed psychokinetic abilities had attracted attention from parapsychologists throughout the world.

Moss chatted with Kulagina but did not see her demonstrate psychokinesis. In Ullman's case, Kulagina came to his Leningrad hotel room; sitting down at a small table, she spent a few hours in a pleasant interview with him. Then, as she quietly began making passes over a matchbox, Ullman and his wife saw the matchbox move. In an interview in *Psychic* magazine, Ullman described what happened next:

> For about an hour she went through a routine of moving small objects— pen tops, clips, wooden matches—by simply making passes with her hands and even moving the upper part of her body over the objects. And they moved.
>
> The pen tops were particularly striking, because they were moving across a rough tablecloth. They remained upright and moved in intervals of about an inch at a time toward her. One pen top was plastic and the other was metal. They also moved independently; she brought one close to the other then moved them both. Then she moved some wooden matches. . . . This brief demonstration . . . in broad daylight in my hotel room was quite

impressive, even though—and I want to stress this—I wasn't there as an investigator setting conditions, but as a guest simply registering interest in what she was doing.

Ullman concluded, in surveying the Soviet psychic scene, "The possibility does exist that at this moment in history the Soviets may have assumed some measure of leadership in the daring and imagination they display. . . . American parapsychology today is associated in the main with proof via the application of refined statistical methods rather than with the demonstration of empirical, concrete, palpable phenomena observed under carefully controlled conditions that was so characteristic of early workers in the field."

Moss went to Alma-Ata as well as Moscow and Leningrad. There, she was met by V. M. Inyushin of Kazakh State University, who showed her the Kirlian photographs he had taken of Alexei Krivorotov, a psychic healer. Before healing, there appeared to be streams of light emanating from Krivorotov's fingertips. During healing, the flares appear consolidated, becoming shorter but denser; in addition, a reddish-orange blotch appeared which was previously absent in the blue and white corona.

Inyushin discussed his concept of "biological plasma" or "bioplasma" with Moss. Physicists customarily speak of four states of matter: solids, liquids, gas, and plasma—the latter found in outer space or in physics laboratories where it can be artificially created. Inyushin's "fifth state of matter" is found only in and around living organisms. It consists of ionized particles mixed with free-floating electrons. It forms a system of its own that can be called the "bioplasmic body." Because the bioplasmic particles are charged, they can affect the electrical fields photographed by the Kirlian apparatus. Inyushin told Moss that the "bioplasmic body" surrounds and interpenetrates the organism's physical body. Therefore, it may be the key to our understanding of psi phenomena and how they operate. Indeed, Ullman was told that a "bioplasma detector" had already been developed by Soviet parapsychologists to detect and to measure the "fifth state of matter."

Ullman's and Moss's interest in Soviet parapsychology had been stimulated by a journalistic account, *Psychic Discoveries Behind the Iron Curtain*, and by the earlier reports which had been brought back from the USSR by J. G. Pratt. In 1962, Pratt made his first of six visits to the USSR. In a visit with Professor L. L. Vasiliev at the University of Leningrad, he was told of the professor's successful attempts to hypnotize subjects at a great distance. Pratt again met with Vasiliev and his colleagues in 1963. Vasiliev discussed Soviet experiments with fish and magnetic fields which indicated that the magnetic field could directly affect the fish's brain. Vasiliev conjectured that a telepathic "field" might work in the same way, bypassing the body's sense organs.

On Pratt's second visit, he met Edward Naumov for the first time. When he returned in 1968, Vasiliev was dead and Naumov was using stationery marked "Institute of Technical Parapsychology." Pratt attended a parapsychology conference organized by Naumov which attracted about thirty scientists from ten countries. On the morning of the conference, an article appeared in *Pravda* attacking Nina Kulagina, with whom Vasiliev had begun to work before he died.

During 1970, Pratt visited Kulagina as well as G. A. Sergeyev, a physiologist who had taken over the experimental program with her after Vasiliev's death. Pratt observed Kulagina perform several dramatic feats of psychokinesis and was allowed to take films of the process.

Pratt's final visit to the USSR took place in 1972. Showing up without warning at Kulagina's home, Pratt and Jürgen Keil, an Australian psychologist, were warmly received. They placed on a table some objects, including a block, that they had brought along. Pratt has written about the subsequent events:

> The block slid about one-half inch forward toward Kulagina but angled toward her left, then it moved again in the same way about five seconds later.

> Both Keil and I saw both motions of the block. We had been seated all the while across the table from Kulagina. She was not expecting the objects to be placed before her, so she could not have made preparations in advance. We saw nothing in the least suspicious in her actions before the block moved.

In retrospect, Pratt has written that Kulagina "has made a real contribution to the problem of psychokinesis acting on static objects. . . . Kulagina's gift, if it is genuine, cannot be unique, and the next scientific step is to apply what she may have taught us in working with others."

An Invitation from the Academy

In discussing their visits with me, both Moss and Ullman had mentioned the interest several Soviet scientists had expressed in some of my research papers. I sent copies of the papers to them and wrote of my desire to visit the USSR someday. Later in 1970, we received word that an inexpensive charter flight was being organized for the first European meeting of the Association for the Psychophysiological Study of Sleep. Richard Davidson and I speculated how simple it would be to go from Belgium, site of the sleep conference, to Moscow, where we could get firsthand information on Soviet parapsychology.

The money for our trip was granted by the Erickson Educational Foundation about the same time as we received a formal invitation from Moscow. The invitation came from the "Institute for Technical Parapsychology" and was signed by its director, Edward Naumov. We were expected in Moscow on June 23, 1971, a Tuesday, and would leave for Leningrad—the home of Nina Kulagina—on the following Monday.

Less than an hour after Davidson and I checked in at Moscow's Intourist Hotel, the telephone rang. It was Larisa Vilenskaya, a Soviet engineer and parapsychologist, welcoming us and saying, "We have arranged for Dr. Krippner to give an address at the Academy of Pedagogical Sciences on Monday. This will be the first lecture on parapsychology ever delivered at the Academy. We have invited over 200 psychologists, psychiatrists, physicists, engineers, space scientists, and cosmonauts-in-training." I explained to Vilenskaya that our flight to Leningrad was scheduled to leave early Monday morning. However, I emphasized how flattered I was by the invitation and that I would change our flight immediately.

Wednesday, June 24

In the morning, we were at Red Square making our first contact with Edward Naumov and Larisa Vilenskaya. We discovered that Vilenskaya had learned to speak English by working with Russian-English dictionaries. Naumov, who had brought along an interpreter, told us, "It is time to integrate parapsychology with the rest of psychology. Your approach at Maimonides has been so rigidly scientific over the years that we feel your talk will be of great assistance." I acknowledged my pleasure at being in the USSR and mentioned that I had long been interested in Soviet parapsychology.

Naumov, a thin, balding man with a genial manner, described for us the terminology he had proposed to make psi phenomena more palatable. Instead of using the terms "extrasensory perception," or "ESP," he suggested "biological information" or "bioinformation."

Naumov's notion of bioinformation took many forms. If a person were to gain information from a telepathic transmitter, this would be an example of "biological communication." If a person were to gain information clairvoyantly (without a transmitter), the term "biological location" (or "biolocation") would be used. One special form of biolocation was "introscopy" in which experimental subjects attempt to identify the contents of sealed containers or envelopes.

Other types of biolocation studied in the USSR, according to Naumov, included dowsing (locating underground oil, metal, or water through presumptively paranormal means, often called the "biophysical effect") and dermaloptical sensitivity or "skin vision." In the latter case, blindfolded psychic sensitives are asked to determine the color of a card either by touching it with their fingers or by touching an envelope in which it is enclosed.

Recalling the trickery I had personally observed in this area over the years, I mentioned the difficulties in pursuing research in skin vision. The blindfold device must come down to the waist to avoid peeking. Further, direct contact with a fixed card could yield correct information through thermal clues; a black card, for example, absorbs more heat than a white card. Naumov told me that Soviet investigators discovered the necessary precautions after one of their most outstanding subjects was caught cheating.

Vilenskaya told us that she had become involved with experimentation in skin vision, even though she doubted that psi is involved in most of its applications. She improved her own ability to identify colors and demonstrated her skills for Thelma Moss in 1970, reportedly holding her fingers half an inch above the colors and letters she identified. Vilenskaya told us that she was currently training a small group of people to heighten their dermaloptical sensitivities. Her goal was to bring them to the point where they could identify the colors and letters even when they were underneath a plastic sheet or in separate envelopes. Only by taking these precautions, she said, could one be sure that psi was involved in the phenomenon.

Another example of bioinformation given us by Naumov was "proscopy," the perception of future events. Nikolai Kozyrev, an astronomer at the Pulkovo Observatory, was mentioned as one scientist who was deeply concerned with the basis of proscopic mechanisms. Kozyrev had worked for many years with gyroscopes and pendulums. It is known that if a weight or a balance beam is suspended elastically and if the base of the balance is vibrated, the weight can be observed to get heavier in proportion to its mass. Kozyrev found that the weight measures the horizontal component of time flow forces caused by the earth's rotation, while the balance measures its vertical component. These experiments produced results that suggested that time not only appears to flow, but that it also has density. Furthermore, it appeared that time density is affected by processes at work in the terrestrial atmosphere, because the effects were observed more easily during winter than in summer. Finally, the density seems to be "stretched" by cause and "compressed" by effect. Kozyrev was of the opinion that these data may eventually explain how consciousness can obtain knowledge of future events.

The terms "biological energy" and "bioenergy" were put forward by Naumov to replace "psychokinesis" and "PK." However, the term "PK" would not be entirely discarded; it would be used to refer to either the spontaneous or experimental action of bioenergy on nonliving things. Examples given by Naumov included psychic photography (the paranormal creation of film images, often called the "bio-optical effect") and the psychokinetic movement of small objects at a distance.

As a global term to describe all parapsychological investigations, Naumov proposed the term "psychoenergetics." He felt that this designation included both the informational and the energetic aspects of psi phenomena. Further, it implied that the field was interdisciplinary, while the term "parapsychology" did not do credit to the physicians, physicists, biologists, and other scientists who were conducting experiments.

Naumov asked us about the funding situation for American parapsychological laboratories. We told him that there had been some improvement over the years; three laboratories now were fairly well assured of constant funding—those at the American Society for Psychical Research, the University of Virginia, and J. B. Rhine's Foundation for Research on the Nature of Man (organized after his retirement from Duke University). As for our own laboratory, we noted that we had six months in which to find additional funding or we would be forced to close.

Naumov was incredulous. He said, "This is extremely important work that you are doing, for it opens the door to creativity and human potential. Your country is a nation of businessmen. Don't they realize that it is good business to support humanitarian efforts?"

Thursday, June 25

Naumov and Vilenskaya returned with Viktor Adamenko, a physicist who had been a boyhood friend of Semyon Kirlian. Adamenko explained to us the principles of Kirlian photography which involves neither a lens nor a camera. Basically, Adamenko told us, it is a technique for making photographic prints or visual observations of electrically conductive objects with no light source other than that produced by a corona discharge at the object's surface in a high voltage, high frequency electric field. The laboratory of Semyon Kirlian and his wife, Valentina, contained an apparatus consisting of a Tesla coil connected to two metallic plates. When Semyon Kirlian placed his hand next to a photographic film an image was obtained when the coil threw a spark.

The Soviet investigators began to use this technique for detecting flaws in metal surfaces and for detecting mineral traces in soil. It was soon discovered that photographic prints of living tissue could be made by using the tissue itself as one of the two electrodes needed. Electric shock and tissue damage were minimized by selecting a low amperage current and by controlling the output of the high voltage power supply (such as a Tesla coil or Oudin coil). The pictures must be taken in a darkroom or by enclosing the film and object to be photographed in a nontransparent envelope, usually constructed from a piece of dark cloth.

On the Kirlian photographs, one sees an image of the object's surface as well as a surrounding corona, "halo," or "aura" which represents a discharge of electrons from the object. There is very little emission from a dead leaf or from the fingertip of a corpse; thus, Adamenko felt that the electron discharge from a living system was a measure of the life processes occurring within that system.

We saw several photographs of plants taken with the Kirlian apparatus. A close inspection of the pictures showed flare patterns emerging from the leaves. If the plant had buds and flowers, more electrical activity seemed to characterize those regions. If the buds and flowers had been cut off, the photograph showed streams of light coming from the severed tip of the plants, resembling a shower of sparks spewing forth from the end of an ignited Roman candle.

Looking at Kirlian photographs of human bodily parts, we again observed the flare patterns. They were especially apparent in the pictures taken of the hands. We were told that these coronas change very quickly if the individual is hypnotized, imbibes alcohol, or is administered drugs. In other words, the Kirlian apparatus allows experimenters to convert non-electrical properties of objects into electrical properties that can be photographed. This is done by sending a low amperage current through the object's surface; electrons are torn from the object, photons of light are emitted by the electrons, and the light exposes the film. Adamenko's colleague in Alma-Ata, V. M. Inyushin, has suggested that when living organisms are photographed, the "bioplasmic body" determines the shape and form the electron discharge will take in the consequent photograph. In this matter, bioplasma can be studied, albeit indirectly, by Kirlian photography.

Work done by Adamenko, as well as by Inyushin and the Kirlians, detected certain points on the skin from which flares emanated more intensely than from the surrounding skin. They checked ancient oriental acupuncture charts and discovered that these areas of the skin corresponded to acupuncture points. Adamenko told us that he had not found an acupuncture point on the skin's surface that could not be photographed with the Kirlian technique.

Adamenko took measurements of the acupuncture points, discovering that they have higher electrical conductivity (thus lower electrical resistance) than other skin areas. Adamenko showed us a device, the "tobiscope," which he invented to detect acupuncture points. We watched as he demonstrated the device, which resembled a small flashlight. Holding a subject's arm with one hand, he pointed the tip of the tobiscope to the subject's face with the other hand. As soon as he touched an acupuncture point, a light went on. A bright light would indicate high electrical conductivity of the point and good health. A dim light would indicate the converse.

Adamenko conjectured that the meridians, which connect acupuncture points on the oriental charts, are areas of high electrical conductivity within the body. He told us that he had invented a device to measure the conductivity of the meridians as well as another instrument named the "biometer," a device which measures the conductivity of the acupuncture points more precisely than does the tobiscope.

Adamenko's research results fired my imagination. While American investigators were arguing about whether acupuncture could be best explained as the result of hypnotic suggestion or the closing of a "gate" in the spinal cord, the Soviets had suggested a physical basis for acupuncture points. The hint that the acupuncture points, and possibly the meridians, had electrical correlates indicated that electrical technology might be a far more useful technique in healing than we had suspected. And if the "bioplasmic body" does indeed exist, perhaps the acupuncture points and meridians provide the framework for its connection to the physical body.

Adamenko then asked Davidson and me about some of our dream experiments at Maimonides. In 1964, he began to collect examples of precognitive dreams. Eventually, he computed that the average time it took for the dream to come true was two days.

I remarked that precognitive dreams are generally more convincing if the predicted event occurs very quickly. In my own experience, I recalled, the interval is one day. For example, I very rarely dream about show business personalities. When I do so, I know that I will see that person's name the following day—usually in the morning. One night I dreamed I was accepting an award on behalf of Helen Hayes and her late husband, Charles MacArthur. The next day, the first piece of mail I opened was an invitation to attend an exhibit of photographs featuring Hayes and MacArthur. One night I dreamed about seeing Joan Blondell at a party; the next morning I turned on the television set and she was being interviewed.

Friday, June 26

The Soviet research in acupuncture, one of the most intriguing discoveries made on our trip, was further discussed. We were informed that Vladimir Raikov, a psychiatrist, had hypnotized several subjects, telling them that the electrical conductivity of certain acupuncture points would increase. Investigation with the tobiscope indicated that Raikov's commands were quickly followed. Furthermore, at the Institute of Clinical Physiology in Kiev, electrophysiologists found that at the moment that solar flares occur on the sun, there are changes in the electrical potential of the skin's acupuncture points.

Several Soviet physicians were reported to have used acupuncture in conjunction with laser beams, combining an ancient medical form with ultramodern technology. An epileptic seizure, we were told, can be stopped immediately if a laser beam is directed at the acupuncture point between the nose and the lip. Severe arthritic pains can be alleviated by directing laser beams at points between the thumb and forefinger. We were told that if the laser beam is correctly applied and precisely directed, no tissue damage occurs to the patient.

We also were told that Adamenko and other Soviet scientists have discovered acupuncture points on animals and plants. In the case of humans, a number of points have been identified that are not on the ancient Chinese charts. Furthermore, some of the traditional Chinese points occupy different positions on different people, hence the importance of the tobiscope and Adamenko's other inventions.

Adamenko introduced radioactive phosphorus into an acupuncture point and did a radiation analysis of the entire body. He found the highest radiation intensity in those regions of the body which coincide with the places of acupuncture on the Chinese charts. This would indicate that the phosphorus moved in definitive channels of the body. In summation, Naumov predicted that the body's acupuncture system would someday take its place with the body's circulatory system, nervous system, and lymphatic system as an important network for physicians to utilize in medical treatment.

Our conversation turned to Nina Kulagina. We noticed sadness in Naumov's voice as he told us of her recent heart attack. He gave us a photograph in which Kulagina appeared to be suspending a small sphere in midair without touching it. He also told us that she moved an entire pitcher of water across a table by PK. In addition, she had separated the yolk from the white of an egg which had been placed in a salt solution six feet away from her. And when a frog's heart was attached to electrodes and Kulagina was told to slow down its heartbeat, Kulagina exerted such a strong effect that the frog's heart stopped completely. These were the types of strenuous activities that apparently led to Kulagina's hospitalization.

We asked if Kulagina's physiology had ever been studied. Naumov told us that several psychophysiological studies had been undertaken by Sergeyev who found that as Kulagina's respiration and heartbeat rate increased, the movement of an object accelerated. Following certain attempts at PK, it was not unusual for Kulagina to weigh less than before; sometimes two pounds or more.

We found out that since her heart attack, Kulagina had been working with psychic photography. Naumov gave us a picture showing about twelve frames of film, half of which were marked with an X. We were told that Kulagina had placed the X marks upon the film through PK, and while the film was in a sealed container several feet away.

Sunday, June 28

We spent Saturday sightseeing. On Sunday Naumov arranged a reception in our honor at the Sports Cinema, a movie theater. I had presented Naumov with a gift from Thelma Moss, a documentary film made in West Germany which portrayed the Maimonides Dream Laboratory, the psychic photography experiments of Jule Eisenbud, and other research projects.

Our hosts had arranged a special showing of "Seven Steps Beyond the Horizon," a Soviet documentary which had run for over two years in Moscow theaters. The film dealt with seven unusual human potentials: "deep" hypnosis, dowsing, dermaloptical sensitivity, a person with the ability to drive a car blindfolded, a guitarist who could improvise songs immediately after being given a topic, a person with the ability to do rapid arithmetic calculations, and a chessmaster who could simultaneously play a dozen games with a dozen opponents.

The film on skin vision began by showing the differentiation of colored cards by inadequately blindfolded subjects. However, one sequence showed a blind girl correctly identifying colors while another demonstrated the accurate identification of colors and letters which were enclosed in metal containers.

Another segment of the film showed a young man who was offered lists of numbers which he would immediately and correctly add—without pencil and paper. He could also take the seventeenth root of a number that had seventy or eighty digits in it. A woman read him a poem of some twelve lines; when she finished, he would tell her how many letters were in the poem.

The segment which showed a blindfolded man driving a car was actually an exercise in "musclereading." It is true that the driver correctly followed a curved pattern of circles and twists in an open field and that he drove through a city in busy traffic. However, there was always someone inside the car with him, usually in physical contact. Even though the passenger may not have intended to give clues, the passenger's change in tension could have been picked up and interpreted as a desire to change direction.

Nevertheless, the demonstration was still remarkable even if it had nothing to do with ESP.

We also saw a short documentary from Czechoslovakia which demonstrated the controversial "psychotronic generators" in action. These small metal constructions had been put together by Robert Pavlita to "store" biological energy and, eventually, to put it to practical use. We saw one generator which resembled a hollow pipe on a rectangular box into which metal filings were poured. After supposedly absorbing the proper amount of biological energy, the filings were transferred into a bottle of polluted water from a dye factory. The pollution eventually disappeared and could not be seen either in the water or on the metal filings.

Another generator looked like a large pencil with a giant-size eraser. As the eraser was directed toward flies and other insects, they reportedly fell to the floor, stunned. Within a few minutes they were dead.

On that somber note, Davidson and I were introduced to the audience. We spoke briefly and answered a few questions on our experimental studies in parapsychology. There was considerable interest in psychic diagnosis and psychic healing, so I described the work of Edgar Cayce and my own observations of Rolling Thunder, Olga Worrall, and other healers I had known. We then adjourned to the reception where we met several interesting people, among them, Nikolaus Minayev, an engineer with the Ministry of the Coal and Mining Industry, and Yuri Nikolayev, a psychiatrist who directed the Gannushkin Institute for Schizophrenics.

Dr. Minayev told me that he had worked for several years placing workers in appropriate jobs. He had developed a personality test which was used for job selection—and which appeared to provide similar data to advice on job placement obtained from psychic sensitives. His personality test involved such areas as logical skills, intuitive skills, artistic skills, esthetic appreciation, moral qualities, voluntary qualities, and ego-strength. He spoke of measuring, through his tests, the conscious mind, the preconscious, the personal unconscious, and the collective unconscious.

Dr. Nikolayev was known to me by reputation through a mutual friend, Allan Cott, a psychiatrist who had done pioneering work in the treatment of learning disability children with vitamins and minerals instead of with stimulant and sedative drugs. Cott had also worked with schizophrenics, giving them large doses of vitamin B_3 and other nutrients in a therapeutic program originally devised by Humphry Osmond. Cott had visited Moscow recently to observe the fasting program carried out at Nikolayev's Institute over the past several years. Cott was impressed and instituted a similar program for his patients who did not show any benefits from the vitamin and mineral program.

Both Cott and Nikolayev felt that the schizophrenics who came to them often suffered from physical ailments—low blood sugar, allergies, improper diets, or nutritional deficiencies. These factors were felt to underlie their delusions, hallucinations, and disordered patterns of thinking rather than early childhood traumas or problems with their parents.

During my conversations with the professors and scientists at the reception, three elderly people came up to me; one of them asked, "What do you think about holding seances and communicating with the dead?" I gave them a stern look, proclaiming, "People who spend too much time speculating about the afterlife don't have enough time to fight for social justice in this life."

Monday, June 29

Viktor Adamenko met us at our hotel and introduced us to his wife, Alla Vinogradava, an educational psychologist, who revealed that she was practicing psychokinesis.

Vinogradava told us that she worked with a small group of people who were attempting to develop PK. After seeing a film of Kulagina in action she became convinced that she could also move objects, but without the stress she observed in Kulagina's face and body movements. She studied yoga, went to Raikov for hypnotic treatments, and attempted to dissociate herself from all surroundings to obtain a relaxed state of mind.

It took only a short period of practice for her to move an object, a cylindrical cigar tube. Soon she was moving the tube more successfully than anyone in the group. Suddenly, her ability stopped and for eight months she could not move anything. She then began to see V. N. Pushkin who arranged for her to practice among a different group of people who encouraged her and who were not competing with her in any way. Soon she was doing better than ever before.

When she starts moving objects, she told us, she tries to direct all the biological energy to her fingers. However, upon occasion, she has been able to move objects with her feet and shoulders as well. Vinogradava also feels energy emanating from the solar plexus, the heart, and the forehead when she works. Sometimes she has the feeling she is connected to the moving object by a rubber band.

Adamenko told us that the people in his training group who had dry skin were generally able to move objects with more facility than other people. All of the subjects had been given sensitive compasses so they could try to move the needles by PK. Adamenko found that it helped if his subjects had a vivid imagination and could think of energy forces streaming from their bodies to move the objects.

When we arrived at the Academy of Pedagogical Sciences, we were greeted by Dr. V. N. Pushkin, a distinguished educational psychologist, and began to fill the blackboard with charts, statistics, and line drawings of brain waves and rapid eye movements. I had brought slides with me which depicted our experimental procedure and I loaded them into the slide projector. The auditorium was filled. Among the people present, I recognized the Soviet Union's star telepathy team: Yuri Kamensky, a biophysicist who had served as a transmitter, and Karl Nikolaev, an actor who served as the receiver.

Kamensky and Nikolaev described the experiments in which they had sent messages by a kind of Morse code consisting of "dots" and "dashes." Nikolaev would often be in another city with electrodes glued on his head so that EEG readings could be made. Kamensky would imagine tickling the actor for a "dot" and punching him for a "dash." On one occasion, Nikolaev received such an emotional wallop that he fell off his chair to the floor, carrying most of the EEG equipment with him.

Another distinguished member of the audience was A. S. Presman, whose work had recently been published in English under the title *Electromagnetic Fields and Life*. Presman had discovered that electromagnetic fields could regulate the spatial orientation of animals, could modulate the rhythms of the organisms' physiological processes, could affect the vital processes of various organisms, and could assist communication between organisms and their environment, between two or more separate organisms, and within living organisms themselves. Presman had concluded that entire organisms are more sensitive to electromagnetic fields than are isolated organs or cells. Thus, future investigations must center upon the effect of electromagnetic fields on groups of organisms as well as whole communities and populations.

I discussed the place of psi phenomena in evolution with Presman. He was of the opinion that psi represented an archaic mode of communicating, rarely used in modern times but perhaps more important than we suspect in less complex forms of life and among primitive tribes.

The time had arrived for my lecture which Davidson and I had titled "Converging Operations in Bioinformation Research." We had written out each word of it so that the interpreter could translate each sentence into Russian as I went along. After a gracious introduction by Naumov, I stood beneath a portrait of Lenin, looking at the portrait of Pavlov on the other wall.

I began my talk by mentioning Joseph Wortis, my colleague at Maimonides who had a long association with Soviet psychology. After noticing smiles and other indications of approval, I cited my deep personal relationship with Gardner Murphy, the first American parapsychologist to visit the Soviet Union (in 1960, following our summer together in Hawaii). Again there were signs of approval. I then noted that one must go back to the writings of I. P. Pavlov to fathom completely our work at Maimonides. I said:

> Learning theorists have maintained that there are two forms of conditioning, classical and operant. In classical conditioning, as demonstrated by the eminent psychologist Pavlov in his laboratories, a conditioned stimulus is presented along with an innate unconditioned stimulus that normally elicits a certain innate unconditioned response. After a time, the conditioned stimulus elicits the same response as the unconditioned stimulus.

I continued:

> In operant or instrumental conditioning, a reinforcement is given whenever the desired conditioned response is elicited by a conditioned stimulus. In classical conditioning, the stimulus and response must have a direct or innate relationship to begin with. In operant learning, the reinforcement strengthens any immediately preceding response. Therefore, a given response can be reinforced by a variety of rewards, and a given reward can reinforce a variety of responses. Operant learning can take place either for responses mediated by the cerebrospinal nervous system or by the autonomic, vegetative nervous system.

I then described biofeedback of autonomic nervous system responses as an example of operant conditioning. In our experiments, I said, biofeedback involves individuals placed in a closed feedback loop where information concerning one of their bodily processes is continually made known to them. When people are given this type of information about a bodily process, they can often learn to control the function. I noted that we have given special attention to the training of control over the EEG alpha rhythm, which occurs most frequently among human subjects who usually are in a state of relaxed alert wakefulness with little visual imagery or cognitive activity.

I then described biofeedback experiments designed by Charles Honorton in which subjects were taught the five-point state report scale to indicate how profoundly their consciousness had changed. During their biofeedback sessions, they attempted to produce alpha as well as to block alpha. At certain times they were asked to identify the markings on decks of ESP cards.

The results indicated that state reports of 2, 3, and 4 were significantly associated to both higher percentages of alpha production and to higher ESP scores.

The results of this study indicate that the degree to which the alpha rhythm is related to bio-introscopy performance is a function of the subject's psychological state during alpha production. The experiment further demonstrates that the procedure of converging operations is effective in identifying and describing a subject's psychological state.

Just as the EEG records used in combination with the state reports demonstrated the use of converging operations in our clairvoyance (or biointroscopy) study, so the rapid eye movement records used in combination with dream reports showed the utility of converging operations in our telepathy (or biocommunication) studies. As an example of this process, I described our recent experiment with Malcolm Bessent and Felicia Parise in which approximately 2,000 persons per night were employed as transmitters. They were attending six consecutive musical concerts at the Capitol Theater in Port Chester, New York, a distance of 45 miles from the Maimonides Dream Laboratory. The concerts featured the Grateful Dead, a musical group with a keen interest in biocommunication and unusual psychological states. The audience at the concerts was informed as to Bessent's participation in the experiment, but was not told about Parise.

I spoke of the target pictures, how they were projected on the screen, and how the 2,000 people in the audience attempted to transmit the pictures to Bessent. The results for Bessent were statistically significant, but not for Parise—perhaps demonstrating the importance of intentionality on the part of the transmitters. I concluded that "this experiment and others like it demonstrate the feasibility of a scientific approach to the study of biocommunication in dreams."

Knowing that there were space scientists and future cosmonauts in the audience, I summarized the experiment in ESP done during the Apollo 14 moon flight by Edgar Mitchell, the sixth American astronaut to walk on the moon.

I described how Mitchell had made preflight arrangements with four subjects for an ESP experiment to be carried out while he was on the Apollo 14 mission. On several different days the subjects were to guess the symbol order in ESP cards being concentrated on by Mitchell. Because the time that Mitchell concentrated on the cards while on the moon did not synchronize with the time the four subjects attempted to identify the ESP symbols, two types of statistical analysis were made. In the first, the experiment was considered a precognition test; the results were statistically significant. In the second analysis, the experiment was considered in terms of the closest time proximity between Mitchell's attempts at "sending" and the subjects' attempts at "receiving." In this instance, the results were also statistically significant, but with more errors than would be expected by chance. Mitchell suggested that the subjects "seemed oriented *away* from the time-matching idea in this experiment, as if they knew it had gone awry."

I finished my presentation by stating:

There are very few scientists in the world who demonstrate a strong enough interest in these unusual phenomena to perform the appropriate scientific research studies. Yet, an understanding of bio-information processing and the production of bio-energy is of critical importance if we are to become aware of human potential in all its varieties. Perhaps the most important advances in this area will be made by those neurophysiologists and biophysicists who are studying the electromagnetic fields of living organisms and those scientists who are attempting to interpret electromagnetic and quantum phenomena. Therefore, it is necessary for those of us who perform experiments in this area to maintain contacts, exchange information, and work together for the benefit of all peoples everywhere.

7

BACK IN THE USSR

It is logical to state that all matter possesses a quality which in fact is related to sensation, namely, the quality of reflection. However miraculous from the viewpoint of common sense the conversion of imponderable ether to ponderable matter may seem, it is but a further confirmation of dialectical materialism.

V. I. Lenin

Picking a Spot

The visits to the USSR by Ullman and me produced an unexpected result: at a small meeting attended by members of the Dream Laboratory staff and subjects, Ullman showed a film of Nina Kulagina. Among the members of the audience was Felicia Parise. Following the film showing, Parise immediately expressed, in no uncertain terms, her conviction in the genuineness of what she had seen.

Later in the week, she began to see if she could produce movement in small objects. First she attempted to move the objects by entering a relaxed, meditative state of consciousness. When that approach failed, she attempted to induce a state of anxiety and project the anxiety onto the target object. This did not work either.

In one of the nighttime experiments Parise had done earlier, she dreamed of seeing her elderly grandmother sitting on the floor in a pool of blood. Returning home the morning after the session, she learned that her grandmother had fallen during the night, cutting her head as she fell. This was only one of several instances in which Parise's psychic abilities were connected with her grandmother's condition.

Another instance occurred during Parise's attempts to exert PK upon small objects. Her grandmother was critically ill and Parise returned home, one night, after visiting her in the hospital. She was just about to work with a small plastic bottle when the phone rang with a message to return to the hospital. Parise reached for the bottle to put it away—and the bottle suddenly moved away from her.

Over the next several months, Parise repeated her success several times. The first outside person to observe the movement was Clark Hubbard, a student research assistant, who visited Parise one night. In a joking manner, Parise instructed Hubbard to watch the bottle. It immediately moved two inches across the table.

Later in 1971, Charles Honorton observed similar movement with the same bottle. Honorton tried to make the bottle move on the same formica surface through other means. He later recalled, "I tried pressing gently and firmly against the sides, top, and underside of the counter; I forcibly jarred the counter top; I moistened the counter and the bottle by spilling some of the alcohol solution. I was completely unsuccessful in getting the bottle to move." Honorton later took a carpenter's level to Parise's apartment and found that the surface on which the bottle had moved was not perfectly level. The bottle had been moving slightly uphill!

Over the next few months, Parise became successful in deflecting the needle of a small compass. Honorton developed the habit of taking Parise's hands unexpectedly and passing them directly over the face of the compass to insure against concealed bits of metal. And on one occasion, the compass needle deflected 90 degrees after Parise had jokingly uttered the word "Abracadabra."

Parise had described the process as focusing her attention on the object to be moved until "that's the only thing there." She would pick a spot on the object and fixate on it until everything else disappeared. She would work up to an emotional excitement in which her desire to make the object move was stronger than anything else. She had described how she would perspire freely during a PK session, how her eyes would run, and how her nose would tremble. After a successful session, Parise would have difficulty speaking for a few moments.

Parise demonstrated before other parapsychologists such as J. G. Pratt and Graham Watkins, one of J. B. Rhine's assistants. She was filmed moving corks which had been placed in a large jar; the cameraman, an amateur magician, examined the environment, inspected Parise, and failed to find anything suggesting chicanery. I personally saw her deflect a compass needle by five degrees.

Parise's last observed session was in 1972, when Honorton saw her move a bottle more than six inches. She discontinued PK work, stating: "It took all of my spare time. PK is something you have to do every day. It's more than just putting it on your schedule. I did it to satisfy myself." Parise also admitted, "I am not the kind of person who can withstand constant criticism." She knew only too well that if she gained a reputation for this type of ability, she would be subjected to the type of vilification directed against Kulagina.

Nevertheless, Parise's performance, stimulated by the Kulagina film, is evidence of what William Schutz and others have called the "Bannister effect." Schutz has written:

> Before Roger Bannister's performance, it was widely believed that a human being could not run a mile in less than four minutes. Elaborate physiological tests were offered to demonstrate this was impossible. Then Bannister ran under four minutes. Within the next several years over a hundred men had broken four minutes. Now it is a rarity if any major mile run is not run that fast. Bannister demonstrated that the limit was a *limit of belief, not of ability*. Human functions of all types are victims of the same limitations.

Search for the New

In the meantime, Thelma Moss and I had sent dozens of copies of Kirlian apparatus schematics to students from all over the United States who had heard of our trips to the USSR. Kendall Johnson , one of Moss's students at UCLA, put together a device and was soon taking pictures. Three of our dream lab research assistants, James Hickman, Ronny Mastrion, and Daniel Rubin, built three different types of Kirlian devices. William Tiller, a physicist at Stanford University, who went to the USSR in 1971, put together a device based on the Soviet information and an original schematic he obtained from Henry Monteith, a faculty member at the University of New Mexico, who had based his design on various translations of Kirlian's articles.

Victor Gioscia, a sociologist at Adelphi University, Judith Skutch, and I knew that the time was ripe for a public meeting to discuss these developments. On May 25, 1972, we convened the First Western Hemisphere Conference on Kirlian Photography, Acupuncture, and the Human Aura in New York City's United Engineering Center. Papers on Kirlian photography were presented by Moss, Tiller, and myself. Hickman and his associate, Larry Amos, showed slides of their electrophotographs. A Rhode Island high school student, Rodney Ross, described a noncontact method for taking electrophotographs which allowed a camera to photograph the Kirlian effect through a microscope. Robert Nelson translated and read a paper sent to us by Viktor Adamenko. Brendan O'Regan, Buckminster Fuller's assistant, commented on the implications of the Kirlian effect for Western science. Max Toth, an EEG technician who had traveled to

Prague, presented a historical overview. He also brought back news that Zdeněk Rejdák, the leading Czech parapsychologist, planned to hold an international parapsychological meeting in 1973.

While I was at the University of Wisconsin, I had a picture of Corinne Calvet, the tempestuous French actress who had starred in such films as *On the Riviera*, on my bulletin board. Nearly two decades later, I met Calvet and discovered that she was a practitioner of sonopuncture, in which high-frequency sound is directed into acupuncture points. At one of her parties, I met J. R. Worsley, an English acupuncturist, and John Fox, the first physician to use acupuncture in an American hospital. I invited all three of them to participate in our 1972 conference. In addition, I arranged for Shizuko Yamamoto to demonstrate *shiatsu*, the Japanese acupuncture massage, on my stepson, Bob, before the assemblage.

The papers were highly technical; yet to our surprise the auditorium was filled to capacity and hundreds of people had to be turned away. The conference opened with a congratulatory telegram from Semyon Kirlian:

> On the opening of the first conference on the Kirlian effect, I personally greet you, all the conferees, and everyone in attendance. . . . From the conference, I hope there will develop significant creative solutions for the blessing of mankind and the affairs of the world. In conclusion, I ask you to please keep in mind the contributions of Valentina Khrisanova Kirlian who devoted all of her conscious energies to the search for the new and the cultivation of the hidden.

Ivy and Electron Flow

To determine whether electrophotography could be used as a parapsychological tool, Daniel Rubin and I visited Rodney Ross, who had volunteered the use of his Kirlian apparatus for an experiment.

Ross had been rescued from an oppressive school situation by the National Foundation for Gifted and Creative Children, an organization I had consulted with over a several-year period. One semester, some of my students in an experimental course at New York University had investigated the practice, commonplace in Rhode Island, of prescribing drugs to children whose overly active classroom behavior was termed "hyperkinetic." When we inspected the tests given the forty-seven youngsters who had been so labeled, we found only two who showed symptoms of brain damage, the underlying cause of hyperkinesis. The others were slow learners, emotionally disturbed, or simply bored.

Rubin and I used the headquarters of the National Foundation for

Gifted and Creative Children as the site for our experiment. We employed the services of three local psychic sensitives as subjects and used the Kirlian device built by Rodney Ross.

Ross tore an ivy leaf from a vine ten minutes before the experiment began and attached it to the Kirlian apparatus. We selected an ivy leaf because Ross's previous work had indicated a minimal dehydration effect over a two-hour time span. This was an important consideration in eliminating dehydration of the leaf as a major variable which might affect in a different way the pictures taken at the beginning and at the end of the experiment.

The Kirlian apparatus was placed in a cellar and was operated by two experimenters who remained in the laboratory during the experiment. The subjects were located in a room on the first floor of the same building. The three subjects were tested individually, were shown several electrophotographs by a third experimenter, were told how the emanations from the leaf often increased just after the leaf had been plucked, and were instructed to attempt to minimize or "hold back" the electron flow.

The experimenters in the cellar took electrophotographs of the ivy leaf every five minutes. In the meantime, the third experimenter tossed a coin every five minutes. If "heads" appeared, the subject would attempt to influence the ivy leaf's corona. If "tails" appeared, no attempt was made to influence the electrophotograph. Thirty electrophotographs were taken for each subject.

Three outside judges were given the electrophotographs and rated each one on a 100-point scale; a rating of 1 indicated a "very weak electrical discharge," while 100 indicated a "very strong electrical discharge." When statistical tests were used to compare the electrophotographs produced when "heads" occurred against those produced when "tails" appeared, it was found that with all three subjects the coronas were smaller for "heads" —when the subjects attempted to "hold back" the emanations. For one of the subjects the results were statistically significant.

Bioenergetic Problems

Edward Naumov had planned a second conference in 1972. Dr. Carmi Harari of the Association for Humanistic Psychology and I sent letters of invitation to scientists and psychologists all over the world. The original responses to my invitation were overwhelmingly positive. Helmut Schmidt, of J. B. Rhine's Foundation, agreed to speak on "Psi Research and Modern Physics." Other parapsychologists who agreed to speak included Montague

Ullman, Charles Honorton, Jule Eisenbud, Gertrude Schmeidler, Karlis Osis, Thelma Moss, Charles Tart, Robert Morris, Alan Vaughan, and Edgar Mitchell. Workers in associated fields expressing interest were Max Toth, Robert Becker, Cleve Backster (the polygraph expert who claimed that he could attach a plant to a lie detector and—at a distance—influence its recorded reactions), Charles Musès (a mathematician), and Khigh Dhiegh (a philosopher). None of these individuals actually followed through on their plans. The reasons were obvious: none of the thirty foundations I wrote to offered any money and Naumov was unable to come up with a sponsor who would legitimize the planned conference and guarantee its occurrence. The letters written by Harari and me to A. R. Luria, the best known Soviet psychologist, as well as those sent to the Soviet-American Friendship House and the Institute of Soviet-American Relations, went unanswered.

When our group left for Moscow in July, we had no idea if there would be a meeting or not. The first group to leave included my stepson, Bob, who had received a travel grant to take photographs of the conference. With him was Richard Davidson, who had just started his doctoral work at Harvard University's Department of Psychology and Social Relations. I traveled with the members of the Association for Humanistic Psychology on a tour which would eventually take us to Tokyo for the Twentieth International Congress of Psychology. My paper on the Maimonides experiments had been accepted for presentation at the Congress as was Adamenko's report on bioenergy. It would be the first time that presentations on parapsychology had been scheduled for an International Congress of Psychology.

On July 16, our group arrived in Moscow. Richard Davidson and Bob had already made contact with Edward Naumov, Larisa Vilenskaya, and Vladimir Raikov who met us at the hotel. In 1971, Naumov's jovial bantering with Vilenskaya had been one of the pleasant memories of my visit. This year, however, Naumov appeared to be tense and worried. "We have been having serious problems," he said. "Until four days ago, we were unsure whether we would have the meeting. We had not received approval but neither had our proposal been turned down. So we decided that we would take a chance and carry on with the meeting just as if it had been approved."

Naumov asked me not to discuss his troubles with the other participants as he did not want to cast a shadow over their visit to Moscow. We agreed that the conference would be called "The International Meeting on the Problem of Bioenergetics and Related Areas" and Naumov told us where to meet the next morning for the first event of the conference.

Monday, July 17

We went to the Gannushkin Institute for Schizophrenics, part of the Moscow Institute of Psychiatry, for a reunion with Yuri Nikolayev whom I had met in 1971. Dr. Nikolayev, in his quiet yet forceful manner, told us about the program:

> Some 8,000 patients have passed through this Institute to be treated; the majority are cured. We have 40 beds for men and 40 beds for women at present. The basic principles of our method are to create a rest for the central nervous system, to free the organism from all poisonous substances, to organize the natural defense forces of the system, and to re-structure the personality of the patients so that they change their habits after treatment —avoiding situations which may lead to addiction to alcohol, tobacco, or narcotics.

When patients arrive at the Institute, they are placed on a fast which lasts approximately thirty days. Although the patients can have as much mineral water as they like, they can have no food. Nikolayev has hypothesized that many types of schizophrenia are caused by toxins in the system which can be eliminated through fasting and a daily administration of an enema consisting of a magnesium solution.

The patients receive a daily massage, occupational therapy, supportive counseling, and are encouraged to walk out of doors in the beautiful gardens. They discuss their personality changes with other patients in regularly scheduled periods of group therapy. In some cases, acupuncture, hypnotherapy, and autogenic training are utilized; however, insulin treatment and drugs are rarely used. In many instances, large doses of vitamins and minerals are introduced at some point during treatment.

Nikolayev told us that his patients' delusions and hallucinations begin to disappear, their emotional reactions become more appropriate, their disordered thinking begins to change to logical thought, and they become more sociable than they had been previously.

He reported that the change in a patient's physiology reflects the changes in the person's behavior. At first, the patient's appetite is very intense; the tongue coats over for about a week as body wastes are discharged. Then the white tongue coating disappears and the skin color improves. The patient's hunger is still great and most of the dreams concern food. During the third week, hunger diminishes and by the end of the fast, about 20 percent of the body weight has been lost.

Once Nikolayev feels that the toxic elements have been eliminated from the patient's body, foods are introduced, beginning with strained fruit and vegetable juices. Buttermilk and salads are sampled. Whenever a food is associated with a recurrence of schizophrenic symptoms, that particular food is removed forever from the patient's diet. As a result, most of the patients must avoid white sugar; many cannot use salt or eat various types of meat.

Following Nikolayev's description, several of the patients spoke to us through an interpreter. In one poignant instance, a student told us that he had been ill for four years. He had lost interest in his studies and discovered he could not make contact with people or answer questions directed to him. Commenting on the treatment, he said that he was planning to return to school; he continued, "My condition is now excellent and I feel that I can overcome obstacles."

Benson Herbert, an English researcher and editor of the *International Journal of Paraphysics,* suggested that some of the patients would make excellent subjects for ESP tests involving dissociated states of consciousness. Vilenskaya agreed and suggested that the paranormal influence of a healthy person over a sick person might be part of the cure.

One of the Americans asked Nikolayev if there was any place in the United States where the fasting treatment was available. He replied, "Dr. Allan Cott uses the treatment at Gracie Square Hospital, in New York City. However, the cost there is one hundred dollars per day, while in Moscow, it is free."

Tuesday, July 18

The meeting at the Moscow Institute of Psychiatry was classified as "official" because it was held in an institution of unquestioned repute. Beginning on Tuesday, our meetings were "unofficial" and we assembled at the May Day Club.

Dr. Eugene Salnikov, director of the Energy Institute of Medical Research in Moscow, gave a welcoming speech. Naumov then traced the history of Soviet parapsychology. Films were presented which showed Nina Kulagina and Alla Vinogradava moving small objects across a table. Viktor Adamenko discussed his work with Vinogradava, and also presented a stunning color film of the Kirlian effect in which moment-by-moment changes in the flare patterns could be observed.

The next speaker was V. M. Inyushin from Kazakh State University in Alma-Ata. I had told the Americans that the trip to Moscow would be worthwhile even if no one showed up but the brilliant Soviet biologist from Alma-Ata whose theories of bioplasma, the "fifth state of matter," offered a possible explanation for psi phenomena. Inyushin did not disappoint us. He began his lecture, continuing Adamenko's discussion of Kirlian photography:

> Many methods apart from the Kirlian technique are being used to register the biological fields existing in and around the living organism. At Alma-Ata, we have been attempting to process the information derived from these registration systems, to estimate the stability of the bioplasmic emission, and to understand their physical parameters. Our aim is to control the bioplasmic processes and to ascertain how these are related to psychic phenomena.

Inyushin went on to describe his ongoing research involving "spontaneous emissions of bioplasma in the ultraviolet spectrum" and the recording of these emissions without subjecting the organism to electrical impulses, as in Kirlian photography.

The technique described by Inyushin involved a special film emulsion sensitive to the ultraviolet spectrum. Selective filters were interposed and all heat effects were held constant. Under these conditions, emanations from the eyes of animals and humans were recorded on the film. Inyushin interpreted the source of these emanations to be "mitogenic radiation," the energy released when cells divide during a process known as "cell mitosis." Therefore, according to Inyushin,

> Bioplasma is emitted from the body and does not come from the atmosphere. A structure in the bioplasmic field is produced which acquires temporary stability, conveying mitogenic information from the living organism. This structure endures for up to five minutes, long enough to make an impression upon the film emulsion. Telepathy, or biological communication, can be looked upon as a product of resonances in the bioplasmic bodies of two organisms.

Inyushin described a series of experiments which he felt were pertinent to understanding the mechanisms of biological communication. Investigators at the State Medical School in Novosibirsk divided healthy tissue from a chicken embryo into two parts. The tissues were placed in isolated metal containers equipped with quartz crystal windows that faced each other. When a toxic virus was put into one metal container the tissue died. Inexplicably, the cells in the other container died also.

It was found that this "mirror effect" did not occur if the windows were made from glass or some material other than quartz. Knowing that quartz will allow ultraviolet photons to pass through its crystals, a sensitive photomultiplier tube was attached to the containers. The tube recorded photons in the ultraviolet range passing from the diseased container to the healthy container. Further, the photon flow surged, then stopped, surged again, then stopped; the pattern of the photon flow corresponded to the stages in which a poisonous virus attacks a healthy cell. Inyushin suggested:

> The biological communication between the tissue cells very much resembles a telepathic model. The emission appears to carry specific information. The possibility thus arises that the information carrier from a contaminated tissue culture may adversely affect a neighboring healthy culture, a possible case of telepathic influence on the cellular level. One can envision the emissions carrying elements of a three-dimensional hologram, conveying with it information relevant to the bioplasmic field of the entire organism.

In the discussion following Inyushin's talk, it was mentioned that G. A. Sergeyev and his associates had invented a device which registered bioplasmic processes in the human body. The apparatus had been used in the Kulagina experiments to record the streams of subatomic particles (felt to comprise bioplasma) that were emitted from the body as she attempted PK. The critical elements of the device were two silver plates and a barium titanate crystal which was polarized—dividing different types of light from one another and sending them in different directions. Sergeyev and V. V. Kulagin (Nina Kulagina's husband) wrote an article for the *International Journal of Paraphysics* noting that the greatest concentration of bioplasma, according to their detector, rests in the cerebral cortex of the brain. In their work with Kulagina, they noted that she was able to expose photographic film which was enclosed in light-proof containers; it was suggested that this was done by a "biolaser effect" brought about by the focusing of her bioplasma.

A final point which emerged in the discussion with Inyushin was that bioplasma interacts with solids, liquids, and gases. From time to time, bioplasma can transform itself to these states of matter, just as water can change into steam or ice. Inyushin conjectured that acupuncture points emit more bioplasma than other areas of the skin; the *Chi* energy described in some ancient oriental texts and the *Prana* discussed by yogis may, in reality, be bioplasma.

During the discussion, Manfred Cassirer, an English parapsychologist, commented on Inyushin's presentation. He suggested that bioplasma could sometimes act as a "pseudopic arm," emerging from a psychic sensitive's body while he or she performs various PK feats. Cassirer speculated that the "ectoplasm" reportedly seen during some of these sessions—and even purportedly photographed on occasion—could be bioplasmic in nature.

The final papers of the day were given by three Americans. Alexander Everett, founder of "Mind Dynamics," described his "mind-control" system and how it could help to enhance relaxation, problem solving, and ESP.

Frank Salisbury, a psychic healer, described his method of keeping his consciousness "in tune" with the "universal energies" during his attempts at healing. Irving Oyle, an osteopath, described the free clinic he started in Bolinas, California, and how psychic healing was one of the treatment modalities he inaugurated there. Oyle described his work with small groups of people, which he had trained to produce a "positive group image" while treating a sick person at a distance through psychic healing.

Wednesday, July 19

Douglas Dean and I presented material on Kirlian photography research in the United States, emphasizing the experiments with psychic healers. I also showed slides taken of the right index fingertip of Ingo Swann, an artist and psychic sensitive living in New York City. When Swann went into the state of consciousness which was associated with psychokinesis, the corona discharge revealed irregular flare patterns. When he shifted to the conscious state associated with "out-of-body" experience, the corona became thick and regular.

O. W. Markley, of the Stanford Research Institute, reported the work done by SRI physicists Harold Puthoff and Russell Targ with Ingo Swann. Under controlled conditions, Swann apparently was able to bend a laser beam.

Markley also spoke of his own work in "futurology"—the monitoring of future trends and events—in the SRI Center for the Study of Social Policy. Naumov said he had also done work in this field, especially in regard to precognition and the choice of alternative futures. Markley stated that what we need "is a new set of methods that would enable humans to use higher levels of consciousness as they grapple with the perennial questions of existence." Markley suggested that psychoenergetics may eventually offer important avenues through which some of these needed understandings may be obtained.

A series of films of the controversial Filipino psychic healers were shown by Gunter Lieb, an Austrian investigator. In the film, healers appeared to thrust their hands into diseased persons, pulling out pathological tissue. Hans Naegeli, a Swiss parapsychologist, and Hans Bender, a parapsychologist from West Germany, had been in the Philippines at the same time and observed the same healers, sometimes side by side. Yet, in discussing the films, Bender claimed that trickery had been used (specifically, a specially prepared plastic foil which was slipped over the abdomen) while Naegeli insisted that many of the phenomena were genuine.

Before the day's session adjourned, I introduced Tina Johnson to the group. I told them about her successful clairvoyance experiment and how, during automatic writing, her EEG record showed a marked increase in high amplitude theta waves.

I also told them how Johnson had presented me with three gummed butterfly decorations on my arrival in Moscow. She said that she saw them in a gift store and bought them on impulse, thinking I would need them, but not knowing why. I told her that I was the only one in the humanistic psychology tour group who had not purchased distinctive stickers for the three pieces of baggage I brought with me. I was hoping I could get some in Moscow to assist in baggage identification. As for the butterfly, just before leaving New York City, I participated in a pilot telepathy session with Martha Harlin, who served as transmitter. I drew a picture of a butterfly which happened to correspond to a painting of a butterfly which Harlin was concentrating on in a distant room.

Thursday, July 20

John Mihalasky of the Newark College of Engineering reported on his study of psi functioning among business managers. Between 1965 and 1971, he had given precognition tests to some fifty groups of business people. The test consisted of having the subjects punch holes in computer cards to match a program which would be automatically punched the following day. The subjects were also asked which of five images they thought best characterized time: a dashing waterfall, a galloping horseman, an old woman spinning, a vast expanse of sky, or a quiet motionless ocean.

Mihalasky found that subjects who selected the waterfall or horseman had significantly higher precognition scores on the computer card tests than those who selected the other images. Furthermore, the business executives with the highest precognition scores increased their company's profits on a year-by-year basis more than those subjects with low precognition scores. Mihalasky concluded, "There is now evidence that the successful 'hunch player' may have something more solid going for him than the odds of chance."

Further sessions were devoted to a discussion of the humanistic psychology movement. Myron Arons described the origins of humanistic psychology, noting the contributions made to the underlying philosophy by such Russian writers as Maxim Gorki and Fyodor Dostoevsky. Vivian Guze, of the Institute of Bio-Energetic Analysis in New York City, gave a demonstration of bioenergetic therapy, pointing out how it evolved from the work of Wilhelm Reich. Carmi Harari led the group in an encounter session —apparently the first one held in the Soviet Union. At the end of the afternoon, a Soviet psychiatrist told Harari, "I learned more about myself today than in all my years of psychiatric training."

Friday, July 21

Our last full day in Moscow was marked by a number of small conferences. Brendan O'Regan was besieged by individuals eager to hear more about the concepts of synergy advanced by Buckminster Fuller; Arons and Guze were questioned about humanistic psychology.

I left to meet Adamenko. With him were Hans Bender, Benson Herbert, Robert Nelson, and James Hickman. Hickman showed his Kirlian photographs. One of the Soviet technicians inspected Hickman's photograph of a leaf and called it "the best example of Kirlian photography I have seen outside of the Soviet Union." We couldn't bring ourselves to tell him that the electrophotograph depicted a marijuana leaf.

Adamenko then showed his film of Alla Vinogradava, after which he introduced her to the assemblage. Vinogradava sat on a chair near a plexiglass table. Adamenko placed a Havana cigar tube on the surface of the table. Vinogradava put her right hand to the side of the tube and it began to move across the table. When it reached the table's far side, she shifted her hand to the other side and it moved back. The tube continued to roll from edge to edge for several minutes; each time it reached the far side of the table, Vinogradava shifted her hand to the other side of the table and the tube moved back.

Adamenko then removed the cigar tube and substituted a heavier tube made from aluminum. She preceded her attempts to move this tube by picking it up and rubbing it briefly—indicating to me that she was initiating an electrostatic charge. This charge would cause the tube to repel from her hand—but through an electrostatic effect rather than PK. The aluminum tube rolled across the table in choppy movements, whereas the cigar tube had moved smoothly.

The next object placed before Vinogradava was a ping-pong ball. In this instance, Vinogradava moved her hand in a circular motion a few inches above the object. The ball obediently followed her hand. I noted that she rubbed her hands briskly before attempting this feat and again wondered whether she was building up an electrostatic charge.

Vinogradava next worked with a film cylinder. Despite its uneven surface, it rolled fairly well across the table. She then placed it on its end to "push" it rather than "roll" it. Adamenko told us that it requires about ten times as much effort for her to "push" rather than to "roll" an object.

Then Adamenko placed a lightweight steel tube on the table which Vinogradava was successful in propelling. Adamenko, at this point, took a small neon light bulb and touched its bottom to the tube. The bulb lit up for an instant—again suggesting to me that some type of electrostatic effect was involved.

Two tubes were then placed on the table. Vinogradava placed her hand above both of them. Adamenko pointed to one of the tubes. With only slight hand movement, Vinogradava was able to move the specified tube while the other one remained still. This ability to move objects selectively indicated the role which her "will" or volition played in the phenomena.

Adamenko took one tube away and Vinogradava rolled the remaining tube back and forth. She then announced that it might be possible for someone else to move the tube. I leaped from my chair, sat down at the table, and, using the identical hand motions I had observed during the demonstration, rolled the tube across the table. I was able to sustain the movement for about thirty seconds; then the motion declined and finally stopped. But the side of my right hand tingled for the next two hours. Vinogradava again initiated movement of the tube, and two other observers took turns rolling it.

Adamenko told me that he could not go to Tokyo to read the paper covering his work with Vinogradava. However, he gave me a copy of his paper so that I could give the presentation. I noticed that the paper was titled, "Objects Moved at a Distance by Means of a Controlled Bioelectric Field." Nowhere in the manuscript was there any claim that the effects were due to psychokinesis. Later, when I read the paper, I was told it was the first time an American scientist had ever read a Soviet scientist's paper at an international conference.

Fiction or Reality?

Back in New York I received a letter signed by A. R. Luria, dated April 1972. Luria noted that he had received letters from Harari and myself concerning the organization of a series of informal meetings on parapsychology in Moscow. Luria stated that the Psychological Society of the USSR could not support this project because parapsychology was not a branch of scientific psychology. Luria mentioned Naumov, stating that he was "unknown" to the Psychological Society.

If we had had this letter earlier, we never would have jeopardized Naumov's safety by pushing ahead with the meetings. Indeed, we began to wonder if we had been used as ploys by Naumov's enemies and became critically concerned about his safety.

We heard very little from Naumov during the following year. And then, in 1973, my Soviet colleagues sent me a photocopy of the first article on psychoenergetics to be published in *Questions of Philosophy*, the official publication of the prestigious USSR Academy of Sciences. The article was signed by V. P. Zinchenko, A. N. Leontiev, B. F. Lomov, and A. R. Luria; it was titled "Parapsychology: Fiction or Reality?"

The article was astonishing. After pointing out the poor work done by certain investigators and the fraud which exists among many "psychic sensitives," the authors concluded almost casually:

> Obviously, some so-called parapsychological phenomena actually do happen. . . . Certainly the time has come to bring order into the scientific research and study of the phenomena described in parapsychology. Much of the research in the field of parapsychology is being done by physicists and engineers. Therefore, it would be expedient to assess, at the Institute for Biophysics in the U.S.S.R. Academy of Sciences . . . the direction . . . of the "biophysical effect" [dowsing]. The electromagnetic fields generated by living organisms could be likewise assessed as a possible means of "biological communication" [telepathy]. . . . If attention is paid to these phenomena from the point of biophysics and information theory, these efforts will help to demystify them.

> The psychological institutes of the U.S.S.R. Academy of Sciences and of the U.S.S.R. Academy of Pedagogical Sciences . . . should also give consideration to the possibility of mounting programs for strictly scientific research into these phenomena. Evidently it would be advisable to organize a laboratory within one of the psychological institutions which would study persons who really do possess unusual abilities.

Three of the four people who signed this report were the leading psychologists in the Soviet Union. With this article, the USSR became the first country in the world whose psychological establishment endorsed the study of ESP and PK.

There were other points of interest in the article. It was noted that the first parapsychological paper to be accepted for delivery at an International Congress of Parapsychology occurred in 1972 when "a report by the American parapsychologist, S. Krippner, was presented." A claim was also made that "the American federal government spends between one-half and one million dollars a year on parapsychological research." One researcher friend of mine exclaimed, "If that's true, no parapsychologist that I know has ever seen it!"

There were also oblique references to Naumov which indicated to me that his fate was sealed. *Psychic Discoveries Behind the Iron Curtain* was denounced as "a low-level work" used to advertise "anti-Sovietism." It was also noted:

> There also exists a category of rather clever persons who often have no seri-

ous background of any kind. These are the very people who assume the role of propagandists and impresarios for those who actually possess unusual abilities. . . . Some of these "experts" declare themselves to be leaders of groups . . . which have never existed in our country. The "Institute of Technical Parapsychology" is an example of such an organization. It is necessary to put an end to the activity of poorly qualified but militant parapsychological "experts" who take upon themselves the role of . . . propagandists and who issue numerous reports and give lectures on parapsychology for audiences which even include scientists. These lectures offer an unscrupulous mishmash of fantasy and fact.

Shortly after the publication of this article, I received word of Naumov's arrest. I was also given three agencies in Moscow to which letters of protest were to be directed. Many of us wrote the letters. Parapsychologists, needless to say, have less political clout than any other scientific group and on March 28, 1974, the wire services announced:

A Soviet specialist in telepathy and clairvoyance has been sentenced to two years at hard labor for refusing to break his contacts with his Western colleagues, dissident sources claimed today. The informants said . . . Edward K. Naumov was convicted following a 15-day trial in a Moscow court. The sources said Naumov was charged with misusing funds of a club that invited him to lecture on parapsychology. . . . According to the informants, the charge was fabricated after Naumov ignored secret police demands that he stop meeting with foreign specialists visiting Moscow.

My tentative interpretation of Naumov's demise was that the Soviet scientific establishment had finally decided to give parapsychology the stamp of approval, albeit a cautious one. Naumov was not a professional scientist. We all knew that his "Institute of Technical Parapsychology" existed only on paper. However, he was the only one we could contact if we wanted information on psychoenergetics in the USSR.

Also, Naumov may have been considered too friendly to foreigners by the secret police; his arrest appeared to be part of a general crackdown on Soviet nonconformists. But unlike most Soviet dissidents, Naumov never criticized the Soviet system or veered from Marxist doctrine. In July 1974, I received an account of Naumov's trial from a Soviet physicist living in Moscow. Regarding the charge that Naumov had misused the funds a club paid him for his lectures, the physicist wrote:

One cannot take seriously the prosecutor's claim that Naumov's receiving payment for a lecture . . . constitutes complicity in "financial gain." . . . What is Naumov really guilty of? . . . Here is what he had dared to do. For many years, he had maintained free, personal, human contacts with many foreign scholars, contacts which were not sanctioned from above. He carried on an extensive correspondence with them and made use of the material he received for disseminating information on parapsychology in the U.S.S.R. On his personal initiative, he organized international meetings and scientific symposiums, became a member of international societies, and presented himself as the representative of Soviet parapsychology at a time when this science was not officially recognized in the U.S.S.R. He created an undesirable precedent and made of himself a dangerous example by taking seriously all the talk about peaceful coexistence and international scientific cooperation. In his wake, other Soviet parapsychologists began to do similar things. . . . Although these actions could not be brought to trial according to law, at the same time they could not be permitted to go unpunished. And so they are punished. Naumov is sent to prison, many other parapsychologists are relieved of their jobs.

In June, 1975, I received word that Naumov had been released from prison on condition that he abandon independent psi research. Although I was pleased to hear the news, I was apprehensive concerning Naumov's future. Naumov, through his efforts, had brought the emerging Soviet interest in psychoenergetics to the attention of the world. He had also forced the ruling scientists to take a position on the subject, a position which was more positive than that taken by official scientific bodies in any other country. Yet Naumov paid a terrible price for listening to the siren's song; parapsychology cannot help but remain in his debt. And perhaps in a more rational time, his heroic stature will be recognized in the Soviet Union.

8

THE SPIRITS OF SÃO PAULO

Science, itself, by investigating alpha-waves, antimatter, holes in space, psychopharmacology, and the dynamics of waves and cycles, may be hoisted by its own petard to the confrontation of a universe very different from what we now imagine. . . . For it does indeed seem that many scientists have a religious fervor and a vested interest in demonstrating that nature is *only* a rather inefficient machine—to which they must paradoxically ascribe their own boastedly superior intelligences.

Alan Watts

The Overlooked Americans

By 1973, my income from the Maimonides Medical Center was down to about five hundred dollars a year. Out of necessity, I was spending much of my time at California State College, Sonoma, helping to initiate an interdisciplinary undergraduate concentration in parapsychology as well as a master's degree emphasizing parapsychology, to be offered through the department of psychology.

I was also involved in creating a doctoral program in parapsychology for the Humanistic Psychology Institute. The required areas of mastery included statistics and experimental psychology, the history of psychical research, developmental psychology emphasizing child and adolescent psychology, personality theory emphasizing psychotherapy and altered states of consciousness, the history and philosophy of psychology stressing humanistic psychology, and a knowledge of prestidigitation (sleight of hand)—to prevent clever "psychics" from using trickery to support their claims to ESP and PK.

One of the graduate students at the Humanistic Psychology Institute was Alberto Villoldo, whom I had originally met in San Juan, where I had served as Visiting Professor for the University of Puerto Rico. Villoldo and

I received a travel grant from the Erickson Educational Foundation to attend the Fourteenth InterAmerican Congress of Psychology in São Paulo and to investigate Brazil's spirit religions.

On April 14, Villoldo and I arrived in São Paulo. The fastest growing city in the world, São Paulo is perched on a plateau, surrounded by the jungle, and serviced by the port city of Santos. The city and the people blend the cosmopolitan and the primitive. Between the skyscrapers there were tiny shops selling spiritist charms. Sophisticated women dressed in the most fashionable and elegant clothes peered at us with dark, primal eyes.

I had always been more attracted to the mythology of the Americas than to that of ancient Europe or the Far East. As I began to study yogic systems and Eastern philosophy, I became very impressed with oriental wisdom. Nevertheless, it was apparent to me that many Americans had overlooked, as practical guidance in their daily lives, the lessons to be learned from Rolling Thunder and other American Indian teachers.

Over the centuries, various American Indian tribes had practiced meditation, lived in communes, spoken of reincarnation, interpreted dreams, developed a healing system which utilized "channels of energy" resembling acupuncture meridians, and originated a series of initiation ceremonies which brought people into contact with the deep levels of their psyches. Many tribes permitted a variety of forms of sexual expression, including multiple marriages, homosexual and bisexual behavior, transsexualism, and transvestism. A concern with ecology permeated American Indian philosophy as did a keen appreciation of altered states of consciousness.

Music and art were used frequently by American Indians to enter altered states of consciousness, and have provided a rich heritage for people to study and appreciate. I knew that we were about to enter a learning experience provided by the "mysterious Americas" in collaboration with the neighboring "darkest Africa" from which many slaves had come to Brazil.

The Yoruba Orishas

Around the corner from our hotel, Villoldo and I discovered a shop which sold various charms and books relating to Brazil's spirit religions. One book noted that the first African slaves had been brought to Brazil about 1550 to work on the plantations in the northeastern part of the colony. The slaves were appropriated, often with the complicity of people from their own tribes, on the West African coast, home of the Yoruba culture. This was also the home of the Yoruba spirits, or *orishas*.

The Yoruba orishas were powerful and terrifying, yet so human that they were talked to, pleaded with, and cajoled through special offerings and gifts. Olorun was the most powerful spirit of them all. He created human beings, but simply did not have the time to deal with them. To speak to humans on his behalf, Olorun created a son and a daughter, Obatalá and Odudua, from a handful of clay. Obatalá, the god of purity, was given charge of the heavens and Odudua charge of the earth. Their children, Aganjú and Yemanjá, had a son named Orungan.

Unlike his father and grandfather, Orungan had no sister for mating purposes. Upon reaching adolescence, he raped his mother. Unlike the hapless Greek mythological figure, Oedipus, Orungan knew full well what he was doing. His mother, Yemanjá, gave birth to a number of orishas: the gods of thunder, the oceans, fertility, vegetables, mountains, wealth, war, and the hunt; the goddesses of the Oshun, Niger, and Obá rivers, the sun, and the moon. Because water flowed from her breasts during this period of multiple births, Yemanjá became known as the "mother of the waters."

A number of other orishas were born later: Sakpata, who prevented disease, Ifá, the hearer of prayers, Exú, the orishas' messenger, and the Ibeji twins, who symbolized the fact that human beings had both an earthly body and a "spiritual" body.

When the slaves were transported to Brazil, they were squeezed into ship quarters so small that they could not stand erect. Many Yorubas died en route, but the slave traders had done a cost analysis on the process discovering that more slaves would survive under inhumane conditions than could be transported in the same ship if the Yorubas had been given more room. Besides, the merchants could advertise the fact that the survivors were undoubtedly healthy, having lived through the cramped conditions of the voyage across the Atlantic Ocean.

On the slaves' part, they prayed to Yemanjá, "mother of the waters," during their horrible ordeal on the ocean. Those who survived thanked Yemanjá for her assistance. But the problems of the Yorubas had just begun. Upon their arrival in Brazil, they were spoken to in Portuguese and separated from their tribal family and friends. Stripped of their homeland, their family, their friends, their language, and their personal freedom, the slaves had only their religion to sustain them.

Although baptized as Christians upon arrival, they were permitted to hold their own religious services. However, they also had to attend the Roman Catholic Mass. Furthermore, they ran into trouble if the priest did not find pictures of Jesus, Mary, and the saints upon the slaves' altars.

So it was that the slaves cleverly adopted the Christian orishas, combining them with their own Yorba orishas. Olorun, god of creation, became Jehova, or God the Father. Obatalá (whose name was shortened to Oxalá), the god of the heavens, was melded with Jesus, while Odudua was forgotten. Their son, Aganjú, was also neglected, but their daughter Yemanjá became identified with the Virgin Mary. When the Portuguese priests noticed a statuette of Mary upon the altar, they smiled with approval, not realizing that the slaves were really praying to Yemanjá—the goddess associated with an incestuous rape and multiple births.

As slaves were put in charge of the plantation owners' children, it was no surprise that the Yoruba religion began to infiltrate the belief system of the European settlers and their descendants. Yoruba tales were related to many young children as bedtime stories by their black nurses; these accounts were much more interesting than the accounts given by priests on Sunday and the children often grew up to be nominal Catholics but practitioners of Yoruba rituals.

A Holistic Worldview

When Villoldo and I arrived in Brazil, we discovered that there were four distinct spirit religions which had grown out of the Yoruba traditions: Candomblé, Umbanda, Spiritism, and Quimbanda.

Candomblé is the oldest of the spirit religions. It is similar to the Yoruba tradition and uses the original Yoruba names for the orishas. However, it has added such Brazilian spirits as the Old Black Slave ("O Prêto Velho"), an archetypal black father image, and the Indians of the Seven Arrows, male and female "noble savages" who embody the best of the indigenous American Indian tradition. Fortunes are told by cowrie shells and religious services are led by middle-aged women, the "Mothers of Saints."

Umbanda places somewhat more of an emphasis on the Christian names of the saints than does Candomblé. It is organized into seven "lines"; each practitioner finds his or her "line" through a process resembling astrology and adopts the foods, colors, numbers, symbols, chants, incense, and perfume of that "line." In command of the "lines" are such orishas as Yemanjá, Oxalá, Ogun, Oxossi, Xangó, and Omulu.

Umbanda developed early in the twentieth century to serve the needs of people who wanted a religion more sophisticated than Candomblé yet more earthy than Spiritism. Umbanda allows both males and females of various ages to serve in its weekly ceremonies. The *macumba* is a Umbanda candle-and-drum ceremony. During the *macumba*, the orishas are contacted and are said to take over one's body for a short period of time.

Spiritism had its roots not only in the Yoruba tradition but also in Franz Anton Mesmer's theories of "animal magnetism." In this regard, the writings of the French Spiritist, Kardec, had been influential. Born on

October 4, 1804, Léon-Dénizarth-Hippolyte Rivail became interested in philosophy at an early age. He began to communicate with "spirits" through the ouija board and was told to use the name "Kardec" when writing the books they would dictate to him.

Kardec's best known volume was *The Spirits' Book*, which was brought from Europe to South America by a member of the Brazilian aristocracy in 1858. It was immediately translated into Portuguese and created a sensation. Celebrated psychic sensitives and mediums were interviewed for their reactions to it by newspapers which ran frequent commentaries on Kardec's point of view.

The Brazilians who had covertly yearned for a religion somewhat more intellectual than Candomblé converted eagerly to Spiritism (or "Kardecismo," as it was sometimes called). Here was a belief system that preserved what their black nurses had taught them, yet circumvented the drum beating, and played down the Yoruba orishas. Kardec proclaimed the immortality of the spirit which was said to enter the body at the moment of conception, choosing the family into which it wishes to be born. If individuals suffer in this life, it is because they are being punished for errors committed in a past life. If one is poor, it is because one abused wealth in a former life and needs to learn the lesson of poverty.

Kardec believed that the "spirit" is enveloped in a semimaterial body of its own, which he named the *perispirit*. The perispirit is composed of a magnetic fluid (or "aura") which contains a certain amount of electricity. Therefore, healing can be accomplished by psychic healers who send magnetic rays from their fingertips into the "auras" of ill persons. A healer can also magnetize water which can be utilized for healing purposes. These techniques involve physical "passes" similar to those originated by Mesmer. Psychic healers may also be mediums and communicate with "spirits," but these "spirits" are usually relatives, or distinguished doctors and teachers rather than orishas.

The practice of Candomblé, Umbanda, and Spiritism is protected by Brazilian law. Quimbanda, the fourth of the spirit religions, is illegal. It centers around the worship of Satan, thus provoking stern opposition from Brazil's Roman Catholic Church. The official Roman Catholic position regarding the other spirit religions is simply that Roman Catholicism and the native belief systems are incompatible.

I thought it possible that the spirit religions allow people to approach nature in an intimate way which is difficult for the more Europeanized Brazilians. The spirit religions may allow their practitioners to get closer to an aspect of reality ignored by "civilized" institutions and traditions. Carl Jung felt that this contact was important for the development of one's creativity, writing that "the poet now and then catches sight of the figures that people the night world—the spirits, demons, and gods. . . . In short, he sees something of that psychic world that strikes terror into the savage and the barbarian."

The image of the Ibeji twins is an appropriate one for the Brazilians who practice the spirit religions, thus uniting the worldly and unworldly planes of their existence. The result is a worldview both esoteric and practical. Further, many Brazilians do not believe in taking chances; like their ancestors before them, they attend Mass at the Roman Catholic church as well as participate in the rituals of the spirit religions.

Biological Organization

On the evening of April 15, we paid the first of several visits to the home of H. G. Andrade, director of the Brazilian Institute for Psychobiophysical Research. Andrade, a civil engineer who had been studying psychical research and Spiritism for four decades, took us to his laboratory to see his "Electromagnetic Space Tension Device." Built by Andrade and three of his sons, the device's purpose was to create a biological field by electromagnetic means. It was built from six electromagnets set in a position perpendicular to one another. Each time the electromagnets were fed by a continuous current, Andrade told us that space was "compressed" at the point where the extremities of the electromagnets converged. Inside the device was a compartment heated by a system of continuously circulating water. A similar stove had been placed in a different position, so as to keep to the same temperature but without being influenced by the electromagnetic field.

In a recent experiment, a bacteria culture was prepared in a nutrient broth. Three samples were taken and placed in sterilized glass containers. An accurate counting of the bacteria in all three containers was made. One of the containers was selected at random and placed in the compartment located in the magnetically compressed region of the device. The other two containers were placed in the other compartment which was shielded from electromagnetic influence. At the end of two hours, the three samples were again inspected. Even though instruments had demonstrated the temperature to be identical in the two compartments, the bacteria in the container subjected to magnetic compression multiplied more rapidly than those bacteria cultures placed in the shielded compartment.

Andrade interpreted these findings as suggestive of the existence of a "biological organizing model." An electrodynamic field, he postulated, surrounds and penetrates all living organisms. His experiment artificially enhanced this field, thus stimulating the growth of the bacteria. Andrade further speculated that the artificial enhancement of an organism's electro-dynamic field might be an excellent way to study the "bioplasmic body" spoken of by some Soviet scientists.

I told Andrade about the work of H. S. Burr, a Yale University profes-sor who set out to understand electrodynamic fields by measuring the differ-ence in voltage between two points on the surface of living organisims. He used a vacuum-tube voltmeter for these experiments because it required a minimum of current for its operation. When measuring the electrodynamic fields of human subjects, Burr usually placed one electrode on the forehead and the other on the chest. Alternatively, the index finger of each hand was dipped into bowls of saline solution connected to the voltmeter.

Among female subjects, these voltage measurements were found to be helpful in measuring the precise moment of ovulation because this event is preceded by a steady rise in voltage, which falls rapidly after the egg has been released. Abnormalities in the voltage measurments were found to give advance warnings of cancer in one study. In another study, high voltages were found to correlate with the subjects' psychological feelings of well-being, while low voltages were associated with negative statements and moods. It was discovered that wounds would change the voltage measure-ments and could serve as a useful measure of healing rate.

Burr referred to the electrodynamic fields identified by these measur-ments as "life-fields" or "L-fields." Noting that L-fields could be used to assess drug effects and the depth of hypnosis, Burr stated:

> L-field measurements are not only useful in diagnosing local conditions; they can also be used to assess the general state of the body as a whole, for these pure voltage differences—independent of any current flow or changes in skin resistance—reveal the state of the whole human force field. . . . And, as the force field extends beyond the surface of the`skin, it is some-times possible to measure field-voltages with the electrodes a short distance from the surface of the skin—*not* in contact with it.

This indicated to Burr that the L-field was a "true" field that was measured.

Burr maintained that L-fields help determine the growth of an organ-ism, just as Andrade hypothesized that there was a "biological organizing model" around each organism. Examining frogs' eggs, Burr noted different voltage gradients across different axes of the eggs. He marked the axis, or line, of the largest voltage gradient and later found, as the eggs developed, that a frog's nervous system always grew along that axis.

Burr found that he could segregate, with his technique, those seeds with superior growth characteristics from the others. And when he placed elec-trodes in the cambium layer of trees, he found correlations with such astro-physical events as sunspot activity. Investigating protoplasm, Burr discovered that a polar reversal of the voltage usually occurs just before there is a directional change in protoplasmic flow. I suggested to Andrade that Burr's L-fields showed close resemblance to his "biological organizing model" and that both appeared to correlate with the "bioplasmic body." One of Andrade's assistants rashly suggested that all three terms were merely scientific terms for the "perispirit" described by Kardec early in the nineteenth century.

There was also a Kirlian photography apparatus in Andrade's laboratory. We discussed a picture he had sent me earlier. It appeared to be the first replication of the Soviets' controversial "phantom leaf," in which the image of a leaf's cutaway portion is still visible when an electrophotograph is taken. We speculated as to whether the "phantom" portion of the leaf might also be evidence of the "biological organizing principle" spoken of earlier by Andrade.

The Federation

While Andrade was investigating Spiritism scientifically, practical application of Kardec's writings were being made at the Spiritist Federation of São Paulo, a large healing center we visited on April 16. Our hostess was Carmen Marinho, a medium who donated several hours of her time each week to the federation.

Marinho explained the procedure to us. Following a quick diagnosis of the visitor's problem, a colored ticket was handed out. The first phase of one's treatment involved a lecture in an auditorium where the sick people were told about Kardec and his belief that physical sickness reflected spiritual sickness. If one did not undergo spiritual growth, the physical sickness might disappear temporarily but would return.

Following the path of these patients, Villoldo and I went to the auditorium for the initial "pep talk" and then to one of several smaller rooms for the second phase of the treatment. A patient's colored ticket directs one to the correct room. In each of the rooms, "magnetic healers" work with one's "perispirit." Marinho guided us to one such room and each of us enjoyed the process. I sat before a smiling "magnetic healer" who began to move her hands and arms rhythmically around my body. I felt some tingling in various parts of my anatomy and was quite refreshed by the end of the treatment.

Villoldo had been suffering from a slight stomach ache and gave the following report:

I go and sit before a very large black woman who is standing directly in front of me. I feel very relaxed and breathe deeply as she proceeds to make certain movements in a criss-crossing fashion over each one of my chakras. I feel a release of tension in my stomach. A very light sensation envelops me. When she is done, she taps me on the shoulder lightly. I walk out of the room feeling very light and bouncy.

The last phase of treatment involved individual counseling with one of the federation's mediums, most of whom had been trained by Carmen Marinho and her husband Jarbas Marinho, an engineer.

The entire mediumistic training program would take three years to complete, including diagnosis, healing, spiritual counseling, and even "exorcism." In the latter cases, the patient would be placed in a circle of mediums, one of whom could "incorporate" an "evil spirit." Another medium, the "indoctrinator," would stand outside the circle and would speak with the "spirit." The "spirit" would be lured out of the patient's body and told to enter the body of the "incorporator." The patient would then be sent home. At this point, the "incorporator" would expunge the "spirit" from his or her own body, telling the "spirit" not to return.

Following our tour of the federation, Marinho took us to see its director, Carlos Jordão, a retired civil servant who donated all his time to the federation. Reputed to be one of the most outstanding psychic sensitives in Brazil, Jordão greeted us warmly and, turning to Villoldo, remarked, "You are originally from Cuba." This statement stunned us because Villoldo had told our friends in São Paulo only that he was Puerto Rican. However, it was true that Cuba had been his place of birth.

Jordão shared with us some impressive statistics; in the past year, over 40,000 patients had been seen monthly. Everyone at the federation was working on a volunteer basis. And the federation is only one of many such centers in Brazil; the number of Spiritist clinics, hospitals, orphanages, libraries, old people's homes, and schools for mentally handicapped children outnumbered those built by the Roman Catholic church and the Brazilian government combined.

Finding a Macumba

The little shop near our hotel contained statutes of the various Yoruba orishas or their Christian equivalents. It was also well stocked with the perfumes and incenses needed by the members of one Umbanda "line" or another. It was through the employees of the shop that we obtained an address of a home where we were able to attend a *macumba*, or drum-and-candle ceremony.

São Paulo, we were told, contains about fourteen loosely affiliated Umbanda bodies, each of which sponsors a number of *macumba* ceremonies. One of the functions of the despacho is to allow a benign "spirit" to enter the body of a medium, and through that medium to diagnose and treat illness. During these ceremonies, drums call the "spirits" to enter the mediums, candles help the mediums to enter altered states of consciousness, and incense purifies the mediums' bodies. Singing and chanting assure the "spirits" that they are respected and welcome.

Adherents to the Umbanda belief system assume that sickness can be dealt with by their rituals because illness is basically a spiritual malaise. One's indisposition can result from religious negligence, from "black magic" as practiced by Quimbanda, aftereffects of a previous incarnation, irregular perturbations in the bodily fluids caused by immature "spirits," undeveloped mediumship (in which case the antidote is to enter training as a medium), or the "evil eye." To ward off the "evil eye," many Umbandistas wear a sacred charm depicting a clenched fist. I later saw this same charm in Pompeii, and discovered that the clenched fist was used there for the same reason over 2,000 years ago.

The "spirits" which enter the Umbanda priests and priestesses may be one of several types. During the first session of the month (or of the week for those groups who meet several times weekly), the Indians of the Seven Arrows are usually present. During the second session, "Os Prêtos Velhos" —the Old Black Ones—make their appearance; these archetypal slaves often give herbal recipes for one's ailments. Next come the crianças, children who have died before the age of five. Later in the month, dead relatives and "spirits" from foreign countries may be present. And sometimes various "evil spirits" attempt to invade the priests' and priestesses' bodies, and must be repelled. The Yoruba orishas are highly respected and their pictures (or those of their Christian counterparts) are widely reproduced. But they could not enter a person's body or that individual would explode from the concentration of power.

I speculated on how the macumba might be the site of a weekly psychodrama in which each of the invading spirits could play a social role. The priests and priestesses could assume father roles as the Old Black Ones and maternal roles as female Indians of the Seven Arrows; they could regress to childhood as crianças and could allow their more exotic tendencies a release as foreign "spirits." The net result must be positive as I was told that the Umbandistas, like the Spiritists, emphasize charity, and run almost as many clinics, rest homes, orphanages, etc., as the followers of Kardec. A number of celebrated psychic healers, such as Dalmério and Isaltina, had their origins in Umbanda. Arigó, however, was a Spiritist; he reputedly performed operations with a pocket knife and, unfortunately, was never adequately studied by physicians or parapsychologists in the twenty years of his career.

As Villoldo and I walked into the home where the *macumba* was in progress, the drums were beating and the candles were flickering. The smell of incense was wafting through the room, and the priests and priestesses were singing to the Old Black Ones. We took our seats with the other spectators.

The altar contained dozens of statues and pictures of the entire panoply of deities and orishas. There were photographs of elderly people; we surmised that these persons were deceased, and that their "spirits" were encouraged to join the ceremonies. There was a high priest who appeared to be in charge of the proceedings as well as four other priests and five priestesses.

As the ritual continued, someone became "possessed," screamed, writhed, and fell to the floor, and eventually rose again and continued dancing. Most of the priests and priestesses were entered by the "spirits" several times over the course of the night.

Toward the end of the session, all the spectators who needed healing were assigned to someone by the high priest. I volunteered for the healing; a priest grabbed my hands, waved them above my head, moved them backward and forward, then quickly massaged my entire body.

The Spiritist healers had avoided contact with the physical body, preferring to work with the "perispirit." Not so the Umbandistas. Villoldo had been suffering from a pain in his back all day; the priest assigned to him moved his hands toward the area immediately and gave it an intensive massage. The pain did not return; both of us felt energized and refreshed even though it was late at night. It had been one of the most meaningful religious services I had ever attended.

A Sound Mind

On Wednesday, I was scheduled to deliver my paper on learning disabilities. I described how an intensive perceptual-motor training program I supervised had increased intelligence test scores of brain-injured children as well as their scores on language development and social maturity tests. Villoldo read the paper for me in Spanish and I delivered summaries in Portuguese and English.

Villoldo and I had dinner with Fiora Paola Filho and Cesário Hossri, two São Paulo psychiatrists. Dr. Paola told us about Mens Sana ("A Sound Mind"), at which he was a consultant. Mens Sana, a private psychiatric clinic, offered treatment based on traditional psychotherapeutic practices. However, Mens Sana utilized psychic sensitives to give an additional diagnosis of each patient.

Dr. Hossri had done pioneering work combining autogenic training with LSD in psychotherapy. He found that the voluntary control of internal states, for the purposes of relaxation, could be learned more quickly if small doses of LSD were administered before the training began. Hossri had also combined hypnosis and acupuncture in treating asthma among children. Instead of using needles, he used *shiatsu*, the Japanese massage, emphasizing six acupuncture points he found especially useful in bringing about relief from asthma.

On Thursday, Andrade discussed *sanskaras* with us, the physical or psychological traits which sometimes carry over from a past incarnation. A person who was strangled in one lifetime may have a neck scar in the next incarnation. The sanskaras carry over into another lifetime because of the "perispirit," the "spirit envelope" of which Kardec wrote. Andrade told us that the "perispirit" is most likely a "biological organizing model"; thus, any change in the "perispirit" would be reflected in the physical body.

I responded that a similar concept exists among the Hindus, who speak of the "Prânamâyakosha," or the vehicle of *Prana*—the vital energy common to all living organisms. In theosophical literature, a description is made of the "etheric body" which forms the basis of psi phenomena as well as serving as a connecting link between the human brain and even more subtle states of existence. Andrade again referred to his work with Kirlian photography and the "Electromagnetic Space Tension Device" in scientifically studying the "perispirit."

An Evening with Dona Regina

Our last evening in São Paulo was spent at a Spiritist center where the famed medium, Dona Regina Moura had agreed to hold a "healing séance" for us. Andrade told us that Dona Regina would be the working medium through whom the healing energy would be channeled. She would "incorporate" the "spirits" who would do the work. The Marinhos and several members of Andrade's family and staff joined us.

Dona Regina was a gentle, but vivacious woman with sparkling, dancing eyes. Although no longer young, she gave one a feeling of youthful strength by her vivacity. We began the session with several prayers asking for "healing power." We then joined hands, forming a healing circle. Soon, our hands began to shake and vibrate; Dona Regina assured us that the "healing power" was present.

Villoldo asked Dona Regina to attempt a healing of a close friend of his in New York City. After receiving the party's name from Villoldo, Dona Regina asked us to send "pink healing vibrations" to the distressed party. The medium then became very still.

A few minutes later, Dona Regina revived and told us that she had taken an "out-of-body" trip to New York, located Villoldo's friend, brought the friend's "perispirit" to São Paulo for healing, then transported it back to New York City. She gave Villoldo a description of his friend, which he confirmed as being accurate, and said that the young woman in question had a serious "spiritual problem" which was the basis for her physical ailment. Villoldo confessed that this was a perceptive statement with which he could agree.

Dona Regina's voice became somewhat strained and she asked us to direct "positive energies" toward her. She stated that these positive energies could be "generated" by visualizing a pleasant scene, a happy memory, or someone we loved. Then she shook violently for a few seconds, as if a wave had broken over her body, sending ripples of movement through every muscle. She clenched the table tightly, then slowly opened her eyes.

Dona Regina's eyes opened wide. Rarely did they blink. She spoke, and her quiet gentle voice was now the strong, deep, throaty vocalization of an old man. She announced that she had "incorporated" the "spirit" of "O Prêto Velho." Words of greeting were given to the Andrades and the Marinhos, whom he recognized from previous séances.

Villoldo and I were introduced to "O Prêto Velho." I was greeted in these words:

> I would like to welcome our visitor from the land of dreams. As a parapsychologist, you know the importance of human consciousness in your studies. But there is one thing you may not know. If the planet is to be saved, there must be an evolution of human consciousness. There must be more concern for humanity and more respect for the earth. Once human beings realize that they are part of the land and part of each other, they will be more loving and less destructive. Parapsychology can demonstrate this unity in scientific ways. And there are important people who will listen to scientists [but] who will not listen to mediums and artists and religious leaders many of whom also know that everything is part of one thing. It is hard work to be a parapsychologist. You have many enemies, both living and dead, who do not want to see parapsychology succeed. Therefore, your enemies will see to it that you are beset with problems—financial, legal, and personal. However, do not let these problems distract you from your goal; you must continue the struggle so that parapsychological findings enter the consciousness of people everywhere.

Villoldo looked at me, smiled, and said, "Right on." "O Prêto Velho" took his leave after telling me one more thing—that I had some psychic potential myself.

Almost immediately, Dona Regina "incorporated" the "spirit" of a man with a very cultured voice who had been a Spiritist leader in the nineteenth century. The voice told us of the need to relate Spiritism to the findings of science. The next voice coming from Dona Regina was less cultured and more brusque; it was purportedly the "spirit" of the same man as had appeared previously—but in a later incarnation. Instead of discussing Spiritism, the voice had personal messages for those present from friends and relatives "on the other side."

As Dona Regina regained her composure, we questioned her about the experiences. As was true of Eileen Garrett, Dona Regina said she remembered little during any of her sessions. However, she spoke with zest of Spiritist theory and how pleased she was that "O Prêto Velho" had made one of his appearances while we were there.

Are We Ever Reborn?

Upon returning to the United States, Villoldo and I agreed that our Brazilian adventure had given us a great deal to think about. One challenge was the concept of reincarnation which Andrade and his fellow scientists took for granted.

I reread some of the cases suggestive of reincarnation meticulously collected by Ian Stevenson over the years. One interesting case involved Suleyman Andary, a Lebanese boy who was born in 1954. As a small child, Andary claimed that he had lived before in a village called Gharife where he had owned an olive oil press. In his sleep he would often mutter the names of his children in the past life.

At the age of eleven, Andary remembered that his previous name had been Abdallah Abu Hamdan and that he had been the *muktar*, or mayor, of his town. Out of curiosity, Andary and his relatives located a village named Gharife and visited it in 1967. They discovered that a man named Abdallah Abu Hamdan had indeed lived in Gharife. He had owned an olive oil press and had been the village muktar for about fifteen years before his death in 1942 at the age of sixty-five. Andary had correctly stated the names of several of Hamdan's children.

Stevenson first studied the case in 1968. Andary was able to identify the building in Gharife which had housed the olive oil press as well as several people who had known Hamdan.

How are these observations to be explained? Perhaps much information had come to Andary before Stevenson first interviewed him, especially during his 1967 visit to Gharife. Perhaps the entire incident was fraudulent, representing an attempt to obtain recognition and money from a foreigner. Perhaps Andary was a psychic sensitive and had clairvoyantly picked up the information about Hamdan in dreams or in waking imagery. Or perhaps, as Stevenson has pointed out, parapsychologists must take the notion of reincarnation seriously.

For me, the most reasonable explanation of reincarnation-type phenomena was put forward by William Wolf, my endocrinologist friend, in one of the last articles he wrote before his death in 1971. His paper, which appeared in the *Journal for the Study of Consciousness*, was titled "Are We Ever Reborn?" In it, he described how during the body's disintegration and diffusion at death, many of the energy complexes and combinations that had constituted the body during its lifetime do not break down completely into elementary particles. Instead, they remained as structured, combined entities for varying periods of time.

Those energy clusters from human beings who lived some years ago, according to Wolf, might well float around in the cosmos, ready to be picked up and then assimilated by some organism that happens to be present. Not only must the organism be present at the right time and place to assimilate the energy complex, but its process of development must be such that the assimilation can take place. If this occurs, the energy cluster becomes a part of the living person and may function as a quality of that person's memory. Wolf described the energy complexes by stating:

> We might best view them as configurations, structures, or organized units of primary undifferentiated energy, which may have become assembled thousands of years ago and may have been part of succeeding generations of human or any kind of nonhuman organism. . . . Such a transmitter might well be an energy configuration, a pattern or template for something like DNA, RNA, an enzyme, a protein, polypeptide or similar compound.

Wolf reiterated that these complexes could be picked up by an organism providing that they would "fit a lock" or "fill a vacuum," reflecting a particular need of the organism.

Wolf's thesis was perfectly consistent with Andrade's description of sanskaras, the psychological or physical marks of a previous life. Wolf's energy complexes could serve as the stimuli for the development of sanskaras. Andrade's belief that one learns in the present life what one had not learned in former incarnations was consistent with Wolf's statement that the energy complexes could be picked up by a living person providing that they fulfilled a need in that organism's development. Wolf's speculations would also explain why in some of the cases collected by Stevenson, the person interviewed gave information about two dead people who lived at the same time rather than one.

Parapsychologists in Collision

Villoldo and I had observed many interesting phenomena in Brazil, but most of them were manifestations of social psychology rather than parapsychology. The psychic healers could have located Villoldo's pains through observing his body movements. Our healing sessions could have revived us through the placebo effect and the power of suggestion. Dona Regina's statement about Villoldo's sick friend was so general it could have applied to many people.

But what about Jordão's correct identification of Villoldo as a Cuban when we visited the Spiritist Federation? And what about the "phantom leaf" produced in Andrade's electrophotography laboratory?

When Villoldo and I brought back news about Andrade's "phantom leaf," Thelma Moss was very encouraged, as she had cut apart hundreds of leaves in a vain attempt to find a "phantom." Furthermore, there had been a statistical study reported by Karen Coen in which fingertip coronas were found to be related to the amount of the skin's surface area exposed, but not to one's health or to one's alcohol intake. Coen concluded, "As pressure increased, surface area increased, corona size decreased and the corona became more sparse."

At the same time, William Tiller reported a simple explanation for the color effects in electrophotography:

> The process for the generation of light in high-voltage (Kirlian) photography is the "streamer" process of corona discharge. This involves the generation and transport of ions in the air space between the driving electrode and the living system. Recombination of ions, notably those of nitrogen, lead to light generation in the blue and ultraviolet range. Thus, film should only show blue and white colors if such radiations are incident on the film emulsion.

However, Tiller continued,

> If film buckling or a film-driving electrode gap of about 0.001 inches were to occur, "streamers" could be developed between the back side of the color film and the driving electrode which exposes the red and green layers of the film to varying degrees. This would provide additional color patterns in the red, orange, yellow, and green range.

While Tiller and Moss were attempting to unravel the complexities of electrophotography, both scientists were attacked by two eminent parapsychologists: R. A. McConnell in the *Journal of the American Society for Psychical Research,* and J. B. Rhine in the *Journal of Parapsychology.* In my own writings on acupuncture and Kirlian photography, I had made it clear that their relationship to psychical phenomena was unknown. However, the possibility that they might some day interface with parapsychology was reason enough to keep in touch with the developing research in these areas. They certainly should not be dismissed unless positively disproven.

While Tiller and Moss were under siege in parapsychology's two most important journals, they found themselves in collision in regard to the "phantom leaf" effect. Encouraged by the reports from Brazil, Moss and her students again started to cut leaves apart. Eventually, one of the students, a laboratory assistant, John Hubacher, produced dramatic pictures which appeared to show the "phantom" effect.

Several procedures appeared to facilitate the emergence of the "phantom": placing a metallic disc on top of the thin glass plate used in electrophotography, and placing two thick glass cover slips under and above the leaf (creating a "sandwich"). Moss then arranged to have a film made of the "phantom." Much to her surprise, she found that it "pulsed"; it would appear vividly, fade away, and then appear once more.

Tiller's reaction to the "phantom leaf" was skeptical. He suggested that the "phantom" pictures which Moss had sent him could just as easily have been due to a discharge from the piece of metal utilized.

Once again, the outcome of an important development in parapsychology was one of frustration. Who was correct? Is the "phantom leaf" one of the great discoveries of the age? Perhaps so. Or perhaps the "phantom" is an artifact resulting from the complexities of the electrophotographic process which themselves are not yet fully understood.

9

PSYCHOTRONICS IN PRAGUE

The human being has a potential that goes beyond it. What all that potential can be, no one yet can know. All of that is the promise of the future. The thing the psi discovery does right now is make the promise. . . . Parapsychological abilities may someday be put to work and if they are, the result can benefit mankind very greatly. But whether or not they ever are, the very fact that they exist opens a big window for man's outlook.

Louisa Rhine

Ping-Pong Balls and ESP

In 1973, Montague Ullman resigned as director of the Maimonides Community Mental Health Center so that he could devote more of his time to parapsychology. The dream lab became the "Division of Parapsychology and Psychophysics"; Charles Honorton and I became senior research associates in the division, and a number of eminent scientists, including T. X. Barber, Barbara Brown, and Gardner Murphy, agreed to serve on the advisory board. Ullman and I wrote a book, *Dream Telepathy*, about our work at Maimonides.

I was still spending less time at Maimonides and more time with the Humanistic Psychology Institute. However, Honorton continued to explore the relationship between ESP and altered states of consciousness, encouraged by a partial replication of his work with hypnotic dreams by Adrian Parker and John Beloff at the University of Edinburgh.

Honorton noted that states of consciousness which facilitate ESP appear to be characterized by a withdrawal of attention from the external world and a shift toward internal thoughts and images. Honorton also recalled that Patanjali and other commentators on yoga called for preparatory exercises to remove impediments to concentration if *siddhis,* or paranormal abilities, were to occur. Apparently, decreasing the irrelevant stimulation of a

186

subject during an ESP test increases the accessibility of psi, which is ordinarily weak and undetectable.

With these ideas in mind, Honorton enlisted thirty volunteer subjects to take part in a telepathy experiment involving the careful regulation of one's perceptual input. A subject was seated in a soundproof room adjoining the lab, with halved ping-pong balls fastened over the eyes. A red light was placed six inches in front of the subject's face and a recording of the seashore was played through headphones; both procedures were designed in an attempt to keep the incoming stimulation the same for all subjects. Before headphones were placed on the subjects' ears, instructions were given to "keep your eyes open" and "report all of the images, thoughts, and feelings which pass through your mind."

In the meantime, a telepathic transmitter in a distant room began to look through a 3-D viewer at the pictures on a randomly selected Viewmaster stereoscopic reel. Following the sessions, subjects selected the Viewmaster reel containing the pictures which corresponded most closely with their imagery. As there were always four reels to choose from, one would expect —by chance alone—seven or eight correct choices by the subjects. Instead, there were thirteen correct choices, a number that is statistically significant.

When the Viewmaster reel was "The American Indian," the subject reported imagery of "a long highway in Mexico" and an "American Indian's arrow." When the reel was "The U.S. Air Force Academy," the subject reported images of "an airplane," "an army uniform," "a mountain range," and "flying through the mountain."

In retrospect, Honorton noted the frequency with which some subjects recalled personal memories that corresponded with the appropriate Viewmaster reel. For example, the subject who talked about Mexico and American Indians associated his images to Carlos Castaneda's book *Journey to Ixtlan,* which he had just read. These observations support the theory that no new information is "sent" during telepathy but that the telepathic receiver is stimulated to recall experiences which correspond to the material being observed by the transmitter.

Honorton also performed a statistical analysis on the results of his study using the "psi quotient" technique designed by Helmut Schmidt, one of J. B. Rhine's associates. A "psi quotient" tests the efficiency of an experiment; therefore, several techniques for producing ESP can be compared to see which one is the most useful. The ping-pong ball technique obtained a "psi quotient" of 148, in comparison to "psi quotients" of 29 for our dream studies, 28 for the witches' cradle experiments, and 8 for the work with hypnotic dreams. It was reassuring to know that an experimental procedure which utilized inexpensive equipment was, at the same time, highly effective in bringing ESP to the surface.

The Happening on Peace Square

In the meantime, I was preparing for the First International Congress on Psychotronic Research, meeting in Prague, having obtained a travel grant from the Erickson Educational Foundation. I agreed to Zdeněk Rejdák's request that I serve as chairperson of the anthropology session. The conference opened on June 18,1973. Over 250 scientists had registered from twenty-one different nations; they gathered on Peace Square in the Railway Workers' House of Culture.

For the next three days, the congress participants attended sectional meetings which covered the relationship of psychotronics (the term they used instead of parapsychology) to such areas as anthropology, physics, education, and biology.

We also saw the first public demonstration of a "psychotronic generator," one of several devices built by Robert Pavlita, a retired Czech engineer. Jana Pavlitova, the engineer's daughter, touched the side of her head and then touched the tip of the generator. After these motions had been repeated several times, a small carousel was placed on the generator's tip. The carousel began to rotate, purportedly because the energy stored in the device was now being "generated" and put to work.

One night Tofik Dadashev, a Soviet psychic sensitive, attempted to demonstrate telepathy. Lois Bird, an American psychologist, served as the subject and decided on a conference participant she would direct Dadashev to identify. Dadashev was blindfolded and, to further rule out visual clues, a hood was placed over his head and tied at the throat.

Dadashev, his hands stretched out before him like a somnambulist, started to walk through the aisles which separated the conference tables. Bird initially followed him, then was instructed to go to the stage and concentrate on the person she had selected. Dadashev eventually stopped near a woman, told her to stand, then asked her to sit down. Dadashev then summoned the man in the next chair to lead him to the stage. The man was Cleve Backster, the American polygraph expert. And Backster was the person Bird had silently selected.

The demonstration was impressive but not conclusive. When I have seen American mentalists do the same thing as a magic trick, they have the subject lead them by the hand, or by a handkerchief both people are holding. The task then becomes one of "muscle reading," in which the mentalist knows by muscular clues when the subject is near the selected person.

The demonstration by Dadashev was successful despite the fact that the subject was not in direct proximity with the psychic sensitive. However, the circumstances do not rule out the possibility that Bird could have emitted clues while she was trailing Dadashev on the auditorium floor. In addition, she could have directed her attention toward Backster from the stage and her unconscious signaling (through gestures and glances) could have been picked up by the audience—and directed to Dadashev. Further, Bird's husband, Christopher, had coauthored a book, *The Secret Life of Plants*, which dealt extensively with Backster, thus making him a likely choice. Alternative explanations need to be carefully considered in the case of Dadashev as he was the man who drove a car blindfolded in the film I had seen in Moscow, a feat which I concluded to be due to "reading" the muscular tension of the person seated beside Dadashev in the automobile.

An impromptu demonstration was given during the day when a Czech dowser lost his glasses. Frances Farrelly, a medical technician and psychic sensitive, was summoned. Farrelly asked for a floor plan of the cavernous Railway Workers' House of Culture. She looked at the floor plan, rubbed her fingers on the table, and asked questions of the floor plan—finding that her fingers stuck to the table whenever a "yes" answer was indicated. A few minutes later, Farrelly went to the third floor, accompanied by a coterie of curious scientists. She pointed to a storeroom. When it was opened, the glasses were inside; a custodian had put the glasses there for safekeeping after finding them the previous night.

Provocative phenomena had characterized Farrelly's appearance at conferences ever since I had known her. The conference participants were additionally impressed with Farrelly when it was mentioned that her talents in psychic diagnosis of medical problems had been described in *Breakthrough to Creativity*, a book by Shafica Karagulla, who was also at the congress. Farrelly, for many years, had worked with physicians, often attempting diagnosis from a single drop of blood sent to her through the mail. The interest of the Eastern Europeans in psychic healing made Farrelly one of the most popular people at the conference.

The East-West Detente

We were curious to see who would attend the congress from the USSR. Adamenko did not attend the Prague meetings, nor did Inyushin, Vilenskaya, or the other researchers I had met in Moscow. However, the Soviet representatives who did show up were an impressive group.

Y. A. Kholodov, a biophysicist, spoke on the work he had done to elucidate the effects of electromagnetic fields on the brain. Kholodov had experimented with birds, rabbits, and fish, discovering that certain portions of their brains were more easily stimulated by electromagnetic fields than were other portions. Further, the motor activity of the organisms increased when they were surrounded by a constant electromagnetic field. However, a number of animals, fish, and birds suffered brain damage if the electromagnetic fields were too strong. Kholodov also noted that living organisms produce their own electromagnetic fields; these fields can even be detected at the cellular level.

Alexander Dubrov advanced the theory that all living organisms emit gravitational waves. This process, he said, may explain the energy relationships during the transformation of cell particles from a liquid state to a crystalline state in the process of mitosis, or cell division. This gravitational effect, referred to as "biogravity" by Dubrov, may also be the mechanism behind PK.

Dubrov then presented evidence from experiments with polarizing microscopes (which divide different types of light for easier observation) to support his theory that high frequency oscillations, or rhythmic movements, of the cell's molecules can generate biogravitational waves and propagate them over long distances. He went on to point out that photons as well as ultrasonic sound can be observed emanating from cells as they divide. He connected these rhythmic events to biogravitational waves and then proposed that the human brain could act as a unit, coordinating the biogravitational waves to produce observable effects. What might some of these effects be? Dubrov listed several:

> . . . to initiate movement of distant objects, to ionize the air during intensive mental activity, to induce fluorescence of crystals in psychokinesis, to expose a film placed at a remote distance from the subject, to generate reactions in plants, and to accelerate or slow down the setting of colloid solutions. It is possible that all the cases mentioned are related to the biogravitational field which is generated by specialized brain structures.

In other words, human consciousness could coordinate the naturally occurring gravitational waves emitted by dividing cells and produce any number of psi phenomena.

How could these waves be detected? Dubrov spoke of the bioplasma detector constructed by G. A. Sergeyev and his associates for use in their experiments with Kulagina. Dubrov stated that the bioplasma and biogravitational waves are closely related.

Dubrov ended his presentation by relating his theory of biogravitation to the research by the Gauquelins in France on planetary effects on human personality and by Jonas in Czechoslovakia on cosmic influences on the menstrual cycle. He said: "We are forced, therefore, to recognize the ability of gravitational forces of cosmic origin to change the parameters of the space-time continuity in which there are genetically important cell molecules."

In conclusion, Dubrov predicted that the organism's biogravitation field would soon join the already acknowledged electrostatic and electromagnetic fields of organisms as important determinants of behavior.

A. G. Bakirov, a mineralogist, noted that he has used rods and other instruments to "dowse," producing what Soviet scientists termed the "biophysical effect." He told about dowsers who had located ore deposits over 3,000 feet underground. Other dowsers, according to Bakirov, have made accurate geological maps from helicopters. Soviet researchers have reported additional work with dowsers, noting that earth tremors had been detected through dowsing, suggesting its possible application as an early warning system for earthquakes.

Several of these scientists were members of the prestigious USSR Academy of Sciences. We speculated that their presence was an invitation for additional cooperation and communication on the topic of parapsychology —but only at the highest levels of scientific respectability.

The Czechoslovak Contribution

Many of the most interesting papers were those presented by Czechoslovakian scientists. In addition to Pavlita's demonstration, a simple PK device was displayed—and moved—by Julius Krmessky, a physicist who "finds a spot" on the object to be moved. He then stares at the "spot" and in many cases the object will begin to indicate movement. Because of the large crowds at his demonstration, however, it was impossible to rule out wind drafts and floor vibration as the sources of the object's movement.

Jiri Bradna described his experiments with the electromyograph or EMG, which measures muscle tension. By attaching the EMG to humans, animals, and plants, Bradna has charted influences from distant organisms. The muscular activity of his pigeons has reportedly been able to affect the movement of philodendron plants over distance through PK. He claimed that a human transmitter could "send" muscle tension to a human receiver, and showed EMG charts in which the transfer could be observed. Bradna claimed that the optimal germination time for seeds is related to the time at which the influence of humans is strongest on the plants from which the seeds came. He explained these phenomena in terms of "bioenergetic fields" which surround human organisms.

Josef Wolf, an anthropologist, held that psychotronic abilities are supportive of human freedom, and of the person's refusal to be subordinated to technology. Wolf predicted that psychotronic factors will someday take their place with the biological and mental aspects of personality. He concluded that psychotronics would be especially useful in the prevention and treatment of psychosomatic illness.

One of the most interesting conference participants was Josef Zezulka, Prague's best-known psychic healer. He maintained that there are three components to personality: psychological, somatic, and the "vital force." Psychic healing, he said, could be used to treat deficiencies in each of these areas.

An American participant, Shelby Parker, complained of severe pain in her hip one morning before our session convened. I asked Zezulka if he would be willing to attempt to alleviate her pain. He agreed, and before the assemblage, performed a laying-on of hands which Parker described as extremely effective in reducing her discomfort.

No Psychotronic Golem

The final day of the congress was June 24 and the sectional chairpersons were called upon to give summaries of their sections' activities. In presenting my remarks on the psychotronics and anthropology section, I expressed the feeling of our group that

1. Psychotronic research must be an interdisciplinary field since it represents an interaction between the person and the environment. The person's physical as well as the person's social environment must be studied. Examples of specific fields which affect this integration are psychosomatic medicine, acupuncture, and Kirlian photography.
2. The end products of a person's psychotronic development are wholeness, an expansion of consciousness, and a heightened awareness. Therefore, if psychotronic phenomena are to be understood in their proper perspective, research should emphasize the healthy aspects of personality functioning, rather than psychopathology.
3. Not only must the person conquer fear when facing his or her psychotronic abilities, but science must conquer fear when deciding whether or not to investigate these phenomena. The difficulty in accepting a changed worldview has held back investigation of psychotronics for many years, but must no longer be an impediment to understanding the entire human system and the part that psychotronics play in that system. Accurate publications in scientific journals and the popular press, as well as suitable presentations in other communication media, can assist this development.
4. Psychotronic research must emphasize the dignity of the person in its experiments. We should oppose any research projects which treat people as objects and as machines. We should urge that an ethics committee be organized by an organization, to be known as the

International Association for Psychotronic Research, to establish guidelines for scientists to follow. This is especially important in doing psychotronic research with primitive people and with the effects of space travel on the psychotronic ability of humans.

5. Eventually, the findings of psychotronic research will be applied to human problems. As this is done, we should insist that psychotronics be used for the enhancement of human freedom and social development, rather than for regimentation and enslavement. Preventive medicine, healing, and creativity represent possible applications of psychotronics.

6. Psychotronics can play a role in contributing to humankind's survival. By emphasizing the connections among all living things, psychotronics can help develop the antiaggressive, peaceful tendencies of the person; psychotronics can underscore the historical development of humans to form societies which advocate social justice and which foster cooperation rather than competition. This cooperation must develop among nations as well as between individuals.

I concluded by recalling the legendary story of Rabbi Low, who investigated paranormal phenomena in Prague centuries ago. Jewish folklore maintains that one of his creations was the Golem, a robot that did the rabbi's bidding, carrying heavy objects, delivering messages, and performing simple tasks. However, Rabbi Low refused to give the Golem orders on the Jewish day of rest and, on one of those days, the Golem ran amuck, terrifying Prague. The Golem had to be destroyed, and the scientific expertise leading to its creation was purportedly forgotten. I stated,

Those of us working in the twentieth century do not wish to create a psychotronic Golem. We must insist that the fruits of our science be directed toward the advancement of human potential and toward the enhancement of life on planet Earth.

Several other conference chairpeople had called for the creation of an International Association for Psychotronic Research. Elections were held; Rejdák was elected president, and I was elected vice-president for the Western Hemisphere.

Dinner in Montreal

One of my duties was to meet with Rejdák in January 1974, to discuss the future direction of the Association. In the meantime, however, another surprise was in store for me. For years, Charlotte Bühler had wanted me to allow my name to be entered for the presidency of the Association for

Humanistic Psychology. In 1973 I agreed and shortly after my return from Prague I was elected.

The annual meeting of the group was held in Montreal and John Levy, the organization's executive officer, had invited Bühler to return from West Germany to give the featured address. In March, she wrote me her misgivings about the proposed speech:

> John Levy invited me in such an honoring way to give this presentation in Montreal. . . . I am not a user of drugs and I am not telepathic and also the other heightened states of consciousness about which you know so much are not available to me. But I could speak about my growing awareness of human beings finding each other and understanding human needs. Tell me frankly what you think about that and whether you would be willing to read a draft of my talk and to be honestly critical about it.

Before I had a chance to reply, Bühler wrote me another letter in which she expressed even graver doubts about her suitability for the address:

> Ever since I accepted the honoring invitation . . ., I am increasingly feeling misgivings about this task. The reason is my impression that in its present development, humanistic psychology is growing in completely new directions which lie, if not beyond my capabilities, certainly beyond any experiences that I can participate in here. I admire the enthusiasm with which the younger group is developing experiments in biofeedback, extension of consciousness, meditation and other new states of mind, but I can speak of none of these things which interest them, from experience. . . . All in all, I wonder whether I should not withdraw from appearing . . . and I ask you . . . to give me your honest opinion.

I wrote Bühler a very blunt letter in which I told her that her concerns were absolutely ridiculous. In the first place, there was nothing important in the realm of human experience that she could learn from drugs, meditation, or biofeedback that she did not already know. In the second place, she had great insight on the very factors that produce expanded awareness: the integration of life experiences, the power of love to transform personality, and the emergence of creativity as proof of an evolved consciousness. "Charlotte," I said in my letter, "what you call the 'younger group' of students and psychologists can learn more about consciousness from you than they can from anybody else. Come to Montreal."

A few weeks later, Bühler replied:

> Your letter was the greatest consolation for me because I think very highly of your judgment. It has consoled me so that now I am quite confident. . . . May I congratulate you also for having been elected president; I wished for that very much. . . . Let us have dinner in Montreal.

Bühler sent me a copy of her address, I made a few suggestions and returned it to her. She came to Montreal, delivered the paper from a wheelchair, and received a standing ovation.

Bühler and I had dinner in Montreal. I gave her a copy of *Dream Telepathy* and she reminisced about her husband, Karl Bühler. Freud had been the best man at their wedding. And once a month, over a period of several years, Karl Bühler met in Vienna with a handful of psychotherapists who were interested in psychic phenomena. Some of their patients had reported dreams which corresponded to incidents in the therapists' personal lives. It was from just such a series of meetings that Montague Ullman developed his plans to investigate telepathic dreams scientifically, thus creating the Maimonides Dream Laboratory.

A Most Joyous Teacher

Upon returning to California, I had a telephone call from Joan Tabernik, Alan Watts's daughter. She was about to open a school for brain-injured children and wanted to meet with me to hear about alternatives to the stimulant drugs characteristically used to assist the concentration of these students. We made an appointment to see each other on November 16 at California State College, Sonoma, where I was scheduled for a talk.

Tabernik did not meet me at the college; her father had died in his sleep that night. It was my sad duty to tell the college community of Watts's death before I spoke. I knew that he would not want us to be sad and solemn, so I recalled some of the joyous events of our long relationship. I told the students how, in 1966, Lelie and I had been married in Evanston, Illinois, in the Presbyterian church which I had attended during my years at Northwestern University. Later that same year, we were married again, in Brooklyn's Spencer Memorial Presbyterian Church. This time, Alan Watts officiated, conducting a strikingly beautiful Buddhist service.

I remembered two pieces of advice he gave us. First, he said, do not expect your marriage partner to change. If anything, people become more eccentric as they grow older, so full acceptance is the key to a happy marriage. Second, do not be possessive. If you are on the beach and try to see how much sand you can hold in your hand, the tighter you hold on, the less you have. If you keep your hand open, much more sand will remain in it. So it is with love; the tighter you hold on, the less you have. Further, if the marriage is truly successful, you will end up loving more and more people as the years go, simply because deep love is contagious and cannot be circumscribed or contained. Thus, possessiveness has no place in a loving relationship.

When the news of Watts's death reached the Esalen Institute, Michael Murphy wrote an appropriate eulogy:

> If you wanted a marriage performed, a building or a bathtub blessed, a mass celebrated (in the High Episcopalian manner, with Roman and Orthodox touches added), a Buddhist prayer invoked for the New Year, or a grace said at meals, he was usually the first person we asked. Sometimes when he came to lead a seminar, we would find him in the kitchen, preparing one of his well-known dishes or admiring the latest vegetable from the Big Sur garden or letting us know that the cooking wasn't up to our usual standards.
>
> So he taught us by who he was. We learned from his infectious, outrageous laughter, from his virtues and his faults, from his sense of play and his eye for the binds we would get ourselves into. He was our gentlest and most joyous teacher.

Biogravitation in Action

Toward the end of 1973, I received news from the USSR concerning two psychic sensitives who had come under recent investigation. Larisa Vilenskaya wrote about someone she referred to as "I.V." A man in his fifties, with little formal education, I. V. had been a psychic healer for three decades.

Vilenskaya, a specialist on the dermaloptical effect (or skin vision), found that I. V. could correctly recite a sentence written on a piece of paper and placed in his hand. I. V. was blindfolded and a shield was placed between his eyes and his hands. Nevertheless, he passed his hand over the piece of paper, crumpled it, and identified the words. Vilenskaya commented:

> We are not dealing here as much with "skin vision" in the traditional sense of the word, as with a special type of "psychometry." By using a piece of paper as a "psychometric" object, I. V. evidently sets up a telepathic contact with the person from whom he has received it.

In regard to I. V.'s psychic healing abilities, Vilenskaya reported that sick people began to feel better when they came into contact with I. V., whether or not they had been told that he was a psychic healer. This would suggest that a field effect took place; possibly I. V.'s bodily bioelectric fields were conducive to the restoration of health.

During formal healing sessions, I. V. entered an altered state of consciousness in which he was hardly aware of his surroundings. In this state, he could move about and even leave the house. On one occasion, he disappeared for three days and had no idea what had happened to him when he finally returned.

The other subject was Boris Ermolaev, a Soviet film director. He was investigated by V. N. Pushkin, the psychologist who had been my host at the Academy of Pedagogical Sciences in 1971. Pushkin wrote:

> Our preliminary work with . . . Ermolaev indicates the presence of psychokinetic phenomena. In a typical experiment, Ermolaev concentrates on a number of objects resting upon a table—a matchbox, a tennis ball, a few pencils. After a period of concentration, Ermolaev directs his attention on one of the objects and it moves from its resting place.

At times, Ermolaev would lift up a spherical object, such as a tennis ball, squeeze it between his palms, and slowly move his hands apart. On several occasions, the object would remain suspended in space. The distance between Ermolaev's hands could extend as far as eight inches and the object would still remain suspended. Further, it was noted that the greater the surface of the object, the longer it remained suspended in the air.

Pushkin explained these phenomena on the basis of the biogravity hypothesis of Alexander Dubrov. If living systems can produce and control gravitational waves, these waves could move the items on the table and keep the ball suspended in the air. A ball with a greater surface area would remain suspended for a longer period of time because there would be more surface for the gravitational waves to act upon than in the case of balls with less of a surface area. Pushkin noted that biogravity may help to stabilize one's perceptual world, then concluded:

> According to the general theory of relativity, gravitation originates in systems in which space has been distorted. Ermolaev is able to distort space to such an extent that a temporary gravitational field is produced in which objects obey his perceptions of them.

Ermolaev was asked how he suspended the objects and responded, "I do not try to get an object to hover; all my energy is concentrated on the way to remove my hands from the object they are holding."

After reading about the two new Soviet psychic sensitives, I was impressed by the role that states of consciousness played in their abilities. Later news from Moscow indicated that Ermolaev had developed healing abilities, especially for individuals suffering from migraine headaches. However, I still wished that the Soviet scientists would prepare well-documented articles for publication in the professional journals, rather than writing letters or filing reports in the popular press.

January in Czechoslovakia

On January 3, 1974, I returned to Prague. I was accompanied on the trip by Mark Rojek, a former student at Kent State University. Rojek and I spent several days with Rejdák and his staff. We discussed current developments in psychotronics and enjoyed hearing several stories concerning Rejdák's investigation of Nina Kulagina in 1968. After examining her entire body with a sensitive compass for hidden magnets, Rejdák asked her to move objects from a distance. She compiled readily, having greatest success with Rejdák's gold wedding ring. Kulagina was reexamined for hidden magnets three more times as she moved matches, dishes, glasses, and a compass needle. Rejdák noted that the Soviet scientists who were examining Kulagina suspected that she unconsciously accumulated bioplasma in certain parts of her body, then "tore it off" and sent it in the direction of an object. As the bioplasma collided with the object, it initiated the object's movement.

On January 5, Rejdák and his staff drove us to Lázne Belchrad, a town famous for its health spa. This community was also the home of Robert Pavlita, designer of the psychotronic generators. As we drove to Lázne Belchrad, Rejdák told us that Pavlita, as an engineer, had directed a development program for the Czechoslovakian textile industry, inventing an entire series of automatic machines to cut and fold material. In his spare time, over a thirty-year period, the engineer had devoted himself to PK experiments, eventually discovering a way in which the human body could impart "psychic energy" to a machine. Pavlita claimed that the machine would accumulate the energy, then transform it into an externally observable effect.

Initially, Pavlita's psychotronic generators were treated with skepticism by the Czech press; Milan Ryzl, the parapsychologist who left Czechoslovakia to take up residence in the United States, suggested that the supposed PK effects were actually caused by air currents. However, Pavlita continued to perfect his generators, finally producing a device which—according to Rejdák—left no doubt as to the psychotronic nature of the effect.

We were given a hospitable greeting by Pavlita, and asked him how he began to study psychotronics. Pavlita, in the company of his wife, his daughter, and his son-in-law, told us that he began his investigations by training himself to do PK, principally by attempting to direct the movement of small pieces of wood floating on water. He soon realized that if an object is moving, the movement must involve energy. If something involves energy, that energy can be inducted, accumulated, generated, and put to work.

Pavlita claimed to have discovered that the body's "psychic energy" or "bioenergy" fields act electromagnetically in some PK experiments, electrostatically in some experiments, and—in still other experiments—in ways that defy either an electromagnetic or an electrostatic explanation.

Any individual can work with a psychotronic generator, according to

Pavlita, because all people have "bioenergy fields." Since his retirement from the textile industry, Pavlita had devoted himself to a study of psychotronics, identifying at least sixty-eight "bioenergy centers" or "biocircuits" in the human body, and inventing a generator to accumulate the energy from each of these centers.

The design of the generators was influenced by Pavlita's study of Egyptian manuscripts and alchemy texts; certain designs in each source corresponded and Pavlita built his devices along those lines. I recalled Carl Jung's interest in alchemy; he stated that the nature of light was the central mystery of alchemical philosophy.

Demonstration #1

Most of our time together was spent in a series of demonstrations of the generators. For the first demonstration, Pavlita placed a compass directly in front of him on a table. He then put a psychotronic generator between himself and the compass. This particular generator consisted of a steel rectangle covered by a cone.

After lifting off the cone (which served as a shielding device) and setting it aside, Pavlita passed the rectangular generator over the compass; the compass needle did not move. Pavlita then began to touch the generator to the right-hand side of his head (an area called the right temporal lobe). He held the generator in his right hand and made contact with his head in a rhythmical manner, explaining that he was "completing a circuit of human bioenergy," thus permitting the generator to accumulate the energy.

After about two minutes of this procedure, Pavlita again held the generator over the compass. This time, the needle moved five degrees, from south to north.

Next, Pavlita removed three of his fingers from the generator, placing them under the palm of his hand. As the generator approached the compass, the south-to-north movement of the needle exceeded fifteen degrees. By altering the position of his fingers on the rectangular form in other ways, Pavlita was able to increase or decrease the effect upon the compass needle.

Demonstration #2

The second demonstration was identical to the first demonstration except that Pavlita held the rectangular generator with his left hand and touched it to the left side of his head. The compass needle, when approached by the generator, moved the same number of degrees as before, except in a north-to-south direction. Then Pavlita lifted the generator with his left hand and placed it in his right hand. The compass needle moved from south to north as the generator approached it. Pavlita moved to the opposite side of the table; approaches to the compass with the left hand then were accompanied by a south-to-north movement of the compass needle, while approaches with the right hand were accompanied by a north-to-south movement.

At one point, the movement of the compass needle was minimal. Pavlita touched the generator to the left side of his head several times; the movement of the compass needle increased upon the next approach. In commenting on the first two demonstrations, Pavlita said that human biological energy is analogous in some ways to the earth's north and south magnetic poles. He also noted that the human "bioenergy field" completely surrounds the body and exists within the body as well.

Demonstration #3

Pavlita placed on the table a metal, scaffoldlike stand which resembled an inverted letter L. A string was tied to the protruding arm of the scaffold and a flat, lightweight bar magnet was tied to the string. A steel psychotronic generator was placed between Pavlita and the stand; the generator was cube-shaped with a small protuberance at its top. Pavlita approached the magnet with the cube; the magnet was not affected and did not move.

Pavlita left the room to demonstrate that he could activate the cube-shaped form from a distance. After about three minutes, he returned. He then picked up the cube and brought it near the north pole of the bar magnet; the magnet moved toward the cube. However, the magnet was repelled when the cube approached the south pole of the magnet.

Pavlita had faced south during the first part of this demonstration. He then moved to the other side of the table and faced north. The experiment was repeated with opposite results, as Pavlita brought the cube near the north pole of the magnet it was repelled, and vice versa. This time he did not leave the room but touched the generator to the right side of his head with his right hand, using a different rhythm than in the earlier experiments and staring intently at the magnet all the while. Pavlita commented that the eyes are important in this experiment and that the results demonstrate a brain "circuit" which is connected to the hands. His comment reminded me of Buckminster Fuller's prediction that the eyes would be found to relate to psychic phenomena more directly than any other part of the body.

Demonstration #4

The same bar magnet and scaffoldlike stand were used for this demonstration, but a different steel generator was utilized. This particular generator was goblet-shaped, but topped by a copper and bronze cover shaped like a holly leaf. Pavlita (facing south) touched his right thumb, first to both sides of his head, then to the cover of the generator, making a rhythmic movement which lasted about one minute. When he approached the bar magnet's north pole, it moved toward his thumb; when he approached the magnet's south pole, it was repelled by his thumb.

Demonstration #5

All the materials were in the same position as for the fourth demonstration. At this point, Pavlita (facing south) placed a mirror in back of the generator. Again he approached the magnet's north pole, placing his finger behind the mirror, but this time the magnet moved away from his thumb. When he approached the south pole, the magnet was attracted to his thumb. Pavlita commented that the body's "bioenergy field" exerted these effects by "passing through the mirror." He stated the results were a function of the relationship forced between an object and its image, reminding me of V. N. Pushkin's ideas concerning biogravitation and perception.

Demonstration #6

Again, the scaffold-shaped stand was used. However, this time a cylindrical-shaped piece of wood, about two inches in length was used. We had seen Pavlita cut it from a longer section of wood which was over a foot in length.

Before the wood was suspended from the stand, it was placed in a wide, cylindrical-shaped psychotronic generator. Diagonal marks could be seen on the outside of the generator; Pavlita remarked that a "biologically activated energy field had been burned into the generator." After the wood was placed in the generator, it protruded slightly; a narrow, rectangular steel bar was placed against the wood so that the end rested on the table and the other end rested on the wood itself. Pavlita called this procedure "closing the circuit."

After about three minutes, the wood was taken from the generator and suspended, by string, from the metal stand.

Pavlita picked up a round magnet and brought it toward one end of the piece of wood. The wood was repelled. He brought the magnet toward the other end of the wood; it was attracted. In other words, the piece of wood gave every appearance of having been magnetized.

Demonstration #7

Pavlita's daughter, Jana Pavlitova, produced a psychotronic generator shaped something like a microphone; it was the same type of device demonstrated at the Prague conference in 1973. A point protruded from the top half of the generator and she touched this to both sides of her head in a rhythmical manner for about three minutes. The generator was then placed in front of a semicircular solid copper screen. A light metal carousel was placed on the top of the generator.

Pavlitova touched the table lightly with the finger of her left hand. The carousel began to revolve from left to right. When Pavlitova removed her fingers, the carousel stopped its motion; when she again touched the table, the carousel resumed its movement. She called this procedure "completing the circuit."

After its motion stopped completely, Pavlitova again touched the generator to the sides of her head. The carousel was again placed on top of the generator and once more revolved for a short period of time.

Pavlita commented that this was an "accumulating-type" generator. He said that all his generators were "purpose-specific" and corresponded to the sixty-eight "biocircuits" of the body which he had identified.

Demonstration #8

Again the metal stand was used and a flat, rectangular piece of wood (resembling the bar magnet in size and shape) was suspended from it. Pavlita produced a rectangular psychotronic generator which fit easily into the palm of his hand. He held the generator with his thumb on the bottom and the other four fingers on top. As it approached the stand, the wood turned to the right. Pavlita then held the generator between his thumb and forefinger. This time when he approached the wood, it turned to the left.

This demonstration was unique in that it was not preceded by any type of body rhythm which would have activated the generator. Later, I was told that the generator involved accumulated energy from the people in the room and did not have to be activated purposively.

The Generator That Backfired

Pavlita told us that when he first began his research, he worked by trial and error. Eventually, he learned the basic principles involved. For example, he became aware of the basic bodily "biocircuits" and how each could be used in a generator.

Once the biological energy field is brought into a generator, Pavlita continued, it stays there permanently. However, a special induction procedure must be used to activate many of the generators. This introduction utilizes what Pavlita referred to as "bodily codes."

Pavlita told us that voltmeters and electrometers do not pick up biological energy. During human transmission of this energy, however, some psychophysiological differences were noted. One's heartbeat rate slows down and breathing becomes irregular. Rejdák told me that additional experiments were being attempted in a Prague psychiatric clinic to observe the brain waves which occurred during the activation of the generators.

No material had been found by Pavlita which could insulate an object against the effect of biological energy. Furthermore, "bioenergy," according to Pavlita, can affect all types of matter to some extent.

Pavlita told us that he has done some work with plants, having moved leaves and flowers at a distance. One type of generator works automatically by absorbing energy from the living organisms around it. This type stimulated the growth of plants; it enhanced seed germination in an experiment with pea and lentil seeds. The other type of generator must have biological energy directed into it; this type appeared to stunt the growth of plants.

The film I had seen concerning a generator which purified waste water from a dye factory was the type which absorbs "bioenergy" automatically. Pavlita reviewed how small pieces of steel were treated by the generator, then put into the polluted water—which became clean again within twelve hours. Pavlita told us that he has thought of trying to treat stones instead of steel, then attempting to depollute a lake or a river.

Pavlita admitted that larger generators could be built but thought that they would be dangerous. Several years ago, a generator "backfired" and his daughter's arm was paralyzed. Pavlita worked around the clock for three days constructing a generator which successfully reversed the effects of this mishap. Pavlita counseled, "Biological energy can turn back upon the human being if one is not careful."

Form Follows Function

Pavlita discussed a number of practical applications of the generators. These included biological communication (when other means of communication are nonoperable), magnetizing materials thought to be impervious to magnetization, testing the contents of unknown materials, facilitating the germination of seeds, and medical diagnosis of the body's "biocircuits." Pavlita stated that his generators could assess the deterioration rate of a dying organism and determine how long an organism had been dead. Perhaps the most important use of the generators, however, would be in assessing healing rates of injured and sick persons. The stronger one's biological energy field, according to Pavlita, the more rapid would be one's recuperative ability.

Pavlita told us that the right side of the body usually attracts, that the left side usually repels, and that left-handed people are not observably different than right-handed people insofar as their psychotronic abilities are concerned.

He spoke of "plus impulses" and "minus impulses" in terms that reminded me of the Oriental concepts of *Yin* and *Yang*, the positive and the negative life forces. From time to time, Pavlita said, he has utilized specialized procedures to produce the desired balance in a person between "plus" and "minus" impulses. An overabundance of one over the other is not uncommon among people and can lead to poor health.

By combining several generators, Pavlita claimed to have combined their functions; some of his experiments involved half a dozen generators or more. The speed at which a function operates supposedly depends upon the induction from the organism to the generator. The principle that "form follows function" is purportedly basic to the design of the generators, many of which are built to channel energy from two poles to a narrow point.

Frank Lloyd Wright also insisted that "form follows function" and used this principle to design buildings. Perhaps, I thought, many architectural and archaeological constructions of the past were attempts to build psychotronic generators. I recalled the "power stones" of primitive tribes which were used to enhance people's psychic abilities. When I returned to the United States, I examined some "power stones" from Papua, New Guinea, in New York City's Museum of Primitive Art Nourished by a coating of pig fat and used to insure success in hunting, fighting, and fertility, the "power stones" bore an uncanny resemblance in shape to Pavlita's generators.

Activation at a Distance

Pavlita had not yet used the psychotronic generators in combination with Kirlian photography, voltage gradient measures, or to study acupuncture points and hemispheric differences of the brain. Yet he did claim that he could affect a person's movements with one of his generators, directing a person to pick up an object with the left hand instead of the right. The dangerous potential of this device, said Pavlita, is one reason he has been cautious about releasing information on their construction. He told us that he wanted to obtain patents first so that the use of his generators could be carefully controlled. He had already obtained a Czechoslovakian patent on his water purification device.

Pavlita told us that he has been able to produce generators which calibrate so well with a person's "biocircuits" that they can be activated at great distances. Once, he claimed, a generator in Karlsbad was activated by a person in Hradec Králové, over 150 miles away. For this type of experiment to be successful, the generator must be carefully adjusted to a person's "bioenergy" field, a process which takes from two to three hours.

In summary, Pavlita, outlined the three components of his psychotronic generators. First are the materials; typically, they consist of steel, iron, brass, copper, and various crystals—his earlier devices relying more on crystalline contents than his later generators. Second in importance is the shape of the generator; a generator could be made of wood instead of steel, but if it were the right shape it could still accumulate a certain amount of biological energy. Of greatest importance is the rhythm or "bodily code" by which the "bioenergy" is transmitted to the generator—with the exception of those devices which quietly accumulate "bioenergy" from their surroundings without anyone making a special effort.

Rojek and I left Pavlita's home in Lázne Belchrad considering that perhaps we had been either completely deluded or that Pavlita's demonstrations were due to his own PK aided by various electrostatic effects. After all, we had imposed no controls on the demonstrations, merely observing what we were shown. However, it was also possible that we had seen one of the most important scientific discoveries of the century. If the generators were valid, parapsychology finally had what it had been searching for—a repeatable experiment which could be performed by investigators throughout the world.

Reich and Priore

When I returned to the United States and told my colleagues about the psychotronic generators, many of them were reminded of the writings of Wilhelm Reich and his devices for accumulating "orgone energy."

Reich's controversial "orgone energy" accumulator was a box-shaped structure, the six sides of which were filled with alternate layers of organic and metallic materials. Reich held that the organic material attracted and absorbed the "orgone energy" from the atmosphere, passing some of it through to the metallic material which radiated it toward the inside of the box. This increased the absorption and radiation of the next dual layer of organic and metallic substances until it reached the space within the box itself. A living organism within this space then absorbed the "energy" through the skin and through breathing, improving one's general health.

In the 1950s, my college psychology professors did not object to Reich's imprisonment, dismissing him as "psychotic" and his followers as "crackpots." Reich died in a federal penitentiary in 1957, the U.S. Food and Drug Administration having ordered his "orgone energy" accumulators destroyed. However, in the 1970s, a new generation of students began to build "orgone energy" accumulators. One of Thelma Moss's students built an accumulator and found that leaves placed in it displayed different Kirlian photography coronas than untreated leaves.

Related work was proceeding in Bordeaux, France, in the laboratory of Antoine Priore. Funded by the World Health Organization, Priore has disclosed few details of his instrument except that it emits "radiation in an electromagnetic field." A report from France's Institute for Cancer Research noted that cancerous rats, when treated with an earlier version of Priore's device, survived while an untreated group died. Priore's instrument was rumored to be a psychotronic generator.

A researcher from the University of Bordeaux carried out an experiment with infected rabbits. Those treated with the Priore device survived; indeed, many developed immunity to further infection. The untreated rabbits, however, deteriorated.

Priore was accused of falsifying the experimental results by substituting animals. So in 1969, a prestigious committee of scientists performed an experiment involving sixty infected mice. Of the thirty treated with Priore's apparatus, twenty-nine survived. Of the thirty untreated mice, twenty-six were dead within five days. A third group of thirty uninfected and untreated mice all survived and carried on their ordinary mice lives.

In the meantime, Priore has stated that his new and greatly expanded machine works through "electromagnetism" and that he built it intuitively from "feeling." And so the matter rests until the new apparatus is completed and outside investigators can closely examine the phenomena.

The Biofeedback Excursion

Later in 1974, I met with Galen Hall, legal counsel for the International Association for Psychotronic Research, who had recently returned from Prague. Hall brought pictures from Prague showing Jana Pavlitova in an experimental laboratory, directing "bioenergy" into a psychotronic generator with electrodes taped to her head. The experimenters were attempting to locate the psychophysiological correlates of the bioenergy transfer.

I thought of Barbara Brown's advice, given when she was the featured speaker at the 1970 meeting of the Parapsychological Association. Brown had suggested that if a biological indicator of ESP or PK were to be found, people could be taught to reproduce this indicator by biofeedback techniques. This process would probably enhance psychic ability, producing what Brown called "a new adventure for biofeedback and . . . the most exciting excursion for mankind."

A step in this direction was taken by Elmer and Alyce Green of the Menninger Foundation. Ten subjects were instructed to spend an hour per day in a biofeedback room where they were interviewed whenever bursts of theta appeared. Theta is slower than alpha, which characterizes certain forms of meditation, but not as slow as delta, which characterizes non-dreaming sleep. Nine of the ten subjects, all college students, were able to increase the percentage of theta while in the biofeedback room.

Some provocative events occurred during the study. Following the bio-feedback sessions, some students would report "heightened sensitivity" and would resolve problems, complete term papers, or study for long periods of time without distraction.

One student, during a biofeedback session, "saw" himself in debate before his committee. The imagery, voices, and words spoken during this experience were so vivid that it seemed as if the drama unfolding in his imagination were actually happening. As it turned out, the experience was a useful and detailed rehearsal for the actual confrontation.

The student also found himself guessing who would be on the phone whenever it rang. He was consistently correct, even when the callers were people he had not heard from for long periods of time.

On another occasion, he "saw" a letter arrive at his apartment with word that he had been accepted for graduate school; as he entered the door, he "saw" his roommate informing him of his acceptance. When the student went home that afternoon, there at the door—just as he had fore-seen—was his roommate, who promptly gave him the good news.

More disturbingly, the student "saw" the shooting of George Wallace a few days before it actually occurred. This premonition came to him not during theta biofeedback training but just before he went to sleep, during hypnagogic imagery—a state of consciousness marked by a high percentage of theta wave activity.

I was excited about the possibilites of reliable control of ESP and PK opened up by combining Pavlita's psychotronic generators with the biofeedback techniques of Brown and the Greens. In 1974, Charles Honorton had written, "I believe we could achieve the goal of at least limited control of psi in the next decade given adequate support, personnel, and—most importantly—a concerted effort to do so. . . . Reliable control of any phenomenon requires knowledge of the antecedent conditions necessary for its occurrence, and obviously, some idea what 'it' is that is occurring. . . ." To me, Honorton's goal seemed nearer to being realized than ever before.

In the meantime, several of the students who had gone to Prague with me attempted to make their own psychotronic generators, searching for clues in the work of Paracelsus (a sixteenth-century Swiss physician and alchemist), Baron von Reichenbach (a technician who conducted experiments with what he called the "odic force" in the latter part of the nineteenth century), Nikola Tesla (the inventor of alternating current whose "Tesla coil" is used in many Kirlian photography devices), and Alexander Gurvich (the Soviet biologist who claimed that "mitogenic radiation" occurs during cell division and can affect other cells at a distance.)

I recalled the stories about the *Kahunas* I had heard in Hawaii. These shamans spoke of a "life energy" called *mana* which can be controlled by the secret *Huna* rituals. There were three elements in the Kahuna practice—substance, force, and consciousness. Psychotronics, defined as the study of interactions among mass, energy, and consciousness, represented an updating of an earlier tradition.

My students seemed to me examples of Margaret Mead's statement in the *New York Times* (March 16, 1969):

> Today all adults are immigrants in a changing world. And in the same measure all children, in whatever part of the world they are growing up, are native to a kind of world in which they take for granted the thinking toward which their parents can only grope. . . . It is technology that has transformed the present world, and it is technology that can help us now in the creation of a shared future for all the peoples of the earth. The special problem we have is how to create a framework within this new and ever-changing world that will help adults become citizens of the community of which their children are the true natives.

Margaret Mead was held in high regard by parapsychologists because, in 1969, she delivered an impassioned speech to the American Association for the Advancement of Science which was considering a bid for affiliate membership by the Parapsychological Association. Mead recalled, "The whole history of scientific advance is full of scientists investigating phenomena that the Establishment did not believe were there. I submit that we vote in favor of this association's work." The vote was affirmative and parapsychology made another advance in its struggle for scientific acceptance.

The Study of Experience

In 1973, I wrote a paper on "The Measurement of Behavior" for a seminar on humanistic psychology. I had stated, almost automatically, that "psychology is the science that studies behavior." I sent the paper to Charlotte Bühler who responded to my chapter:

> You begin, "Psychology is the science that studies behavior." No. Psychology also studies "inner experience" and "products" or "creations." If you do not believe me, when my whole study of the course of human life is

based on these three aspects, and if you don't believe Karl, whose most famous book is on these three aspects of psychology . . ., then believe all the psychologists who study "perception," "thinking," and "emotions. . . ." It is farfetched to call this "behavior. . . ." Psychology is the science of behavior, inner experiences, and the resulting products or creations . . ., all the three. Many greetings, warm regards, and, please, let yourself be converted!

The following day I received another letter from Bühler. It stated:

In continuation of my letter of the other day: What are you doing when you study dreams? The behavior is that the person sleeps, but the important thing is his or her inner experiences. What do you measure? Only group comparisons or external details, not the main thing—the content of the experience. That you describe.

If Uri Geller sits there and breaks the spoons, his behavior is just the sitting there. Yet he has inner experiences which have not even been described and we have a production which we understand less than other productions.

When I sit here and write this letter, my behavior is only sitting and writing. But I have inner experiences of thoughts which are supposed to reach your thinking after I produce the letter in which they are put down. What do you want to measure in all this? Only unimportant details of this can be measured.

I hope we understand each other. The singular unique experience is a datum which even modern statistics is beginning to accept.

Those of us who were working with the Humanistic Psychology Institute made plans to bring Bühler back to the United States to participate in the program. Our program for granting graduate degrees had been approved by the State of California; Carl Rogers had hailed HPI and a similar institute, the Union Graduate School, as among the most important developments in graduate education in recent years. He continued:

[The] graduate schools . . . permit a student to achieve a doctor's degree through an honest program of independent study by the student, advised and aided by a group of his faculty and peers. They were both swamped by an incredible number of applications, and have attracted the highest type of true scholar, but both intend to keep themselves small.

In February I received word that Charlotte Bühler had died peacefully from a stroke. Her presence was missed at the annual meeting of the Association for Humanistic Psychology in New Orleans which Carie and I attended. In my presidential address, I recalled how political militants were fond of saying, "If you're not part of the solution, you're part of the problem." I asked, "Is psychology part of the problem?"

In my address, I noted how psychologists had aided the oppression of ethnic minorities by classifiying many of their children "mentally retarded" after giving them tests which were standardized on middle class, white children. I described young people as the most oppressed minority in history and told about the psychologists who encouraged the use of psychoactive drugs to "calm down" children who were disruptive in school classrooms.

I described the way women's talents had been thwarted by psychologists who considered a woman's principle functions to be a wife and mother. I noted psychology's insistence that there was only one "normal" type of sexual behavior and the resulting notorious treatment of homosexuals, bisexuals, transsexuals, and asexuals.

I recalled that 300,000 people are arrested on marijuana charges each year and that many psychologists play major roles in treatment programs for the "rehabilitation" of marijuana users. Other psychologists work in government-sponsored research programs attempting to find harmful effects from the substance that would prevent marijuana's eventual decriminalization or legalization. I complained about psychosurgery, the suppression of parapsychological data in college courses, the inadequate treatment given to old people, the manipulation of consumer purchasing through psychologically based advertising techniques, and the lack of attention paid to the psychological needs of the Vietnam veterans and of the expatriate antiwar protesters seeking amnesty.

Perhaps it is psychology itself that should seek amnesty. But in the meantime, humanistic psychology should do what it can to offer support to America's oppressed people: blacks, Chicanos, Puerto Ricans, American Indians, Asian-Americans, children, old people, women, users of unpopular drugs and practitioners of unorthodox sex, war veterans, war protesters, mental patients, and parapsychologists!

10

JOURNEY TO THE EAST

*INCREASE. It furthers one
To undertake something.
It furthers one to cross the great water.*
I Ching

Separating the Yins from the Yangs

Western science is based on assumptions of cause and effect that were not
shared by many oriental philosophers. Thus, it is only recently that such
Eastern procedures as acupuncture have been scrutinized with experimental
methodology. At Maimonides, Charles Honorton brought together the East
and the West by initiating the first scientific study of the *I Ching*. He solicited the assistance of forty staff members at Maimonides, most of whom
knew very little about the *I Ching*. They were asked to think of a personal
problem for which they had no immediate answer. They were also queried
as to their attitude in regard to ESP. Then they were given a cup containing
three coins and were asked to throw the coins six times while thinking of
their problem.

Later, each subject was given two Kua. One Kua, or hexagram, corresponded to the coins they had thrown. The other Kua was selected arbi-
trarily by using a table of random numbers. The subject was asked to rate,
on a ten-point scale, the degrees to which each passage was relevant to the
problem.

The twenty-four subjects with a positive attitude toward ESP gave a
higher score to the correct Kua than to the incorrect Kua. But the thirteen subjects with a negative attitude toward ESP gave a higher score to the
incorrect Kua. The difference between the two groups was statistically significant.

The East and West were also brought together at the Second Western

211

Hemisphere Conference on Kirlian Photography, Acupuncture, and the Human Aura which was held in New York in February 1973. The speakers included Edgar Mitchell, William Tiller, Don Parker, Victor Gioscia, and John Pierrokas, who had started to replicate some of the Soviet work on "bioluminescence" by measuring light emanations from the human body with photomultiplier tubes. Thelma Moss's associate, Kendall Johnson, spoke on the influence of psychic healers on leaves; in one instance, Olga Worrall concentrated on a leaf and its image disappeared from the film, giving rise to the name of Moss and Johnson's paper—"Now You See It, Now You Don't."

David Bresler discussed the clinical work with acupuncture he had done at the UCLA acupuncture clinic. Lok Yee-kung, whom I had met the previous year in Hong Kong, gave the theoretical basis for the effect, based on acupuncture meridians and the "Yin-Yang" balance of the body. However, T. X. Barber pointed out several overlooked factors in acupuncture:

1. Belief in acupuncture's effect is crucial to its success; in the People's Republic of China, readings from Mao Tse-tung often precede acupuncture, further strengthening the patient's belief system.
2. During surgery in China, local anesthetics and sedatives are often given as well as acupuncture anesthesia.
3. Most tissues and organs of the body are insensitive to pain when they are cut; the Western overreaction to pain does not exist throughout the world.
4. In China, patients are typically exposed to special preparation and indoctrination for several days prior to surgery.
5. Acupuncture needles actually can distract patients from surgical pain.
6. Suggestions are given the patients which often convince them that acupuncture will reduce the pain. These suggestions produce a powerful placebo effect.

Barber criticized the "gate control theory" which maintains that acupuncture closes a spinal "gate" which prevents transmission of pain sensation. Barber did not see how this theory would explain the reduction of pain when needles were inserted into the head. He concluded that the psychological factors which he had cited would have to be considered in the formulation of a comprehensive acupuncture theory.

A few months after our conference, another critical report was delivered by J. J. Bonica, chairperson of the Ad Hoc Committee on Acupuncture of the U.S. National Institutes of Health. Following a tour of China, Bonica admitted that acupuncture "does relieve pain and other symptoms in some patients," but that Chinese claims of widespread benefit "are not based upon data derived from well-controlled clinical trials." The American Medical Association also reported that of the sixty-six cases their investigators had studied in which acupuncture has been used to treat deafness, not a single patient showed any improvement.

Much as I had disagreed with the AMA throughout the years, I was sympathetic to their cautionary statement on acupuncture. I had seen a flurry of weekend courses being offered to physicians, complete with acupuncture charts and "do-it-yourself" kits containing acupuncture needles. After two or three days of study, physicians—and even nonphysicians—would begin to stick needles into patients.

Much of the improvement, I was sure, was due to a placebo effect. But to use acupuncture effectively, the entire fabric of traditional Chinese medicine must be understood—a legacy unknown even to many contemporary Chinese practitioners both in and out of China.

Portions of the classic Chinese book on acupuncture, the *Nei Ching,* may have been written about 1000 B.C.; however, the practice of acupuncture dates back to at least 3000 B.C. Acupuncture was one of several treatment modalities which evolved in ancient China, the others being herbal medicine, physical exercises, breathing exercises, massage, and the burning on the skin of *moxa*—small cones made from an oriental plant.

The Taoist philosophy, which exerted a strong influence on Chinese medicine, held that all things created in the universe are composed of two forces, the *Yin* and the *Yang.* Disease is created by an imbalance of the Yin, which is a passive, receptive force responsible for bodily repair, and the Yang, an active, dynamic force. The interaction of Yin and Yang produces *Chi,* a "body energy" that flows through the meridians which, like electrical circuits, connect the acupuncture points. The practitioner, it is felt, can pass his or her own *Chi* to the patient; the acupuncture needle serves as the channel through which the energy is passed.

The Data Transmission System

When I was in the Soviet Union, I learned about the research by Viktor Adamenko and others which had succeeded in identifying acupuncture points with Kirlian photography, the tobiscope, and the biometer. Acupuncture points were conceptualized as areas of low skin resistance and high electrical conductivity on the surface of the body, while meridians were thought of as pathways of electrical conductivity within the body.

An attempt to replicate the Soviet findings was reported in 1973 by two biomedical engineers. Abraham Noordergraaf and Dennis Silage. They used electrodes to measure skin resistance and electrical conductivity—and found no acupuncture points which demonstrated resistance markedly smaller than the surrounding area.

Then they turned over the measurement device to an acupuncture practitioner; in this case, the resistance of the acupuncture points was lower than nonacupuncture points on the skin. However, the investigators felt that the acupuncturist had applied a different amount of force when touching the electrode to the acupuncture point than when touching other parts of the skin. When they held the amount of force constant, the difference between acupuncture and nonacupuncture points diminished. Therefore, Noordergraaf and Silage's data did not confirm the Soviet work.

At this point, another investigator, Robert Becker, reported research done with a different technique. Becker was influenced by the theories of Albert Szent-Györgyi that cells might have electronic properties that would help regulate life processes. Becker carried out a number of experiments which indicated that there is a "data transmission system" in the human body which operates on the "steady state" principle of direct current (D.C.). One limb of this system interacts with the nervous system while the other limb interacts with the body cells.

Becker felt that his findings explained the fact that salamanders can regrow a severed tail or leg, and even part of a truncated heart or brain. Further, anatomical regeneration in salamanders and bone healing in humans has been enhanced by surrounding the healing bodily part with an electric field. The tissue which is of critical importance in these effects is composed of Schwann cells. Becker stated:

> We are obliged to conclude, therefore, that the control over local regenerative healing does not reside in the neurones themselves, but in their accompanying "supportive" structures, the Schwann cells, and we propose that these cells are the tissue responsible, in part, for the generation and transmission of the D.C. electrical control signals.

Becker went on to hypothesize that the Schwann cells were important elements in the body's "data transmission system," a system which probably antedated the nervous system in evolutionary development. Becker then used D.C. measurements with both electrodes and electrometers to study acupuncture points. He found them to be "sources of D.C." and suggested that they may be "spaced generating sources." If this were so, Becker continued, the meridians could be Schwann cell transmission lines. Therefore, the body's acupuncture network would, as Adamenko predicted, be a part of a separate system comparable to the nervous system, the circulatory system, and the lymphatic system.

Becker concluded that the "data transmission system" involving such components as acupuncture points, meridians, and Schwann cells,

> is involved in the receipt of damage or injury stimuli which we perceive as pain and in the control of the various processes of repair, including regeneration. Its nature renders it susceptible to perturbation by electrical and magnetic fields and it is proposed that it furnishes the linkage mechanism between biological cycles and geomagnetic cycles.

Becker was of the opinion that a proper understanding of this system would increase the use of "induced energy" in treating human disease while decreasing the use of pills and drugs.

Additional research would have to be done before it would be clear if the Chi energy written about by the ancient Chinese physicians existed and could be measured. But some tantalizing data were sent to me by V. M. Inyushin. Using photomultiplier tubes to measure the photons of light which emanate from the human face, Inyushin discovered that "acupuncture points give the greatest luminescence yield." He further found that the photon flow varied predictably during the twenty-four-hour cycle.

I knew that Inyushin suspected a relationship between body luminescence and bioplasma. Was it possible that bioplasma was the modern-day equivalent of Chi energy? If so, the photons detected flowing from the skin's acupuncture points might eventually relate to Becker's "data transmission systems." One of the hypothesized functions of bioplasma is that of carrying information to various parts of the body as well as from the environment to the body. And Becker spoke of his hypothesized system serving as a "linkage mechanism" between biological and geomagnetic cycles.

The Grad Experiments

I hoped that the research studies reported by Adamenko, Becker, Inyushin, and Pierrokas could provide an impetus for studies of psychic healing. While acupuncture was being developed in China, an Egyptian architect named Imhotep became chief physician to the pharaohs. When Imhotep died, about 3000 B.C., his tomb became a shrine for pilgrims seeking recovery from their illnesses. So many individuals made dramatic recoveries that Imhotep became regarded as a god.

Other ancient physicians—Galen in Greece, Thrita in Persia, Dhan-Wantari in India—were reported to have had psychic healing powers. Jesus included the "laying-on of hands" as part of his ministry and told his disciples to "heal the sick." However, a few hundred years after Jesus's crucifixion, the Roman Catholic church began to persecute psychic healers, regarding them as witches or heretics. In modern times, orthodox medicine has taken the church's place in debunking reports of paranormal healing.

One of the most celebrated American psychic sensitives, Edgar Cayce, gained renown—and controversy—for his attempts at paranormal diagnosis. Once Cayce had closed his eyes and entered an altered state of consciousness, he would be given the name and location of a subject. Within a few minutes, Cayce would give a detailed diagnosis of the ailment and would suggest a treatment.

One physician, Wesley Ketchum, gave Cayce 180 names and, in 1910, announced the results before a meeting with the Boston Clinical Research Society. Ketchum reported that Cayce had made only two errors in diagnosis; the suggested treatment procedures emphasized herbs and diet. Unfortunately, no scientist did extensive work with Cayce when he was alive. However, two physicians, William and Gladys McGarey, began to integrate Cayce's treatment suggestions into their medical practice and, in 1970, opened a clinic specializing in the Cayce procedures.

The first extensive controlled experiments in psychic healing were carried out at McGill University by Bernard Grad. Working with Oskar Estebany, a Hungarian healer, Grad noticed that the sprouting of grains, a plant's height, or the yield of plant material could be significantly increased (as compared with control seeds in other vessels) by watering them with a solution that had been exposed to Estebany's hands.

After obtaining significant results in four separate experiments, Grad wondered if Estebany would have the same effect upon mice. To find out, Grad cut out, with scissors, an oval of skin about one-half inch in diameter at the base of each mouse's spine. The area of the wound was measured by placing a piece of thin transparent plastic over it and tracing the outline with a grease pencil.

The mice were divided into three groups, each containing 16 animals. The first group was treated with Estebany's laying-on of hands, the second was untreated, and the third was heated by an electrothermal tape for the same length of time and to the same degree as those warmed by the heat from Estebany's hands. Measurements of the wounds were made by the paper outline method on the first, eleventh, and fourteenth days following the making of the wounds.

There were no significant differences in the size of the wounds among the three groups on the day the wounds were made or on the day after. Nor were there any significant differences between the untreated group and the electrothermally heated group eleven or fourteen days after the wounds were made. However, the wounds of the group treated by Estebany were significantly smaller than those of the other two groups both eleven and fourteen days afterwards.

The experiment was repeated by Grad with similar results and was replicated at another university under stricter conditions. For example, Estebany was not allowed to touch the mice; each animal was placed in a cage and the cage was placed in a bag. Half of the bags were kept open and the other half were closed. Instead of using the electrothermal tape, medical students duplicated Estebany's procedure; again, half the mice were in open bags and half were in closed bags. No significant differences were observed among the various groups up to the twelfth day after wounding. Some significant differences favoring Estebany's mice in the open bags were noted until the eighteenth day. The experiment was terminated two days later.

Grad hypothesized that Estebany was able to pass some type of "energy" to both the sprouts and the mice; he conjectured that this force might resemble the *Chi* energy written of by the ancient Chinese, the *Ka* of the Egyptian physicians, the *Prana* of the Indian yogis, the *Ylur* of Tibetan monks, the *Mana* of the Hawaiian Kahunas, the "magnetic fluid" of Anton Mesmer, or the "orgone energy" of Wilhelm Reich.

The Smith Experiments

During several visits to Buffalo, when I gave lectures and workshops at the Human Dimensions Institute, I met Justa Smith, a biologist. She had previously discovered that the activity level of trypsin, an enzyme, was increased by a magnetic field, but damaged and slowed down by ultraviolet radiation. Therefore, she decided to investigate whether Estebany could effect trypsin by a laying-on of hands.

Solutions of trypsin were divided into four portions. One was treated by Estebany who put his hands around a covered glass flask containing the enzyme for a maximum of seventy-five minutes. Another sample was exposed to ultraviolet light at a wave length determined to be the most damaging for enzymes, and then treated by Estebany. The third sample was exposed to a high magnetic field for three hours. The final sample was used as a control and was untreated.

The most striking finding of Smith's study was that the effect of Estebany's treatment of the undamaged sample was similar to that of the enzyme's exposure to a high magnetic field. The effect of Estebany on the damaged sample was similar but not as dramatic.

Smith repeated the study with three other psychic healers and three individuals who did not claim to have any healing powers. In no instance were the effects significant. Another experiment with Estebany also yielded nonsignificant results.* However, arrangements were made with a local physician for Estebany to attempt healing with twenty-four of the physician's patients. Estebany said he could not work with two of the twenty-four, suggesting that they obtain psychotherapeutic help. Of the remaining twenty-two, twenty-one stated that they felt "much better" following psychic healing. Smith told me that there was no way to discover how much of the patient's stated improvement mirrored bodily changes, and to what degree placebo effects entered into the results. Yet, she noted, "I don't believe too many physicians have that kind of batting average!"

Smith's next study involved three additional psychic healers. Again, trypsin was used; the results resembled those obtained by Estebany in that the activity level of the samples worked with by the healers increased significantly. However, work was also done with two other enzymes; nicotinamide-adenine dinucleotide (NAD) and amylase-amylose. NAD regulates the production of adenosive triphosphate, an energy-releasing compound involved in bodily healing. Amylase-amylose is also a body enzyme but plays no part in the healing process.

The psychic healers had no idea which enzyme was which or what their functions were. The healers had no effect on amylase-amylose, but significantly decreased the activity level of NAD. In the body, a decrease of NAD occurs when it regulates adenosive triphosphate, thus facilitating bodily healing. In other words, the healers' effects on the three enzymes were exactly what one would predict if they were functioning in the body to combat illness.

The Watkins Experiment

It occurred to me that the best way to eliminate some of the problems involved in psychic healing research would be to attempt healing at a distance. As long as one attempts laying-on of hands with sprouts, animals, or people, the possibility exists that the effect is due, at least in part, to the healer's bodily heat, electrostatic field, or electromagnetic field.

One experiment which involved working at a distance was reported by two of J. B. Rhine's assistants, Graham and Anita Watkins, who obtained the services of twelve people, most of whom did not profess to have any paranormal healing abilities. The task given these individuals was to arouse mice more quickly from anesthesia than would be expected under ordinary circumstances.

---

*Estebany later participated in two studies with Dolores Krieger in which his attempts at healing were associated with an increase in hemoglobin count among the patients.

Pairs of mice were simultaneously rendered unconscious with ether. The pairs were of the same sex, of the same size, and had been litter mates. After both mice were unconscious, they were placed in plastic containers. One mouse was placed before a "healer" who was asked to "awaken" the animal while the other mouse served as a control.

Tests were conducted under various circumstances. In some cases, the "healer" and the mouse were in one room and the control mouse was in another room. In some cases, the "healer" and both mice were in the same room. In some instances, both mice were in the same room with the "healer" looking through a window. And in some instances, the "healers" were blindfolded. In no instance was the "healer" allowed to do a laying-on of hands with the unconscious mouse.

The over-all results of this study were statistically significant; the animals who were assigned to the "healers" required an average of 13 percent less time to revive as did the control animals. There were no clear-cut differences among the various conditions; however, when the mice were viewed through a window, the unblindfolded "healers" did significantly better than the blindfolded "healers."

The Watkinses found three "healers" who did exceptionally well in reviving the mice, so much so that in twenty-four attempts their mice revived significantly more quickly than did the control mice. An additional subject also produced significant results; but in that instance, the control mice revived more quickly. Perhaps this unusual finding suggests that some people should stay away from psychic healing!

The LeShan Experiment

Lawrence LeShan's work in parapsychology originated with his exposure to Bernard Grad's experiments in paranormal healing. Having authored several excellent papers in psychical research, LeShan decided that unorthodox healing offered the greatest potential for the application of psi phenomena. After interviewing and observing dozens of healers, he arrived at a theory on its operation and began to apply the theory first by learning psychic healing himself, then by teaching others.

LeShan felt that most instances of psychic healing occur when the healer is in an altered state of consciousness—one in which a "merging" with the patient occurs. This "merging" is done with a sense of love and concern; at an unconscious level, the patient's self-repair mechanisms are stimulated to function in an accelerated manner.

With one of his students, Joyce Goodrich, LeShan designed an experiment in which healers would attempt, at various times, to "merge" with patients who were several miles away. The patients would keep a journal and would note those times when they felt the presence of the healer. The results were statistically significant; independent judges were able to identify correctly the times that the healers were at work from reading the journals of the patients or, as LeShan referred to them, the "healees."

LeShan has described the state of consciousness experienced by the healer in his book, *The Medium, the Mystic, and the Physicist:*

> It is essential that there be a deeply intense caring and a viewing of the healer and oneself as one, as being united in a universe . . . in which this unity is possible. . . . This is a perfectly valid set of beliefs about reality. Since at this moment of intense knowing on the part of the healer it was valid and the healee was an integral and central part of the system, the healer knew it too.

LeShan noticed that there were other types of healing which required very little modification of consciousness. In these cases, the healer consciously attempts to heal through creating a "healing flow." LeShan admitted that these efforts are often successful but that he would not know how to teach the process.

My wife and many of our friends took LeShan's healing seminars, which typically lasted ten hours per day for six days. The exercises involved learning such skills as mental discipline, alterations of time and space concepts, and techniques of entering the special state of consciousness LeShan associated with psychic healing. In one exercise, the students imagined that each of them was alone with a patient inside a bubble. In another, the students held matches and attempted to "merge" with them.

LeShan has stated that psychic healing is a basic human potential and is something that almost anyone can develop to some extent. On the other hand, an ill-prepared person can do harm; like all human abilities, psychic healing needs structure and discipline to be effectively handled.

Anthropological Efforts

One logical place to study psychic healing would be among primitive peoples, many of whom depend upon shamans to alleviate their illnesses. Anthropologists frequently encounter psychic phenomena in their observations but often dismiss them as fraudulent.

A few anthropologists such as Margaret Mead have been impressed by some of the events they have observed. Weston LaBarre has attributed the ability to handle snakes among members of Appalachian cults as being due, in part, to psychokinesis. LaBarre has also hypothesized that psychic phenomena may sometimes play a role in the religious ceremonies of American Indians. A. E. Jensen, in commenting on primitive healing, has stated that "there can be no doubt that man actually possesses such abilities." And the expert on shamanism, Mircea Eliade, has taken the following stand:

> We now touch upon a problem of the greatest importance . . . , that is, the question of the reality of the extrasensory capacities and paranormal powers ascribed to the shamans. . . . Although research into this question is still beginning, a fairly large number of ethnographic documents has already put the authenticity of such phenomena beyond doubt.

Few scientists have studied paranormal phenomena using anthropological techniques. One exception, Carlos Castaneda, stressed the importance of "entering worlds other than our own," noting that the experience teaches us that in these worlds of "nonordinary reality," space does not always conform to Euclidean geometry and that time does not always form a continuous unidirectional flow.

A few formal experiments with ESP cards have been undertaken with primitive peoples such as Manitoba Indians and natives of New Guinea; above-chance results were obtained in both cases although in the latter instance, they were not statistically significant. Ronald Rose tested Australian aborigines and New Zealand Maoris in a series of telepathy tests with ESP cards, obtaining highly significant results. His tests with Samoan natives were less impressive, a result he attributed to the repressive elements of the Christian missionaries to stamp out native beliefs in paranormal phenomena.

Robert Van de Castle and Malcolm Bessent, visited the Cuna Indians of Panama in 1972. Bessent discussed his psychic abilities with the local shamans while Van de Castle devised tests which employed special ESP cards (picturing such objects as conch shells and canoes). Van de Castle's overall results with adolescents revealed significant sex differences with the girls making more correct guesses than the boys. By the time they left Panama, Bessent had become well known for his abilities as a psychic healer and each day was asked to assist a number of ailing natives.

I suspected that primitive people could produce more impressive phenomena than card-guessing. On the other hand, I was wary of the extravagant, undocumented claims often emanating from the jungles and deserts of barely accessible parts of the globe.

Phenomena in the Philippines

Shortly after I moved to New York City, Zelda Suplee introduced me to Harold Sherman who was in town for a lecture. Sherman had formed his own foundation, ESP Research Associates, in Little Rock, Arkansas, and we became good friends. Sherman was well known for his long distance ESP experiment, in 1937, with Sir Hubert Wilkins, the explorer. Each day, Wilkins attempted to transmit telepathically impressions of what had happened on his expedition to the Arctic. Sherman wrote down his impressions and sent them to Gardner Murphy. When Wilkins returned, after nearly six months, his log was checked against Sherman's impressions; a 70 percent accuracy rate was claimed by Wilkins.

In 1967, Sherman published a book, *"Wonder" Healers of the Philippines,* in which he described his observations of two alleged Filipino "psychic healers." In one case, Sherman suspected sleight of hand; in the other case he reported "operations" in which the patient's body seemed to open up while a Filipino named Antonio Agpaoa appeared to remove a diseased piece of tissue, after which the body opening seemed to close.

In his book, Sherman presented opposing points of view as well. One of the dissenters was Sherman's associate, S. S. Wanderman, a cancer and arthritis specialist, who spent three days observing Agpaoa. When offered the tumor allegedly taken from the body of a patient, Dr. Wanderman said he did not need to examine it. He could tell "at a glance" the specimen was several days old and that the liquid was not actually blood.

Sherman also noted that the Philippines Medical Association, in 1962, had denounced Agpaoa as a "conjurer," stating that tissue removed by Agpaoa during an "appendectomy" turned out to be a piece of chicken intestine when scrutinized in a laboratory. Sherman concluded that he could not personally recommend the "psychic surgery" operation until further studies had been made.

In 1973, two important reports were published bearing on the Filipino healers. The *Parapsychology Review* revealed that an Italian neurologist had traveled to the Philippines to film Agpaoa's "operations." On his return, the neurologist and his team reported:

1. One of the tricks we detected was that the "blood" produced on the patient's body was smuggled into the operation room in little vials that were deftly broken open at an opportune moment. The red liquid, which appeared during the "operations" was examined in a laboratory at Turin University and found to be neither human nor animal blood.

2. Two renal stones emerged during an "operation" on an Italian journalist. On examination in a laboratory at Rome University, they were found to be a lump of kitchen salt and a piece of pumice.

3. Pieces of bone which seemed to emerge from patients' bodies during the "operations" were later examined and found to be bones in an advanced state of decomposition. Tissue which was produced during the "opera-

tions" was also found to be decomposed. The Italians doubted that organic matter in this state could have come from the human body.

4. The neurologist complained that he never succeeded in seeing with his own eyes an "opening" in the patient's skin; the operation field invariably remained covered by Agpaoa's hands.

The cameras brought over by the Italian group remained focused upon the "operation" but failed to produce satisfactory evidence that an "opening" was ever made.

Also in 1973, a journalist, Tom Valentine, published *Psychic Surgery,* an account of his own impressions of the Philippine phenomena. Valentine had read the negative accounts of Agpaoa, one stating that he held a small bag of animal blood in his hand, squeezing it out as he kneaded the skin, and another claiming that the "blood" was actually a chemical compound produced by a mixture of one substance mixed with the alcohol and other hidden material in the cotton swabs he used. He also heard the explanation that a pig's membrane is spread over the patient's skin to simulate an exposure of the internal organs.

Valentine wrote of his interview with W. J. Monaghan, an investigator for the American Medical Association. Monaghan showed Valentine a file of clippings which were critical of Agpaoa as well as a letter from Ian Stevenson, the prominent psychiatrist and parapsychologist. Agpaoa avoided Stevenson but a meeting was arranged with another healer, Eleuterio Terte. Stevenson witnessed an operation for gallstones, and later had the stones analyzed by two laboratories. One laboratory found them to be organic, and thus presumably genuine; the other report, however, labeled them limestone. Valentine decided to go to Manila for a firsthand look at the phenomena.

He found at least one instance when Agpaoa did resort to trickery. Valentine had been told that when Agpaoa's powers "go on vacation, he can't do anything, so he's dishonest about it and perpetrates a hoax. . . ." Valentine reported that Agpaoa, whose letterhead referred to him as "Pontifex Maximus," rarely charged fees but that the "donations" from foreigners sometimes exceeded one thousand dollars. Agpaoa's father had even gotten into the act, charging fifteen dollars for massage treatments—with special attention given to female customers.

However, Valentine saw Agpaoa work on many patients who reported that they were healed. Valentine also visited some of the less publicized healers, such as José Mercado about whom he wrote:

The most astonishing operations . . . I witnessed were performed . . . in the Pangasinan lowlands. . . It was in his crowded chapel that we encountered the curious phenomenon of "spiritual injection. . . ." Those who wanted injections lined up along a wall, and Mercado went to work. . . .

My turn arrived, and my left shoulder was the target. Mercado, grinning from ear to ear, pointed his right forefinger at my upper arm. There was nothing in his hand and nothing protruding from the tip of his finger, yet when he made a slight jerking motion with his hand, I felt a distinct needle jab. A tiny welt and a droplet of blood appeared on the spot.

The "injections" were part of the diagnostic procedure and preceded the "operations."

Later, I met a West German physicist who lined up for the "injection," having placed four sheets of polyethylene foil under his shirt. After Mercado gave the physicist an "injection," a tiny amount of blood spurted from the sheets which then had holes in the center. To me, this was a potentially impressive experience as there had been witnesses to it, and because the polythene sheets had been examined microscopically. The physicist said that he was convinced that no needle had been injected and that there was no trickery. One of the most interesting items in *Psychic Surgery* is Valentine's account of taking two genuine gallstones to a laboratory in the Philippines. He told the technicians that the stones had been removed by a "psychic operation." When the laboratory report came back, it carried the flat statement that the stones were not organic. This event points out the importance of preconception and belief even on the part of those who do laboratory analysis.

Film Festivals

The publication of Sherman's and Valentine's books and the controversy surrounding them, created interest on the part of many parapsychologists in the Filipino phenomena. It was apparent to many psychical researchers that if the reports from the Philippines were valid, the healings were extremely important psychokinetic occurrences that simply had to be investigated. The interest primarily centered around the allegation that the body appeared to open up during the healing sessions. For example, Sherman had written in his book that "the 'surgeon' . . . makes incisions, does whatever surgery is required, and then closes the openings he has made in the bodies. . . ." Further, Sherman quoted Henry Belk as stating, in reference to Agpaoa:

He will begin to knead this part of the flesh as though he is mixing dough. The next thing you know, blood begins to come out. . . . The flesh rolls back. He sloshes around with the guts. . . . When he locates the tumor—*bam*—out it comes—still no knife! Then he sloshes around again and . . ., instantaneously—*bam*—the stomach is healed back up. . . .

I continued to be unmoved when I saw some films of Agpaoa's "operations" at the Fourth Annual Interdisciplinary Conference on the Voluntary Control of Internal States which was held in Kansas during April 1972. The material Agpaoa appeared to pull from the bodies of his patients looked suspiciously like the poultry innards I had seen on my parents' farm when we prepared a chicken for Sunday dinner or a turkey for Thanksgiving. In addition, the patients exposed so little of their anatomy that it would have been a very simple procedure to slide some foreign matter from under the table, under the patients' clothes, and onto the patients' skin. Indeed, I observed instances of blatant chicanery which were apparent even in the film.

My reaction to the Austrian films of Agpaoa I viewed in Moscow was similar. Indeed, I was surprised at Dr. Hans Naegli's spirited defense of the Filipino phenomena. He admitted that some "healers" used trickery all of the time, and that many of them used trickery some of the time—especially on days when their abilities were on the wane. Nevertheless, Naegli insisted, there were enough genuine instances of paranormal phenomena to give this area a high priority in parapsychology.

The Fifth Annual Interdisciplinary Conference on the Voluntary Control of Internal States was held in Kansas in May 1973. Among the participants were Don Westerbeke, a California business executive, and his wife, Patty Westerbeke. They told me about his skiing accident in 1972, and his subsequent hearing and vision problems. A physician identified a pituitary tumor and advised an operation, using a technique of entering the brain's frontal lobe through the forehead. While making plans for the operation, Westerbeke saw a film of Antonio Agpaoa's "operations." A few days later, he arrived in Manila. After a talk with Agpaoa, and after witnessing several "operations," Westerbeke found himself on a table in a Manila hotel. Westerbeke recalled the events of July 22:

> Two cotton pads were put over my eyes and we were on the way. I felt stroking of my forehead and application of oil and grease, and then a pulsing or vibration of Tony's hands. . . . Suddenly, there was a movement of hands on my forehead—sort of a "pushing it all back in" movement—and Tony said, "We are finished."

His hospital operation had been scheduled for July 21. It would have taken close to ten hours, followed by several days in intensive care, ten days in the recovery room, and at least a month at home recovering. Agpaoa's "operation" took no more than ten minutes and Westerbeke went for a walk in the sunshine later that same day.

On the following day, Agpaoa performed a second operation to improve

Westerbeke's vision. Eyewitnesses described it as a partial "removal" of the eyeball from its socket, a "wiping" of the nerve, and a "replacement" of the eyeball in the socket. The process took only a few minutes.

Agpaoa promised to give Westerbeke the "tumor" he had removed during the first operation, but claimed to have lost it. However, Westerbeke returned to the United States feeling that he had lost the symptoms which physicians had attributed to the tumor. Westerbeke's film of his first operation certainly did depict a great deal of red fluid pouring down his head as well as a chunk of white matter in Agpaoa's hand following the kneading of Westerbeke's forehead.

When visiting Westerbeke in 1974, he told me that he had not had a recurrence of any ailments. Further, he had returned to the Philippines several times to visit other healers and to compare the various approaches used.

Caliraya

It was now obvious that I needed to reevaluate my total rejection of the Philippine phenomena. In a conference on paranormal healing sponsored by Judith Skutch's Foundation for ParaSensory Investigation, I briefly reviewed the controversy over the Filipino healers and concluded that even if 99 percent of the cases were fraudulent, the remaining 1 percent would still be worthy of investigation. This statement appeared in a 1973 issue of the *Newsletter of the American Society for Psychical Research;* I thus became the first member of the Parapsychological Association to call publicly for an investigation of these healings—the most controversial of the paranormal phenomena.

It was apparent to me that I would have to go to the Philippines for a firsthand look at the healers. If there was anything at all to the secondhand reports I had been hearing, and the home movies I had been viewing, no parapsychologist could pass up the opportunity to make a personal observation. I even asked the *I Ching* for counsel regarding a trip to the Philippines: Kua 42 appeared stating, "It furthers one to cross the great water."

At the same time, I received an invitation from Maximo Kalaw, Jr., to be the final speaker in the Caliraya Conference on Higher Consciousness and the Environment, a series of seminars sponsored by the Caliraya Management and Development Foundation in Manila. Included in the invitation was a promise to take me to see a number of the healers while I was in the Philippines.

Maximo Kalaw, Jr. met me at the Manila airport and took me to a hotel. He asked if I would like to rest or go directly to a psychic healing center. Even though I was dreadfully tired from the trip, the decision was easy to make. Accompanying us on our tour was Dr. Hiram Ramos, a clinical psychologist whose experiences in a Japanese prison during the World War II occupation of the Philippines had made him appreciate life so intensely that he could not rule out any healing modality—including psychic healing—that might alleviate human suffering. Ramos served as my translator, as most of the morning's dialogue was in Tagalog, the national language of the Philippines.

"Savior of the World"

Our first stop was at 56 Dr. Pilapil Street in Pasig, the capital of Rizal province. This was the site of "Savior of the World," the local chapter of the Christian Spiritists' Union of the Philippines, an organization which for over fifty years has represented most of the nation's psychic healers. Antonio Agpaoa represented a notable exception, having never joined the union.

We were greeted by Juan Blance and his assistant, Felipe Biton. Blance told us how he used to detest the Spiritists—as did many members of the Roman Catholic church in his neighborhood who were told by the priests that Spiritists were involved in "the work of the devil." Indeed, Blance remembered throwing rocks at the Spiritists when he was a boy.

In 1957, Blance witnessed a serious crime and was afraid that he would be unjustly arrested for complicity. Terrified, he went to several people for help but they could offer him little in the way of advice or solace. Finally, he talked to a Spiritist who correctly predicted that he would be approached by the police to act as a witness to the crime, but would not be accused of complicity. In gratitude, Blance became a convert to Spiritism and about two months later, he successfully attempted psychic healing. He told us that for four years he would enter an altered state of consciousness when he began healing and would not remember the experience at its conclusion. As the years went by, he still went into an altered state during healing, but was able to remember the events once the session was over.

Felipe Biton discussed his own serious interest in psychic healing which went back four years to an incident in which a blind man recovered his sight after Biton prayed over him. He then began to specialize in "magnetic healing," a procedure which resembled that used by the Spiritists I had visited in Brazil.

As we entered Blance's center, we noticed a group of ailing people sitting patiently in the waiting room. I learned that the room doubles as a sanctuary for the Spiritist services that were held there once a month. At these services, I was told, an abundance of spontaneous cases of automatic writing, mediumship, and speaking-in-tongues had been observed. I had a chance to observe several healing sessions in the small treatment room which was separated from the sanctuary by a curtain.

The first patient was a middle-aged woman who complained of an indigestion problem. Blance asked her to lie down on a high, narrow table, baring her abdominal region. He rubbed some coconut oil on his right thumb. He closed his eyes, as if in prayer, and pressed firmly on the skin. Slowly, a pool of milky fluid appeared around the woman's navel. While continuing the pressure with one hand, Blance reached for a tablespoon with the other. As he ladled the fluid into a bucket, we observed some thick, foamy, light-colored material. Dr. Ramos told me that this material had been analyzed by a Manila laboratory and found to be pus in some cases and a sugary substance in others.

Blance wiped the remaining fluid from the woman's abdomen with a towel. She then pointed to a mole which protruded slightly from her neck, asking that it be removed. Blance applied some coconut oil to it, then picked it off with his hands. A tiny portion still remained, but this too was removed with his second attempt. There were a few drops of blood which Blance wiped off with a swab of cotton; a bit of cotton was left on her neck to absorb any other blood that might appear.

What was I to make of this? The removal of the mole did not seem unusual, although it did seem a highly dangerous procedure, medically, in that it could have led to considerable pain, bleeding, and possible infection. As for the appearance of the milky puslike fluid, this could have been stored in a capsule or vial which Blance had hidden in his palm and then broken. However, I looked in vain for the remains of the container. Also, I had been watching Blance's hands carefully, once he folded them in prayer. From the prayer, the hands went to the woman's abdomen. So if there had been a hidden capsule, Blance would have needed to hold it during several different manual operations. Could a capsule have been hidden under the spoon? Perhaps. However, the fluid had already appeared by the time Blance reached for the spoon. Nevertheless, some of the fluid could conceivably have been hidden in a capsule taped to the spoon. This procedure would have necessitated the existence of two capsules large enough to contain the three tablespoons of liquid which Blance eventually ladled into the bucket.

Another of Blance's patients was a woman suffering from asthma. Instead of spending much time on her nose, Blance had the patient remove her blouse and lie down on her stomach. After folding his hands and uttering a silent prayer, Blance indicated, by gesture, that I should extend my right hand and my forefinger. He then took my right hand and aimed my forefinger at the woman's back. He brought my finger to a point about six inches from the skin just underneath the shoulder blade. Suddenly, he made an abrupt motion with my forefinger, then released it.

I had not taken my eyes off the woman's skin as this procedure was transpiring. I maintained my attention because I knew that Blance was reputedly able to cut skin at a distance as part of a "purification" ritual. And I noticed a slit on the woman's skin at the exact area beneath my finger position. Within a few seconds, a thin ribbon of blood filled this slit. It appears to me as if the cut were superficial, barely scratching the first layer of skin.

How was this phenomenon to be explained? Blance could not have used his left hand physically to cut the skin as it was clasping my right hand. Blance's right hand was resting by his side. Just possibly, he could have concealed a knife or razor blade in his right hand, making the slit while I was distracted and looking elsewhere. However, I knew only too well the distraction techniques of magicians, and resolved not to let my eyes wander from the woman's skin from the moment I approached the table and gave Blance my hand.

Could the scratch have been produced before this? Perhaps. Blance could have slit the woman's skin before I approached the table. But if that had happened, why did I not notice the scratch earlier? The slit was clearly visible just as soon as the cutting motion had been made by my finger. If the incision had been made earlier, why did the bleeding not start until after my hand had completed making its abrupt movement? The possibility does exist that Blance scratched the skin before I observed the process; if so, the timing would have had to have been extremely precise so as to precede the flowing of blood.

Blance then proceeded to place a Filipino coin on the slit, tore a small piece of cotton from a roll, dipped it in alcohol, and lit the cotton with a match. He then placed a glass cup over everything. The skin quickly rose to fill half the cup because of the partial vacuum which had been created. There was profuse bleeding and the cup and cotton were removed.

Blance, at this point, dipped his thumb into coconut oil and proceeded to squeeze and press the skin around the incision. An irregular disclike piece of matter could be observed in the middle of the blood. It resembled melted wax, and I noticed there were specks of foreign material in the disc. Ramos told me that he had examined several of these discs, finding such material as blood, small pieces of bone, and sugar deposits.

Blance showed the disc to the patient, then dropped it in a basin of water. He told me that the process "purified" the body in some way. I had not known about the disc and did not expect it to appear; conceivably,

Blance could have secretly placed it under the coin as he put the coin on the slit in the skin. This procedure was not repeated, so I had no chance to examine another disc more closely as to its appearance.

The next patient was a young girl, the palm of whose right hand was disfigured by a mole which was about the size of a quarter. Blance closed his eyes in prayer and asked the girl to pray as well. He then soaked a wad of cotton in alcohol. He lit the end of the cotton and, while it was still burning, pressed the cotton firmly onto the girl's palm. After Blance removed the cotton, it was apparent that the mole had puffed up slightly. Then Blance, with a pair of scissors, cut out the portion of the mole which had risen above the skin. He repeated the process so that the remainder of the mole could be cut away.

I asked the girl if the process had hurt her and she replied, "Not very much." Blance stated that, "When there is little pain, the healing power is greater than if there is much pain." This incident, of course, could be adequately explained on the basis of what has been discovered in hypnosis research. If a patient is hypnotized, or spoken to reassuringly, the experience of pain is lessened considerably.

"Merciful Endeavors"

From Blance's center, we drove to 63 St. Mary's Street in Quezon City. There we visited "Merciful Endeavors, Inc.," a conglomerate of psychic healers and mediums affiliated with the Association of Psychic Healers, a small group operating outside of the Spiritists' Union due to policy disagreements. The leader of the group was Nemesio Taylo; Ben Bustamante was the other healer we observed, while Rosario Gerard, Cornelio Miranda, and Perla Ocampo worked as mediums and "magnetic healers." The patients in the room appeared to represent a wide spectrum of social and economic classes.

The treatment room contained three "operating tables" above which hung illuminated pictures of Christ and Mary. Another painting showed a dove above which had been written the words "Christ the Healer" and below which were printed the words, "The Spirit of Man Is the Candle of the Lord."

As we came into the room, an elderly lady was brought forward by her relatives, none of whom she recognized. Taylo had her lie down on a table, and proceeded to bring his large diamond-chip ring to the tips of her toes and fingers. Every time Taylo did this, the woman would wince with pain. When he brought the ring close to her forehead, she grimaced horribly. "Possession by evil spirits," Taylo muttered, and went to work.

For about five minutes, Taylo massaged various parts of the old woman's body, moving limbs upward and downward as he proceeded. He then uttered a silent prayer and brought his ring near to the woman's body parts again. This time she demonstrated no reaction. Instead, she smiled at her relatives and, as Taylo pointed to each one, she called out the correct name.

In the meantime, Miranda was praying over a woman on the table at the far left and Bustamante was rubbing a young man's stomach on the middle table. Suddenly, a thick strip of white fabric emerged, apparently from the proximity of his navel. Bustamante kept massaging the abdominal region with one hand, while pulling out three additional strips of fabric with the other. When Bustamante finished, the young man's stomach pains had ceased; the stomach as well as Bustamante's hands were cleaned with alcohol and the next patient came up to the table.

This was a young woman who complained of backaches; again, Bustamante had her lie on her back as he poured a small amount of water on her stomach. Within seconds, his hands were rubbing the water around the woman's navel; out popped a polyethylene strip approximately an inch wide and six inches long. This was followed by a second strip of about the same dimensions.

The first phenomenon could have been the result of the fabric strips being "palmed," the way a clever magician "palms" an object later "produced" from thin air. However, I watched Bustamante's hands very closely between operations. When he washed his hands with alcohol, the fingers were spread widely apart. At no time did he touch his hands to the table or his pockets (where he might have had the polyethylene strips hidden). Instead, he moved directly to the next patient.

With patients on every table in the center, I faced the same problem I had encountered at a three-ring circus in my youth—which area should I concentrate upon? I directed my attention back to Taylo. He was now working with an adolescent suffering from a case of swollen testicles. After pouring some water over the abdominal area, Taylo motioned for some cotton. As his assistant was not immediately available, I reached for the box, handed him the cotton, and remained standing directly in front of the patient during the entire session.

As Taylo pressed firmly into the abdominal area, he again motioned for cotton and as I gave it to him, I leaned so far over the patient that I was only a few inches from the site. As Taylo took the cotton, I could see nothing in his hands. After he wiped some of the water from the boy's body, I could see nothing in either hand. Then, Taylo appeared to grasp a strip of material and began to pull it. The material was about five inches long; upon examination it seemed to be a band of elastic. The sides of the elastic were coated with clay. Indeed, small lumps of clay floated to the surface of the pool of water surrounding the patient's navel and dissolved into the water which dripped down the side of his body.

Taylo's hands never left the boy's body. Taylo did not reach under the table or into his pockets. Unexpectedly, another piece of elastic appeared and Taylo seemed to pull it from the small pool of water on the patient's abdomen. All this occurred while I was handing cotton to Taylo. I had a large enough piece of cotton in my hand so I could keep a constant watch on Taylo's fingers. He would take a small piece of cotton as it was needed and wipe the clay from the boy's side.

Taylo deposited the two strips of elastic in a wastebasket as well as the clay-encrusted pieces of cotton. He poured alcohol on the boy's abdomen, wiped it off with cotton, and massaged the entire area with his hands. He told the boy's mother that her son had been "hexed" but that the "hex" was now removed. Nevertheless, if the swelling of the testicles did not go down, then she should return with her son for an additional treatment. After the two of them left, he told me, "Of course, this was not necessarily a 'hex'; the ailment could have been the result of the boy's anger or of resentment that he was unable to express."

Taylo's next patient was a young woman whose neck was swollen from goiter. Again, I stood ready with the cotton, this time placing myself in a different position so I could see Taylo's hands from the side rather than from the front. Taylo asked for some cotton, placed it on the woman's throat, and it soon began to become discolored with a red fluid. Taylo poked a hole in the center of the cotton and I could see several small, dark red, solid objects which resembled blood clots. This piece of cotton was discarded, a fresh piece was substituted, and the same phenomenon occurred.

Finally, Taylo wiped the area with alcohol, placed a fresh piece of cotton on the woman's neck, bandaged it with a piece of cloth, prescribed a special type of herbal tea and compresses of coconut oil, and suggested she return in a week. I noticed there had been no change in the size of the swelling on the woman's neck.

Later that day, I reflected on my experiences and the several unusual phenomena I had witnessed. In one instance, I had seen a slit appear in the epidermis of a person's skin for no apparent reason, save the healer's moving of my finger at a distance of several inches above the patient's body. In other instances, I had seen various fluids, waxlike and puslike substances, fabrics, polyethylene strips, and elastic material appear when a healer rubbed a patient's abdominal area. The diagnostic aspects of the process were, no doubt, important for healing to take place but did not hold the possibility of being paranormal in nature. However, many of the healing phenomena themselves were either psychokinetic in nature or incredibly sophisticated sleight of hand effects.

"Teleportation" and the "Bioplasmic Body"

I revisited the two centers the next day and later that afternoon Kalaw, Ramos, and I drove to Caliraya where I began my seminar. For three days, I spoke of our work in the dream laboratory, of Kirlian photography, about altered states of consciousness, and of the parapsychological research I had observed in Czechoslovakia, the Soviet Union, and Brazil. Inevitably, someone asked me for an explanation of the phenomena manifested by the Filipino healers. I had been giving the matter considerable thought since my observations of Blance, Taylo, and Bustamante, so I offered a few hypotheses.

In the first place, I observed, there is not one phenomenon but several phenomena. On the films, I had observed outright trickery. At "Merciful Endeavors," I had witnessed prayer and supportive counseling. At both centers, "magnetic passes" were utilized. All of these procedures, including legerdemain, could result in healing but were not necessarily paranormal in nature. Possibly paranormal, however, were the scratches made by Blance on human skin. I conjectured that this may have been the result of focusing bodily fields, "psychic energies," or a combination of the two, in the way that a magnifying glass focuses sunlight to produce a burned hole on paper.

What of the sudden appearance of material such as the red liquid and the waxlike substance? Did not this suggest some sort of "materialization" that would violate the laws in physics of conservation of matter? Not necessarily. Each of the items I saw was a common one. Why could they not have been "teleported" from a nearby butcher shop (in the case of the red liquid), church candle (in the case of the solidified wax), or clothes closet (in the case of the elastic)? I then reminded the group of the Soviet theories concerning a "bioplasmic body." Perhaps this was the matrix for the "teleportation." An item could simply vanish from one spot and travel through the patient's "bioplasmic body"—extended by the action of the healer several feet or several miles into space.

I further suggested that the "bioplasmic body" may interact with the person's acupuncture points and meridians, found by the Soviet researchers to be areas of high electrical conductivity. This would explain why Taylo's patients winced in pain when the ring made from diamond chips was brought near to their acupuncture points. Apparently, either their bodily fields or "psychic energies"—or both—were out of balance. The healing ritual was needed to restore the energetic balance.

Tom Valentine, in his book, had quoted Dr. Hiroshe Motayama regarding Juan Blance's scratching of the skin from a distance: "He accomplished a depletion at a viscera-cutaneous reflex point, which is a kind of treatment often done in acupuncture." Therefore, I was not the first one to see a connection between the Philippine healing process and acupuncture. Nor was I the first to suspect some sort of "teleportation" as a mechanism; Dr. Lee Sanella, of the Academy of Parapsychology and Medicine, stated a similar opinion following his visit to the Philippines earlier in 1974.

In addition to the healers' ability to affect their patients' "bioplasmic bodies," I observed considerable knowledge of healing itself. If one believes that a certain procedure will help one get well, that patient is already on the road to recovery. The Filipino healers appeared to speak in terms of their patients' belief systems, especially in regard to "spirits," even though Bustamante and Taylo had made side remarks to me that were more understandable in terms of a traditional Western belief system.

For example, Blance's patients suffered from a number of ailments which usually have strong psychosomatic components: indigestion, asthma, and respiration difficulties. Perhaps all that some of the patients needed from Blance was assurance, through his attempts at psychokinesis, that he had "healing power." Thus, they allowed their own self-healing capacities to begin functioning. In the successful healing of infants and animals, this explanation would not suffice by itself. However, I suspected that self-healing was a very important part of the Philippine phenomena.

Shrewd application of psychological principles also played a part. I remembered the old woman who, upon coming into "Merciful Endeavors," could not identify her relatives. Her memory returned after Taylo massaged her limbs, and after her relatives paid her some attention—perhaps after years of ignoring her.

A Protégé of St. Michael

Ramos and I later drove to Baguio City to see Antonio Agpaoa's healing center, "Dominican Hill." However, we were informed that the center, largely financed by West German funds, was in legal difficulty and that a lawsuit had already been served against Agpaoa's wife. Clearly, this was not the best time to visit "Dominican Hill." Instead, we drove to the small hamlet of Villasis in the province of Pangasinan. The majority of the Filipino healers were from this province and the most highly recommended healer was Josephina Sison.

Leaving the main highway, we drove a few miles down a dirt road to the home of Josephina Sison, her husband, and her two children. We entered the small concrete chapel which served as the "Orduha" branch of the Spiritists' Union, and Sison appeared. Because of heavy rains the usual flood of patients had not yet arrived, so we had a chance to visit and ask questions.

Born on All Saints' Day in 1941, Sison told me that she had her first visitation with "spirits" when she was thirteen years of age. She recalled, "My parents thought that I was crazy," but at the age of twenty-two Sison began her "holy work" or psychic healing. She remarked that she was guided to move in this direction by the "Holy Spirit" which manifests itself in the form of St. Michael, the archangel. "Sometimes," she said, "St. Michael takes me on a white horse to other planets. And he gives me precious stones which are very beautiful but which don't last very long."

Sison and her husband have had two children. St. Michael told her that she would need to have a physician's help for the delivery of her first child. So Sison went to the hospital and it developed that a Caesarean birth was necessary. When she again found herself pregnant, Sison was told by the physicians she should have another Caesarean. St. Michael told her otherwise and she had her baby by natural childbirth. Then she decided that she wanted no more children and St. Michael instituted a "spiritual birth control program" for her. Since that time, she has had sexual intercourse but no children, merely by praying to her patron before making love.

When I asked her about the healing process itself, she said, "There is much about it I do not understand." However, she was of the opinion that the blood which reportedly appears during her work "carries disease out of the body" and that often she removes foreign materials from the body that "have been placed there by witchcraft." I asked if any people have come for healing who are skeptical about her ability; Sison replied, "It is easier to heal if they believe, but if they are doubters I swallow my pride and heal them anyway."

I observed two tables, one wooden and one plastic. Sison told me that the plastic table was brought from the United States by the Academy of Parapsychology and Medicine early in 1974 when several of their members filmed her at work. The transparent property of the plastic would have disclosed any hidden objects. Sison said, "At first the table gave off a strange vibration, but then I performed a ritual of consecration and found that I could work quite well with it."

Sison noted that she could do her "holy work" for hours without becoming fatigued. However, heavy manual work in the garden would sometimes exhaust her and St. Michael would tell her to rest or the labor might diminish her healing ability. She has disobeyed St. Michael when overly eager to finish a task of manual labor only to be stung by an insect, bitten by an animal, or cut by a garden implement in a self-inflicted accident. Sison admitted that sometimes she disobeyed on purpose, "just to test St. Michael and make sure he still knows what he is talking about; after all, sometimes I have a hard time believing all of this myself!"

The Cotton Vanishes

As no patients had arrived, I asked Sison if she would like to perform a healing on me, telling her of my gastrectomy in 1965. She eagerly accepted the invitation and said she would first do a diagnosis. Taking a pencil and paper, she appeared to enter an altered state of consciousness and began to do automatic writing. Three lines of unusual script appeared which vaguely resembled Chinese calligraphy. She interpreted the writing to indicate only minor problems associated with my operation, but a liver ailment which was just developing.

I unbuttoned my shirt, spreading it out so far that nothing could be secreted in the folds. I also loosened my pants, lying down on the wooden table with my head on a Bible. Sison bowed her head in prayer and folded her hands. As she opened her hands, I could see that the fingers were wide apart. As the hands touched my abdominal area, small red drops of fluid began to appear. Soon, streams of red fluid trickled down my sides. The fluid appeared to come from the part of my skin which came into direct contact with Sison's hands. There were no clotlike objects and she later took this to mean that the ailment was not serious.

After wiping her hands and my abdomen with cotton, Sison tore a fresh piece of cotton from a roll and dipped it in coconut oil. Earlier, she had observed that coconut oil was used by Christ's apostles for healing because "it helps direct the power of the Holy Spirit." Sison pressed the wad of cotton, which measured about one inch by half an inch, to the right side of my abdomen. While I watched, the cotton appeared to vanish into the skin until only a small tuft remained. As Sison gave this a pat, it also disappeared. Still standing at the right side of my body, Sison moved her hands to the left side of my abdomen. I looked at her hands carefully and they seemed to be empty. Again, the fingers were not pressed together and the palms were open.

As Sison brought her fingers to my side, a piece of cotton appeared to protrude from my skin. She began to pull it up and I could see that it was streaked with red. I moved my body to get a better look. Sison stopped pulling, removing her hand from the cotton. And for that moment, the cotton appeared to be sticking halfway out of my body. Then she finished removing the cotton and I could see traces of red fluid on either side of it

—but no coconut oil. She told me that the fluid was "impure blood" and that the coconut oil remained in my body to complete the healing process. I felt very alert and somewhat euphoric. I also noticed half a dozen patients who had arrived during my session and who were ready to receive healing themselves.

I stood by Sison's table as an elderly man was placed on his back. He was blind in both eyes. As Sison rubbed the right eye, fluid poured down the side of his face. She repeated the procedure with his left eye then thrust a wad of oil-soaked cotton in his left ear. As she poked it in his ear, it appeared to disappear completely. Moving her hands, she seemed to pull a wad of cotton from his right ear. The cotton had the same shape and size as the wad which had apparently entered the left ear; the oil could not be seen and there were no red streaks on the cotton. Sison predicted that sight would begin to return to his left eye in three weeks.

Another patient was a young man complaining of a stomach problem. As he bared his abdomen, I could see a gastrectomy scar similar to my own. Sison rubbed his abdomen until the red fluid appeared, then had him turn over. She appeared to poke the cotton into a carefully selected spot on the man's back until it disappeared. After a short period of time, she seemed to withdraw it from a point on the opposite side of his back.

I asked Sison about her treatment of opiate addiction and alcoholism. She told me that she used the cotton technique to "clean the blood" but that at least three visits were necessary. For alcoholism, she has prescribed a special herbal tea. Sison mentioned that she had frequently used herbs in her work and gave me a bundle of twigs from the Zepa rosebush which she recommended as a heathful tonic to prevent disease.

Could Sison's effects have been the result of legerdemain? For this position to be defended, one would have to conjecture that small capsules of red fluid had been "palmed" by Sison before she touched a patient's skin. The empty capsules would have had to accumulate somewhere—on the floor or on the table—unless she returned them to the drawer on the table where she kept her supplies. When I gave Sison a donation for her work, I noticed that she opened the drawer. It was quite empty, as she had run out of cotton, and I could see no capsules, empty or full. As for her clothing, she wore a short-sleeved smock devoid of pockets, during the work. The capsule hypothesis, therefore, could not be reasonably maintained unless it were determined where the containers were hidden before and after the red fluid appeared. Also, I had observed her hands so closely, and from so many different angles, that the "palming" procedure appeared highly unlikely.

The cotton phenomenon would also be difficult to ascribe to legerde-main. Sison would have had to "palm" a piece of cotton after it appeared to enter the body. To produce the red streak on the cotton, which I noted after it had appeared to reemerge from my abdomen and that of one of the other two patients I saw, Sison would have had either to substitute cotton or break a capsule of red fluid on the same piece after it reemerged. And what about the time when I appeared to see the cotton protrude from my flesh even when Sison was not touching it? This could have only been explained in terms of a hypnotic effect, and I simply did not feel that anyone was overtly or covertly making an attempt to alter my perceptions of the exter-nal world.

The only other alternative explanation to the Filipino phenomena would have been an enlistment of several Filipino "stooges" who came to the three centers I visited with objects already hidden on their bodies, or flesh-colored tape (or a thin overlay of animal skin) from which objects could be removed or suddenly appear. Why anyone would have wanted to go to the expense of hoaxing me is a question for which I found no sensible answer. But whatever validity this conjecture might have is destroyed by the fact that I was a participant in a session myself—and with no plastic coating over my abdomen.

Of course, I knew that I could easily be accused of making up the whole story. Again, however, it would be difficult to find a motive. Indeed, my stature as a hard-nosed, skeptical parapsychologist would have been enhanced if I had been able to expose the Filipino healers as tricksters. Instead, I knew that some of my own colleagues would shake their heads in dismay, concluding that the pressures of my financial problems had finally affected me, that with advancing years I had lost my scientific rigor, or simply that I had taken one LSD trip too many. There was nothing for me to gain by urging an open-minded approach to the Filipino phenomena and much for me to lose.

However, if Sison's phenomena were genuine, how would they fit into the hypothesis I outlined at Caliraya? The red bloodlike liquid could have been "teleported" from a dye factory, painting shop, hospital, or butcher shop. But the disappearing cotton needed to be explained somewhat differ-ently. One might have conjectured that the cotton had entered the "bioplas-mic body," possibly through an acupuncture point. Quite possibly it traveled along a meridian and emerged from another acupuncture point. Of course, acupuncture points are rather tiny under ordinary circumstances; but under extraordinary circumstances, could they not expand as the skin electricity changed? And could not acupuncture points and meridians be the frame-work which held together the physical body and "bioplasmic body"?

A Psychic Placebo Effect

When I left Manila a few days later, I was convinced that a full-scale investigation of the healers by parapsychologists was essential. Indeed, other disciplines would also benefit from a research effort. The paranormal phenomena involved seemed, to me, to be only indirectly involved in the healing itself. It was my suspicion that much of the healing that occurred was self-healing, inspired by the healer's psychic pyrotechnical displays. Therefore, medicine could learn a great deal from what was going on in the Spiritists' centers, even if they remained skeptical about the psychic nature of the incidents themselves. I guessed that even fraudulent healers could bring about healing in much the same way that a physician administers a sugar pill when the patient's complaint appears to be psychosomatic. In other words, the "placebo effect," which accounts for a sizable proportion of "cures" in Western medicine, also applies to psychic healing and pseudopsychic "healing."

Lessons applicable to psychotherapy also emerged from a number of specific practices I observed. Taylo had spoken to an ailing boy's mother of a "hex," but had told us that the young man's swollen testicles could have been the result of anger or resentment "that he was unable to express." This may have been a case of psychic healing which also involved the emotions; it would be important to follow up the case to see if the swelling of the boy's testicles went down as he began to deal with his feelings more directly.

While at "Merciful Endeavors," I also observed a healer at work with a young boy who was losing hair. As medical treatment had been ineffective, and skull X rays had been inconclusive, one could certainly posit a psychosomatic reason for his disturbance. The healer dropped melted candle wax into a bowl of water, telling the boy and his mother that the shape of the solidified wax would resemble the "spirits" who were causing his trouble. Once the three blobs of wax had solidified, the healer told the mother that they should be placed under the boy's pillow at night and that incense should be burned during the day. In an aside to me, the healer noted that the shapes "represented things the boy is afraid of" and that his advice, if taken, would "help him overcome his fears."

I interpreted the waxen shapes as serving a projective function similar to that of Rorschach inkblots. The boy, consciously or unconsciously, would project the images of his fears into the blobs. The act of placing them under his pillow would force the boy to confront his fears; the burning of incense would force him to attend to this task by day—either consciously or unconsciously. Thus, a resolution of his fears was entirely possible through these procedures; once his fears were worked through, his hair might even start to grow back.

Psychology is another field which could benefit from studying the Filipino phenomena. In fact, three psychologists (Don Parker, Shelby Parker, and Mary Jane Ledyard) visited the healers a few months after I did and brought back similar impressions. Why does each healer demonstrate slightly different phenomena? The explanation might rest in the healer's personal psychodynamics. Blance had a record of violence in his personal history which included throwing rocks at the Spiritists when he was a boy. Perhaps this aggression was sublimated in his purported laser beamlike scratch.

Although I did not know enough about Bustamante's and Taylo's earlier lives to conjecture how their psychodynamics tied into their healing processes, there were several correspondences between their patients' histories and the foreign objects which surfaced at "Merciful Endeavors." In the case of a gardener, it was pebbles and clay that emerged. In the case of an eighty-three-year-old man, a withered brown palm leaf appeared. Perhaps the presumptively "teleported" objects related to the psychodynamics of the patient, the healer, or both.

Some Misconceptions

For the suggested scientific investigations to proceed properly, some misconceptions would have to be laid aside. For example, I was warned that the healers would be wary of a scientist and would not deviate from their set patterns on behalf of scientific research. On the contrary, I found that I could inspect anything in the room, stand as close to the patient as I liked, make any simple requests, discuss the process with the healers, and even assist in the procedures—affording me a closer look. I had explained to the healers that, as a scientist, I was searching for the truth—and that I intended to spread the news of my findings in ways that would assist other sick people.

I had also been told that the Filipinos were too modest to allow much of their skin to be exposed; hence it would be difficult to check for trickery. However, the healers I observed removed much more clothing from the patients than did the healers in the films. It was not unusual for a woman to be completely nude from the waist up. When the removal of this much clothing was required, the patient could request that a cloth be held between her and the other patients in the room—a request I only observed on one occasion. Exposure of the pubic area was more unusual, for both men and women, but it was often necessary to pull down the pants or skirt to expose as much of the abdominal area as possible.

Another misconception involved the so-called "opening" and "closing" of the body wall. With the exception of the small scratch produced by Blance, never once did I see this happen. In fact, the "opening" may not be in the physical body at all, but in the "bioplasmic body," allowing the viewer to see the bioplasmic counterparts of the physical organs. A change in the "bioplasmic body" might well affect a change in the physical body; therefore, this procedure could be extremely useful in certain cases.

Harold Sherman has given a possible explanation of the supposed "opening" of the physical body. The hypothesis states that cell structures can be separated and then reunited by the electromagnetic power of the healer. Although I would prefer my own explanation (which places the phenomena at the bioplasmic level), the notion put forward by Sherman, following a conversation with a European physicist, is provocative.

Another misconception involves the impression that no adequately trained scientists, physicians, or magicians have felt the Filipino phenomena to be genuine. While in Manila, I was given a long list of professional people who had visited the healers. It is true that many of them observed blatant examples of fraud and chicanery. However, a number of healers—including those I observed—had elicited wonderment from some magicians who admitted they could see no sign of trickery.

Finally, some scientists and physicians ran tests which convinced them that, in some cases, the phenomena were real. However, these individuals —chiefly from West Germany and the United States—have refused to make a public statement of verification or to publish their findings. Their excuse? It would damage their professional reputations. I was furious to hear of this situation. I knew the statements of the Filipinos were true because two of my scientific colleagues had returned from the Philippines, convinced that some of the healers actually did have unusual abilities—and both refused to share their impressions with the scientific community.

In my own case, I discussed my visit to the Philippines in public a week after my return. At the end of my banquet address to the annual meeting of the Jersey Society of Parapsychology, I stated that the healers I had seen may indeed have possessed psychokinetic ability and that the possible paranormal phenomena they manifested were among the items most worthy of scientific study that I had observed in my travels to various places in the world. However, I could not make a conclusive statement because I merely observed and did not impose any controls.

To many people, the most convincing incidents involved the cotton that, at one point, seemed to be half inside of me and half outside. I found out that Don Westerbeke had observed the same phenomenon while visiting Sison. He said, "If you ask her to stop, she will pause and the cotton seems to be protruding from the skin." How could "palming" explain such a process?

A bizarre reaction to psychic healing in the Philippines was made by William Nolen in his 1974 book, *Healing: A Doctor in Search of a Miracle*. In the book, Nolen made frequent disparaging remarks about the Philippines. For example:

> I'd suggest that if you're thinking of visiting the Philippines—that is, if after you've had your head examined you still want to go, you lock yourself in a sauna for two weeks instead; weatherwise, you'll know exactly what it's like to visit the Philippines . . . and you'll have saved yourself about $2,000.

He then proceeded to describe his visits to various "healers," describing how each one of them used legerdemain—palming an animal eye for an "eye operation," using betel-nut juice to simulate blood, scratching the body with a hidden piece of mica to resemble a "psychic opening," etc.

The crux of Nolen's diatribe against the healers was a lengthy account of an interview with a "Dr. Louis Martinez," described as "a practicing clinical psychologist" to whom physicians "refer patients for psychoanalysis" and to whom obstetricians send "pregnant women who need training in preparation for natural childbirth." Martinez is cited, in the book, as claiming to know most of the "healers" personally. He also is quoted as saying:

1. There are about twenty "healers" altogether.
2. Antonio Agpaoa operates in Manila; he is afraid to go back to Baguio for fear he will be assessed for back taxes.
3. The psychic healing phenomenon began to occur about thirty years ago.
4. Juan Blance makes an incision with a sharp object before he starts to knead the skin. The cut shows up as he applies pressure to the body.
5. Josephina Sison has betel nuts in her kitchen. Imitation blood can be made from betel nuts. Thus, Sison's effects are explainable by sleight of hand.

Martinez concluded the interview by saying:

> This psychic surgery business is getting out of hand. It may be bringing money to our country, but it is also giving us a bad reputation with respectable people from abroad. Something needs to be done. I hope you can do it.

The uninformed reader dipping into Nolen's book will not realize that there are considerably *more* than twenty Filipino healers, that Agpaoa *did* go back to Baguio City, that psychic healing in the Philippines goes back *hundreds* of years, that Blance, in my presence, *did not* knead the body after the incision appeared, and that I had observed no container large enough to hold all of Sison's purported betel nut juice during the morning I had observed her at work.

Furthermore, there does not seem to be such a person as "Dr. Louis Martinez." None of my friends in Manila had heard of him, nor could they locate him in the phone directory. Nolen admits to using pseudonyms in his book, but one should not use a false name of the purportedly intelligent professional person whose word is accepted as evidence. In view of this serious flaw in Nolen's account, his other charges have to be viewed with extreme skepticism.

I have repeatedly stated the need for caution when discussing the Filipino controversy; I do not doubt that most of the purported "operations" are done by sleight of hand. The phenomena which I observed could have been paranormal or they could have been clever illusions. I knew enough about magic and about visual perception when I arrived in the Philippines not to trust all the information given to me by my eyes. However, some of the events I witnessed were remarkable enough to demand further investigation, and the healers I spoke to expressed their willingness to cooperate with science. The facts simply are not yet in, and it is better to be open-minded than to close our options. In the meantime, it is as irresponsible to publicize false information as it is to perform fraudulent "operations."

The Lopsided View

For Carie's birthday in 1974, I took her with me to Carlin, Nevada, the home of Rolling Thunder and his wife, Spotted Fawn. Corinne Calvet went along with us as did my long-time assistants Michael Bova and Alberto Villoldo.

Rolling Thunder taught us the snake dance and stopped the pain associated with a gall bladder problem which had been bothering Calvet. He interpreted the images which Villoldo had received during a recent dream series. He discussed the theory behind psychic healing with Bova, a student in Lawrence LeShan's healing seminars. And he initiated me into the sweatlodge ceremony. I experienced one of the most profound altered conscious states of my life as the water was poured over the hot rocks, as the steam filled the hide structure or *wickiup*, and as we cleansed ourselves by chanting, praying, and sweating out our impurities.

Rolling Thunder told us of a recent case in which he touched a sick person's stomach and several pebbles appeared to emerge. I told him about the similarity of this event to the Philippine phenomena; Rolling Thunder stated that the stones were symbolic of the disease, the sick person being "hard" and "dense"—thus liable to get sick again until a personality change took place.

Rolling Thunder also told us about treating a young man who had been labeled a "hopeless schizophrenic" by a physician after the young man had set fire to his parents' home. He was taken to a hospital in a strait jacket and his parents telephoned Rolling Thunder.

The medicine man told them, "Your son will come home soon, and I will come to see him." A week later, the young man was sent home for a visit, even though the psychiatrists had originally decided to confine him to the hospital for six months.

Rolling Thunder and the other members of his party (who later corroborated the incident), arrived at the young man's home at a prearranged time. Rolling Thunder rubbed a white herb on their faces to protect them from the "evil forces."

After talking with the young man, Rolling Thunder asked his father to buy some raw meat. He began to burn herbs to purify the room. When the raw meat arrived, Rolling Thunder asked the young man to stand on it. The shaman then brought an eagle claw and feathers from his bag and moved around the room slowly, chanting in an Indian dialect.

The young man cringed whenever the eagle feathers came near him, and finally—as Rolling Thunder passed the feathers over the young man's head —he screamed and flung himself to the floor.

As the young man writhed on the floor, the medicine man began to whimper like a dog, sniffing and growling. The young man's body stiffened, he screamed again, and began to shiver. Rolling Thunder's body also stiffened; he turned quickly and coughed up a black substance which he expectorated into a can.

Five hours after the ritual began, the young man began talking in a relaxed manner and said he felt "totally relieved." The incident occurred almost a year before our visit; the young man's illness had not returned. One of the members of our group suggested that this might have been an "exorcism" and that Rolling Thunder may have excised an "evil spirit" from the young man's body.

Rolling Thunder continued his discussion of psychic healing by referring to Edgar Cayce as "a great medicine man among the white people." He said that all healers, "have to be in accord with the Great Spirit when they-work." Among primitive people, he noted, "ESP is common. Scientists will eventually discover what savages have always known." This comment, and our visit to Carlin, Nevada, reminded me of Jule Eisenbud's contention:

The price man has paid for his by now quite devitalized and concomitantly lopsided view of matter and motion in a world bristling with unresolvable paradoxes is incalculable. The price is a world that the primitive, who was fairly comfortable with his simple belief in the efficacy of his volitions, including his death wishes, would no doubt view as one of unimaginable horror. At the same time the price is a world in which we no longer have the means of comprehending all the dimensions of causality and determinism in the natural stream of life's events, in which may be imbedded influences now undreamed of.

Eisenbud wisely suggested that the place to begin such a restructuring of our worldview "would be with a deeper study of the psychology of the paranormal."

11

BE NOT DECEIVED

Just because fake mediums sitting in darkened rooms can induce
gullible dupes to shake hands with cold, sand-filled rubber gloves,
there is no reason to deny the reality of psychic phenomena we
cannot yet explain. . . . The temptation to produce hoaxes and
the temptation to believe that what is strange and not understood
must be a hoax are equally human vulnerabilities. And so in
exactly those fields in which human beings are exploring possibilities that boggle the mind, it is most likely that some people
will perpetrate hoaxes and that others, as one way of protecting
themselves from anxiety, will suspect that they are being hood-
winked. But this does not mean that the whole thing is a hoax.
It means only that one recurrent response to fear of the unknown
is insistence that it's all some kind of trick.

Margaret Mead

A New Code

By 1974, the funding problems at Maimonides were critical. At one point
during the year, we discovered that there was only enough money left to
sustain our operation until August 16. On August 8, just as plans were being
made to close the laboratory, a private donor agreed to give us a research
grant.

This development gave us a chance to refine further our judging procedures for the dream studies. Gardner Murphy had frequently told me that
his main criticism of our work was that the scoring process was not objective enough; different judges would produce different ratings depending on
how impressed they were with the correspondences between the dream content and the pictures being transmitted. Our "units of meaning" procedure
was an improvement; each "unit" in a dream transcript was inspected for
correspondence with the art print. This proved to be more objective, but
also more time-consuming.

246

Finally, Charles Honorton devised a judging technique which was both objective and efficient. He selected ten categories from Calvin Hall and Robert Van de Castle's book, *The Content Analysis of Dreams*. He then assigned art prints a number indicating how many of these content categories they possessed. If an art print had none of the categories, it would be coded with ten zeros: 0000000000. If it contained all the categories, it would be coded with ten ones: 1111111111.

The ten categories were color, activity, mythical characters, animals, human characters, implements, food, body parts, architectural objects, and nature scenes. Thus, Van Gogh's *Portrait of Lieutenant Milliet,* a colored art print of a bearded army officer, was coded 1000100000, indicating it contained color and a human character. A subject in one of Honorton's hypnotic dream experiments had the following imagery: "I had the impression that this was a close-up of a face—probably that of a woman or child, half profile, facing to the right. I tried to see more and I see kind of an orange and gold cobble." According to the coding system, this report contains items from only two of the content categories, human characters and color. The report is thus coded 1000100000, which is a perfect match with the target. This procedure allowed for a more precise determination of ESP when we used art prints, photographs, and other pictorial material.

The Structure of Reality

While Honorton was devising the new coding system for future research, Roy Dreistadt, a student research assistant, was using the "units of meaning" system to explore the nature of psi. Lawrence LeShan, in his writings, had concerned himself with how an individual's perception of reality influences his or her acquisition of information. In his work with Eileen Garrett, LeShan noted that while functioning as a psychic sensitive, she perceived the world differently than when she was perceiving the structure of reality in her ordinary state of consciousness. LeShan referred to this process as "clairvoyant reality" as opposed to "sensory reality."

LeShan also discovered that Garrett and other psychic sensitives perceived "clairvoyant reality" in much the same way that mystics wrote about their experiences and in a similar fashion to the descriptions of reality produced by certain theoretical physicists. From all three vantage points, there is a unity of all things, relationships are more important than single events, observers cannot be separated from what they observe, cause-and-effect relationships lose their meaning, time and space limitations are minimized, and one's ordinary perceptions are seen as not producing a valid picture of reality.

For LeShan, ESP operates when the subject slips into viewing one world in the modality of "clairvoyant reality." This condition is marked by a passive, but alert, state of mind. Therefore, LeShan predicted, "In dream material showing evidence of psi, this evidence will appear far more frequently when the dreamer reports that, in the relevant section of the dream, he was an *observer* of the action, than when he reports that, in the relevant section of the dream, he was a *participant* in the action."

To check out LeShan's hypothesis, Dreistadt and I had one judge take the dream transcripts of William Erwin, Robyn Posin, Theresa Grayeb, and Robert Van de Castle, dividing them into "units of meaning." A second judge compared each "unit of meaning" to the art print used that night to see whether there was a correspondence; if so, it was considered an "ESP unit," if not, it was considered a "non-ESP unit." A third judge evaluated each "unit of meaning" and determined whether the subject was a "witness," a "participant," neither, or both. In making this determination, the judge used the "witness" and "participant" scoring categories from Hall and Van de Castle's, *The Content Analysis of Dreams,* which read:

> WITNESS: This variable is considered to be present if the subject reports a dream in which he served as a witness of the event.
>
> PARTICIPANT: This variable is considered to be present if the subject reports a dream in which he participated in the event.

These descriptions matched LeShan's notation of an "observer of the action" and "a participant in the action." Thus, we felt they could be used to confirm or deny LeShan's prediction.

Taken together, the three studies with Posin, Grayeb, and Van de Castle, and the two studies with Erwin produced 1,602 "units of meaning" in which the subjects witnessed the event. Of these, 37 percent were "ESP units." There were 2,826 "units of meaning" in which the subjects participated in the event. Of these, 33 percent were "ESP units." The difference, although not dramatic, was statistically significant, verifying LeShan's prediction.

More dramatic results were obtained when each experimental series was analyzed. For the first Erwin study, 61 percent of the "units of meaning" in which he was a witness contained ESP as compared with 35 percent of the participant units. In the second Erwin study, the difference was even more dramatic: 92 percent for the witness units and 39 percent for the participant units. In the case of Van de Castle, 32 percent of the witness units contained ESP versus 24 percent of the participant units. In all three cases, the results were statistically significant.

For Posin, the score was 51.3 percent and 51 percent; for Grayeb, it was 26 percent and 23 percent. In neither instance was the difference statistically significant. The original statistics for these studies had produced similar data; Erwin's and Van de Castle's experiments had been statistically significant but Posin's and Grayeb's studies had yielded chance results.

According to LeShan, while a subject is in "clairvoyant reality," he or she cannot act but can only observe. Our analysis had confirmed LeShan's hypothesis and had demonstrated how theoretical material can be put to an experimental test. Fortunately, all the laboratory work had been done before LeShan announced his theory, thus refuting the criticism that we found only what we expected to find, unconsciously biasing our studies to produce the expected result.

The Banerjee Affair

Humanistic psychologists have frequently noted that the problem of unconscious experimenter bias is a major difficulty underlying all scientific research. The eminent physicist, Werner Heisenberg, has noted that scientists cannot help but be a part of what they study; therefore, the very act of examining an event results in altering that event. Robert Rosenthal's experiments have demonstrated that the information given to teachers about students often changes the teachers' attitudes toward the students, hence altering the students' behavior. If these effects operate in physics and psychology, they certainly operate in parapsychology where the dividing line between the observer and the observed, between the researcher and the phenomenon, is even more fluid.

In addition to the possibility of unconscious bias, science needs to be perpetually vigilant against conscious fraud. As a student at the University of Wisconsin, I learned about the "Piltdown Man," a creature thought to have lived half a million years ago. The existence of the "Piltdown Man" had been based on skull fragments and teeth found in Southern England by Charles Dawson and his associates—one of whom was Pierre Teilhard de Chardin. It was not until 1953 that scientific analysis proved that the jaw of the "Piltdown Man" had been artificially colored and aged; in reality, it was the jaw of an orangoutang. A tooth uncovered by Teilhard was also found to have been artificially colored. In retrospect, the evidence suggests that Dawson originated the hoax to insure his place in scientific history, planting fragments in the archeological site for himself, the unsuspecting Teilhard, and others to "discover."

In 1964, K. Ramakrishna Rao read a five-year report of the Seth Sohan Lal Memorial Institute of Parapsychology in India. These projects had been largely financed and supported by J. B. Rhine in his attempts to internationalize psychical research. While reviewing a series of experiments conducted with mothers and their children by H. N. Banerjee, Rao noted a strange pattern in the ESP "hits." Rao observed that the initial guess by the subject was frequently correct. He also found out that Banerjee left the first scoring space blank on a test sheet observed by J. G. Pratt. Rao wrote:

> This raises the question whether the experimenter may not have made a practice of leaving the top call space blank . . ., allowing it to be filled in after ascertaining the target for it.

Rao also discovered that when Pratt observed the sessions, the number of ESP "hits" decreased. After he excused himself, leaving Banerjee to his own devices, the number of ESP "hits" showed a dramatic increase.

Ian Stevenson objected to the tone of Rao's review and Pratt insisted that he should have been consulted before his name was used in Rao's critique. Banerjee objected to Rao's suggestion of fraud, proposing that the decline in ESP "hits" during Pratt's visit was due to the "general state of tension" in India "related to the Chinese invasion." Rao replied, "But one wonders why the Chinese invasion did not interfere with the subject's performance when Pratt excused himself and left Banerjee and his assistant to work." In any event, J. B. Rhine withdrew his support from Banerjee and the controversial researcher was no longer given serious attention by the parapsychological journals.

The Levy Affair

In 1974, ten years after the controversy over Banerjee had erupted, J. B. Rhine wrote an editorial in the *Journal of Parapsychology* titled "Security Versus Deception in Parapsychology." In his article, Rhine noted that concern over the security and the reliability of an experiment involves four questions:

1. Have the experiments been firmly controlled against counter-hypotheses such as sensori-motor leakage?
2. Have the statistics been appropriate?
3. Would the problem logically permit a definite conclusion if significant results were obtained?
4. Has the research been adequately secured to guard against experimenter deception?

Rhine gave several examples of attempted fraud in psychical research— most of them involving neophytes in the field. He spoke of checking ESP and PK scoring patterns as a method of identifying possible chicanery and concluded by stressing the necessity to "close in on the experimenter-deception problem."

Rhine's editorial was well-timed, coming on the heels of the scandal at the Sloan-Kettering Institute for Cancer Research. William Summerlin had reported grafting white skin onto black animals, black skin onto white animals, and skin from humans onto mice. However, some of his colleagues became suspicious and charged that Summerlin had dyed the animals' skins to make it appear that new tissue had been transplanted. A committee of Sloan-Kettering scientists investigated the case, verified the charges, and recommended that Summerlin leave the Institute.

A few months later, the Institute for Parapsychology, at the Foundation for Research on the Nature of Man, was hit by a similar scandal. In 1973, Rhine had named, as director of the Institute, W. J. Levy, Jr., a physician who had made his mark in parapsychology by testing the PK ability of rats. In one of his experiments, for example, Levy had implanted electrodes in the brains of rats in a zone where stimulation gave the rats intense pleasure. The rats were stimulated at random intervals by a computer. Without any outside influence, the computer would stimulate the rats' pleasure zones 50 percent of the time. If the rats could influence the computer by PK to deviate from randomness, their pleasure score would exceed 50 percent.

Earlier in 1974, Levy had reported a significant 54 percent pleasure score. Then one of Levy's assistants became suspicious, noticing Levy loitering needlessly about the equipment. With two colleagues, the assistant decided to check his intuition. From a hiding place, one of them observed while the others helped Levy run a test. The observer saw Levy tamper with a recorder, causing the scores to run above 50 percent. Another set of instruments had been installed without Levy's knowledge—and recorded the expected 50 percent score.

The three assistants reported the situation to Rhine, who confronted Levy. Upon resigning, Levy said that he had been under great pressure to produce positive results and insisted that this was the only time he had falsified data. Rhine cautioned other parapsychologists not to rely on any of Levy's work and began to reexamine his earlier findings.

Levy's deception was a cruel blow to Rhine, who had turned over the Institute to Levy in order to enjoy a well-deserved semi-retirement. In his editorial, Rhine had remarked that "apparatus can sometimes be used as a screen to conceal the trickery it was intended to prevent."

To me, the incident was yet another demonstration of the need for replicability in psi experimentation. If an experiment can be repeated at another laboratory under the same conditions, the possibility of fraud is considerably lessened. The fact that Levy's assistants detected his chicanery and that Rhine immediately took action demonstrate once again that parapsychologists are their own best police and critics.

The incident also may have sounded the death knell of attempts to explore psi phenomena through the rigid, old-fashioned methods of behavioristic psychology. Levy took this approach to its extreme, found that it simply did not work, and had to fabricate results to support his position. I hoped that the demise of Levy would also mean the demise of sterile, unimaginative experimentation in parapsychology.

And what about Levy himself? Levy had been the only prominent parapsychologist with whom I had not enjoyed a warm personal relationship. After his duplicity had been found out, several parapsychologists told me that they had never trusted Levy.

Another of my colleagues wrote me, "As for the Levy scandal, I am neither shocked nor surprised. . . . Ever since I visited Durham. . . , I have been fairly convinced that Levy's work was suspect." Indeed, some parapsychologists simply did what I had done over the years; we omitted all references to Levy's experiments in our own articles and reviews of the literature in psychical research.

Criticism and Regrets

The first book length critique of parapsychology to appear in the 1970s was *ESP: The Search Beyond the Senses,* by Daniel Cohen. Several criticisms of our work at Maimonides appear in the book. For example:

> Doctors Ullman and Krippner and the staff at the dream laboratory have tried to reintroduce the missing "emotional element" into their studies.
>
> By bringing in the emotional element, however, the dream researchers have opened their experiments to charges that significant results are not due to ESP but to an over-generous interpretation of what is supposed to be significant. Then, too, there is always the possibility of fraud. Is there no way that some of the subjects of the Maimonides experiments could have known what the target word would be, or somehow have made sure that a particular target picture would be chosen?
>
> . . . The researchers at the dream laboratory have been reluctant to allow skeptical outsiders to monitor their experiments too closely. Like many psychical researchers they believe that the overbearing presence of skeptics tends to disrupt ESP.

Cohen's attack is a splendid example of the "shotgun approach" of criticism; if you fire a blast in all directions, you might hit something and no one will notice those shots that go astray. Cohen did not explain how emotionally toned targets open up an "overgenerous interpretation"; if the statistical methods are rigid enough, such target pictures as a severed head and a crucifix can be employed just as effectively as cards containing a circle and a cross.

Cohen asked if there might be a way in which the subject could know the identity of the target before the experiment starts, or make sure that a certain picture is chosen. However, he gave no specific methods by which such deception could take place. Cohen also charged that we have been reluctant to allow skeptical outsiders to monitor our experiments—but provided no instance where this had happened. In fact, the opposite has been the case. Frequently, I have allowed professional research workers to observe the entire experimental process. And some of the student research assistants who have run the EEG and done the evaluation of the results have been very skeptical regarding the existence of ESP.

Cohen's treatment of our work at Maimonides reached a point of bankruptcy when, in discussing the PK abilities of Nina Kulagina, he wrote, "Dr. Krippner . . . claims that he, too, has been able to master the ability to move small objects about and that the ability improves with practice." Cohen's statement, like so many others in his book, had no basis in reality as I had never made such a claim.

I would be the last person to assert that we made no mistakes at Maimonides. One of my greatest regrets has been that we never had the time or the money to reevaluate all of our dream studies with identical statistical procedures to gain a solid basis for comparison. We constantly revised and improved our evaluative procedures over the years, but did not go back and inspect our earlier studies with the revised techniques.

The gravest single mistake I made at the Dream Laboratory occurred in the summer of 1969. I was heavily in debt, working at three other part-time jobs in order to raise money. A high school student showed up who wanted to do a research project which he could submit in a competition for a college scholarship. I put him to work counting rapid eye movements, in an attempt to see if the number of eye number movements bore any relationship to the "activities" category as described in Hall and Van de Castle's *The Content Analysis of Dreams*. I showed the student how to do the statistics, asking him to do them twice to be sure he had not made a mistake.

In between my trips to and from New York City, the sequence of events got completely out of hand. The student claimed to have gotten statistically significant results linking the number of eye movements to a dream's activity level. Wanting to make as much of an impression on the scholarship committee as he could, the student submitted his report to a medical journal. The editor of the journal, knowing me personally and assuming that the paper had my approval, rushed it into publication. I looked over the statistics, found that the student had made the identical mistake twice, and phoned the editor, telling him not to publish the article. It was too late. A week later, the journal arrived containing the claim that significant data emerged from a study in which the correct statistics would have produced nonsignificant results.

Shortly after publication, the editor received a letter from William Dement, one of the world's leading sleep researchers. He had taken the numbers reported in the article, recomputed the data, and had also obtained nonsignificant results. I wrote to Dement, accepting responsibility for the fiasco, and promised to publish an article containing the correct information. The only pleasant memory of the entire disastrous situation was a cordial note from Dement telling me not to feel too badly about it because the same thing had happened to him.

Science cannot make allowances for events in one's personal life to result in shoddy research. The incident taught me a lesson in administrative control that I have never forgotten. I am only grateful that the embarrassing incident occurred in one of our non-ESP studies rather than affecting an ESP article where the results would have caused even greater damage.

Oracles, Playing Cards, and Phantom Hands

Psychic phenomena have been reported since ancient times. And trickery among psychics is just as old. For example, the Oracle of Delphi began to assume an important role in Greek culture about 800 B.C.; nothing of importance was carried out unless the oracle was consulted. However, it was not long before the temple was flanked by a marketplace where pilgrims could buy souvenirs and religious objects. Further, the Oracle's messages became more and more ambiguous and open to a variety of interpretations. In the fifth century B.C., the king of Lydia asked the oracle if he should wage war against Persia. The oracle predicted that the war would destroy a great empire. Confidently, the king marched off to battle. But his army was decimated, and his own empire destroyed. Nevertheless, the oracle's prediction was considered confirmed.

In 1882, the British Society for Psychical Research was formed and its founder, William Fletcher Barrett, read a provocative report concerning apparent thought transference. Five young girls had been tested; when one was out of the room, the investigators selected an object which the girl would name upon her return. Barrett told how a white penknife, a box of almonds, and five playing cards had been guessed correctly. As soon as

Barrett's report appeared in print, a scorching criticism was made by Henry Donkin, an astute physician. The girl who had left the room was not blindfolded and she could have been given clues by the others upon her return. Thus, psychical research in Britain had not chosen an auspicious incident to inaugurate its history. However, better controls were gradually introduced and the society's later experiments were conducted more rigorously.

In 1895, the British Society for Psychical Research brought the controversial, exhibitionistic occultist Eusapia Palladino from her native Italy to London for a series of sessions. Palladino had been investigated by a host of experts in Italy, France, Poland, and Russia, but opinion about her ability was divided. Nor was the dispute settled in Britain. As she sat before a table, with her hands and feet held by the investigators, the room was darkened and bizarre phenomena occurred. Tables soared, objects descended from a cabinet behind her, and phantom hands appeared over her head. One investigator claimed that Palladino gradually moved her hands together, eventually lifting her left fingers and putting her right fingers in their place. This ploy gave Palladino free use of her left hand. The leading British conjurer of the day, John Nevil Maskelyne, agreed with this explanation after seeing Palladino perform.

Nevertheless, Palladino was soon on her way to the United States, purportedly for scientific experimentation. However, no representatives of the American Society for Psychical Research had been invited to Palladino's premiere performance in New York City in 1909. Soon after the session began, raps were heard, the table tilted, and a drumlike sound was produced. The evening was considered a triumph for the Italian visitor.

Once scientists were brought into the picture, the situation changed. During a later session, two investigators, clad in black from head to toe, crawled into the room when the lights were dimmed and hid under the chairs. With their heads close to Palladino's feet, they saw her strike the table leg with her shoe to produce raps. They also saw her put her left foot under a table leg to tilt it to the right. When she lifted her other foot, all four table legs rose from the floor.

On the other hand, certain of Palladino's sessions were acclaimed by the investigators. Howard Thurston, America's leading stage illusionist, observed Palladino and wrote, "I am convinced that the table was levitated without fraudulent use of her hands, feet, knees, or any part of her body, or by any mechanical device." He offered a thousand dollars to anyone who could prove that she cheated. Joseph Rinn, one of the investigators who had hidden beneath Palladino's table, made a counteroffer of a thousand dollars to Palladino if she produced paranormal phenomena while laced up in a canvas sack. Neither sum was ever awarded; Palladino refused to enter the sack and her detractors were unable to catch her cheating once the offer had been made.

Palladino returned to Italy in 1910. She was revisited by E. E. Fielding, an investigator for the British Society for Psychical Research who had filed a highly favorable report on her in 1908. This time he sadly concluded that she resorted to trickery.

It is unfortunate that Palladino felt that she had to produce dramatic phenomena at each sitting; whatever genuine ability she might have had could easily be attributed to the fraudulent methods that were known to characterize at least some of her operations.

A Bender of the Keys

During my trip to Brazil, I heard many provocative stories about the late Ze Arigó, the psychic healer first brought to my attention by Andrija Puharich who had visited Arigó several times but who had never made a formal scientific study of him. After Arigó's death in 1971, Puharich wrote:

> I had failed both Arigó and humanity by not completing my studies of Arigó's healing work. I realized that I should have dropped my other work in 1963 and concentrated all of my efforts on Arigó. I was sure there would never be another Arigó in my lifetime. But if there were, I would not fail the next time.

Later that same year, Puharich, while in Israel, watched Uri Geller perform before an audience. Preceded by musical numbers, jugglers, clowns, and comedians, Geller demonstrated what he claimed to be ESP and PK. After a series of private meetings with Geller, Puharich was convinced that he had found another Arigó.

In collaboration with Edgar Mitchell and Judith Skutch, Puharich brought Geller to the Stanford Research Institute in California. In 1973, Jean Mayo and I were invited to see Geller demonstrate his abilities at the home of Jeffrey Smith, a philosopher with a long-time interest in psychical research.

Geller asked volunteers from the audience to write numbers and names on a blackboard while he faced the audience. He correctly identified what was written, but this did not impress me because he was not blindfolded and could have quickly looked at the board while distracting the audience's attention. Further, he had friends in the audience who could have given him clues as to the identity of the material.

More impressive was Geller's PK demonstration. While a member of the audience grasped the earpiece of a pair of glasses loaned to Geller by another spectator, Geller held the volunteer's hand. I was sitting in the front of the room; as far as I could see, Geller did not touch the earpiece itself. Soon, the *other* earpiece began to bend as if tremendous heat was being applied. The volunteer removed her hand from the earpiece and the bending continued over the next few minutes, even though neither Geller nor the volunteer was touching the pair of glasses.

Events moved very quickly. Alan Vaughan held a hotel key while Geller touched Vaughan's hands. The key bent even though Geller had not touched it. At 10:00 A.M. one day, Edgar Mitchell removed his watch and placed his hand over it. Geller concentrated on the watch for thirty seconds, then told Mitchell to inspect it. The hour and minute hands of both the watch and its separate Greenwich time dials had been moved back one hour and eight minutes.

While Geller was visiting Wernher von Braun, the scientist's secretary informed him that his small electronic calculator was not operating. Geller held the calculator between his palms for two brief intervals and its function was restored.

When Geller and I appeared on the Barbara Walters television show, "Not for Women Only," I saw him bend a key and a spoon while stroking them. These feats, of course, could have been duplicated by a clever magician. Not so easily explained is a key that bent while someone in the audience was holding it at a distance of several feet, unless she was a confederate of Geller's.

At the Stanford Research Institute, two physicists, Harold Puthoff and Russell Targ, were unable to obtain satisfactory PK data from Geller but did obtain ESP results which were statistically significant and which were published in the prestigious British scientific journal *Nature*. Russell Targ and Jean Mayo served as cotransmitters during some of the telepathy tests. In one instance, Targ randomly selected the word "farmer" to transmit to Geller. Mayo drew the picture of a farmer with a pitchfork, then whimsically added horns, a tail, and the word "devil." Geller drew a picture containing two pitchfork-shaped objects, a snake, an apple with a worm in it, and the words "God" and "The Ten Commandments." When he observed the picture which Mayo had drawn, he noted that the word "devil" never is mentioned in a Jewish temple and that he would not have written the word down even if he had perceived it.

No Show

Puthoff and Targ produced a film documenting some of their work with Geller and I was invited to SRI to preview it. Parts of the film showed well-controlled tests designed to eliminate sensory clues or motor effects; in one experiment, Geller several times predicted which number would turn up on a die kept in a closed container which was shaken. However, other aspects of the film disturbed me. Geller was able to identify correctly which of several metal containers had been filled with water—but a water-filled container is discernibly different than neighboring containers which are empty. Also, Geller correctly drew a picture that a telepathic transmitter was looking at; however, they were both in the same room and any number of clues could have been given unconsciously. In all, I detected twelve flaws in the film which I urged the SRI investigators to correct. Puthoff and Targ were sympathetic to my criticisms, but the film had already gone into production and it was too late to make the changes.

Shortly after this incident, I was in California when Judith Skutch and her son, Jonathan Cohen, telephoned me. They had just taken a series of Kirlian photographs of Uri Geller's fingertip while a person in a distant room telepathically transmitted a letter or a number. In most instances, the correct letter or number showed up on the electrophotograph in the middle of the corona around Geller's fingertip! As Geller excitedly joined the conversation from an extension telephone, I described what additional controls would have to be added to create an experiment worth publishing. For example, a random selection of the letters and numbers was needed, and the number of attempts would have to be decided in advance.

Skutch, Cohen, and Geller agreed to carry out my proposed experiment the following week. However, Geller never showed up.

Nevertheless, Skutch raised the money to have Geller investigated at Maimonides. Charles Honorton devised a series of ESP and PK tests based on previous experiments conducted at the laboratory. Randall Zwinge, a magician known professionally as "The Amazing Randi," arrived one day to see if he could use legerdemain to simulate ESP and PK.

Zwinge failed. Honorton's safeguards and controls did not permit the magician to pass a single test. The only effect left in his wake was a scratched desk; Zwinge had attempted to distract Honorton and bend a key against a desk. Honorton was not distracted and the key did not bend. Zwinge, one of Geller's most severe critics, concluded that if Geller could perform under Honorton's conditions, he might have to revise his opinion concerning the Israeli psychic.

Here was Geller's chance to vindicate himself. His ESP successes at SRI were dismissed by some critics because of the Institute's inexperience in parapsychological testing. Russell Targ, although an amateur magician who supposedly would be on guard against sleight of hand, had an eye defect which suggested to some skeptics that he could not carefully observe what Geller was doing. Furthermore, if Geller could execute the PK tests which had been prepared for him at Maimonides, he would have exceeded the repertoire of talents he had exhibited at SRI.

But Geller did not show up at Maimonides. Several times the appointments were rescheduled and several times Geller found more important appointments. Zwinge gleefully predicted that Geller would never appear at Maimonides because the controls were too tight.

The Limits of Personal Experience

Geller would not allow Honorton to test him, but he did agree to see the celebrated psychiatrist, Andrew Weil. While sitting in the same room with Weil, Geller "telepathically" perceived a geometric figure which Weil had drawn. Geller then tried to bend a key; after holding it for a considerable length of time—and while conversing with other people in the room—Geller put the key down. Later in the session, he picked it up again and it appeared to bend almost immediately. Weil, in a report appearing in *Psychology Today,* told how more images were drawn and more pieces of metal were bent. On the basis of several personal experiences with Geller, Weil concluded, "I have no doubt that Geller is real."

But then Weil went to see Randall Zwinge. Before Weil's eyes, Zwinge appeared to bend a nail and correctly copied a drawing done in private by Weil. Zwinge also gave his explanation for one of Geller's other effects:

> He asked a woman to write a foreign capital on the blackboard, and she wrote "Denver." The whole audience was annoyed at her for not following instructions. At one point you could just see every head in the audience turn to glare at her, and right then old Uri just shot a glance at the blackboard. It's that simple. And when he broke a zodiac ring at the end, he said, "Let's try two rings at once." What he did was to click off his microphone for an instant, wedge one ring into the other, and gave a hard squeeze so that the zodiac ring broke where the setting was joined.

Zwinge also criticized SRI for not including a professional magician as a consultant in their studies of Geller. Zwinge claimed, "Scientists are the people *least* qualified to detect chicanery. . . . If you want to catch a burglar, you go to a burglar, not to a scientist. If you want to catch a magician, go to a magician."

After Zwinge appeared to bend one of Weil's personal keys, Weil wrote, "My faith in Geller lay in pieces on the floor." What Zwinge had done was to distract Weil's attention and bend the key against a chair. Weil concluded:

> I can't say with certainty that Uri Geller doesn't have the powers he claims.
> . . . I am not sure that stage magic can explain completely everything I saw

him do. And that is just about as far as I can go without getting very confused.

In my opinion, Weil would have been less confused had he set up some elementary scientific safeguards before Geller performed, or simply refused to make a premature judgment on the basis of his observations. I remembered the conversation in Kansas when Weil told Abraham Maslow that he was not interested in doing research on the Tarot cards because his own personal experience had convinced him of their validity. I would be the last one to deny the importance of personal experience, but in psychical research, one must learn to combine personal experience with a scientific approach—especially when dealing with a Eusapia Palladino or a Uri Geller.

The Case of the Hamilton Pocket Watch

In 1974, Judith Skutch arranged a meeting between Uri Geller and W. E. Cox, J. B. Rhine's long-time associate in North Carolina. I had always felt that Cox was one of the brightest people on Rhine's staff; not only was Cox a careful researcher, he was also a magician and the chairperson of the Society of American Magician's National Occult Committee. Cox prepared several PK tests and gave his analysis of them at the 1974 convention of the Parapsychological Association.

Cox reported:

> The first test was with a flat steel key of the safety deposit box type, much too hard to bend by hand. . . . He laid my key on the glass (coffee table), we both noted its absolute flatness. I placed my right forefinger lightly on the larger end, and Geller gently stroked the remainder with his right forefinger. The key began to bend slowly at a point just before my finger. . . . Any pressure of his naturally would have been against the direction of the bend. . . . No semblance of fraud was detected. . . .
>
> [Another] experiment involved my Hamilton pocket watch. It was handed to Geller, with its chain. I had proposed this earlier by telephone, wherein I had said only that I was going to alter the speed regulator and challenge him to readjust the same so that the watch would run again. . . . He expressed uncertainty, held it to his ear, did not shake it unduly, kept it clearly within my view, then again listened and ejaculated, "It's ticking, it's ticking!" . . . This watch had been specially prepared in advance. . . .
>
> A strip of tinfoil . . . was inserted upon the balance wheel bridge. . . . Ten minutes before my interview I depressed the shorter portion into the spokes of the wheel and thereby stopped it.
>
> Following Geller's accomplishment, I retrieved the watch. . . . On opening the back, we found the regulator arm to have been moved slightly. . . .

> This had pulled the shorter end of foil with it, up out of the wheel. The
> remaining . . . tinfoil was separated and had itself been moved. . . . This
> dual effect within my watch was even more impressive to me than the
> keys. . . . Insofar as the question of deception by Geller is concerned, I
> believe . . . that it has been ruled out as the explanation of these three
> effects.

Cox expressed his regrets that Geller seemed to be "more interested in
entertainment and publicity" than in science. The answer given by Puharich
was that Geller's mission on earth was to serve as an intermediary between
cosmic intelligence and human beings. Why waste one's time with scientists
when unidentified flying objects and extraterrestrial intelligence have greater
plans in store?

Heat at a Distance

Following the Geller controversy as carefully as I could, I reached the conclusion that he might possess genuine psychic talent. Some of the criticisms of
Geller were outrageous—including an allegation that Puharich had planted
a hearing aid in Geller's tooth. And in any case, the shielded room used at
the Stanford Research Institute would have prevented this device from
functioning even if it had been used.

Unfortunately, Geller was not above using sleight of hand when he was
nervous, tired, or when his powers faded. However, I reached a different
conclusion in regard to Ingo Swann, an artist and another of SRI's research
subjects. Swann simply refused to attempt ESP or PK when he was not in
the mood. His record of parapsychological accomplishments, therefore, is
both impressive and immune to criticism.

Swann recalled "zooming out of the body" as a child. When he had his
tonsils removed at the age of three, he claimed to have "watched the doctor
perform the whole operation from out of my body." After the operation, he
stunned the physician by correctly telling him that the removed tonsils were
now in a side cabinet behind two rolls of paper.

In 1971, some friends took photographs of Swann in a darkened room
when he was trying to produce "energy" that could show up on a special
type of infrared film. Swann recalled, "I felt that I was going out of my
body and from there directing the energy to form balls of light in my
hands." The photograph did appear to show balls of light. Zelda Suplee, a
friend of Swann's, showed me the picture and also shared it with Gertrude
Schmeidler. Both of us were impressed. Schmeidler asked Swann to participate in a PK experiment and he enthusiastically agreed.

Four thermistors (extremely sensitive devices which measure heat) were used in the experiments. Swann sat in a chair about three feet in front of the machine on which the temperature changes in the thermistors could be observed. One thermistor was randomly selected for Swann to affect through PK. A typical sequence of attempts was "Rest, Make it hotter, Rest, Make it colder, Rest, Make it colder, Rest, Make it hotter." Each attempt lasted forty-five seconds. A total of five sessions was held. Significant differences between Swann's "Make it hotter" and "Make it colder" attempts were observed on the selected thermistor during four of these sessions. Schmeidler concluded that Swann's scores "demonstrated a significant PK effect."

I visited Swann when he was serving as a research subject at SRI; he told me how he had been able to both increase and decrease the movement in a magnetometer—one protected by superconducting shields thought to be impervious to any outside influence. He also suggested that some of my students do a pilot study on Kirlian photography with him as a subject. A team of four students spent a day with Swann attempting to determine if he could affect leaf and fingertip coronas at a distance. The results were extremely dramatic. By changing his state of consciousness, Swann appeared to change the width, pattern, and color of the corona discharge of the objects being photographed. I observed the session and felt that Swann was one of the most gifted and cooperative subjects I had ever witnessed.

Out of the Body

Swann also worked with Janet Mitchell and Karlis Osis at the American Society for Psychical Research. An eccentric miner had left a large sum of money to be used "to study the human soul." A court decided to award the bequest to the society. Swann's claim that part of his consciousness could "leave" his body made him a perfect subject for these experiments.

Each day before Swann arrived, a laboratory assistant would place several three-dimensional items on a platform suspended from the ceiling. There was a partition in the platform allowing objects to be placed on both sides. Swann would then enter with electrodes glued to his scalp; Mitchell would connect the electrodes to a junction box to measure his brain waves as well as control his movements so as to have proof he did not leave the chair.

Swann would attempt to "leave his body." Upon returning to an ordinary state of consciousness, he would draw what he thought was on the suspended platform. He would also note the direction from which he saw the objects; this information was needed to see if his impressions matched the side of the platform on which the corresponding objects had been placed.

Swann frequently drew pictures which matched objects on both sides of the platform. For one session, the objects on one side of the platform were a black leather holder for a letter opener placed on a red paper heart. On the other side, a bull's-eye had been made from construction paper. Swann drew the platform and divided it in half. On one side he drew a red oval which came to a point at the end. On it, he drew a long black form which corresponded to the shape of the black leather holder. Swann drew a bull's-eye on the other side of the platform. Again the colors matched the actual object, but they were reversed.

There were eight sessions in this experiment and an outside judge was able to match correctly each of Swann's eight drawings to the correct set of objects. The expectation of this happening by chance is one in 40,000.

Primary colors seemed to be perceived more clearly by Swann than pastels. Familiar forms seemed to come through more readily than unfamiliar forms. And materials such as leather, fabrics, and clay seemed to work better than plastic, glossy paper, or glass.

Swann's success in this experiment did not *prove* that he was "out of the body"; he might have used precognition, telepathy, or clairvoyance to identify the objects. However, there did seem to be a change in Swann's brain-wave patterns when he was experiencing an "out-of-body" state. A decrease in the activity of the brain's left hemisphere was the most noticeable change reported.

Charles Tart had previously studied two subjects who went "out of the body" while asleep. Although the EEG records of the two subjects differed, both showed a "flat" EEG record with a dramatic slowing down of alpha-wave activity. One of the subjects claimed that her consciousness "rose" to the top of the room; she correctly identified a five-digit number which Tart had placed on a platform. The other subject, Robert Monroe, felt his consciousness "drift" to an adjoining room; he correctly described events which were taking place in that room at the time.

In 1970, Tart visited Monroe in Virginia. Staying overnight, Tart told Monroe to take him along if he went "out of the body" that night. Late the next morning, Tart began to awaken, feeling what he described as "a sense of vibration." He thought he should try to get "out of the body" then lost consciousness. A while later, he awakened feeling that he had almost had the experience but had failed.

Perhaps not. That same morning, my stepdaughter, Carie, was on her way to school in Manhattan when she thought she saw Tart waving to her from a restaurant. She was late to school so did not stop to talk with him, thinking that he would undoubtedly visit me later and that she would see him again then. Carie returned home that evening, reported the news to me, and I was quite puzzled—knowing that Tart avoided New York City because of his dislike for the place. I wrote Tart and we discovered that his "vibrations" occurred at about the same time that Carie was on her way to school.

Carie and Tart always had a close rapport and enjoyed each other's company very much. So if Tart did get "out of the body," he found a way to visit Carie without exposing his physical body to the pollution, noise, and crowds of New York City!

12

THE PUZZLE OF PSI

I have no personal doubt that we can communicate from mind
to mind in a way that does not involve our organs or senses in
the usual way. I, therefore, continue to hope that new scientific
explanations, however impartial or critical they may appear,
will offer one day fresh hypotheses. . . . One lives a fuller life
when one comprehends the world of dreams, psychic impulses,
urges, and even conscience itself. . . . Without those who have
helped me pursue the light within, I would still be knocking on
the outer doors of insight that lead to the untapped sources of
energy which . . . I regard with both awe and veneration.

Eileen Garrett

What Have We Learned?

Geraldine Lenz spent her birthday at Maimonides, running the polygraph
and studying the EEGs of subjects in one of our biofeedback studies. Suddenly, she was grabbed from behind, a pillowcase was slipped over her
head, and she was carried—kicking and screaming—into a darkened room.

Lenz's fear turned into puzzlement as the pillowcase was removed. A
single candle on a birthday cake illuminated the scene. A dozen figures surrounded her, all draped in white sheets. All wore pillowcases which came to
a point at the top. Pleasant music played in the background. Had Lenz been
kidnaped by the Ku Klux Klan? No, she was welcomed to a secret meeting
of the MOPs—the Mysterious Order of the Pointees.

Lenz recalled attending a showing of the classic film, *Freaks*, earlier that
summer. Most of the dream lab staff had been with her—and enjoyed the
antics of three sisters with pointed heads. We had immediately named them
the "Pointee" sisters, and joked about how they must have been caught in a
pencil sharpener during their formative years. A few weeks later, one of the

dream lab staff members had her first LSD experience, and imagined that her head was growing a point.

After the birthday cake had been eaten in a ritual of silence, all of us went into Manhattan to introduce Lenz to our magnificent leader, the Grand Pointee. By this time, Lenz too had a point at the top of her skull—a birthday party cap on her head underneath the pillowcase.

Lenz was ushered into one of the environments designed by Aleksandra Kasuba and used previously by Michael Bova and me in an ESP experiment. By this time, she had identified several of the Pointees—Bova, Stuart Fischer, Clark Hubbard, Richard Davidson, and myself. But who was the Grand Pointee? The masked figure was sitting on a throne at the far end of the environment, wearing the tallest point of anyone.

Lenz's pillowcase was removed and she was given three chances to guess the identity of the Grand Pointee. If she failed, her point would be removed and she would be banished in disgrace. Lenz noticed that the Grand Pointee's hands were very small—barely large enough to hold the circular ball which was spewing colored lights throughout the environment. Lenz also noted a strand of long, dark hair emerging from beneath the Grand Pointee's hood. She asked the imposing figure, "Are you Carie?" She was correct.

Later we mused how fortunate we would be if the siren of psychic phenomena would give us as many clues as had the Grand Pointee. After nearly a century of careful observation, laboratory experimentation, and statistical evaluation, just what had we learned about ESP and PK?

In 1964, two social scientists, Bernard Berelson and G. A. Steiner, produced a volume containing 1,045 scientific findings about human behavior. They also cited four additional findings from parapsychology, noting that the evidence, though persuasive, had not yet been accepted by the majority of scientists. These four general statements were representative of the collected parapsychological data and the "state of the art" when I became director of the Maimonides Dream Laboratory in 1964:

1. ESP and PK exist, in one form or another. The typical ESP study involves a pack of twenty-five cards of five different types. The subject guesses the identity of each in a series of runs through the pack. In telepathy, the cards are visible to a sender but not to the receiver. In clairvoyance the subject guesses the identity of cards in another location. In precognition, he or she predicts the order of future cards. ESP is indicated by a number of hits significantly above the chance expectancy of five per run. Most PK experiments have dealt with mental attempts to influence dice, thrown either by hand or by independent mechanical devices.

2. People vary in their extrasensory capacities; relatively few are

"highly sensitive." The highly sensitive are so designated because they consistently do somewhat, although not very much, better than chance. For example, a highly sensitive subject may guess consistently at the rate of seven correct out of twenty-five cards, where five correct would be the chance expectancy.

3. ESP seems to be related to the belief in its existence. In one series of studies, subjects who reported for experiments with the belief that ESP is possible, did better than skeptics. Some efforts to replicate this finding, however, have been negative.

4. ESP and PK performance is often better in the initial stages of an experiment, or under novel or spontaneous conditions. PK, particularly, shows a striking and consistent decline from the early to the later trials in a series.

Berelson and Steiner concluded that "there are a large number of specific findings regarding the relative effectiveness of various sizes of cards or dice, distances between subject and sender, subjects with various personality patterns as measured by tests, and the like. But none of these, to date, is as well established . . . as are the above mainline findings."

I was of the opinion that Berelson and Steiner had done an excellent job of summarizing the scientific data emerging from parapsychology at that time. I was also interested in their observation that the inventory "has rather little to say about central human concerns: nobility, moral courage, ethical torments, the delicate relation . . . of the marriage state, life's way of corrupting innocence, the rightness and wrongness of acts, evil, happiness, love and hate, death, even sex." These concerns, of course, were central to humanistic psychologists such as Charlotte Bühler and Abraham Maslow who were just then beginning to gain wide attention for their efforts to broaden and deepen the scope of science to include consciousness, values, creativity, and other human potentials and concerns.

In 1971, Gertrude Schmeidler conducted an informal survey of Parapsychological Association members in an attempt to assess what had been learned in the field. The consensus was that ESP was firmly established and that it occurs in the various forms designed as clairvoyance, telepathy, and precognition. Strong argument was also expressed that PK occurs.

There was a striking agreement that psi is a general ability rather than one limited to a few individuals. The information provided by ESP is partial rather than total. The systematic errors which often occur in psychic experimentation (such as significant below chance scores, "decline" effects, and significant "displacement" of one's ESP to the incorrect target) can ultimately provide useful information about the process involved. It was agreed that negative attitudes and social withdrawal tend to be associated with low ESP scores while belief, interest, and enthusiasm are conducive to high scores. Neither retrocognition (psychic knowledge of past events) nor survival after death had been experimentally demonstrated. And finally, the parapsychologists in Schmeidler's survey conceded that the physiological processes of ESP input and PK output are unknown.

Applying Basic Concepts

The issues raised in both of these overviews convinced Gardner Murphy and me that we should further study the topic. This resulted in a paper, "Humanistic Psychology and Parapsychology," in which we discussed the basic theoretical concepts of humanistic psychology outlined by Charlotte Bühler and applied them to psychical research.

Bühler emphasized the importance of studying the person as a whole. Parapsychology, however, has usually focused its attention upon observed responses of subjects who guessed the order of cards or who tried to influence the fall of dice. Few parapsychologists have shown an interest in the total human being whom they study, or the process involved by which a subject manifests ESP or PK. Exceptions to this pattern have been the psychoanalysts who have written clinical reports of psychic sensitives or of their patients who occasionally demonstrate psychic phenomena. Ira Progoff's study of Eileen Garrett is a case in point, as well as the superb clinical descriptions by Jule Eisenbud, Jan Ehrenwald, Montague Ullman, and others, of psi in the psychotherapeutic relationship. The work of W. H. C. Tenhaeff stands as another exception. While holding the prestigious chair in parapsychology at the State University of Utrecht, Tenhaeff studied some 40 Dutch psychics intensively, discerning "a great sensitivity for everything coming from the outside world" and an ability "to identify with nearby persons and objects."

The second concept stressed by Bühler was the importance of studying the entire course of human life. Again, parapsychology has ignored this task, focusing instead on what a group of people are able to do in one experiment or what psychic sensitives can demonstrate in a few observations. It is often said that children are better subjects in psi experiments than adults; in J. B. Rhine's early research, a nine-year-old girl made correct guesses on all twenty-five ESP cards in a deck. However, no one has taken the trouble to compare ESP or PK responses of people at various ages, or to design a developmental study which would trace the psychic performance of an individual from childhood to maturity. Some clues can be gained by studying the autobiographies of celebrated psychics; Eileen Garrett's autobiographical writings describe how psychic phenomena entered her life and how they developed over the years.

Bühler's third emphasis was on human intentionality and choice. And Abraham Maslow once described how the person with a fragile sense of self typically possesses a limited capacity for self-determination. Gertrude Schmeidler and R. A. McConnell had studied the self-concept of high-scoring and low-scoring ESP subjects using Rorschach inkblots. They found that high-scoring subjects had a higher degree of "psychological self-sufficiency" than low-scoring subjects. The high scorers also displayed more of a readiness to accept new experiences—and were less rigid in their perception of the environment which they saw in less stereotyped ways than the low scorers. In addition to this type of research study, parapsychologists often speculate on the question of "free will," as do humanistic psychologists. K. Ramakrishna Rao, for example, has claimed that parapsychological data support the concept of human choice; to Rao, PK indicates that human volition can change external objects.

The importance of human motivation and goal setting was the fourth theoretical aspect of humanistic psychology stressed by Bühler. In one of Gertrude Schmeidler's experiments, believers in ESP tended to score higher than nonbelievers, presumably because of personal motivation. And Martin Johnson, at the State University of Utrecht, attempted to manipulate the scoring direction of college students by increasing their motivation. Johnson gave one group of students a stack of sealed envelopes, stating that some of them contained questions which would be used in their final examination for a psychology course. The students attempted to identify those envelopes through ESP. A second group of students was told merely to find the envelopes in a stack which had been randomly selected previously. The scores of the first group were significantly higher than those of the second group.

Bühler's fifth emphasis was on the human being's propensity to search for meaningful experiences and to establish a set of values which would assist the integration of one's entire personality. I recalled my several meetings with Eileen Garrett, whose psychic experiences appeared to be integrating factors in her life which provided meaning and value. I also recalled how she discouraged people from embarking on psychic development prematurely. At one of her conferences, a young woman attempted to enter a mediumistic trance, and became overwhelmed with anxiety which she could not handle. A psychologist and a psychiatrist who were attending the conference finally pulled the neophyte together and Garrett advised, "Until you have more personal stability and emotional maturity, psychic development is not for you."

In 1973, I was interviewed by *Psychology Today,* and stated:

People often ask me how they can learn to do telepathy or PK. My response is that I would first want to make sure that they had developed the capacity to love, to show compassion to other human beings, to have worthwhile human relationships. They should also engage in some sort of creative, fulfilling work. Next, I would like to see them develop some sort of social consciousness, some way in which they can make a contribution toward making this a more humane world. Then if they want to develop their paranormal abilities, fine. But that goal ought to be pretty far down the list.

In addition, I told the *Psychology Today* interviewer how values must be an integral part of scientific investigation. All scientists, including parapsychologists, have moral responsibility for their acts; "If you can use psychic energy or bioplasma to heal someone, then you can also use it to hurt someone."

The sixth assertion made by Bühler was that creativity, more than any other human behavior, demonstrates that the human brain is an "open system" with a certain freedom of operation as well as a capacity for change. In our article, Murphy and I noted that there had been a host of experiments which demonstrated a link between creativity and psychic phenomena; further, psi also demonstrated the brain's existence as an "open system." In one of these experiments, Charles Honorton had used ESP cards, finding a significant difference in precognition success between high-scoring and low-scoring subjects on a creativity test. Murphy had often commented that creativity and psi both were characterized by positive motivation, relaxation, and dissociation. One recalls the story of Archimedes leaping from a bathtub shouting, "Eureka!" Just as the solution came to Archimedes while relaxing in a warm bath, many creative insights and telepathic messages have emerged while people are dreaming, meditating, or engaged in other activities which permit one aspect of consciousness to relax while another portion retains its concern over a problem to be solved or a loved one to be contacted. Often, the breakthrough comes while there is a "shift" from relaxation to activation, as several of our research studies at Maimonides demonstrated.

Bühler's final theoretical statements in regard to humanistic psychology concerned the importance of person-to-person relationships in psychotherapy and education. Any number of psychoanalysts, such as Joost Meerloo, Berthold Schwarz and Montague Ullman had written about cases in which their patients dreamed about events in the psychoanalysts' private lives. More recently, leaders of therapeutic "encounter groups," such as Paul Bindram, Steve King, and William Schutz have told me of apparent ESP occurring between patient and patient, or between patient and therapist in these settings. In 1974, I was invited to give a series of lectures at the University of Wisconsin Hospitals; in a meeting with the psychiatric staff, I discussed ways in which person-to-person encounters appear to facilitate ESP, and how these incidents often indicate that the patient is ready to move ahead in therapy and develop an even more open relationship with the therapist.

As for education, a similar phenomenon can take place; Margaret Anderson and Rhea White have found that students who liked their teachers scored higher on ESP card-guessing tests in which the teacher supervised the experiment than the students who did not like their teachers. In addition, the high-scorers obtained better grades in school than the low-scorers, leading one to conjecture that successful education and successful psychotherapy may have an ESP component.

Murphy and I concluded that humanistic psychology and parapsychology had much to learn from each other. The humanistic psychologist can accept psychic capacities as another human potential which is worthy of attention in research, in psychotherapy, and in education. Parapsychologists can enhance their findings by studying psychic sensitives as they develop and change over a several-year period, as well as considering them as total human beings.

Finally, Bühler, Maslow, Tart, and others have pointed out ways in which psychology can be enriched so as to more easily encompass the study of psi. Examples would include the conceptualization of the brain as an "open system," the scientific study of unusual but meaningful human potentials such as "peak experiences," and the development of "state-specific sciences" in which more attention is paid to altered states of consciousness.

A Decade of Dreams

I had another chance to reflect upon my ten years at Maimonides when preparing two papers for the Fifth International Conference on Humanistic Psychology at Andhra University in Vishakhapatnam, India.

James Hickman and I gave a paper on the American Indian and humanistic psychology; in it we noted the traditions shared by the two movements—a concern for the natural ecology, a respect for individuality (exemplified in the attention paid to the special gifts of both children and elderly people), an emphasis on altered states of consciousness (as in the "vision quest"), a concern for one's inner life (as demonstrated by the importance of dreams in many Indian tribes), and a unique sharing of decision-making power with women.

Hickman and I did not claim that the American Indian culture was perfect; there were superstitions, petty rivalries, and bloody sacrifices that marred their record. Indeed, some of the rivalries persisted. When Rolling Thunder spoke at a California college, I invited the local "Red Power" group to attend. They refused because Rolling Thunder was not a separatist; he treated sick people regardless of their ethnic background, and worked to better the lot of many oppressed people, not solely Indians.

My other paper was a review of the Maimonides experiments from 1964 to 1974. I summarized all of our dream studies—those with Erwin, Bessent, and Van de Castle which yielded highly significant results, those with Posin and Grayeb which produced no evidence of telepathy, our screening studies, hypnotic dream studies, and pilot studies, as well as the complex experiments which attempted to tell us more about ESP through using several pictures during the night or through contrasting emotional and nonemotional films. I ended the paper by presenting several conclusions which Ullman and I had reached, and which were open for verification or refutation from other scientific laboratories:

1. ESP in dreams can be demonstrated in a laboratory setting. Most of our own studies had yielded statistically significant results, and the majority of experiments in laboratories which had attempted to repeat our work were also successful.

2. For ESP to occur in dreams, it is important to emphasize the role of expectation, motivation, and emotion. For example, subjects who are "open" to a telepathic experience are more likely to dream about the picture being transmitted than subjects who are uncomfortable with the thought of having their dreams invaded by someone else.

3. Altered states of consciousness appear to be favorable for the occurrence of ESP. Collections of people's experiences with psi indicate that most of them occur in periods of altered awareness, such as dreams or drowsiness. This finding emerged not only from Louisa Rhine's collection, but from records collected over the years by both the American and British societies for psychical research. Our work with self-report scales indicated that the greater the alteration in consciousness reported by our subjects, the more likely they were to score well on an ESP test, whether awareness was altered by sensory isolation, sensory bombardment, relaxation, electrosleep, or a colorful environment. Further, a noticeable "shift" from one state of consciousness to another produced the highest ESP scores of all.

In other words, we had demonstrated that real-life experiences, such as telepathic dreams, could be recreated in a laboratory setting and scientifically studied by researchers who wanted to understand psychic phenomena. The impact of our work was dramatically revealed to me before I left for India. Upon receiving the program for the 1974 convention of the Parapsychological Association, I noted that of the sixteen experimental papers, eight were to be presented by Maimonides staff members or were attempts by other laboratories either to replicate our work or to expand on it. It was apparent that Ullman, Honorton, and I had profoundly influenced the direction of parapsychology.

Of course, this did not happen by accident. Throughout the years, we had shared our findings with other researchers through personal contact, through the mail, and by presentations at both parapsychological and non-parapsychological scientific meetings. We had been extremely careful in the area of public relations, not allowing our research to be sensationalized and popularized, but always cooperating with programs that would educate the public with accurate material and in a low-keyed manner. It was a great compliment for us to receive a letter from J. B. Rhine, stating:

> I have said several times over the years . . . that I think there has been a better educational presentation of the Maimonides dream work than of any-thing else of which I know in the field of parapsychology. This began very noticeably back in the case of the first publication. It went into a number of forms of presentation and . . . holds true over the continuing course. . . .

I looked back over the ten years in the dream lab, wincing at my mistakes, shuddering at the obstacles, smiling when recalling most of our experiences, and glowing when considering our accomplishments.

The Road to Amritsar

In July 1974 Lelie and I left for India. Accompanying us were James Hickman, Martha Harlin (who planned to lead a "psychic development" workshop at the conference), two college students, and three American Sikhs who were making a pilgrimage to Amritsar, the international headquarters of their religion.

Our first stop was Delhi, where I was told about a previous visitor, David McClelland—the psychologist who had brought Timothy Leary to Harvard. Having heard much about Maharaji from Baba Ram Dass, McClelland and his wife visited the guru's temple. Finding it deserted, they were about to leave when Maharaji appeared, invited them in, and proceeded to tell McClelland specific details about his childhood. The next morning, McClelland's wife awakened with a very high fever. No physician could be found and McClelland called upon Maharaji for assistance. The temperature subsided following a period of psychic healing, and the McClellands proceeded on their way. Within a few months Maharaji was dead, but he had altered McClelland's view of human potential more than either Leary or Ram Dass had succeeded in doing.

Delhi is the site of Jantar Mantar, an astronomical observatory built at the command of Maharajah Swami Jai Singh II in 1710. We examined several portions of the observatory which still remain—a horizontal sundial, an instrument for marking the declination of the sun, and a device for computing noontime at four different observatories around the world. We also inspected a complex device which could be used to reconstruct the position of the sun, moon, and planets at the time of one's birth, enabling an astrologer to cast a person's horoscope. This structure reminded me of the data scrupulously collected by Michel and Françoise Gauquelin which demonstrated the effects of planets on one's temperament. Perhaps planetary positions, sunspots, and phases of the moon had a more important effect on ESP and PK than most parapsychologists have suspected; if so, these cyclic variations need to be taken into account when experiments are designed.

Our next stop was Agra, home of the incredible Taj Mahal, the most beautiful piece of architecture I have ever seen. The Mogul emperor Shah Jahan built the Taj Mahal as a tomb for his wife, who died after giving birth to their fourteenth child. One of Shah Jahan's sons, Jahangir, later seized power and imprisoned his father in a nearby tower. We had used a picture of Jahangir in our second dream telepathy study with William Erwin —accompanied by Indian costumes to heighten the emotional involvement of the telepathic transmitter. The beauty and the tragedy embodied in the Taj Mahal, as well as the successful experiment with Erwin, impressed upon me the importance of studying psi in natural settings, or at least designing experiments which incorporate emotionality and other human concerns that characterize many real-life occurrences of ESP and PK.

Upon arriving in Amritsar, we were greeted by a delegation of Sikhs and taken to the Golden Temple, a spectacular building which rests on a lake. Devotees of Sikhism bathe in the lake as its waters are reputed to have healing powers. The large number of people we saw enter the water confirmed my belief that research in psychic healing should have a larger priority among parapsychologists. It is no doubt true that most of those who report improved health from the waters of Amritsar, the shrine at Lourdes, the Spiritist clinics in Brazil, or the healing centers in the Philippines are moved by expectation, devotion, charisma, suggestion, or self-delusion. Nevertheless, a small number of cases are difficult to explain away as are the results of the laboratory experiments reported in this complex area.

The Sufi and the Pandit

From Amritsar we flew to Srinigar where we were met by Saint Suber Singh, leader of the Sikhs in Kashmir. The white-bearded Sikh patriarch told us that he had awakened that morning with the thought in his mind, "I must go to the airport." Once he arrived, he noticed our three Sikh companions, who were wearing their turbans. Singh enhanced our stay in Kashmir, teaching us a great deal about the philosophy of Guru Nanuk, founder of the Sikh religion. Singh's impulse upon awakening, to leave for the airport, may have been ESP; if so, it serves as another example of how psychic phenomena are often manifested during "shifts" in consciousness. These "shifts" need to be thoroughly scrutinized if the manifestations of ESP and PK are to be understood.

One morning we drove to a small village to meet a Sufi teacher widely acclaimed as a psychic healer. The Sufis represent an esoteric mystical wing of the Moslem religion. At the 1972 Menninger Foundation Conference on internal states, I had developed an interest in Sufi dances, Sufi meditation, and Sufi stories. One story, used at the 1972 conference, seemed especially appropriate for scientists investigating altered states of consciousness:

> Once upon a time, there was a monkey who was very fond of cherries. One day he saw a delicious-looking cherry, and came down from the tree to get it. But the fruit turned out to be in a clear glass bottle. After some experimentation, the monkey found that he could get hold of the cherry by putting his hand into the bottle by way of the neck. As soon as he had done so, he closed his hand over the cherry; then he found that he could not withdraw his fist holding the cherry, because it was larger than the internal dimension of the neck.
>
> Now all this was deliberate, because the cherry in the bottle was a trap laid by a monkey-hunter who knew how monkeys think.
>
> The hunter, hearing the monkey's whimperings, came along and the monkey tried to run away. But because his hand was, as he thought, stuck in the bottle, he could not move fast enough to escape.
>
> But, as he thought, he still had hold of the cherry. The hunter picked him up. A moment later he tapped the monkey sharply on the elbow, making him suddenly relax his hold on the fruit.
>
> The monkey was free, but he was captured. The hunter had used the cherry and the bottle, but he still had them.

This Sufi tale reminded me of the difficulty we have in bringing specific tangible ideas and thoughts back from certain episodes of altered consciousness. Sometimes a person hears a lovely song in a dream but cannot retrieve it upon awakening. At other times people claim to be given tangible objects during prayer by a "spirit guide," but find that these objects are not present when the prayer is over. The Sufi tale indicates that sometimes it is better to appreciate the altered state while it lasts—to enjoy looking at the cherry in the bottle—rather than attempting to bring it back to ordinary reality.

These impressions came to mind as we drove to the outskirts of a small

Kashmiri village and parked our cars. We walked down the earthen streets and entered a grass-thatched house. We found spots on the floor; joining a dozen people who were already sitting there. The Sufi, a moon-faced man of middle age, entered and sat with legs crossed on a mat at one end of the room. He smiled at us and, through our translator, conjectured, "You have come this way in your quest for knowledge and your search for peace." He said very little more. After lunch, he walked us to the street and asked if we had any questions. Nobody responded. He concluded, "It is just as well that you do not ask me questions. Look into yourselves and you will find all the answers."

A naive observer might have been puzzled at the morning's proceedings. However, we interpreted the events as an intricate healing service permeated by human ecology. Several times, the Sufi had taken money from one person to give it to another. He had also attempted to distribute his "healing energies" in a number of ways—through the food and beverages that were served, and through the steady gaze of his dark eyes toward those who were ill or troubled.

Returning from our visit with the Sufi, we had only a brief amount of time to rest before keeping an appointment with Pandit Gopi Krishna. The Pandit had experienced what he called an "awakening" of the "Kundalini energy" during the earlier part of his life, and had devoted his subsequent years to studying the implications of this "enlightenment" for the evolution of higher consciousness. He was convinced that the "Kundalini awakening" altered one's reproductive cells in such a way that children born to parents who had experienced "enlightenment" would represent a significant leap forward in evolutionary development.

During our conversation, Gopi Krishna spoke about a rush of *Prana* or "biological energy" up the spine as the mechanism involved in one's "Kundalini awakening." He was familiar with the Soviet concept of a "bioplasmic body" and compared it with the "pranic spectrum" spoken of by ancient Indian philosophers. It is this "pranic spectrum" that is a component of all life; it is involved in psi phenomena and could probably be observed during psychic healing.

Because of his own experience of "enlightenment," Gopi Krishna was in a unique position to suggest scientific approaches to the study of "Kundalini." He told us, "A strange phenomenon occurs after the awakening of Kundalini; the consciousness becomes a most intriguing, a most fascinating, and a most mysterious entity—and one never tires of studying oneself." As I listened to Gopi Krishna, I thought of the scientists who have called for an elimination of the line between the experimenter and the experiment, between the observer and the observed. Parapsychology could benefit from Gopi Krishna's program of self-study.

A Dream Grows in Vishakhapatnam

K. Ramakrishna Rao met our airplane in Vishakhapatnam and told us that psychologists had arrived from all over India for our meetings. Rao welcomed the visitors and informed the audience that he and I were time twins —having been born on the same day of the same month of the same year (October 4, 1932), and both ending up in humanistic psychology and parapsychology. He also discussed his commitment to strictly controlled experiments in parapsychology while seeing an equally great need to pay attention to people's experiences in real-life situations which might provide insights which have not been obtained in laboratory tests.

Rao later took me on a tour of his departmental offices, library, and a research laboratory named after Eileen Garrett, a long-time friend of Rao's. It was encouraging to hear that one of Rao's graduate students, Shanti Piasad, had attempted to study ESP in dreams. After collecting dreams from one subject for several nights, she had judges attempt to match the dreams with those pictures concentrated on by a telepathic transmitter. The results were statistically significant, yielding another example of paranormal dreaming under experimental conditions. As Rao's graduate students told me of the ambitious program of experiments they had planned for the future, I realized that even if we ran out of money in Brooklyn, our dream would continue to grow in Vishakhapatnam.

The last day of the Conference was highlighted by a demonstration of yoga. It was presented by T. S. N. Murty, a retired educator and school administrator—a black-haired man in his seventies, who demonstrated astonishing control over his body musculature. As Murty twisted his body into unusual positions, and as he gave advice on breathing exercises and diet, I was reminded of the skeptical attitude most scientists had toward yogis until biofeedback experiments demonstrated that many people could be trained to control their brain waves, relax their muscles, alter their heartbeat, and lower their temperature. Further, if specific brain waves and other physical recordings could be found which accompanied psi, could not biofeedback training be used to improve a person's psychic abilities? Some of the leading experts in the field seemed to think so.

A Missing Piece

The last city we visited in India was Hyderabad, home of the Patanjali Yoga Institute, the imposing Qatar dynasty tombs, and the magnificent Hyderabad Museum. As we walked through the art collection housed in the museum, I noticed many paintings which looked familiar because we had used some reproductions of them as materials for our telepathic transmitters at Maimonides.

I recalled how subjects would often distort a telepathic message to conform to their own backlog of experiences. Van de Castle dreamed of cowboys when the transmitter was looking at a painting from India, *Man with Arrows and Companions*. An Iranian student dreamed of a Zoroastrian temple when the transmitter was concentrating on a painting of a Protestant church. Perhaps ESP provides us with no new stimulation, instead enabling us to recall memories—or combinations of memories—appropriate to the distant event we appear to perceive.

Our memory bank, if this were true, could be stimulated by informational fields extending from a given person or object. Space, then, could not be considered "empty" but as a connecting matrix for these psychic fields. The most appropriate memory available for recall would be elicited by these fields, just as a jigsaw puzzle requires a missing piece. Sometimes the piece fits well, sometimes the memory matches the event, and sometimes the appropriate memory is simply not available. Parapsychologists could design tests which consider the past experiences of the subjects, selecting ESP materials which are most likely to correspond to the subject's personal interests and stored memories.

Premature Discoveries

Looking back over my years in parapsychology, as well as the decades which had preceded my entry into the field, I concluded that the field had developed quite well. The progress of parapsychology is especially surprising, considering the outside opposition it has encountered, the fraud it has discovered within its own ranks, and the perpetual lack of funding with which it has had to contend.

Thomas Kuhn, in studying how science advances, noted that new discoveries are typically rejected until a "paradigm" or explanation is put forward which will accommodate them. In the meantime, the people who have made these discoveries cannot expect that their rejection will be overcome simply by the accumulation of stronger evidence in favor of their reality. An English parapsychologist, R. H. Thouless, has commented on the implications of Kuhn's ideas for parapsychology:

> It would . . . be a misunderstanding . . . of Kuhn's ideas to infer that our task now is to think out a new paradigm. It is not thus that scientific revolutions have taken place in the past. The call is rather to more detailed and more precise research. As we know more about the psi phenomena and as our knowledge becomes more exact, the shape of the future paradigm will gradually become clear. . . . Then an individual like Darwin, Newton, or Einstein will put forward a new explanatory system in terms of which the

phenomena of psi will not merely be explained, but will be shown to be such as we should have expected.

Thouless's statement made good sense to me, and I began to speculate on what directions psychical research should take in the future.

I discussed some of the possibilities for future psi research at a panel on humanistic psychology organized by Carmi Harari, Alberto Villoldo, and me at the Fifteenth InterAmerican Congress of Psychology. Held in Bogotá, Colombia, during December 1974, this was the first InterAmerican Congress to present a panel on humanistic psychology and to air the topic of parapsychology. I suggested that there were at least two ways that breakthroughs in parapsychology could occur. In one instance, parapsychologists could keep refining their technique until a repeatable experiment emerges. Gardner Murphy has suggested replication will only come once the entire context of the psi event is well understood. Once it comes, the factors could be disentangled—one at a time—for close study. Eventually, after moving from wholes to parts and back to wholes, a pattern would emerge that fits into a rational theory. I suggested that this could lead to further experiments which would eventually place parapsychology into the arena of existing knowledge about the world. Until then, psi phenomena are premature discoveries, events stumbled upon before they can be easily understood and therefore ignored or rejected by most of the scientific community.

A second possibility is that other psychological researchers, in the course of their work, will run into psi phenomena which they will not only acknowledge, but continue to explore until they are understood. Investigators in such fields as psychedelic drug and biofeedback research have already reported anecdotal instances of psi which they have observed, while psychotherapy researchers have noted it on a clinical level. Eventually, experimental data may occur which can only be explained by the existence of ESP and PK.

For example, a research psychologist in Canada found that specific brain waves would appear whenever a telepathic message was sent from a distant room. Inaugurating a formal experiment, he obtained significant results which he published in *New Horizons* under the title "Objective Events in the Brain Correlating with Psychic Phenomena." Unfortunately, he had to publish the paper under a pen name because he knew he would face censure, and possibly dismissal, from his university if his superiors knew he had been engaged in psychical research.

Gary Schwartz, a psychologist at Harvard University, was invited to address the Parapsychological Association at its 1974 convention. He suggested that ESP might actually be ESCP—"Extra-Sensitive Cortical Perception"—which would respond to ultraweak "signals" of which science is currently unaware. Schwartz suggested that the notion of psi phenomena is not as bizarre as many scientists think. We already know that the brain responds to subliminal stimulation, material that is perceived unconsciously rather than consciously. In addition, some organism's cells are responsive to changes in the moon despite the great distance between them. And various types of electromagnetic fields can influence the brain, thus changing behavior. Schwartz concluded that possible models for ESP, or ESCP, already exist in psychology; brain researchers may begin to encounter psi phenomena as they proceed along these lines of research.

Psi, for example, may be observed by the psychologists who study the differences between brain hemispheres. Roger Sperry, David Galen, Robert Ornstein, and others have observed that the brain's left hemisphere controls the right hand side of the body and is predominantly involved with language, mathematics, and logical thinking. The right hemisphere, which controls the left side of the body, is primarily responsible for art, music, fantasy, spatial orientation, and intuition. There are many exceptions to this generalization; for example, one group of researchers discovered that people with musical experience recognized melodies better in the right ear than the left, while the reverse was true for inexperienced listeners. Therefore, the experience of a person must be considered before making simplistic statements about the brain's hemispheres and ESP. However, in an experimental study, William Braud and Lendell Braud reported an association between right hemisphere functioning and high scores in psi tests. Further work in this area is certainly needed.

Another area worth pursuing for its possible interface with psi phenomena is the study of cybernetics which explores the similarities between computers and the human brain. One computer, designed by Lawrence Pinneo at the Stanford Research Institute, portrays a dot's movements on a screen while a subject, attached by electrodes to the computer, tries to direct the dot by thinking about it. The computer recognizes seven different commands—up, down, left, right, slow, fast, and stop—by matching subjects' brain waves with patterns stored in its memory bank. At some point, an investigator might have subjects attempt to move the dot on a similar computer, using PK instead of electrode connections.

In the meantime, cybernetics can help us to develop models which may explain how psi operates. And with computers, we can examine the scoring patterns made by psychic sensitives on ESP card tests to help determine the underlying process. J. G. Pratt has stated that spontaneity is the basic characteristic of psi in all of its manifestations. If so, this should be kept in mind when cybernetics and computer technology are utilized by parapsychologists.

A Psi-Conducive Syndrome

I also told the psychologists in Bogotá about the vast series of psychological and physiological tests administered to subjects by psychical researchers. Although the results have not been consistent, and in some cases have been contradictory, ESP does appear to be associated with such personality traits as "extroversion," "expansiveness," and "spontaneity." In other words, the ability to "let go" would appear to be of value if a subject in an ESP test wants to make a high score. (Is the same thing true for psychokinesis? We simply do not know, because very little work has been done on personality traits of high-scoring PK subjects.)

As for physiological tests and the states of consciousness which accompany them, William Braud has described a "syndrome" which appears to be conducive to psi. Physically, it consists of muscle relaxation, a slowing down of brain waves, and a reduction of heart rate, blood pressure, oxygen consumption, breathing, blood lactate level, and electrical conductivity of the skin. A low level of blood lactate usually accompanies a reduction of anxiety and anger as do many of the other factors noted.

The "psi-conducive syndrome," similar in many ways to an LSD trip, also consists of a blurred perception of where one's body leaves off and where the environment begins. Other accompanying psychological processes include an increased ability to think in terms of images and wholes, to have access to intuition and the unconscious, and to turn one's attention inward. There is a decrease in logical, abstract thinking, in analyzing the environment, and in making judgments. One's time sense changes and the boundaries between past, present, and future fade away. If "extraverted," "expansive," and "spontaneous" people can be trained to enter this state of internally oriented awareness, high ESP scores should result.

Braud's "psi-conducive syndrome," of course, reflects our findings at Maimonides using dreams, hypnosis, biofeedback, etc., to explore altered states of consciousness. The fact that we have not always been successful indicates that certain factors need to be considered in addition to the presence or absence of a "psi-conducive syndrome." One of these factors involves the experimenter. Michael Polanyi, a philosopher of science, noted that scientific knowledge is never impersonal knowledge but depends upon the values, biases, and investigative techniques of the scientist. And Robert Rosenthal conducted dozens of psychological experiments which demonstrated the unconscious effect a researcher has on an experiment. When Rosenthal addressed the 1971 convention of the Parapsychological Association, he raised this issue and applied it to parapsychology.

Since then, a number of parapsychologists have studied the "Rosenthal effect" in their laboratories. Much to their surprise, it proved to be an important factor. For example, Charles Honorton designed an experiment at Maimonides in which one group of subjects was treated in a friendly, informal manner, while another group was handled formally and distantly. Even though the words used were exactly the same, the first group made higher ESP scores than the second group.

In another study, J. G. Craig, at the University of Waterloo, randomly assigned rats to two experimenters. Each experimenter picked his rat from a cage and deposited it at the beginning of a maze. The running time of each rat was recorded. After the experiment was concluded, half of these rats were randomly selected for "extinction." The doomed rats run by one experimenter took no longer to run the maze than his rats who were chosen to survive. But the rats handled by the other experimenter ran the maze significantly more quickly if they were later placed in the survival group rather than the extinction group.

Craig concluded that unless the effect of the experimenter is measured, parapsychologists cannot make any definite conclusions regarding the nature of psi in animals. In Craig's experiment, the rats later marked for extinction could have precognitively realized their fate, thus becoming listless and running more slowly through the maze than the rats who survived. But the fact that this occurred for only one experimenter's animals suggests that it may have been the experimenter who was precognitive rather than the rats. If so, did the experimenter influence the rats to slow down through telepathy? Through psychokinesis? And if the "Rosenthal effect" occurs in parapsychology, will we ever be able to study psi processes without considering it? Probably not. The experimenter is an integral part of the experiment. Parapsychologists as well as other scientists must realize this fact and design their research projects accordingly.

The Synergistic Relationship

K. Ramakrishna Rao, after surveying the parapsychological literature with one of his students, sadly concluded that "there are far too many variables influencing the subject's ESP performance to be adequately dealt with by the experimenter." J. G. Pratt has conjectured that psi might represent "an area of nature in which nonpredictability and nonrepeatability are the rule." And Emilio Servadio has stated that our attempts to circumscribe psi within our customary reality "could be compared to the efforts of a natural scientist who should want by hook or by crook to study fishes only by taking them systematically out of the water, to establish the 'reality' of fishes within the boundaries of a world without water." I would hope that a repeatable experiment in ESP or PK can be found. However, if this search proves fruitless, there are a number of other options open to psychical researchers—and upon my return from Colombia, I began to study them.

Many sciences are based upon careful observation of phenomena rather than on laboratory experiments. Great strides have been made in geology, archeology, paleontology, and astronomy without the benefit of repeatable experiments. Parapsychology, therefore, could pay more attention to real-life situations (such as poltergeist phenomena) and engage in more field studies (such as observing the Filipino healers). In addition, the enigmas of psychical research might finally succumb to researchers if an intensive interdisciplinary study were made of special instances of psi. For example:

1. Jule Eisenbud has noted that amino acids have been produced by electrically sparking a mixture of water vapor, methane, ammonia, and hydrogen. He has suggested that a psychic sensitive with powerful PK ability attempt to do the same thing. If psychic sensitives are able to produce amino acids, they should then attempt to produce (from the same mixture) self-replicating molecules. In so doing, we might be able to understand more about both psi processes and the origin of life on the earth.

2. When a psychic sensitive alters a physical object through PK, that object should be intensively studied. For example, Uri Geller attempted to demonstrate PK for Eldon Bird, a metallurgist in the U.S. Naval Ordinance Laboratory. Bird reported that with "just a touch of his fingers," Geller bent Nitinol, a nickel-titanium alloy. Nitinol ordinarily springs back to its original shape when placed in hot water after being bent. But after Geller released the metal, it continued to bend to a 90-degree deflection, even after being immersed in hot water.

    Geller was also investigated by Wilbur Franklin, a physicist at Kent State University, and succeeded in breaking a spoon and a ring. In the case of the ring, Geller did not touch it until after the first fracture appeared. Using a scanning electron microscope, Franklin noted "an unusual viscous appearance" along the crack of the spoon. The cracked ring was also examined; one portion of it "appeared like incipient melting." Franklin's observations might ultimately help to separate fraudulent attempts from actual PK as well as help to explain the process which occurs at the molecular level during psychokinetic effects.

3. Several Kirlian photography effects need to be closely analyzed for their relationship to psi. The "phantom leaf effect," the appearance of letters and numbers under a fingertip, and the influence of a dis-

tant psychic on a Kirlian electrophotograph, should be attempted. The "Kirlian effect" in parapsychology could be investigated at several laboratories. Motion pictures would enable us to explore these effects more closely as would the noncontact Kirlian process in which the object to be photographed does not touch the film.

Thelma Moss has claimed she found major changes in fingertip coronas following eye-to-eye meditation. The fingertip coronas also changed following sessions with psychic healers. Kirlian photography may become a useful tool for studying many poorly understood phenomena—but first we need to understand Kirlian photography better.

4. A number of scientific instruments have started to be explored for their possible utility to psi researchers. Olga Worrall is said to have affected the pattern of subatomic particles in a cloud chamber at a laboratory in Agnes Scott College while holding her hands around the chamber and, later, while 600 miles away. Nina Kulagina apparently influenced a hydrometer in a session with Benson Herbert. Ingo Swann, at the Stanford Research Institute, deflected a magnetometer. In the case of Kulagina, the effects were accompanied by strong breathing and signs of great physical exertion, but not for Worrall or for Swann. In fact, Swann remarked, "There are two types of psychokinesis in my view. One is the application of direct force to an object—such as making a compass needle move by a movement of the hand. In the kind I've now been working with, I sit very quietly and, at a distance, effect a small change in an object." It is important to investigate Swann's ideas; among the instruments that might be helpful is the voltage gradient meter devised by H. S. Burr to detect changes in the electrodynamic fields of living organisms. It has never been used in psi research although I suspect it might prove to be far more useful than the better known procedures of Kirlian photography.

5. The patterns of chemical reactions have been given considerable attention by several Soviet researchers. A. M. Zhabotinsky and A. N. Zaikin noted that when ions of the metal cerium affect an organic substance dissolved in water, there is a cycle of change from a yellow to a colorless fluid twice a minute. They also noted circular chemical waves produced by other reactions, creating changes in color and form. Many of the cycles move in spirals or in rings that vanish before perfect symmetry is reached. These patterns are delicate yet predictable. It would seem that a psychic sensitive might be able to alter these patterns by PK. It would also seem that other

forms of matter with delicate patterns or structures would be amenable to PK influence. Liquid crystals should be especially amenable to psychokinetic influence, because they are extremely sensitive to temperature changes, electromagnetic fields, stress, and radiation. An examination of these changes, if they occur, might yield considerable information about psi processes.

6. Electromagnetic and electrostatic fields which occur in nature have measurable effects upon the central nervous system; for example, one's general alertness and ability to visually discriminate degrees of brightness improved under the influence of an electrostatic field in experiments conducted by A. S. Presman, whom I met in Moscow. Another Soviet scientist, Y. A. Kholodov, whom I met in Prague, found that brain activity could be affected by an electromagnetic field, with specific areas responding more strongly than other areas. Could these fields exert an effect upon psi?

7. Rather than being the simple structure scientists once thought, the living cell is actually quite complex; the cell wall, for example, is typically folded and convoluted in such a way as to make it an excellent conductor. Indeed, scientists have identified more than 100 distinct chemical reactions that occur as a cell develops. And computer specialists at the University of Toronto have made a mathematical model of the cell nucleus, thus creating a "computer cell." When the mathematical equivalent of a virus was introduced into the "computer cell," the cell died. When disturbances were introduced into the ribonucleic acid (RNA) of the "computer cell," it displayed all the earmarks of cancer. If such research could provide a model of the changes which occur in enzymes and red blood cells during psychic healing experiments, the mechanisms of both distant healing and laying-on of hands might become apparent. Tools such as the cathode-ray tube and the photomultiplier unit can detect light emerging from cells; the bioluminescence phenomenon may also play an important role in psychic healing, and needs to be explored.

8. Such scientists as Alexander Dubrov and Haakon Forwald have conjectured that gravity plays an important role in psi phenomena. Experiments could be designed to explore the propositions that gravitational waves are influenced by human consciousness and that gravity acts upon consciousness. Dubrov believes that organisms produce biogravitational effects which can be consciously influenced. Forwald holds the position that once the role of gravity in PK is understood, scientists will not have to conjecture the existence of new "energies." Although the concept of psychic "energies" is an

appealing one, there are various types of gravitational forces that should also be considered by psychical researchers.

Human beings live in what Buckminster Fuller has called a "synergistic" relationship with their environment. The human environment relationship will eventually have to be viewed as an entire system by parapsychologists. In the meantime, the use of biochemical and biophysical indications may help us obtain information about psi which has been ignored by the psychological and mathematical procedures in vogue for so many years. To explore psi from this vantage point, I initiated a new journal in 1974, *Psychoenergetic Systems*; Arthur Hastings, Viktor Adamenko, Gladys McGarey, and Robert Becker joined me on the editorial board.

Many parapsychologists would be aghast at the idea that biochemical and biophysical approaches represent a better way of studying ESP and PK. What could be learned by employing these alternative methods? If psychical researchers were to abandon the search for a repeatable experiment and devote themselves to careful observation of the occurring phenomena, they might discover that:

1. A crystallike structure in the nerve cells changes from liquid to solid during psi.
2. The organism emits a series of weak gravitational waves during psi.
3. The organism's electrostatic and electromagnetic fields shrink during ESP but expand during PK.
4. There are electrodynamic properties of organisms which do not conform to the conventional laws of time and space; furthermore, they can stimulate the memory banks of organisms.

These are examples of some of the findings that might emerge. They are also examples of findings that might not emerge, but there is no way of knowing until we look for them.

Trapping a Photon

Quantum physics can be explored by psychical researchers for clues that will help them solve the puzzle of psi. One investigator who has taken this approach is Arthur Young, inventor of the Bell helicopter. Young was struck by the observation that photons are "packages of light energy," whole units of action. Human acts and decisions also come in wholes—and it is these actions that comprise experience, not distance, time, mass, and other measurable properties that are secondary to the acts. In parapsychological research, the intention of the subject is a whole act, corresponding to the photons in quantum physics. When a physicist observes a photon of light, it is annihilated; when a parapsychologist attempts to discover psychic "laws," the phenomena often disappear.

If this is so, how does one trap a photon? How does one capture psi? How does one tame a siren? If Young is correct and "purpose" and "intention" form the kernel of psi phenomena, how can they be adequately studied? It is here that we must seriously consider the possibility that there are several types of psi that occur in different ways on various levels of reality. What is appropriate for one type of psi may be completely inappropriate for the study of another type.

Telepathy at short distances may be a function of high frequency radiations which transmit information. But long distance telepathy may result from an interaction of the transmitter's and receiver's electrodynamic fields; when they resonate, a matching item in the receiver's memory bank is stimulated, emerges into awareness, and is reported.

Psychokinetic movement of small objects may result from the focusing of a person's electrostatic or electromagnetic field. But the movement of large objects through PK may represent biogravitation at work.

Precognitive knowledge of events a few hours or days in advance might be explained through the hypothesis that time has density, and that consciousness can sometimes approach time's outer limits, bringing back information. If precognition occurs several years in advance of the event, we may have to explain it through synchronicity, as a "meaningful coincidence."

Clairvoyance for an item in a sealed envelope one is holding may represent special qualities of the cells in the skin that cross the information barrier and elicit data. But clairvoyance for objects several hundred miles away might depend upon holographic characteristics of the brain when focused upon a distant item that is conceptualized as part of one's total available imagery.

The Soviet experiment with chicken embryos serves as an example of parapsychology's need for various strategies. When the embryo was cut apart and put in two different containers, the experimenters might have thought they had a splendid way to test for cell-to-cell telepathy. When one container was infected, the cells in both containers died. The experiment was replicated several times and if the investigators had stopped there, parapsychology would have had its repeatable experiment.

But the scientists went a step further. By placing photomultiplier tubes between the quartz windows of the containers, they were able to detect ultraviolet radiation which, in coded form, sent fatal instructions from the infected cells to the healthy cells. As a result, the phenomena of distant cell-to-cell communication no longer belonged to the realm of parapsychology.

It would be my feeling that this incident will be repeated many times as science investigates other unusual phenomena. For example, dowsing might eventually be explained as the result of a sensitive person responding to the radiation field of underground metal or oil. This, of course, would not explain "map dowsing," in which the sensitive marks on a map the most likely places for exploration. Here, then, we would have a case in which one type of human behavior felt to be paranormal would leave the field of parapsychology while another type—"map dowsing"—would remain.

Even those psi events which occur on other levels of reality might eventually be assigned to more orthodox fields of study once "state-specific sciences" are developed. Charles Tart has listed the four basic rules of scientific method, noting all of them could apply to "state-specific sciences":

1. The scientist is committed to observe as well as possible the phenomena of interest. Many important phenomena associated with altered states of consciousness have been ignored because they have been labeled "subjective." However, once we realize that there is no such thing as a "detached observer" in science, we will be more willing to deal with subjective realities using, of course, the best possible ways of making our observations.

2. The scientist knows that observations must be described in sufficient detail so that others may either duplicate them or have similar experiences. In "state-specific sciences," a considerable period of training might be necessary for one observer to have the same experiences as a previous observer. However, Lawrence LeShan's studies in psychic healing demonstrate that this procedure is possible, and his training program for healers (which involves entering altered states of consciousness) suggests that a large number of observers can be produced to study similar events.

3. A scientist must develop theories that account for what has been observed; the theory must have a logical structure that other scientists can understand. A person in one state of consciousness might develop a theory which seems invalid to a scientist in another state of consciousness. However, once that scientist reaches the same state of consciousness as the theorist, the theory might appear extremely logical. Many of Carlos Castaneda's theories about his experiences with don Juan Matus would appear bizarre to someone who has never shared Castaneda's state of consciousness; once this state is attained, Castaneda's entire theoretical structure might seem quite valid indeed.

4. Any theory a scientist develops must have observable consequences; from that theory, it must be possible to make predictions that can be verified by observation. Thus, a workable theory in a "state-specific science" might predict events extremely well even if it is based on internal "subjective" data.

A major obstruction to the development of "state-specific sciences" is the objection to considering internal events as scientific data because they are too subjective. However, Sir Cyril Burt, the illustrious British psychologist, has pointed out that the human sense organs are millions of times more sensitive in detecting energy than they are in discriminating weight, matter, and mass. In other words, our distinction between "energy" and "matter" may result from the extreme sensitivity we have for seeing a beam of light or hearing a musical tone versus the lack of sensitivity we have for perceiving a grain of sand falling on the skin or feeling tension in our muscles while lifting a feather. These differences may have led to the differentiation of "energy" and "matter" as well as the division between "external" and "internal" events. If our sense of touch were as delicate as our sense of vision, the puzzle of psi would have long since been solved and "state-specific sciences" would have already been developed.

Song of the Siren

In examining special instances of psi, researchers will frequently encounter gifted subjects. If these individuals can be cajoled into working with scientists, and if the money can be obtained for intensive study, parapsychology may break through many of the impasses that hinder its progress. Perhaps one or more of these psychic sensitives could manifest a phenomenon that is repeatable. If not, perhaps a subject could at least occasionally produce an effect that would be observed by scientists of unquestioned eminence, leaving in its wake data available for close analysis and inspection. Perhaps observational techniques will supplant the search for repeatable experiments in parapsychology. Or perhaps a combination of observation and experimentation will prevail. In either event, the gifted subject could be of inestimable value to psychical research. And once a practical application of ESP or PK is discovered, technicians who have made a practice of avoiding the field may suddenly take an interest. At the present time we use a variety of products—from electricity to aspirin—on a daily basis without fully understanding how they work. An application of ESP or PK, in such a field as psychic healing, could force skeptics to pay serious attention to psi and its manifestations.

Until then, parapsychologists must resign themselves to being the outcasts of science. Over the years, I have seen psychical researchers ridiculed by professors and castigated by magicians. Parapsychologists are sought after by the media—but are typically exploited and rarely remunerated. In addition, occultists and "gurus" have made light of parapsychologists' attempts to study phenomena which have been "proved" long ago by the founders of "religious" and "spiritual" cults. Typically, the media are eager to popularize the views of the debunkers, even though their statements might be totally untrue. Where is the "new consciousness" that is supposed to permeate the culture and bring about a fair hearing for psi? As Jerry Garcia has observed, "The news that there has been a change of consciousness on the planet is slow getting out."

So why do we do it? Why do parapsychologists spend their time studying science's most elusive phenomena? The usual professional rewards rarely seem to come our way. Instead of fame, fortune, promotions, awards, and honorary degrees, we usually find ourselves involved in controversy, debts, job insecurity, and the admonition that we are wasting our time studying ESP and PK when so many vital problems face science which would yield their secrets more easily.

Speaking for myself, I devoted ten years of my life to parapsychological research because of a lifetime curiosity concerning the scope of human consciousness as well as a commitment to the development of human potential. The findings about ESP and PK, sparse though they may be, suggest that there exists in the universe a dimension that is ignored, unacknowledged, and virtually unexplored. This dimension of existence could teach us more than we know about time and space. It could reveal new ways of maintaining health and treating disease. It could expand our development of intellect, emotion, intuition, and creativity. It might even demonstrate that human beings do not end at the boundaries of their skin, but exist as part of a network of consciousness which connects one person to other people distant in space and time.

Curiosity and commitment, however, are only the cornerstones of a career in psychical research. Support from external sources is also essential. Early in 1975, as I had finished unpacking files, books, and materials sent to my California office from the dream lab in Brooklyn, I fell asleep. I awakened later, having dreamed that I returned to Brooklyn and found nothing in my old office but a cardboard box. Upon opening the box, I noticed a shoestring.

One cannot do research on a shoestring indefinitely. In my case, ten years was more than enough. The resentments and frustrations that build up over time cannot facilitate the environment in which ESP and PK blossom and become available for study. And so I stopped conducting experiments in parapsychology, deciding instead to stimulate the development of psychical research through teaching and writing. Montague Ullman had accepted a visiting professorship at the University of Göteborg in Sweden; Charles Honorton remained at Maimonides, doing excellent research but fighting the ever menacing battle of the budget.

Nevertheless, the progress made by parapsychology in those ten eventful years was significant and encouraging. The battle is difficult, the rewards are small, but the progress becomes increasingly visible. This progress continues because parapsychologists, like Ulysses, have learned hard lessons over the years. Our discipline involves steering a middle road between noncritical acceptance of strange phenomena and dogmatic rejection of anything unusual. It involves grounding oneself when lured to abandon scientific methodology or to announce conclusions prematurely. As a result of this discipline—which amounts to a yoga for the science of consciousness—psychical research slowly advances. Each year, parapsychology courses increase in colleges and universities. Every month, new experiments are reported from a growing number of laboratories around the world. And on each succeeding day, one can hear in one form or another, the song of the siren echo across the land.

REFERENCES

CHAPTER 1

Chance, P. "Skeptic Among the Spooks: A Sketch of Stanley Krippner." *Psychology Today,* October 1973.
Hastings, A., and Krippner, S. "Expectancy Set and 'Poltergeist' Phenomena." *ETC.* 18 (1961):349–360.
Huxley, A. "The Case for ESP, PK, and Psi." *Life,* January 11, 1954.
Krippner, S. "Coding and Clairvoyance in a Dual-Aspect Test with Children." *Perceptual and Motor Skills* 20 (1965):745–748.
Murphy, G. *Human Potentialities.* New York: Basic Books, 1958.
Pratt, J. G.; Rhine, J. B.; Smith, B. M.; Stuart, C. G.; and Greenwood, J. A. *Extrasensory Perception After Sixty Years.* Somerville, Ma.: Humphries, 1940.
Price, G. R. "Apology to Rhine and Soal." *Science* 175 (1972):359.
———. "Science and the Supernatural." *Science* 122 (1955):359–367.
Rao, K. R. "The Preferential Effect in ESP." *Journal of Parapsychology* 26 (1962):252–259.
Rhine, J. B. *Extrasensory Perception.* Somerville, Ma.: Somerville, 1934.
Rhine, J. B., and Pratt, J. G. *Parapsychology: Frontier Science of the Mind.* Springfield, Ill.: Thomas, 1957. Rev. ed.: Thomas, 1962.
Rhine, L. E. *Hidden Channels of the Mind.* New York: Sloane, 1961.
Wright, F. L. *A Testament.* New York: Bramhall, 1957.

CHAPTER 2

Baba Ram Dass *Be Here Now.* New York: Crown, 1971.
Clark, W. H. *Chemical Ecstasy.* New York: Sheed & Ward, 1969.
Cottle, T. J., and Klineberg, S. L. *The Present of Things Future.* New York: Free Press, 1974.
Garnett, A. C. "Matter, Mind and Precognition." *Journal of Parapsychology* 29 (1965):19–26.
Hayakawa, S. I. *Language in Thought and Action.* New York: Harcourt, Brace, 1949.
———. "The Quest for Instant Satori." *ETC.* 22 (1965):389–392.
Huxley, A. *The Doors of Perception.* New York: Perennial Library, 1954.
Jung, C. G. Foreword to the *I Ching.* Translated by R. Wilhelm. New York: Pantheon, 1950.

Jung, C. G., and Pauli, W. *The Interpretation of Nature and the Psyche*. New York: Pantheon, 1955.

Koestler, A. *The Roots of Coincidence*. New York: Random House, 1972.

Krippner, S. "An Adventure in Psilocybin." In *Psychedelics*, edited by B. Aaronson and H. Osmond, pp. 35–39. New York: Anchor, 1970.

———. "An Expansion of Consciousness and the Extensional World." *ETC*. 22 (1965):431–462.

———. "The Cycle in Deaths Among Presidents Elected at Twenty-Year Intervals." *International Journal of Parapsychology* 9 (1967):145–153.

Krippner, S., and Davidson, R. J. "Religious Implications of Paranormal Events Occurring During Chemically-Induced 'Psychedelic' Experience." *Pastoral Psychology* 21 (1970):27–34.

Leary, T. "Drugs, Set and Suggestion." Paper read at the annual convention, American Psychological Association, New York, N.Y., 1961.

———. *High Priest*. New York: New American Library, 1968.

———. *Jail Notes*. New York: Douglas, 1970.

Leary, T.; Metzner, R.; and Alpert, R. *The Psychedelic Experience*. New Hyde Park, N.Y.: University Books, 1964.

Masters, R. E. L., and Houston, J. *The Varieties of Psychedelic Experience*. New York: Holt, Rinehart & Winston, 1966.

Rogo, D. S. "Psychedelics and ESP." *Psychic*, August 1973.

Watts, A. *In My Own Way*. New York: Pantheon, 1972.

CHAPTER 3

Belvedere, E., and Foulkes, D. "Telepathy in Dreams: A Failure to Replicate." *Perceptual and Motor Skills* 33 (1971):783–789.

Foulkes, D.; Belvedere, E.; Masters, R. E. L.; Houston, J.; Krippner, S.; Honorton, C.; and Ullman, M. "Long-Distance 'Sensory-Bombardment' ESP in Dreams: A Failure to Replicate." *Perceptual and Motor Skills* 35 (1972):731–734.

Freud, S. "Dreams and Telepathy." *International Journal of Psychoanalysis* 3 (1922):283–305.

Globus, G. G.; Knapp, P. H.; Skinner, J. C.; and Healy, G. "An Appraisal of Telepathic Communication in Dreams." *Psychophysiology* 4 (1968):365.

Hall, C. S. "Experiments with Telepathically-Influenced Dreams." *Zeitschrift für Parapsychologie und Grenzgebiete der Psychologie* 10 (1967):18–47.

Honorton, C. "Significant Factors in Hypnotically-Induced Clairvoyant Dreams." *Journal of the American Society for Psychical Research* 66 (1972):86–102.

Krippner, S. "An Experimental Study in Hypnosis and Telepathy." *American Journal of Clinical Hypnosis* 11 (1968):45–54.

———. "Electrophysiological Studies of ESP in Dreams: Sex Differences in Seventy-Four Telepathy Sessions." *Journal of the American Society for Psychical Research* 64 (1970):277–285.

Krippner, S., and Ullman, M. "Telepathy and Dreams: A Controlled Experiment with Electroencephalogram-Electro-oculogram Monitoring." *Journal of Nervous and Mental Diseases* 151 (1970):394–403.

Ross, C. "Telepathy and Dreams: An Attempt at Replication." Mimeographed. Princeton, N. J.: Princeton University, 1972.

Schmeidler, G. R., and LeShan, L. "An Aspect of Body Image Related to ESP Scores." *Journal of the American Society for Psychical Research* 64 (1970):211–218.

Strauch, I. "A Method for Investigating Telepathy in Dreams." *Zeitschrift für Parapsychologie und Grenzgebiete der Psychology* 8 (1965):55.

Ullman, M.; Honorton, C.; and Krippner, S. "Comparison of Extrasensory and Presleep Influences on Dreams." A Paper Presented at the Annual Convention of the Parapsychological Association, St. John's University, N.Y., 1974.

Ullman, M., and Krippner, S. "Dream Studies and Telepathy: An Experimental Approach." *Parapsychological Monographs*, no. 12. New York: Parapsychology Foundation, 1970.

Ullman, M.; Krippner, S.; with Vaughan, A. *Dream Telepathy*. New York: Macmillan, 1973.

Van de Castle, R. L. "The Study of GESP in a Group Setting by Means of Dreams." *Journal of Parapsychology* 35 (1971):312.

Witkin, H. A., and Lewis, H. "The Relation of Experimentally-Induced Presleep Experiences to Dreams: A Report on Method and Preliminary Findings." *Journal of the American Psychoanalytical Association* 13 (1965):819–849.

CHAPTER 4

Castaneda, C. *A Separate Reality*. New York: Simon & Schuster, 1972.

Davidson, R. J., and Krippner, S. "Biofeedback Research: The Data and Their Implications." In *Biofeedback and Self-Control: 1971*, edited by J. Stoyva et al., pp. 3–34. Chicago: Aldine/Atherton, 1972.

Freud, S. *The Major Works of Sigmund Freud*. Chicago: Encyclopedia Britannica, 1952.

Homer. *The Odyssey*, translated by S. Butler. Chicago: Encyclopedia Britannica, 1952.

Honorton, C.; Drucker, S. A.; and Hermon, H. "Shifts in Subjective State and ESP under Conditions of Partial Sensory Deprivation: A Preliminary Study." *Journal of the American Society for Psychical Research* 67 (1973): 191–196.

Houston, J. "The Psychenaut Program: An Exploration into Some Human Potentials." *Journal of Creative Behavior* 7 (1973):257–262.

Jones, R. M. *The New Psychology of Dreaming*. New York: Grune & Stratton, 1970.

Krippner, S., and Bova, M. "Environmental Influences on Clairvoyance and Alterations in Consciousness." *International Journal of Paraphysics* 8 (1974):48–56.

Krippner, S.; Hickman, J.; Auerhahn, N.; and Harris, R. "Clairvoyant Perception of Target Material in Three States of Consciousness." *Perceptual and Motor Skills* 35 (1972):439–446.

Krippner, S.; Honorton, C.; and Ullman, M. "An Experiment in Dream Telepathy with 'The Grateful Dead.'" *Journal of the American Society of Psychosomatic Dentistry and Medicine* 20 (1973): 9–17.

Krippner, S.; Honorton, C.; Ullman, M.; Masters, R.; and Houston, J. "A Long-Distance 'Sensory Bombardment' Study of ESP in Dreams." *Journal of the American Society for Psychical Research* 65 (1971):468–475.

Krippner, S., and Hubbard, C. C. "Clairvoyance and Alterations in Consciousness." *International Journal of Paraphysics* 7 (1973):5–17.

Krippner, S., and Zeichner, S. "Telepathy and Dreams: A Descriptive Analysis of Art Prints Telepathically Transmitted During Sleep." *A.R.E. Journal* 8 (1973):197–201.

Moss, T., and Gengerelli, J. A. "Telepathy and Emotional Stimuli: A Controlled Experiment." *Journal of Abnormal Psychology* 72 (1967):341–348.

Murphy, G. "Research in Creativeness: What Can It Tell Us About Extrasensory Perception?" *Journal of the American Society for Psychical Research* 60 (1966):8–22.

Osis, K.; Turner, M. E., Jr.; and Carlson, M. L. "ESP Over Distance: Research on the ESP Channel." *Journal of the American Society for Psychical Research* 65 (1971):245–288.

Stanford, R. G. "EEG Activity and ESP Performance: A Replicative Study." *Journal of the American Society for Psychical Research* 65 (1971):144–154.

Trungpa, C. *Mudra.* Berkeley: Shambala, 1972.

White, R. A.; Krippner, S.; and Ullman, M. "Experimentally-Induced Telepathic Dreams with EEG-REM Monitoring: Some Manifest Content Variables Related to Psi Operation." In *Papers Presented for the Eleventh Annual Convention of the Parapsychological Association,* edited by H. Bender, pp. 431–443. Freiburg: Institut für Grenzgebiete der Psychologie, 1968.

CHAPTER 5

Aaronson, B. S. "Hypnotic Alterations of Space and Time." In *Psi and Altered States of Consciousness,* edited by R. Cavanna and M. Ullman, pp. 42–54. New York: Garrett Press, 1968.

Bennett, J. T., and Barth, J. R. "Predicting Human Behavior: A Spirited Approach." *Journal of Irreproducible Results* 20 (1973):5–6.

Boyd, D. *Rolling Thunder.* New York: Random House, 1974.

Brown, F. A., Jr. *Biological Clocks.* Boston: American Institute of Biological Sciences, 1962.

Bühler, C. "Human Life Patterns and Potentialities." In *Explorations in Human Potentialities,* edited by H. Otto. pp. 19–35. Springfield, Ill.: Charles C. Thomas. 1966.

————. *Values in Psychotherapy.* New York: Free Press, 1962.

Burroughs, W., and Ginsberg, A. *The Yagé Letters.* San Francisco: City Lights Books, 1963.

Cavanna, R., and Ullman, M., eds. *Psi and Altered States of Consciousness.* New York: Garrett Press, 1968.

Darwin, C. *The Descent of Man and Selection in Relation to Sex.* Chicago: Encyclopedia Brittanica, 1952. Originally published in 1891.

Fischer, R. "A Cartography of the Ecstatic and Meditative States." *Science* 174 (1971):897–904.

Friedman, H.; Becker, R. O.; and Bachman, C. H. "Geomagnetic Parameters and Psychiatric Hospital Admissions." *Nature* 626 (1963):200.

Gauquelin, F. *The Cosmic Clocks.* New York, Avon, 1969.

―――. "Terrestrial Modulations of the Daily Cycle of Birth." *Journal of Interdisciplinary Cycle Research* 2 (1971):211–217.

Gauquelin, M. *Cosmic Influences on Human Behavior*. Briarcliff Manor, N.Y.: Stein & Day, 1973.

―――. "Possible Planetary Effects at the Time of Birth of 'Successful' Professionals: An Experimental Control." *Journal of Inter-disciplinary Cycle Research* 3 (1972):381–389.

Green, E., and Green, A. "The Ins and Outs of Mind-Body Energy." In *Science Year, 1974*, World Book Science Annual, pp. 137–147. Chicago: Field Enterprises, 1973.

Hamer, J. R. *Biological Entrainment of the Human Brain by Low Frequency Radiation*. New York: Northrup Space Laboratory, 1967.

Hernández-Peón, R. "A Unitary Neurophysiological Model of Hypnosis, Dreams, Hallucinations, and ESP." In *Psi and Altered States of Consciousness*, edited by R. Cavanna and M. Ullman, pp. 178–193. New York: Garrett Press, 1968.

Krippner, S. "The Plateau Experience: A. H. Maslow and Others." *Journal of Transpersonal Psychology* 4 (1972): 107–120.

Krippner, S.; Becker, A.; Cavallo, M.; and Washburn, B. "Electrophysiological Studies of ESP in Dreams: Lunar Cycle Differences in 80 Telepathy Sessions." *Human Dimensions*, Fall 1972.

Krippner, S., and Nell, R. "Clairvoyance and the Lunar Cycle." *International Journal of Paraphysics* 7 (1973):180–186.

Kuhn, T. S. *The Structure of Scientific Revolutions*. 2nd ed. Chicago: University of Chicago Press, 1970.

Leiber, A., and Sherin, C. "Homicides and the Lunar Cycle." *American Journal of Psychiatry* 129 (1972):101–106.

Luce, G. G. *Body Time: Physiological Rhythms and Social Stress*. New York: Pantheon, 1971.

Maslow, A. H. *Motivation and Personality*. 2nd ed. New York: Harper & Row, 1970.

―――. *Religions, Values, and Peak-Experiences*. 2nd ed. New York: Viking, 1970.

―――. *The Psychology of Science: A Reconnaissance*. New York: Harper & Row, 1966.

―――. *Toward a Psychology of Being*. 2nd ed. Princeton: Van Nostrand-Reinhold, 1968.

Puharich, A. *Beyond Telepathy*. New York: Doubleday, 1961.

Ravitz, L. J. "Electrometric Correlates of the Hypnotic State." *Science* 112 (1950):341–351.

Rubin, F. "The Lunar Cycle in Relation to Human Conception and the Sex of Offspring: An Account of the Work of Dr. Eugen Jonas." *Astrological Journal* 9 (1967):1–16.

Sechrest, L., and Wallace, J. *Psychology and Human Problems*. Columbus, Ohio: Charles E. Merrill, 1967.

Watts, A. W. "Virginia Glenn—1931–1970." *Bulletin of the Society for Comparative Philosophy*, November 1970.

Wolf, W. "Introductory Remarks: Rhythmic Functions in the Living System." *Annals of the New York Academy of Sciences*, 98 (1962):755.

CHAPTER 6

Adamenko, V. G. "Electrodynamics of Living Systems." *International Journal of Paraphysics* 4 (1970):113–120.

Adamenko, V. G.; Kirlian, V. K.; and Kirlian, S. D. "Detection of Acupuncture Points by the Biometer." In *Galaxies of Life: The Human Aura in Acupuncture and Kirlian Photography*, edited by S. Krippner and D. Rubin, pp. 129–131. New York: Gordon & Breach, 1973.

Behkterev, V. M. "Experiments in Influencing 'Mentally' the Behavior of Animals." *Problems of Study and Education of the Personality* 2 (1920):230–265.

Brozek, J. "Soviet Psychology's Coming of Age." *American Psychologist* 25 (1970):1057–1058.

Inyushin, V. M. "Biological Plasma of Human and Animal Organisms." In *Symposium of Psychotronics,* edited by Z. Rejdák, et al., pp. 50–53. Downton, Wiltshire, England: Paraphysical Laboratory, 1971.

Kogan, I. M. "Is Telepathy Possible?" *Radiotechnika* 21 (1966):8–14.

Kozyrev, N. A. "Possibility of Experimental Study of the Properties of Time." Washington, D.C.: Joint Publications Research Service, U.S. Department of Commerce, 1968.

Krippner, S., and Davidson, R. J. "The Use of Convergent Operations in Bio-Information Research." *Journal for the Study of Consciousness* 5 (1972):64–76.

Leonidov, I. "Russians Photograph Life and Death." *Fate*, September 1962.

Mitchell, E. D. "An ESP Test from Apollo 14." *Journal of Parapsychology,* 35 (1971):89–107.

Moss, T. "Searching for Psi from Prague to Lower Siberia." *Psychic*, June 1971.

Murphy, G. "Parapsychology: New Neighbor or Unwelcome Guest." In *Readings in Pyschology Today*, 2nd ed., pp. 52–56. Del Mar, Cal.: CRM Books, 1972.

Naumov, E. K., and Vilenskaya, L. V. *Bibliographies on Parapsychology (Psychoenergetics) and Related Subjects.* Springfield, Va.: National Technical Information Service, 1972.

Newland, C. *My Self and I.* New York: Coward-McCann, 1961.

Ostrander, S., and Schroeder, L. *Psychic Discoveries Behind the Iron Curtain.* Englewood Cliffs, N.J.: Prentice-Hall, 1970.

———. "Psychic Enigmas and Energies in the U.S.S.R." *Psychic,* June 1971.

Pratt, J. G. *ESP Research Today: A Study of Developments in Parapsychology Since 1960*. Metuchen, N.J.: Scarecrow Press, 1973.

Presman, A.S. *Electromagnetic Fields and Life*. New York: Plenum, 1970.

Raikov, V. L. "Artificial Reincarnation Through Hypnosis." *Psychic,* June, 1971.

Tiller, W. A. "Some Energy Field Observations of Man and Nature." In *Galaxies of Life: The Human Aura in Acupuncture and Kirlian Photography,* edited by S. Krippner and D. Rubin, pp. 70–111. New York: Gordon & Breach, 1973.

Ullman, M. "Fragments of a Parapsychological Journey." *Newsletter, American Society for Psychical Research,* Summer 1971.

Vasiliev, L. L. *Mysterious Phenomena of the Human Psyche.* New Hyde Park, N.Y.: University Books, 1965.

Vaughan, A. "Interview: Montague Ullman, M.D." *Psychic,* June 1971.

CHAPTER 7

Adamenko, V. G. "Objects Moved at a Distance by Means of a Controlled Bioelectric Field." In *Abstracts, Twentieth International Congress of Psychology*. Tokyo: International Congress of Psychology, 1972.

Asher, J. "Soviet Psychologists Reverse Stand, Urge New Action on Psychic Research." *APA Monitor*, April 1974.

Cott, A. "Controlled Fasting Treatment of Schizophrenia in the U.S.S.R." *Schizophrenia* 3 (1971):2–10.

Ebon, M., ed. *Psychic Discoveries by the Russians*. New York: New American Library, 1971.

Herbert, B. "Parapsychology in U.S.S.R., 1972." *International Journal of Paraphysics* 6 (1972):181–225.

Honorton, C. "Apparent Psychokinesis on Static Objects by a 'Gifted' Subject." In *Research in Parapsychology, 1973*, edited by W. G. Roll; R. L. Morris; and J. D. Morris, pp. 128–131. Metuchen, N.J.: Scarecrow Press, 1974.

Kaznacheyev, V. P.; Shurin, S. P.; Mikhailova, L. P.; and Ignatovish, N. W. "Distant Intercellular Interactions in a System of Two Tissue Cultures." In *Ultraweak Biochemiluminescehce*, edited by A. I. Zhuravlev, pp. 224–227. Moscow: Nauka, 1973.

Kirlian, S. D., and Kirlian, V. K. "Photography and Visual Observation by Means of High-Frequency Currents." *Journal of Scientific and Applied Photography* 6 (1961):397–403.

Krippner, S. "Experimentally-Induced Paranormal Effects in Dreams and Other Altered Conscious States." In *Abstracts, Twentieth International Congress of Psychology*. Tokyo: International Congress of Psychology, 1972.

Krippner, S.; Davidson, R. J.; and Peterson, N. "Psi Phenomena in Moscow." *Journal of Contemporary Psychotherapy* 6 (1973):79–88.

Krippner, S., and Rubin, D., eds. *The Kirlian Aura*. New York: Anchor, 1974.

Krippner, S.; Silverman, R.; Cavallo, M.; and Healy, M. "A Study of 'Hyperkinetic' Children Receiving Stimulant Drugs." *Academic Therapy* 8 (1973):198–222.

Markley, O. W., ed. *Changing Images of Man*. Menlo Park, Ca.: Stanford Research Institute, 1974.

Mihalasky, J. "The Role of Proscopy in Managerial Decision-Making." *International Journal of Paraphysics* 7 (1973):19–34.

Ostrander, S., and Schroeder, L. *Handbook of Psi Discoveries*. New York: G. P. Putnam's Sons, 1974.

Oyle, I. *Magic, Mysticism, and Modern Medicine*. Bolinas, California: Mesa Press, 1973.

Possony, S. T. *Lenin Reader*. Chicago: Regnery, 1956.

Schutz, W. C. "Wishes for the Future of Psychotherapy." *Voices* 9 (1973–1974)14–16.

Sergeyev, G. A., and Kulagin, V. V. "Psychokinetic Effects of Bioplasmic Energy." *International Journal of Paraphysics* 6 (1972):18–19.

Sergeyev, G. A.; Shushkev, G. D.; and Gryaznukhin, E. G. "The Piezoelectric Detector of Bioplasm." *International Journal of Paraphysics* 6 (1972):16–18.

Zinchenko, V. P.; Leontiev, A. N.; Lomov, B. F.; and Luria, A. R. "Parapsychology: Fiction or Reality?" *Questions of Philosophy* 27 (1973) :128–136.

CHAPTER 8

Andrade, H. G. *Experimental Parapsychology*. São Paulo: Edição Calvario, 1967.
Bastide, R. *The African Religions of Brazil*. 2 vols. São Paulo: Livraria Pioneira Editôria, 1971.
Burr, H. S. *The Fields of Life: Our Links with the Universe*. New York: Ballantine, 1973.
Coen, K. "An Exploratory Study of High-Frequency Photography with a Modified Kirlian Apparatus." *International Journal of Paraphysics* 7 (1973):187–193.
Flew, A. "Is There a Case for Disembodied Survival?" *Journal of the American Society for Psychical Research* 66 (1972):129–144.
Hossri, C. M. *Experiments in Autogenic Training and LSD*. São Paulo: Editória Mestre Jou, 1968.
Jung, C. G. *The Collected Works of C. G. Jung*. Vol. 10. Princeton, N.J.: Princeton University Press, 1970.
Kardec, A. *The Spirits' Book*. São Paulo: Lake, 1950.
McConnell, R. A. "Parapsychology and the Occult." *Journal of the American Society for Psychical Research* 67 (1973) :225–243.
Pressel, E. "Umbanda in São Paulo: Religious Innovation in a Developing Society." In *Religion, Altered States of Consciousness, and Social Change*, edited by E. Bourguignon, pp. 264–320. Columbus, Ohio: Ohio State University Press, 1973.
Rhine, J. B. "Is Parapsychology Losing its Way?" *Journal of Parapsychology* 36 (1972):170–176.
St. Clair, D. *Drum and Candle*. Garden City, N.Y.: Doubleday, 1971.
Stevenson, I. "Some New Cases Suggestive of Reincarnation. III. The Case of Suleyman Andary." *Journal of the American Society for Psychical Research* 67 (1973):244–266.
———. "Twenty Cases Suggestive of Reincarnation." *Proceedings of the American Society for Psychical Research* 26 (1966):1–362.
Tiller, W. A. "Human Auras and Buckling Film." *Prevention*, March 1974.
Watts, A. *The Book: On the Taboo Against Knowing Who You Are*. New York: Pantheon, 1966.
Wolf, W. "Are We Ever Reborn?" *Journal for the Study of Consciousness* 3 (1970):137–148.

CHAPTER 9

Andrès, P., and Kiefer, W. "The Prague Conference on Psychotronics." *Swiss Bulletin for Parapsychology*, March 8, 1974.
Bird, C. "Psychotronics: On the Horizon of Science." *East-West Journal*, June 1974.

Bradna, J. "Interpersonal Relations and Energetic Transfer." In *Proceedings, First International Conference on Psychotronics,* edited by Z. Rejdák, pp. 172–179. Prague: Cerven, 1973.

Brown, B. B. *New Mind, New Body.* New York: Harper & Row, 1974.

Drbal, K. A., and Rejdák, Z. *Telepathy and Clairvoyance.* Prague: Nakladatelstui Svoboda, 1970.

Greenberg, D. S. "The French Concoction." *Saturday Review,* May 1973.

Greenfield, J. *Wilhelm Reich Vs. the U.S.A.* New York: W. W. Norton, 1974.

Herbert, B. "International Congress: Prague, June 18–24, 1973." *Parapsychology Review* 4 (1973):17–19.

Honorton, C., and Harper, S. "Psi-mediated Imagery and Ideation in an Experimental Procedure for Regulating Perceptual Input." *Journal of the American Society for Psychical Research* 68 (1974) :156–168.

Jung, C. G. *Alchemical Studies.* Princeton, N. J.: Princeton University Press, 1967.

Karagulla, S. *Breakthrough to Creativity.* Los Angeles: DeVorss, 1967.

Kholodov, Y. A. *The Effect of Electromagnetic and Magnetic Fields on the Central Nervous System.* Moscow: Nauka, 1966.

Krippner, S. "Is Psychology Part of the Problem?" *Newsletter, Association for Humanistic Psychology,* September 1974.

Krippner, S., and Hickman, J. "West Meets East: A Parapsychological Détente." *Psychic,* June 1974.

Long, M. F. *The Secret Science Behind Miracles.* 2nd ed. Los Angeles: DeVorss, 1954.

Mann, W. E. *Orgone, Reich and Eros.* New York: Simon & Schuster, 1973.

Parker, A., and Beloff, J. "Hypnotically-Induced Clairvoyant Dreams: A Partial Replication and Attempted Confirmation." *Journal of the American Society for Psychical Research* 64 (1970):432–442.

Pushkin, V. N. "The Autogravity Hypothesis as a Possible Explanation for Psychokinetic Phenomena." *Socialist Industries,* September 9, 1973.

Rejdák, Z. "What is Psychotronics?" *International Journal of Paraphysics* 8 (1974):26–29.

Reich, W. *The Discovery of the Orgone.* New York: Noonday Press, 1970.

Rhine, L. E. *ESP in Life and Lab: Tracing Hidden Channels.* New York: Macmillan, 1967.

Rogers, C. R. Cited in "Ph.D. Program, Humanistic Psychology Institute." San Francisco: Association for Humanistic Psychology, 1974.

Rørvik, D. "The Theta Experience." *Saturday Review,* May 1973.

CHAPTER 10

Becker, R. O. "Electromagnetic Forces and Life Processes." *Technology Review* 75 (1972):2–8.

———. "The Significance of Bioelectric Potentials." Paper presented at the Second International Symposium on Bioelectrochemistry, Pont à Mousson, France, 1973.

Castaneda, C. *The Teachings of Don Juan: A Yaqui Way of Knowledge.* Berkeley: University of California Press, 1968.

Chaves, J. F., and Barber, T. X. "Acupuncture Analgesia: A Six Factor Theory." *Psychoenergetic Systems* 1 (1974):11–20.

Editorial Committee for Acupuncture and Moxibustion. *Basic Acupuncture Techniques.* Peking: The People's Health Publishing House. San Francisco: Basic Medicine Books, 1973.

Eisenbud, J. "Some Notes on the Psychology of the Paranormal." *Journal of the American Society for Psychical Research,* 66 (1972):27–41.

Eliade, M. *Shamanism: Archaic Techniques of Ecstasy.* Princeton, N.J.: Princeton University Press, 1966.

Grad, B. "A Telekinetic Effect on Plant Growth." *International Journal of Parapsychology* 5 (1963):117–133.

———. "The 'Laying-On' of Hands: Implications for Psychotherapy, Gentling, and the Placebo Effect." *Journal of the American Society for Psychical Research* 61 (1967):286–305.

Hammond, S. *We Are All Healers.* New York: Harper & Row, 1973.

Inyushin, V. M., and Inyushina, T. P. "On the Investigation of Some Electrobioluminescence Properties of Plants, Animals and Man." In *Ultraweak Luminescence in Biology,* edited by A. I. Zhuravlev, pp. 91–93. Moscow: Nauka, 1972.

Jensen, A. E. *Myth and Cult Among Primitive Peoples.* Chicago: University of Chicago Press, 1963.

Krieger, D. "The Response of In Vivo Human Hemoglobin to an Active Healing Therapy by Direct Laying-On of Hands." *Human Dimensions,* Fall 1972.

Krippner, S. "Research in Paranormal Healing: Paradox and Promise." *Newsletter, American Society for Psychical Research,* Autumn 1973.

Krippner, S., and Rubin, D., eds. *The Energies of Consciousness.* New York: Gordon & Breach, 1975.

La Barre, W. *They Shall Take Up Serpents.* New York: Schocken, 1962.

LeShan, L. *The Medium, the Mystic, and the Physicist: Toward a General Theory of the Paranormal.* New York: Viking, 1974.

McGarey, W. A. *Acupuncture and Body Energies.* Phoenix, Arizona: Gabriel, 1974.

Nolen, W. *Healing: A Doctor in Search of a Miracle.* New York: Random House, 1974.

Noordergraaf, A., and Silage, D. "Electroacupuncture." *IEEE Transactions of Biomedical Engineering,* September 1973.

Rogo, D. S., and Bayless, R. "Psychic Surgery." *Journal of the* (British) *Society for Psychical Research* 44 (1968):426–428.

Rose, R. *Living Magic: The Realities Underlying the Psychical Practices and Beliefs of Australian Aborigines.* New York: Rand McNally, 1956.

Rubin, L. and Honorton, C. "Separating the Yins from the Yangs: An Experiment with the *I Ching.*" In *Proceedings of the Parapsychological Association, 1971,* edited by W. G. Roll, et al. Durham, N.C.: Parapsychological Association, 1972.

Sherman, H. *Thoughts Through Space.* London: Frederick Muller, 1971.

———. *"Wonder" Healers of the Philippines.* Los Angeles: De Vorss, 1967.

Silverman, J. "Shamans and Acute Schizophrenia." *American Anthropologist* 69 (1967):21–31.

Smith, M. J. "Paranormal Effect of Enzyme Activity Through Laying-On of Hands." *Human Dimensions*, Summer 1972.

Steiger, B. *Medicine Power*. New York: Doubleday, 1974.

Szent-Györgyi, A. *Introduction to a Submolecular Biology*. New York: Academic Press, 1960.

Valentine, T. *Psychic Surgery*. Chicago: Henry Regnery, 1973.

Van de Castle, R. L. "Anthropology and ESP." *Psychic*, February 1974.

Veith, I., ed. *Huang Ti Nei Ching Su Wen: The Yellow Emperor's Classic of Internal Medicine*. New ed. Berkeley, California: University of California Press, 1970.

Watkins, G. K., & Watkins, A. M. "Possible PK Influence on the Resuscitation of Anesthetized Mice." *Journal of Parapsychology* 35 (1971): 257–272.

Yunker, B. "AMA Study Gives the Needle to Acupuncture." *New York Post*, June 17, 1974.

Zorab, G. "From the European Press," *Parapsychology Review*, May–June 1973.

CHAPTER 11

Angoff, A. *Eileen Garrett and the World Beyond the Senses*. New York: William Morrow, 1974.

Banerjee, H. N. Letter. *Journal of Parapsychology* 28 (1964):261–264.

Boring, E. G. "Paranormal Phenomena: Evidence, Specification, and Chance." Introduction to *ESP: A Scientific Evaluation* by C. E. M. Hensel. New York: Charles Scribner's Sons, 1966.

Carrington H. *Eusapia Palladino and Her Phenomena*. New York: B. W. Dodge, 1909.

Christopher, M. *ESP, Seers, and Psychics*. New York: Thomas Y. Crowell, 1970.

Cohen, D. *ESP: The Search Beyond the Senses*. New York: Harcourt Brace Jovanovich, 1973.

Cox, W. E. "A Scrutiny of Uri Geller." Paper delivered at the annual convention of the Parapsychological Association, Jamaica, New York, 1974.

———. "Parapsychology and Magicians." *Parapsychology Review*, May-June 1974.

Eisenbud, J. *The World of Ted Serios*. New York: Morrow, 1967.

Fuller, J. G. *Arigó: Surgeon of the Rusty Knife*. New York: Thomas Y. Crowell, 1974.

Hall, C., and Van de Castle, R. L. *The Content Analysis of Dreams*. New York: Appleton-Century-Crofts, 1966.

Hanlon, J. "Uri Geller and Science." *New Scientist*, October 17, 1974.

Honorton, C. "Objective Determination of Stimulus Incorporation in ESP Tasks with Pictorial Targets." Paper delivered at the annual convention of the Parapsychological Association, Jamaica, New York, 1974.

"Interview: Ingo Swann." *Psychic*, March–April 1973.

Krippner, S. "Paranormal Communication: Dreams and other Conscious States." *Journal of Communication* 25 (1975): 173–182.

Krippner, S.; Cavallo, M.; and Keenan, R. "Content Analysis Approach to Visual Scanning Theory in Dreams." *Perceptual and Motor Skills* 34 (1972):41–42.

Krippner, S., and Dreistadt, R. "Electrophysiological Studies of ESP in Dreams: Content Analysis of Witness-Participant Variables." *Human Dimensions*, Fall–Winter 1973.

LeShan, L. "Toward a General Theory of the Paranormal." *Parapsychological Monographs*, no. 9. New York: Parapsychology Foundation, 1969.

Levy, W. J., Jr. "One View: Dream Telepathy." *Journal of Parapsychology* 38 (1974):86–89.

————. "Possible PK by Rats to Receive Pleasurable Brain Stimulation." Paper presented at the annual convention of the Parapsychological Association, Charlottesville, Virginia, 1973.

Mead, M. "UFOs—Visitors from Outer Space?" *Redbook*, September, 1974.

Mitchell, J. "Out of the Body Vision." *Psychic*, March–April 1973.

Monroe, R. *Journeys Out of the Body*. Garden City, N.Y.: Doubleday, 1971.

Pratt, J. G. Letter. *Journal of Parapsychology* 28 (1964):258–259.

Puharich, A. "Uri Geller and Extraterrestrials." *Psychic*, May–June 1974.

Rao, K. R. Book review of *Five Years Report of Seth Sohan Lal Memorial Institute of Parapsychology* by S. C. Mukherjee. *Journal of Parapsychology* 28 (1964):59–62.

————. Letter. *Journal of Parapsychology*, 28 (1964):265–273.

Rauscher, W. "Mentalism and Extra-Sensory Perception." *Psychic*, March–April 1974.

Rhine, J. B. "Security Versus Deception in Parapsychology." *Journal of Parapsychology* 38 (1974):99–121.

Rieth, A. *Archeological Fakes*. New York: Praeger, 1970.

Rosenthal, R., and Jacobson, L. *Pygmalion in the Classroom*. New York: Holt, Rinehart & Winston, 1968.

Schmeidler, G. R. "PK Effects Upon Continuously Recorded Temperature." *Journal of the American Society for Psychical Research* 67 (1973):326–340.

Stevenson, L. Letter. *Journal of Parapsychology* 28 (1964): 259–261.

Swann, I. *To Kiss Earth Goodbye*. New York: Hawthorn, 1975.

Targ, R., and Puthoff, H. "Information Transmission Under Conditions of Sensory Shielding." *Nature* 251 (1974):602–607.

Tart, C. T. "A Psychophysiological Study of Out-of-the-Body Experiences in a Selected Subject." *Journal of the American Society for Psychical Research* 62 (1968):3–27.

————. "A Second Psychophysiological Study of Out-of-the-Body Experiences in a Gifted Subject." *International Journal of Parapsychology* 9 (1967):251–258.

Ullman, M.; Krippner, S.; and Vaughan, A. *Dream Telepathy*. Baltimore: Penguin, 1974.

Weil, A. "Parapsychology: Andrew Weil's Search for the True Geller." *Psychology Today*, June 1974; July 1974.

CHAPTER 12

Anderson, M. L., and White, R. A. "ESP Score Level in Relation to Students' Attitude Toward Teacher-Agents Acting Simultaneously." *Journal of Parapsychology* 22 (1958):20–28.

Berelson, B., and Steiner, G. A. *Human Behavior: An Inventory of Scientific Findings.* New York: Harcourt, Brace & World, 1964.

Bever, T. G., and Chiarello, R. J. "Cerebral Dominance in Musicians and Non-musicians." *Science* 185 (1974):537–539.

Braud, W. G., and Braud, L. W. "Further Studies of Relaxation as a Psi-Conducive State." *Journal of the American Society for Psychical Research* 68 (1974):229–245.

Braud, W. "Psi Conducive States." Paper delivered at the annual convention, Parapsychological Association, Jamaica, N.Y., 1974.

Bühler, C. "Basic Theoretical Concepts of Humanistic Psychology." *American Psychologist* 26 (1971):378–386.

Burt, C. "Psychology and Parapsychology." In *Science and ESP*, edited by S. Book, pp. 27–35. London: Routledge & Kegan, 1967.

Castaneda, C. *Tales of Power.* New York: Simon & Schuster, 1974.

Chance, P. "Parapsychology is an Idea Whose Time Has Come." *Psychology Today*, October 1973.

Craig, J. G. "The Effect of the Experimenter on Precognition in the Rat." Paper presented at the annual convention of the Parapsychological Association, Jamaica, N.Y. 1974.

Ehrenwald, J. *Telepathy and Medical Psychology.* New York: Norton, 1948.

Eisenbud, J. *Psi and Psychoanalysis.* New York: Grune & Stratton, 1970.

Forwald, H. "Mind, Matter, and Gravitation." *Parapsychological Monographs* no. 11. New York: Parapsychology Foundation, 1969.

Franklin, W. "Is There Physics in ESP, Mimeographed. Kent, Ohio: Kent State University, 1974.

Garrett, E. J. *Many Voices: The Autobiography of a Medium.* New York: G. P. Putnam's Sons, 1968.

Honorton, C. "Creativity and Precognition Scoring Level." *Journal of Parapsychology* 31 (1967):29–42.

———. "ESP and Altered States of Consciousness." In *New Directions in Parapsychology*, edited by J. Beloff, pp. 38-59. London: Paul Elek, 1974.

Johnson, M. "An attempt to Manipulate the Scoring Direction of Subjects by Means of Control of Motivation of the Subjects." *Research Letter of the Parapsychological Division of the Psychological Laboratory, University of Utrecht*, December 1971.

Koestler, A. "The Perversity of Physics." *Parapsychology Review*, May–June 1973.

Krippner, S. "Induction of Psychotronic·Effects in Altered States of Consciousness." *Impact* 24 (1974):339–346.

Krippner, S. "To the Question of Distant Excitation of Dreams." In *Psychical Self-Regulation*, edited by A. S. Romen, pp. 346–347. Alma-Ata, USSR: Kazakh State University; 1974.

Krippner, S., and Murphy, G. "Humanistic Psychology and Parapsychology." *Journal of Humanistic Psychology* 13 (1973):3–24.

Krishna, G. *Higher Consciousness—The Evolutionary Thrust of Kundalini.* New York: Julian Press, 1974.

Kuhn, T. S. *The Structure of Scientific Revolutions.* Chicago: University of Chicago Press, 1962.

Lloyd, D. H. "Objective Events in the Brain Correlating with Psychic Phenomena." *New Horizons* 1 (1973):69–75.

McCallan, E., and Honorton, C. "Effects of Feedback on Discrimination Between Correct and Incorrect ESP Responses: A Further Replication and Extension." *Journal of the American Society for Psychical Research* 67 (1973):77–85.

Meerloo, J. A. M. *Intuition and the Evil Eye: The Natural History of a Superstition.* Wassenaar, Netherlands: Servine, 1971.

Moss, T. *The Probability of the Impossible.* Los Angeles: J. P. Tarcher, 1974.

Murphy, G. "The Problem of Repeatability in Psychical Research." *Journal of the American Society for Psychical Research* 65 (1971):3–16.

Musēs, C., and Young, A. M. eds. *Consciousness and Reality: The Human Pivot Point.* New York: E. P. Dutton, 1972.

Pratt, J. G. "Some Notes for the Future Einstein of Parapsychology." *Journal of the American Society for Psychical Research* 68 (1974): 133–155.

Progoff, I. *The Image of an Oracle: A Report Into the Mediumship of Eileen J. Garrett.* New York: Garrett–Helix, 1964.

Rao, K. R. "An Autobiographical Note." *Parapsychology Review*, July–August, 1973.

––––––. *Mystic Awareness: Four Lectures on the Paranormal.* Mysore, India: University of Mysore, 1972.

––––––. "Psi and Personality." In *New Directions in Parapsychology,* edited by J. Beloff. pp. 60–76. London: Paul Elek, 1974.

Reich, C. and Wenner, J. *Garcia: A Signpost to New Space.* San Francisco: Straight Arrow, 1972.

Roll, W. G. "ESP and Memory." *International Journal of Neuropsychiatry* 4 (1966): 505–521.

Rosenthal, R. *Experimenter Effects in Behavioral Research.* New York: Appleton-Century-Crofts, 1966.

Sailaja, P., and Rao, K. R. "Experimental Studies of the Differential Effect in Life Setting." *Parapsychological Monographs,* no. 13. New York: Parapsychology Foundation, 1973.

Schmeidler, G. R. "ESP in Relation to Rorschach Test Evaluation." *Parapsychological Monographs,* no. 2 New York: Parapsychology Foundation, 1960.

––––––. "Parapsychologists' Opinions about Parapsychology." *Journal of Parapsychology* 8 (1971):117–145.

Schmeidler, G. R., and McConnell, R. A. *ESP and Personality Patterns.* New Haven: Yale University Press, 1958.

Schwartz, G. E. "Biofeedback, Meditation, and Cognitive Self Regulation of Patterns of Response." Address to the annual convention of the Parapsychology Association, Jamaica, N.Y., 1974.

Schwarz, B. E. *Parent-Child Telepathy.* New York: Garrett, 1971.

Servadio, E. Comment. *Parapsychology Review.* March–April 1974.

Shah, I. *Tales of the Dervishes.* New York: E. P. Dutton, 1967.

Tart, C. T. "States of Consciousness and State-Specific Sciences." *Science* 176 (1972):1203–1210.

Tenhaeff, W. H. C. "Summary of the Results of a Psychodiagnostic Investigation of Forty Paragnosts." *Proceedings of the Parapsychological Institute of the State University of Utrecht,* no. 2, 1962.

Thouless, R. H. "Parapsychology During the Last Quarter of a Century." *Journal of Parapsychology* 33 (1969):283–299.

Whiteman, J. H. M. "Quantum Theory and Parapsychology." *Journal of the American Society for Psychical Research* 66 (1973):341–360.

Winfree, A. T., "Rotating Chemical Reactions." *Scientific American,* June 1974.

Young, A. M. "The Acceptance of ESP." *Psychic Times,* February 1974.

Zhabotinsky, A. M., and Zaikin, A. N. "Autowave Processes in a Disturbed Chemical System." *Journal of Theoretical Biology* 40 (1973):45–61.

INDEX

ACID, *see* Altered Consciousness
    Induction Device
Acupuncture, 155, 212–215
    acupuncture points, 213, 214
        photographing of, 142
        physical basis for, 142–143
        solar flares and, 144
    Soviet research on, 142–145
Altered Consciousness Induction
    Device (ACID), 70, 71
American Indian culture:
    humanistic psychology and,
        271–272
Astrology:
    parapsychology and 113–134
Automatic writing:
    paranormal phenomena and, 70–74

Bannister effect, 154
Behavior, human:
    voluntary control of internal states,
        101–105, 111–112
Bioenergetic fields, 191
Bioenergy, 140, 198–203, 206
Biogravitation; biogravity, 190–191, 197
Bioinformation:
    defined, 139
    research, 148–151
Biolocation:
    defined, 139
Biological clock; biological compass, 123
Biological energy, 140
Bioluminescence, 212
Bioplasma concept, 137, 159–161, 215
Bodhisattva:
    significance of, 107

Clairvoyance, 9, 287
    clairvoyant reality, 247–249
    hypnotic dreams and, 59–60
Coma, 41
Consciousness, ordinary, 44
Consciousness expansion and altered
        states, 4, 43–44
    extensional world and, 29–31
    ESP and, 186–187
    "group shelter" experiments, 80–84
    Millbrook experiment, 33–45
    nondrug, 40
    paranormal phenomena and, 70–96
    patterns of, 40–44
    research on, 31
    "the sensory" environment experiments,
        80–84
    shifts in, and ESP, 74–77, 79, 80–96
    Sufi belief and, 275–276
    "writing shelter" experiments, 80–84
    see also Altered Consciousness
        Induction Device
Cortical perception, 279–280
Creativity:
    ESP and, 14–15, 270
Cybernetics, 280

Daydreaming, 43
Dowsing, 191
Dreams, 40
    bodily changes accompanying, 85–87
    clairvoyance and hypnotic dreams,
        59–60
    color and, 87–90
    emotion and, 87–90
    ESP and dream telepathy, 50–52,
        64–66

Dreams (Continued)
  interpreting, 15
  judging technique for dream
    transcripts, 246–277
  precognitive, 61–62
  research summarized, 272–273
  telepathic, 45–67, 69, 90–93

Education:
  learning-disability programs, 15–17,
    179–180
  state-specific learning, 108–111, 289
Electrosleep, 77–80
ESP, see Extrasensory perception
Extrasensory perception (ESP), 6, 44,
    94, 96, 100, 166, 206, 207, 248,
    257, 289, 290, 291
  Apollo 14 experiment in, 150–151
  assessment of, 266–268
  conscious fraud in experimentation,
    249–252
  creativity and, 14–15, 270
  dream telepathy and, 50–52, 64–66
  effect of researcher on experiment,
    281–282
  hypnosis and, 52–53
  lunar cycle and, 127–134
  personality traits associated with, 281
  physiological processes and, 84–87
  shifts in consciousness and, 74–77, 79,
    80–96
  states of consciousness and, 186–187
  unconscious bias in assessing, 249
  yoga and, 99

Fragmentation, 42–43
Futurology, 162

Healing, psychic, 217–245
  and altered state of
    consciousness, 219–221
  from a distance, 218–219
  in Philippines, 162, 221–245
    assessment of Filipino experience,
      239–243
Horoscopes, 115, 274
Humanistic psychology, 163–164,
    112–113, 208–210
  American Indian culture and, 271–272
  foundations of, 112–113
  psychical research and, 268–271
Hyperalertism, 41
Hyperkinesis, 155
Hypnagogic consciousness, 41, 69, 70
Hypnopompic consciousness, 41, 69, 70

Hypnotism:
  "by candlelight," 3
  clairvoyance and hypnotic dreams,
    59–60
  ESP scores and, 52–53
  shifts in consciousness, 74
  space-time alterations through, 99
Hysteria, 42

IFIF, see International Federation for
    Internal Freedom
Illness:
  physical vs. spiritual, 176–179
Imprinting, 35–37
Internal scanning, 41
International Federation for Internal
    Freedom (IFIF), 32–33

Kirlian effect:
  conference on, 154–156
  see also Photography, Kirlian
Kundalini awakening, 276

League for Spiritual Discovery, 59
Learning, see Education
Lethargy, 41
Levitation, 255
LSD, 21, 30, 31, 32, 266
  government intervention in research
    with, 44–45
  imprinting and, 35–37
Lunar cycle:
  parapsychology and, 115, 127–134

Marijuana, 210
Meditation, 43
  American Indian practices, 170
  paranormal phenomena and, 70–74
  Zen, 70–74
Memory:
  "stored memories," 41–42
Mescaline, 30
Muscle tension, 191
"Musclereading," 145–146

Orgone energy, 205–206
Orishas (Yoruba spirits), 170–172
"Out-of-body" experiences, 43, 108, 162,
    262–264

Parapsychology (psi phenomena):
  American Association for Advancement
    of Science and, 208
  anthropology and, 192–193
  areas of future study, 279–280

Parapsychology (Continued)
  basic concept of humanistic psychology
      applied to, 268–271
  critiques of, 252–254
  doctoral program for, 169
  fraudulent practices, 249–261
  interdisciplinary studies suggested,
      282–290
  opposition to, 7–8, 10–12
  Soviet studies, 136–151; 158–168,
      196–197
Personality:
  components of, 192
"Phantom leaf" phenomenon, 176
      184–185
Photography:
  Kirlian, 141–142, 154–156, 160, 176,
      184, 212, 214, 258, 262, 284
  psychic, 141
PK, see Psychokinesis
Planetary temperaments:
  parapsychology and, 115–134 passim
Poltergeists, 13, 15
Pranic spectrum, 276
Precognition, 10, 26, 287
  experiments with business managers,
      163
  human intervention and, 26–29
  precognitive dreams, 61–62
Proscopy, 140
Psi-conducive syndrome, 281
Psilocybin, 19, 30
  experiments with, 20–24, 31–33
Psychic photography, 141
Psychoenergetics, 141, 166–168
Psychokinesis (PK), 6, 9–10, 44, 94, 96,
      112, 141, 147, 166, 197, 206, 207,
      253, 256–257, 261, 262, 281, 285,
      286, 287, 289, 290, 291
  assessment of, 266–268
  tests analyzed, 260–261
Psychotronic generators, 146, 188, 198,
      206–208
  demonstrations of, 199–203
  uses for, 203–204
Psychotronics, see Parapsychology

Rapture, 42

Reality:
  clairvoyant reality vs. sensory reality,
      247–249
Realizing one's potential, 98–99
Regression, 42
Reincarnation, 180, 182–183
Reverie, 43

Sanskaras, 180
Schizophrenia, 146–147, 244–245
  Soviet treatment, 158–159
Scientific method:
  basic rules of, 288–289
Shiatsu, 155, 180
Skin vision, 140, 145, 196
Sonopuncture, 155
Spirit religions (Brazilian), 169–185
  physical vs. spiritual sickness, 176–179
  scientific investigations into, 174–176
State-specific sciences:
  development of, 289
  see also Learning
Statistics:
  "statistically significant" defined, 9n
Stored memories, 41–42
Stupor, 41
Suggestibility, 43
Synchronicity:
  defined, 24–25
  examples, 25–26

Telepathy, 9, 287
  conference demonstrations of, 188–189
  dream telepathy, 45–67, 69, 90–93
  dream transmission from a distance,
      90–93
  "resonance" vs. "build-up" theories, 64
  role of transmitter in dream telepathy,
      62–64, 66–67
Thought transference, 254–255
Trypsin experiments, 217–218

Witches' cradle, 75

Yagé, 98
Yoga:
  ESP and, 99

Zen meditation:
  paranormal phenomena and, 70–74